Beyond the Cubicle

Beyond the Cubicle

*Job Insecurity, Intimacy and
the Flexible Self*

Edited by Allison J. Pugh

OXFORD
UNIVERSITY PRESS

OXFORD
UNIVERSITY PRESS

Oxford University Press is a department of the University of Oxford. It furthers
the University's objective of excellence in research, scholarship, and education
by publishing worldwide. Oxford is a registered trade mark of Oxford University
Press in the UK and certain other countries.

Published in the United States of America by Oxford University Press
198 Madison Avenue, New York, NY 10016, United States of America.

Library of Congress Cataloging-in-Publication Data
Names: Pugh, Allison J., author.
Title: Beyond the cubicle : job insecurity, intimacy and the flexible self /
Allison J. Pugh.
Description: New York, NY : Oxford University Press, 2016. |
Includes bibliographical references and index.
Identifiers: LCCN 2015013934| ISBN 9780199957767 (hardcover : alk. paper) |
ISBN 9780199957781 (pbk. : alk. paper) | ISBN 9780199957774 (ebook)
Subjects: LCSH: Unemployment—Psychological aspects. |
Precarious employment—Psychological aspects. |
Unemployed. | Industrial sociology.
Classification: LCC HD5708 .P837 2016 | DDC 306.3/6—dc23
LC record available at http://lccn.loc.gov/2015013934

1 3 5 7 9 8 6 4 2

Paperback printed by Webcom, Inc., Canada
Hardback printed by Bridgeport National Bindery, Inc., United States of America

CONTENTS

ABOUT THE AUTHORS

Allison Alexy is an Assistant Professor in the Department of Asian Languages and Cultures at the University of Michigan. Her research explores intimacy, family norms, and law in contemporary Japan. She is finishing a book exploring these topics, *Divorce and the Romance of Independence in Contemporary Japan*, and has completed research about international child custody disputes and abductions involving Japanese citizens. With Richard Ronald, she co-edited *Home and Family in Japan: Continuity and Transformation* (Routledge 2010) and will soon publish *Intimate Japan*, co-edited with Emma E. Cook. Her research has been supported by Fulbright IIE fellowship, the Japan Foundation, and an Abe Fellowship administered by the Social Science Research Council.

Enobong Hannah Branch is an Associate Professor of Sociology and Director of Diversity Advancement for the College of Social and Behavioral Sciences at University of Massachusetts-Amherst. Her research interests are in race, racism, and inequality; intersectional theory; work and occupations; and historical demography. She is the author of *Opportunity Denied: Limiting Black Women to Devalued Work* (2011), which provides an overview of the historical evolution of black women's work and the socioeconomic structures that have located them in particular and devalued places in the US labor market. Her work has also appeared in *The Sociological Quarterly; Sociological Perspectives; Social Science History; Journal of Black Studies;* and *Race, Gender, & Class*. Her current research, supported by the National Science Foundation, investigates rising employment insecurity in the postindustrial era through the lens of racial and gender inequality.

Orfeu M. Buxton, PhD, is Associate Professor at Pennsylvania State University where he directs the Sleep Health and Society program in the Department of Biobehavioral Health. He also serves as adjunct associate professor at the Harvard School of Public Health, a lecturer on medicine at Harvard Medical School, and as an associate neuroscientist at Brigham and Women's Hospital. He currently serves as co-chair of the Steering Committee for the Work, Family, and Health Network. His research focuses on the causes of sleep deficiency in the workplace, home, and society, and the health consequences of sleep deficiency.

Edgar Cabanas received his PhD in Psychology at the Universidad Autónoma de Madrid, Spain. He has published several works such as "The Roots of Positive Psychology" (2012) and "Positive Psychology and Self-Help Popular Literature: A Historical, Psychological And Cultural Romance" (2014) on the political, economic, and social uses of the psychological studies of human happiness. He currently holds a postdoctoral position in the Centre for the History of Emotions at the Max Planck Institute for Human Development in Berlin, where he explores the relationship between "spaces" and "emotions" from a historical, cultural, and psychological perspective. He was also a visiting scholar in The Hebrew University of Jerusalem in 2011 and 2013.

Sarah M. Corse is Associate Professor of Sociology at the University of Virginia. Her work focuses on the ways through which cultural artifacts acquire meaning and value. She has analyzed the relationship between literature and the political process of nation-building (*Nationalism and Literature: The Politics of Culture in Canada and the United States*, Cambridge University Press, 1997); the involvement of particular narratives in the identity politics of race and gender; and the dynamics of class transmission. Her current project, *Picture This: The Meaning of Art in the Home*, is based on interviews about the art people display in their homes.

Michal Frenkel is an Associate Professor of Sociology at the Hebrew University of Jerusalem. She was a visiting fellow at Harvard University's Center for European Studies, a scholar-in-residence at the Hadassah-Brandeis Institute at Brandeis University, and a visiting professor at Smith College Her research focuses on the transformation of local and transnational social orders, in the context of the "globalization" of management practices. Her empirical and theoretical publications, which have appeared in top international and Israeli journals, have looked at work–family reconciliation and the role of globalization in transforming the discourse and practices associated with workers' attempts to synergize the two, both in Israel and in the context of multinational corporations; other publications look at the role of geopolitical and center–periphery power relations in the cross-national transfer and translation of management practices within multinational corporations and across national boundaries.

Kathleen Gerson is Collegiate Professor of Sociology at New York University, where she studies work–family connections and their links to the structuring of gender inequality. The author of numerous books and articles, her most recent book, *The Unfinished Revolution: Coming of Age in a New Era of Gender, Work, and Family* (Oxford, 2011), is an award-winning study of how new generations have experienced and responded to the rapidly unfolding gender revolution of the last several decades. Gerson is now at work on a study of "work and care in the new economy," which examines how today's women and men are navigating the increasingly uncertain occupational and family waters wrought by economic change. She has held visiting positions at the Stanford Center for Advanced Study in the Behavioral Sciences, the Russell Sage Foundation, and the Bremen Center for Status Passages and Risks in the Life Course. She is the recipient of the American Sociological Association's Jessie Bernard Award for distinguished contributions to the study of women and gender, the Rosabeth Kanter Award for excellence in work–family research, and the Eastern Sociological Society's Distinguished Merit Award for lifetime contributions.

Eva Illouz is Professor of Sociology at Hebrew University of Jerusalem. She served as the President of the Bezalel Academy of Arts and Design from 2012 to 2015. She is the author of eighty articles and book chapters, and nine books translated in sixteen languages, which have received international awards in philosophy and sociology. She was a member of the Wissenshaftskolleg zu Berlin in 2007, and a visiting Professor at the Ecole des Hautes Etudes en Sciences Sociales in Paris and in Princeton. Her books include *Why Love Hurts; Cold Intimacies: The Making of Emotional Capitalism; Consuming the Romantic Utopia;* and *Hard-Core Romance: "Fifty Shades of Grey," Best-Sellers, and Society.*

Jack Lam is a postdoctoral research fellow at the University of Queensland Institute for Social Science Research and its Life Course Centre in Brisbane, Australia. His research focuses on issues of work, family, and health over the life course. His work has appeared in journals such as *The Sociological Quarterly, Social Sciences and Medicine, Society and Mental Health, Work and Occupations,* and *the Journal of Occupational Health Psychology.*

Carrie M. Lane is an anthropologist of the United States who teaches in the Department of American Studies at California State University, Fullerton. Her research concerns the changing nature of work in the contemporary United States. Her first book, *A Company of One: Insecurity, Independence, and the New World of White-Collar Unemployment* (Ithaca, NY: Cornell University Press, 2011), documents the experiences of laid-off high-technology workers and was awarded the 2012 Book Prize of the Society for the Anthropology of Work. She is currently writing a book on the professional organizing industry.

Shi-Rong Lee is a PhD candidate in the Sociology Department at the University of Minnesota. Her research interests include finance, work and organizations, health, and life course studies.

Phyllis Moen is McKnight Presidential Endowed Chair and Professor of Sociology at the University of Minnesota, which she joined in 2003 after twenty-five years at Cornell University. She has published numerous books and articles on careers, retirement, health, gender, policy, and families as they are institutionalizing, transforming, and intersecting over the life course. Dr. Moen's latest (2016) book is *Encore Adulthood: Boomers on the Edge of Risk, Renewal, and Purpose* (Oxford: Oxford University Press).

Allison J. Pugh is a sociologist at the University of Virginia who writes about how economic and intimate life intertwine. Her most recent book, *The Tumbleweed Society: Working and Caring in an Age of Insecurity* (Oxford 2015), investigates the effects of job insecurity—as filtered through gender and class—on how people view their obligations to others at work and at home. Pugh's first book, *Longing and Belonging: Parents, Children, and Consumer Culture* (Berkeley: University of California Press, 2009), was awarded the 2010 William J. Goode award of the American Sociological Association. Pugh has had visiting positions in France, Germany, and Australia, and her research has been funded by the National Science Foundation, the Alfred P. Sloan Foundation, and the Bankard Fund for Political Economy.

Laura Robinson is Associate Professor in the Department of Sociology at Santa Clara University and affiliated faculty at the UC Berkeley ISSI. Her work has been published in journals including *Sociological Methodology, Sociology, Qualitative Sociology and Information,* and *Communication & Society*. She earned her PhD from UCLA, where she held a Mellon Fellowship in Latin American Studies, and also received a Bourse d'Accueil at the École Normale Supérieure. In addition to holding a postdoctoral fellowship on a John D. and Catherine T. MacArthur Foundation-funded project at the USC Annenberg Center, Robinson has served as a visiting assistant professor at Cornell University and visiting scholar at Trinity College Dublin. She is Co-Series Editor for Emerald Studies in Media and Communications and a past chair for the American Sociological Association (ASA) Communication, Information Technologies, and Media Sociology (CITAMS) section. Her research on new media in Brazil, France, and the United States has earned awards from CITAMS, Association of Internet Researchers (AOIR), and the National Communication Association's International and Intercultural Communication Division (NCA IICD).

Jeremy Schulz is a visiting scholar at the UC Berkeley Institute for the Study of Societal Issues. He is also an affiliate at the UC San Diego Center for Research on Gender in the Professions and has served as a Council Member of the ASA Section on Consumers and Consumption. Previously, he held an NSF-funded postdoctoral fellowship at Cornell University after earning his PhD at UC Berkeley. He has published on a broad range of topics, including consumption, work, family, culture, and inequalities. His recent publications include "Talk of Work," published in *Theory and Society* and "Shifting Grounds and Evolving Battlegrounds," published in the *American Journal of Cultural Sociology*. His article "Winding Down the Workday," published in *Qualitative Sociology*, received the Shils-Coleman Award from the American Sociological Association Theory Section. His current research examines peer-to-peer consumption, wealth trajectories, indebtedness, and innovative qualitative methods.

Jennifer M. Silva is Assistant Professor of Sociology at Bucknell University. Her book, *Coming Up Short: Working-Class Adulthood in an Age of Uncertainty* (Oxford: Oxford University Press, 2013), examines how working-class young men and women navigate the transition to adulthood in a world of disappearing jobs, soaring education costs, shrinking support networks, and fragile families. Her previous work has explored class gaps in extracurricular activities (*The ANNALS of the American Academy of Political and Social Science* 2015), working-class identity (*American Sociological Review* 2012), and gender negotiation in the military (*Social Forces* 2008). Additionally, she has written for the New York Times "Great Divide" series, the *Chronicle of Higher Education*, and the *Boston Review*.

Jennifer Utrata is Associate Professor of Sociology at the University of Puget Sound. Her research focuses on how economic and social transformations shape gender and intimate relationships. Her book, *Women without Men: Single Mothers and Family Change in the New Russia* (Ithaca, NY: Cornell University Press, 2015), illuminates Russia's "quiet revolution" in family life through examining the puzzle of how single motherhood, frequently seen as a social problem in other contexts, became taken for granted in Russia. *Women without Men* won the 2016 Mirra Komarovsky Book Award from the Eastern Sociological Society. Utrata has published articles in the *Journal of Marriage and Family* and *Gender & Society*, and in 2012 her article on the intersectionality of gender and age power relations between grandmothers and single-mother daughters won the Distinguished Article award from the ASA's Sex and Gender section. Her current research focuses on how grandmothers' unpaid care work shapes both the transition to parenthood and the economic mobility of families in the United States.

Elizabeth Ann Whitaker is a sociologist at Central Michigan University whose research focuses on the work/family interface, family financial decision making, and aging—all with gender as the main organizing principle. Her most recent work looks at retirement decision making in its changing economic and demographic context. Whitaker holds an M.B.A. from Villanova University and a PhD in Sociology from Michigan State University.

Christine L. Williams is the Adams Centennial Professor of Liberal Arts at the University of Texas at Austin. She is a specialist in the sociology of gender, sexuality, and workplace discrimination. She has written on gender inequality in a wide range of organizational settings, including most recently on low-wage jobs in the retail industry and on scientific careers in the oil and gas industry. Williams received the Feminist Lecturer Award (2012) and the Feminist Mentor Award (2013) from Sociologists for Women in Society. In 2014, she was awarded the Jessie Bernard Award from the American Sociological Association for her lifetime contributions to research on gender.

Beyond the Cubicle

Introduction

The Broader Impacts of Precariousness

ALLISON J. PUGH

When social scientists set out in 1931 to study Marienthal, the Austrian company town laid bare by the Great Depression, they tripped over a major finding: unemployment unraveled men's sense of time and schedules, but not women's, even when they had also been factory workers. The women still rose at 6 a.m., lit the fire, prepared the meals, their mending tasks greatly lengthened by tighter budgets so they spent "the whole day patching and darning to keep [the children] looking decent" (Jahoda et al. 2002 [1971]: 76). In contrast, the men were adrift, disinclined to pick up the slack on the domestic front, yet unable to find paid work. Family life suffered from pinched budgets, the shadow of shame over every decision about shoes or school lunches that threatened public exposure, raised voices boiling up from contempt or worry—or worse, the resignation of defeated hope. The book *Marienthal* is heralded as one of the first of its kind to systematically study the broader impacts of unemployment, to chronicle how one's relationship to paid work shapes one's experience of home, to interrogate how gender and work combine to generate the shifting sense of what people owe each other when the job becomes unmoored. In a time diary, one unemployed thirty-three-year-old man narrated his day, observing flatly (68): "In the meantime, midday comes around."

Almost a century later, massive layoffs are once again part of the daily news, and some of the same trends are visible; the *New York Times* in 2015 reported that unemployed women spend twice as much time on housework and caregiving than unemployed men, who are more likely to watch TV and movies or engage in other leisure activities. Of course, there are important differences: *Marienthal* documented the shock of workers accustomed to stability and predictability at work so that, before the study, "dismissals were rare; once settled in Marienthal, the whole family would be employed in the factory" (13). In contrast, as a recent review (Datta et al. 2010: 282) concluded, employee downsizing, once confined primarily to the United States, "has become the norm in many countries." Most important, job insecurity affects even the employed, even while they are employed (Smith 2001). Yet while its historical and geographical contexts differ, *Marienthal* points us to a useful angle of vision: what are the broader impacts of work precariousness, the tensions and contradictions reaching out from within the factory to the city streets and playgrounds, to the families, indeed, to workers' very selves? How does job insecurity make us into women and men, and how does it shape those places where men and women come together, where obligations are contested, negotiated, wrested, or given freely? How do people adapt themselves and their relationships to what feels to them like economic necessity, descending all around them like a night they cannot see beyond?

This volume brings together a host of essays that consider these questions from different angles. The contributors come from sociology, anthropology, American studies, and other fields, while the chapters attend to workers who vary by age, class, race, and gender; sites ranging from Texas to California to Japan, Russia, and Israel; and analytic targets from gender, class, and racial and ethnic inequalities to plans for the future to questions of stress and health. Yet despite the variety, the cumulative finding is of the powerful broader impacts of the new ways of organizing work, particularly upon emotions, individualism, and inequality beyond the workplace. Most of all, the chapters offer a pointillist portrait of how people construct self and subjectivity under the "extreme mundane" conditions of pervasive insecurity.

WHY EXPLORE THE BROADER IMPACTS OF WORK?

In the last forty years, employers have transformed the organization of work, and in particular their relationship to workers, increasingly relying on such options as downsizing, outsourcing, and the use of contract or part-time labor, in order to gain more control over (and flexibility in) their labor costs. These actions violated an implicit social contract between employers and workers involving mutual long-term commitment, which subsequently dissolved, ushering in a new era of widespread mobility and fluidity, benefiting some workers while penalizing others (McCall 2004). One crucial end result is that, overall, workers' job tenure has been steadily declining, with men suffering the most significant drops; these trends have been masked by married women's increased labor force attachment (Hollister and Smith 2013). In tandem with these changes, workers' *perceptions* of their job insecurity has risen in the United States and in Europe; in one OECD survey, more than 50% of workers in France, Japan, the United Kingdom, and the United States reported dissatisfaction with their job security (OECD 1997, as cited in Sverke, Hallgren, and Naswall 2006).

We know what job insecurity—defined as the sense that one may lose one's job involuntarily—does to workers at work, thanks to decades of research by sociologists, economists, and other scholars (De Witte 1999, Greenhalgh and Rosenblatt 2010). Job insecurity tends to lower productivity and performance, increase turnover, and decrease job satisfaction and morale. Contrary to conventional wisdom, which seems to view job insecurity as some sort of medicine against the ills of globalization—a lamentable but necessary antibiotic for employers steeling themselves against the ravages of competition—downsizing does not lead to higher productivity, nor even to increased value for shareholders, as stock prices tend to go down after layoffs (see Datta et al. 2010 for a review). Instead scholars have found that layoffs are best at prying us away from each other, tending to depress worker wages and to increase profits, and contributing to the growing inequality of the last decades (Baumol, Blinder, and Wolff 2003).

What we know less about, however, is how job insecurity affects other dimensions besides work, other realms besides the workplace, other people besides the worker. Nonetheless, there are some clues suggesting that the impact of such changes does not stop at the workplace door.

Scholars have documented links between the organization of Fordist work and such consequential practices as the family wage and the male-breadwinner-and-female-caregiver family model that depended upon it (Thistle 2006); the very notion of a stable (male) adulthood (Lee 2001); and the mechanics of class reproduction, such as the paradoxical ways in which working-class lads secured respect by failing at school even as in doing so they ensured their own futures as factory laborers (Willis 1977). Given these and other extensive repercussions of one kind of employment relationship during the era of its cultural dominance, we need to ask: what are the wider implications of the new ways of organizing work for the self, for relationships, for community?

The relatively spare but intriguing scholarship that ventures into this area seems to apply different metaphors to job insecurity: as a symptom, in which insecurity at work reflects the increased precariousness elsewhere, prevailing on a systemic level (Giddens 1991); as a contagion, spreading precariousness from work to other areas (Wallulis 1998, Streeck 2008, Sennett 1998); or as a vaccine, wherein people strive to fend off from other spheres the insecurity they accept at work (Pugh 2015). Much research focuses on the impact of job insecurity on less advantaged people: recently, for example, scholars have found that union membership signals job security, which in turn enhances members' marriageability compared to other working-class men (Schneider and Reich 2014); that the threat of losing their jobs makes low-level employees strive to adapt their family lives to the wearing demands of work, including its routine schedule unpredictability (Clawson and Gerstel 2014, Henly and Lambert 2014); that the primacy of family needs made the demands of some kinds of precarious jobs unworkable (Young 2008); and that the "casualization" of work for the working-class reinforces and is reinforced by a "casualization" of family life (Cherlin 2014). Together, these and other studies suggest job insecurity affects people's ability to form families, the kind of family lives they have once they form them, and the capacity of these families to endure.[1] In tandem with these vitally important discoveries, contributors to this volume draw our attention to three cross-cutting areas that generate important findings and rich commentary about the broader effects of job insecurity: a changing emotional geography; the radical individualism of the neoliberal era; and the interplay of gender, race, and class inequalities.

A CHANGING EMOTIONAL GEOGRAPHY

Job insecurity is emotional tinder, in part because of the paramount importance of paid work. In the United States, paid work is both moral measure and common language, a claim to citizenship and a means of signaling honor (Lamont 2002, Muirhead 2007). Paid work is one of the last remaining signs of adulthood, since marriage, a house, and children are no longer culturally compulsory signals of having come of age (Douglass 2005, Silva 2013, Newman 2012). The honor imbued in paid work is how the working-class distinguish themselves from the poor (Sherman 2009); how the rich distinguish themselves from the middle-class (Blair-Loy 2003, Blair-Loy and Wharton 2004); and how men distinguish themselves from women, particularly women with children (Williams 2000). The moral deservingness of those who work is why some government benefits such as welfare are "handouts" to the needy, while others, such as unemployment insurance or social security, are prerogatives, a distinction among recipients that scholars have described as between the "pitied" and the "entitled" (Gordon 1994). Work exaltation is behind the cultural contempt for the stay-at-home mother (Crittenden 2002) and the flexibility stigma (Williams, Blair-Loy, and Berdahl 2013). Despite certain contrary indicators (Cherlin 2014), many Americans remain in the cultural thrall of paid work, making it all the more piercing when they are released involuntarily from its hold (Lane, this volume).[2]

Emotions act as a crucial prism through which we can view job insecurity and its impact. Social scientists and historians have long established the social character of emotions, deconstructing notions of feelings as purely psychological or biological entities (Hochschild 1979, Hochschild 1983, Stearns 1994). Instead existing cultural ideas and practices—such as the powerful moral meanings of work in America, Japan, and other countries—generate and intersect with emotional regimes that render certain feelings more culturally acceptable. People then exert great effort to shape their feelings in line with the emotional regime in which they find themselves (Diaz and Illouz, this volume). Yet all this shaping has its own social, collective effects, because as people use culture to discipline their selves, they generate emotional contradictions that suggest potential stores of cultural resistance or change (Pugh 2013). Thus in the search for the broader impacts of job insecurity, emotions act as both method and outcome, as signal for the cultural collisions caused by job insecurity, and also as the site of those impacts (see, for example, Lam et al. and Lane's contributions to this volume).

The emotional impacts of precariousness are drenched in gendered meanings, with three major implications. First, insecurity impairs people's capacity to fulfill conventional gender norms, and part of its pain is located in the shame, guilt, and betrayal of those who cannot meet historically and culturally generated expectations (Branch, this volume). If, as West and Zimmerman (1987, 2009) argued, we are held accountable for the gender we "do," then widespread understandings of what counts as honorable behavior—the mix of paid work and caregiving that men and women owe to each other—serve to discipline us when we transgress these norms, even when we do so in response to broad structural changes in the economy (Pugh 2015). Second, gender inequalities shape the emotions available to men and women adapting to job insecurity; men whose provider role is battered by economic dislocations can enjoy constructing themselves as a modern subject with a breadwinning spouse, while women's retreat from earning is felt also as an unwelcome retreat from modernity (Lane 2011).

Finally, pervasive cultural ideas and language arising out of precariousness impede or discourage the gendered emotions of empathy and care, dismissing mercy as "enabling," castigating "dependence" as a moral wrong, and celebrating "self-reliance" as the ideal (Fraser and Gordon 1994, Utrata this volume). The effect here is to pry compassion out of ordinary feeling, as the anxiety of insecurity inures us to the plight of others; compassion becomes not commonplace but instead an often gendered accomplishment of those who refuse to ignore its call (Pugh 2015).

INSECURITY CULTURE AND RADICAL INDIVIDUALISM

"Insecurity culture" refers to the constellation of contemporary economic and political practices that emphasize market solutions, a shrinking role for government, and a narrative of individual risk and responsibility, often gathered under the rubric "neoliberalism" (Harvey 2005). As Ortner (2011) writes, it rests on two related shifts, the first of which involving a new way of thinking about the relationship between the state and the economy, in which the government plays less of a role in regulation and providing public goods. But the second shift is the dissolution of the temporary truce between capital and labor that existed during mid-century Fordism. Instead, Ortner (2011) argues, "the truce is over, and labor has become dispensable, disposable, and replaceable."

Embedded in insecurity culture, workers adapt to its conditions by developing and maintaining what Utrata (this volume) dubs "socially necessary selves," addressing structural changes with a form of radical individualism, trumpeting their self-reliance and renouncing their need for undependable others. Carrie Lane (2011, this volume) outlines the contours of a neoliberal subjectivity, as workers exert a certain discipline on themselves to curate their own "brand," to exhibit a remarkable understanding about their employers, whose firing practices are all that they might expect in a globalized world, and to endure the resultant depression and self-blame when their makeovers do not actually resolve the structural problems that have rendered them disposable.

These trends affect different workers differently, as class, gender, and other inequalities refract the impact of insecurity. Elite workers benefit from flatter, more nimble company hierarchies and looser hiring practices that increase opportunity, while low-income workers struggle with decreased benefits, work speed-ups, more surveillance, and greater demands for round-the-clock availability, with little recourse when jobs are lost due to weaker unions and reduced expectations of employers (Fligstein and Shin 2004). Furthermore, due to the retreat from social provisioning, when low-income workers endure disruption they have less of a cushion for their fall.

As Utrata (this volume) demonstrates, among single mothers in Russia neoliberalism makes work seem like the path to a cherished independence, but because it is insecure work, the women strive to develop the flexible, adaptable selves they need. Furthermore, they compel their own submission to discriminatory practices. Developing neoliberal subjectivity has become a moral imperative, ushered into being, as Cabanas and Illouz (this volume) argue, by the marriage of a popular psychology of happiness and consumer capitalism, even as that marriage reflects and enables the very precariousness that dislodges workers in the first place.

Job insecurity also shapes family life directly, not only through the selves that workers develop and hone and carry to and from work, but also through the particular configurations of providing and caring that particular jobs, and the political economy in which those jobs are embedded, make possible. Insecurity culture has meant that job precariousness makes the male-breadwinner-and-female-caregiver family even harder to sustain for disadvantaged men and women, thus complicating the resonance of cultural ideals about intimacy—as Branch (this volume) shows—particularly for African American and low-income couples. In contrast to the greater homogeneity of family life during the Fordist mid-century, then, new economic practices that disenfranchise the less advantaged, new relationships between the economy and the state, and new understandings about human nature have led to a new heterogeneity in family life (Gerson, this volume). This transition has been even more pronounced in Japan, where the "salaryman" and his household once epitomized the separate spheres generated by the Fordist/Keynesian system, but have been edged aside by a new diversity of domestic configurations (Alexy, this volume).

Of course, family heterogeneity is itself not a problem, as global evidence suggests a broad diversity of human configurations of domesticity and desire (Stacey 2011). But job insecurity appears to generate a mismatch between the kind of families at least some couples, particularly working-class ones, want to have at this time and place, and the kind they are able to support (Pugh 2015, Cherlin 2009). As Corse and Silva (this volume) suggest, low-income women and men find the outlook of marriage skittering far out of reach along with the prospects for their stable earnings, while middle-class couples have tools to protect themselves from the destabilizing impact of job insecurity—tools they consider a form of "private insurance" against the relationship insecurity that bedevils the less advantaged.

This is the stratification of endurance; insecurity culture privatizes not just access to stable families, but also the means to keep them.

Insecurity culture is not just an amorphous and unitary ethos, of course, but a very specific set of economic, political, and cultural relations, put into practice in different ways in different contexts, shaped by what came before (Gershon and Alexy 2011). The meanings of single mothers' independence in Russia, for example, are overlaid upon entrenched narratives of "strong" women dating from the Soviet era, while in Japan, the coinage of a new term that signifies "spouse-hunting," invoking a consumerist model of self-improvement and willful intent, makes sense because it maps onto prior understandings of job-hunting. Yet Frenkel (this volume) finds that in Israel, state support for the unemployed made job insecurity easier to survive, and also attenuated the language of self-blame and responsibility so prevalent in the United States (Pugh 2015, Lane 2011, Sharone 2014). While global in its reach, insecurity culture varies in its local expression of the broader impacts of job precariousness, with preexisting ideas acting as a cultural seedbed, fostering the growth of some effects while inhibiting others.

THE IMPACT OF INSECURITY UPON INEQUALITY

Job insecurity has a complex relationship to social inequalities such as gender, race, and class. First, job precariousness is spread unevenly: women's job tenure has not gone down, or at least not as much as men's, and when you restrict analysis to married women, their job tenure has increased (Farber 1998, 2008; Hollister 2011). Of course, these trends tell us more about the increasing work attachment of more advantaged women than they do about any employer propensity to keep women on and let men go, as women's labor force participation is increasingly full time and year-round, and married women have moved from earning "pin money" to enabling their families to keep up with cost of living increases given stagnant male wages (Zelizer 1997; Aveilar and Smock 2003; Parker 2013). One physical therapist I interviewed for *The Tumbleweed Society* (2015) captured the import of this change when she characterized what her earnings paid for: "from piano lessons to the electricity." For less advantaged women, as scholars have demonstrated, work has long been underpaid and insecure; while precariousness is not new for women, particularly for minority and low-income women, it nonetheless continues to shape the working conditions for many (Branch 2011). In my own research, I found that women tell stories about their fathers' jobs, and their fathers' expectations of security, borrowing from their fathers' histories to take on the cultural feeling of labor's loss. Even as women's jobs have long been more uncertain, then, women take precariousness more personally than their own work records would predict (Pugh 2015).

Outside the workplace, job insecurity has powerful implications for gender. There is considerable evidence that job precariousness unsettles traditional family structures, leads to new gender bargains in couples, and in some cases disrupts intimate partnerships (Pugh 2015; see also chapters by Gerson, Corse and Silva, and Alexy in this volume). On the one hand, these changes unshackle women and men from the rigidities of the male breadwinner-female caregiver configuration, enabling them—even compelling them—to find new understandings of gendered commitment and responsibility. The growing heterogeneity of family forms attests to these new freedoms. On the other hand, the shrinking state support for low-income households—the reductions in income subsidies, unemployment benefits, and the like—sharpen the impact of job precariousness upon low-wage working people, rendering job insecurity even more menacing for those at the bottom of the class ladder, including single mothers and their partners.

Moreover, amid the spread of the precariousness of paid work, women continue to retain primary responsibility for paid and unpaid care (despite the involvement of some men), making any trend that affects the delivery of that care profoundly consequential. In households with married parents, mothers spend an estimated fifty hours a week with children, as opposed to an estimated thirty-one hours a week for fathers (Raley, Bianchi, and Wang 2012). Single mothers, 60% of whom are nonwhite (Pew 2014), still comprise the overwhelming majority of single-parent families, at 85%. Women comprise about 70% of informal caregivers for the elderly, including care given as spouses and as adult children (Bianchi, Folbre, and Wolf 2012). Of paid home care workers, women make up 90% of the labor force (Glenn 2010). Women do the bulk of caregiving, and thus any change that affects how care happens—including how that care is supported—profoundly and disproportionately affects women's lives.

Through "patriarchal bargains," women worldwide exchange their own curtailed autonomy for support for their caring labor and individual security; with the unraveling of Fordist work, the family wage, and gendered job security, the terms of those bargains are being renegotiated as women respond to a changing landscape of care support (Kandiyoti 1988). Thus job insecurity, embedded in insecurity culture, is particularly gendered, as women find themselves with diminished access to men's wages, and withering state support for their unpaid carework (Thistle 1996). They do have improved access to work, but the terms of that work have degraded overall, particularly for the working class. In essence, the trends of job insecurity propelled women, and those in their care, from a patriarchal shelter—a halfway house of imprisonment and protection that classified them as not-quite-adults—out into the open, where, shielded or not, with whatever resources they have at their disposal, they face mercurial weather conditions on their own.

Some of these gender inequalities shape the way couples interpret and respond to job precariousness. Cultural ideas of gender collide with historical employment patterns to create expectations of the other that vary by race, as Branch (this volume) documents. Gendered experiences in work and love generate different paths couples take to resolve the conundrum of how they are going to support and care for their families (Gerson, this volume). Counterintuitively, for example, men's greater employment insecurity can make couples prioritize men's jobs, as when couples together acquiesce to male employee relocation, even when women's employment distinctly suffers, in order to forestall any punitive employer reaction against male workers (Whitaker, this volume).

For less-advantaged people, however, gender inequalities act less like glue than like a solvent upon their romantic partnerships under the stress of job precariousness. As we have seen, the increase in job precariousness within a context of insecurity culture has reduced support by men (through marriage) and the state (through social programs that were mostly available to the unmarried) for women's unpaid caring labor (Thistle 1996). Nonetheless, that labor still has to happen—children still have to be raised, the elderly still have to be tended—and less-advantaged women struggle to accomplish these tasks and support themselves with the low-wage jobs to which they have access. At the same time, they are largely able to disentangle themselves from poor prospective partners, whose insecure employment trajectories mean their contribution to the household is sometimes unclear. Job insecurity thus relies upon and amplifies class and racialized inequalities, making the chasm between more- and less-advantaged women or men often more significant than that between men and women.

ORGANIZATION OF THE BOOK

These three overlapping areas of interest—the changing emotional geography, insecurity culture and radical individualism, and the impact of insecurity on inequalities—are interwoven across the chapters that follow, which explore them from different perspectives. While each of the chapters stands alone, the book is organized in two broadly construed sections: "culture, emotions, and the flexible self" and "insecurity and inequalities." In the first section, we first meet two chapters that consider how changes at work affect workers' selves—in happiness and in health. The section then branches out to think about how cultural ideas and practices about work affect people's intimate lives— through the emotional inflections of their interpretations of insecurity, their notions of the good self, and their aspirations toward flexibility. In the second section, we consider the broader impacts of insecurity across different kinds of inequality, from gendered and racialized arrangements within heterosexual couples, to class variations in how children and couples perceive and prepare for an insecure future.

The book starts off with a broadly theoretical and ambitious account of how precariousness produces and relies upon a new emotional regime at work. Corporations' need for particular traits among their workers—self-reliance, flexibility, resilience, and the like—was aided and abetted by the positive psychology movement, argue Edgar Cabanas and Eva Illouz. They contend that academic work provided the scientific basis—through an emphasis on the causal links between happiness and success—for the new organization of work, which devolved greater responsibility but also greater risk to the individual worker. The focus on happiness has thus acted as a sort of midwife for job insecurity and other changes at work, serving employers and corporations more than the individual workers. These trends have ultimately had large cultural ramifications, Cabanas and Illouz argue, since happiness becomes "a sort of moral imperative," part of the legacy of insecurity culture: a dominant and pervasive vision of human nature.

The second chapter also focuses on the effects of precariousness upon workers, taking advantage of a rare opportunity to study the impact of job insecurity in action. A team of researchers from Minnesota and Harvard Medical School—Jack Lam, Phyllis Moen, Shi-Rong Lee, and Orfeu M. Buxton—were in the right place at the right time to be able to examine the longitudinal impact of precariousness on workers of different ages and levels of supervisory responsibility. Their team was already ensconced in a large electronics firm, conducting another study, when the firm announced that it was merging with a different company, and that its workforce would be absorbed within the other firm. Lam and his colleagues found that workers who learned about the merger after their first interview exhibited higher levels of emotional distress in their second interview, while those who knew about it from the beginning showed diminished emotional exhaustion, suggesting that perhaps workers can simply become used to the prospect of impending uncertainty. Their research hints at the psychological impact of job insecurity and how it varies by time, age, and worker position; the dynamism of the symbolically constructed domains of "work" and "family"; and how workers vary in which domain they strive to protect from the emotional fallout.

The rest of the book leaves the workplace to think about how precariousness extends its impact beyond its walls. Carrie Lane provides an account of the effects of insecurity culture—the broad-based cultural apparatus that supports and enables job insecurity—upon the self. Based on her in-depth and long-term immersion in the lives of the unemployed in Texas, Lane is able to document the costs to their finances and their family lives, reporting that most did not find jobs that paid as well, and many endured rocky relationships. Lane focuses the bulk of her attention on a subtler target, however—the struggle of people trying to live up to the ideal of the flexible, unencumbered worker, who must constantly acquire new skills to meet the ever-changing needs of the employer, while also being prepared to amiably depart should the employer require. People strive to develop the neoliberal self that they perceive as the key to success, even though such efforts have taken on the aura of magical thinking, incantations in the hopes of enacting some measure of control over a labor market that has been "radically reconfigured to disadvantage individual workers."

Changes in the organization of work bear implications not just for the self, but also for the intimate relationships we conduct, as Allison Alexy demonstrates in her analysis of the political economy of intimacy in postwar Japan. The iconic salaryman, a white-collar man who worked long hours for years in return for lifetime employment, was once an economic hero credited with the unprecedented growth of the Japanese economy. Yet his efforts on behalf of his employer were only possible with the support of a full-time caregiver such as a nonworking wife, who did not require much of his presence in the marriage or the household. Outside of marriage, salarymen were often conscripted into late-night socializing for the company that involved "sexualized play" at hostess bars; Alexy notes that this form of intimacy similarly helped to shore up the dominant employment relation. Tracing the fall of the salaryman as an iconic masculine ideal, Alexy argues that a recently coined word for "marriage-hunting" reflects the resonance of security today in Japan, coupled with the rise of calls for personal responsibility.

If Japan has swung "from social contract to employee covenant" (Pugh 2015), wherein employees still feel bound to jobs that employers now feel free to rescind, Russia's insecurity pendulum has swung even farther, as Jennifer Utrata explains. The single mothers she interviewed recall a Soviet era when they shouldered the entire second shift, but at least had guaranteed employment and a range of state protections. Now, faced with what they describe as insecure workplaces, weakened state support, and unreliable men, they embrace the dogma of personal responsibility, "going it alone" like their counterparts in the United States (Gerson, this volume), convinced that both men and the state will fail them.

The second section of the book explores the broader impacts of insecurity refracted through different social inequalities. Kathleen Gerson explores the way gendered patterns of labor at home and work contribute to an increasing heterogeneity of intimacy patterns in her chapter on Silicon Valley workers. Gerson delves into case studies that reveal how work pressures, gendered obstacles, and economic forces shape each person's configuration of work and family. Ultimately, she demonstrates, work-and-care strategies are the product of one's access to stable work, one's partner's access to stable work, and the ability to establish a steady romantic life. Insecure work also has ramifications across the life course, as women and men negotiate pathways of provisioning and care.

The very notion of what counts as ideal arrangements of provisioning and care, and the impact of insecurity upon these ideals, varies by race, as Enobong Hannah Branch demonstrates in her chapter. Branch uses extensive interviews with white and African American women to explore racialized conceptions of masculinity and intimacy, in light of the spread of precarious work. She finds that even as both groups of women spoke of a persistent cultural ideal of the breadwinning male partner, African American women's expectations were grounded in a historical understanding of black men's more precarious employment. Thus when they invoked flexible gender ideals, Branch contends, "it was a continuation of a flexible past." Branch's work shows how views of history shaped the women's expectations: precariousness has a racialized record, which informs the impact of its present.

Job insecurity shapes and reshapes gender among relocating couples as well, according to Elizabeth Ann Whitaker. Women married to men who are relocated by their employers—rendered compliant by the ambient threat of insecurity, or the recent experience of it—make significant compromises to prioritize their husbands' careers, Whitaker finds. When women were the relocated employees, however, they were far more educated and had more specialized skills, giving them greater leverage; for this reason, their moves involved less duress and their husbands had to make fewer sacrifices as trailing spouses. Overall, despite improvements in women's labor market position, when relocating in an insecure age "men's continued dominance in paid labor can become both more visible and reinforced," Whitaker concludes.

The gendered negotiations between couples are shaped by structures of gender in the workplace and at home, to be sure, but the terms of those conversations are themselves set by state policies and practices determining what options look more available than others, Frenkel reminds us. Relying on interviews, focus groups, and surveys in Israel, with mostly women employed in the high-tech sector, Frenkel finds that her informants did not evince much of a discourse of personal responsibility and resilience. Instead she found that laid-off technology workers viewed their dismissals as an "outcome of stronger structural forces beyond their control." Shielded by a social democratic welfare regime that sought to lessen the impact of work disruption, Israeli tech workers seemed to view the primacy of family as more salient than individual responsibility, independence, or resilience. Frenkel's work usefully complicates what we know about the spread of insecurity culture among those living with precariousness, by helping us see how the state might play a mitigating role.

Class and gender combine together to generate the pathways that teenagers cultivate in response to the adult work trajectories they observe, according to Jeremy Schulz and Laura Robinson. Schulz and Robinson interviewed several hundred rural high school students of diverse class and racial and ethnic origins in California to see how they viewed the task ahead. The authors develop the concept of security-autonomy-mobility roadmaps—or plans the youth cultivate for how they will make a living, support themselves and/or loved ones, raise a family, and end up better off than their parents. For many teenaged children looking down the road of adulthood, job insecurity looks like a speed bump that threatens to slow down or stop their trajectories; when they bear witness to job precariousness in the lives of the adults around them, it shapes the direction of their own plans for training, their hopes for autonomy, and their sense of efficacy.

Class inequality also affects the impacts precariousness can have on marriage and relationships, according to Sarah Corse and Jennifer Silva, who argue that middle-class workers with college educations enjoy the material and cultural resources that can turn insecurity into opportunity, while less educated workers struggle with the privations that accompanies precarious work, the decline of labor unions, and the disappearance of benefits. In their chapter, Corse and Silva find that among the working class, many men and some women yearn for a neotraditional arrangement but fear that men's jobs cannot sustain the model, while other women seem to desire a more mutual sharing but shy away from relationships that founder on lack of trust. The middle class, meanwhile, used their more extensive resources to cushion the blow of insecurity, and to help their relationships endure and grow through material investments, strategies that Corse and Silva dub "private insurance," too costly for working-class couples.

These chapters share a common theme—the broader effects of job insecurity—but generate a few contradictions, even amid the similarities. On the one hand, the Corse and Silva chapter seems to find sizable evidence of young men and women with little hope for their futures—this contrasts with the findings of the Schulz and Robinson chapter, wherein even young men and women who have lived with much scarcity make big plans for the future. Lane discusses men and women who have lost jobs and know there is no security left, which contradicts with other chapters (such as Gerson's Silcon Valley workers) in which there remains faith that job security is not a thing of the past.[3] On the other hand, time and again across the chapters we see men and women labor to fashion flexible selves that can bend and sway before the winds of precariousness, struggle with the pressure of traditional gendered ideals, and forge new kinds of intimacy, with new expectations shaping new negotiations. While perceptions of hope and optimism might vary, insecurity seems to create some similar challenges, and point the way to similar solutions, across dramatically varying situations.

In the afterword, Christine Williams warns of the elusiveness of the necessary political solutions to prevailing job precariousness. She points out the cultural changes that must happen first: workers must be able to see beyond self-blame to the external causes of such structural economic changes, and workers must develop a sense of pride and self-worth. "Feminism has an important role to play," she argues, not just in pressing for good jobs and living wages, but also in heralding the inherent value of work and care, enabling women and men to articulate what they need to survive insecurity culture.

CONCLUSION: FUTURE RESEARCH ON THE FUTURE OF WORK

Marienthal revealed how the absence of work colonizes the rest of the social world. In this century, after our own Great Recession, as work is reorganized into an everyday precariousness, we can see the broader implications of this change: beyond the worker, beyond the workplace. This volume pulls together much of the work on the wider impacts of job precariousness, but there remain many questions for future scholarship to explore. The most promising attend to three particular issues: context, interpretation, and compliance.

Context. Work in this volume and elsewhere suggest that some factors—class advantage in the United States (Pugh 2015), social welfare regimes in other states (Frenkel this volume)—filter, mediate, or block the effects of job insecurity on intimate life. For many families, however, these factors seem to shore up neotraditional configurations of work and care (see also Clawson and Gerstel 2014). Thus when workers do not feel like their livelihoods are at risk—either because they have resource advantages born of class or state policies cushioning their fall—they appear to withstand the anxiety that otherwise bleeds into domestic lives. Scholars could usefully interrogate further the links between insecurity and innovative or neotraditional domestic configurations. When do people rewrite cultural scripts impelled by anxiety, and when do they do so enabled by its absence? Furthermore, future research is needed to broaden and extend this finding to other forms of intimate life. How might job precariousness shape and reflect the adaptations of queer families, families that involve more than two parents, multigenerational families, or those that combine multiple households?

Interpretation. Some of the most interesting work done in the work-family field attends closely to how people define and interpret "work" and "intimate life," and how that varies under different conditions, as opposed to simply considering the impact of one upon the other. How does job insecurity affect the varying shape and weight people give to these domains? There are some indications, for example, that younger generations are trying to reduce the cultural space allotted to work (Twenge 2010). Yet at the same time, the encroachment of work into nonwork spaces, either by technological developments (Perlow 2012)—or by a new blurriness of what counts as work and what counts as consumption (Ritzer 2010), play (Grimes 2015), faith (Miller 2007), or other practices—suggests that the project of measuring the impact of job insecurity must contend with varying definitions of the "job." How do the broader impacts of insecurity intersect with new and various interpretations of "work" and "intimacy"?

Resistance. What are the sources and kinds of resistance to these trends? With union membership at all-time lows (less than 7% for private sector union membership in the United States in 2014, for example [Bureau of Labor Statistics 2015]), the conduits for worker organization against these deleterious trends are harder to see. Those who count unemployment rates, for example, sometimes caution against too much optimism when rates decline because those rates do not count those who have stopped looking for work. Media reports of declining men's labor force participation note that men in the prime working age (twenty-five to thirty-nine years old) show levels of disaffection from work that are unprecedented. The inchoate

Occupy movements, the WTO protests, the populist rhetoric of some political elites—there is evidence of widespread discontent with insecurity. How do insecurity's broader impacts enable or discourage resistance where its disparate sources are coalescing and to what ends?

The contributors to this volume focus on the impacts of job insecurity from different perspectives and from a range of disciplines, data, and international contexts. Their work covers the broader impacts of job precariousness, from the poignant compromises individuals make in disciplining their selves to fit the new era, to the intersections of job trends with inequality, such as the stratification of family endurance. They form a nascent field analyzing the broader impacts of precariousness, stepping outside the traditional silos of scholarly inquiry to view critically a crucial contemporary phenomenon and its consequences for emotions, individualism, and inequality—indeed for the construction of the modern self.

ACKNOWLEDGMENTS

This volume grew from discussions with a number of its contributors at conferences and meetings, in which the contours began to emerge of a nascent field of scholars who were thinking about prevalent changes at work and their nonwork effects. I am grateful to the contributors for their responsiveness and patience; to James Cook at Oxford University Press for his support of the volume; to two anonymous reviewers and Steven Vallas for their particularly thoughtful commentary on the manuscript; as well as to Jennifer Petersen, Jennifer Cyd Rubenstein, Stephen Sellers, Denise Walsh, and Christine Williams for their helpful feedback on earlier versions of this introduction. Funding for its writing was provided by the University of Virginia Faculty Summer Research Award in Humanities & Social Sciences.

NOTES

1. Existing work-family scholarship is only just starting to focus on the new ways of organizing work. Until recently the "flexibility" with which that field has largely concerned itself, for example, is not that which employers reserve for themselves—the "flexibilization" that serves as one of the primary handmaidens of job insecurity—but instead the access to parental leave and other accommodations that some (mostly privileged) workers enjoy (Blair-Loy et al. 2015). Yet while women's labor force participation has been transformative, particularly for middle-class women who did not work for pay before and for their families, flexibilization and related

changes have surely been just as transformative, and particularly so for more disadvantaged populations (Fligstein and Shin 2004).

2. Some scholars argue that the moral power of work is waning for certain populations (working-class men, low-income young adults [see Cherlin 2014]); the evidence on this is mixed, however, with other studies showing an increased pull of work for working-class adults (Clawson and Gerstel 2014; Damaske 2011). The differences may reflect gendered samples, but the area needs more study.

3. Thanks to an anonymous reviewer for this point.

REFERENCES

Avellar, S., and P. J. Smock. (2003), "Has the Price of Motherhood Declined Over Time? A Cross-Cohort Comparison of the Motherhood Wage Penalty." *Journal of Marriage and Family* 65(3): 597–607.

Baumol, William J., Alan Blinder, and Edward N. Wolff. 2003. *Downsizing in America: Reality, Causes, and Consequences.* New York: Russell Sage.

Bianchi, Suzanne M., Nancy Folbre, and Douglas Wolf. 2012. "Unpaid Care Work." In *For Love and Money: Care Provision in the United States,* edited by Nancy Folbre, 40–64. New York: Russell Sage.

Blair-Loy, Mary. 2003. *Competing Devotions: Career and Family Among Women Executives.* Cambridge, MA: Harvard University Press.

Blair-Loy, Mary, Arlie Hochschild, Allison J. Pugh, Joan C. Williams, and Heidi Hartmann. 2015. "Stability and Transformation in Gender, Work, and Family: Insights from *The Second Shift* for the Next Quarter Century." *Community, Work, and Family* 18(4):435–454.

Blair-Loy, Mary, and Amy S Wharton. 2004. "Mothers in Finance: Surviving and Thriving." *Annals of the American Academy of Political and Social Science*, 596(1):151–171.

Branch, Enobong Hannah. 2011. *Opportunity Denied: Limiting Black Women to Devalued Work.* New Brunswick, NJ: Rutgers University Press.

Bureau of Labor Statistics. 2015. "Union Members Summary." United States Dept. of Labor, Economic News Release. January 28. http://www.bls.gov/news.release/union2.nr0.htm. Accessed March 10, 2015.

Cherlin, Andrew J. 2009. *The Marriage-Go-Round.* New York: Knopf.

Cherlin, Andrew J. 2014. *Labor's Love Lost: The Rise and Fall of the Working-Class Family in America.* New York: Russell Sage Foundation.

Clawson, Dan, and Naomi Gerstel. 2014. *Unequal Time: Gender, Class and Family in Employment Schedules.* New York: Russell Sage Foundation.

Crittenden, Ann. 2002. *The Price of Motherhood.* New York: MacMillan.

Damaske, Sarah. 2011. *For the Family? How Class and Gender Shape Women's Work.* New York: Oxford University Press.

Datta, Deepak K., James P. Guthrie, Dynah Basuil, and Alankrita Pandey. 2010. "Causes and Effects of Employee Downsizing: A Review and Synthesis." *Journal of Management* 36(1): 281–348.

De Witte, Hans. 1999. "Job Insecurity and Psychological Well-Being: Review of the Literature and Exploration of Some Unresolved Issues." *European Journal of Work and Organizational Psychology* 8(2):155–177.

Douglass, Carrie B. 2005. "'We're Fine at Home': Young People, Family and Low Fertility in Spain." In *Barren States: The Population Implosion in Europe*, by Carrie Douglass, 183–206. Oxford, UK: Berg.

Farber, Henry S. 1998. "Are Lifetime Jobs Disappearing? Job Duration in the United States, 1973-1993," NBER Working Paper No. 5014, National Bureau of Economic Research, Inc. February 1995.

Farber, Henry S. 2008. "Short(er) Shrift: The Decline in Worker-Firm Attachment in the United States." In *Laid Off, Laid Low: Political and Economic Consequences of Employment Insecurity,* edited by K. S. Newman, 10–37. New York: Columbia University Press.

Fligstein, Neil, and Taek-Jin Shin. 2004. "The Shareholder Value Society: A Review of Changes in Working Conditions and Inequality in the United States, 1976–2000." In *Social Inequality,* edited by K.M. Neckerman, 402–432. New York: Russell Sage.

Fraser, Nancy, and Linda Gordon. 1994. "A Genealogy of Dependency: Tracing a Keyword of the U.S. Welfare State." *Signs* 19(2):309–336.

Gershon, Ilana, and Allison Alexy. 2011. "Introduction: The Ethics of Disconnection in a Neoliberal Age." *Anthropological Quarterly* 84(4):799–808.

Giddens, Anthony. 1991. *Modernity and Self-Identity: Self and Society in the Late Modern Age.* Cambridge, UK: Polity.

Glenn, Evelyn Nakano. 2010. *Forced to Care: Coercion and Caregiving in America.* Cambridge, MA: Harvard University Press.

Gordon, Linda. 1994. *Pitied but Not Entitled: Single Mothers and the History of Welfare 1890–1935.* Cambridge, MA: Harvard University Press.

Greenhalgh, Leonard, and Zehava Rosenblatt. 2010. "Evolution of Research on Job Insecurity." *International Studies of Management and Organization* 40(1):6–19.

Grimes, Sara M. 2015. "Playing by the Market Rules: Promotional Priorities and Commercialization in Children's Virtual Worlds." *Journal of Consumer Culture* 15(1):110–134.

Harvey, David. 2005. *A Brief History of Neoliberalism.* Oxford: Oxford University Press.

Henly, Julia R., and Susan Lambert. 2014. "Unpredictable Work Timing in Retail Jobs: Implications for Employee Work-Life Outcomes." *Industrial and Labor Relations Review* 67(3):986–1016.

Hochschild, Arlie R. 1979. "Emotion Work, Feeling Rules and Social Structure." *American Journal of Sociology* 85(3):551–575.

Hochschild, Arlie R. 1983. *The Managed Heart.* Berkeley: University of California Press.

Hollister, Matissa N. 2011. "Employment Stability in the U.S. Labor Market: Rhetoric vs. Reality." *Annual Review of Sociology* 37:305–324.

Hollister, Matissa N., and Kristin E. Smith. 2013. "Unmasking the Conflicting Trends in Job Tenure by Gender in the United States, 1983–2008." *American Sociological Review.* 79(1):159–181.

Jahoda, Marie, Paul F. Lazarsfeld, and Hans Zeisel. 2002 [1971]. *Marienthal: The Sociography of an Unemployed Community.* New Brunswick, NJ and London: Transaction Publishers.

Kalleberg, Arne L. 2009. "Precarious Work, Insecure Workers: Employment Relations in Transition." *American Sociological Review* 74(1):1–22.

Kandiyoti, Deniz. 1988. "Bargaining with Patriarchy." *Gender & Society* 2(3):274–290.

Katz, Josh. "How Nonemployed Americans Spend Their Weekdays: Men vs. Women." *The New York Times,* "The Upshot," Jan. 6, 2015. http://www.nytimes.com/interactive/2015/01/06/upshot/how-nonemployed-americans-spend-their-weekdays-men-vs-women.html?_r=0&abt=0002&abg=0. Accessed March 9, 2015.

Lamont, Michèle. 2002. *The Dignity of Working Men.* Cambridge, MA: Russell Sage Foundation.

Lane, Carrie M. 2011. *A Company of One: Insecurity, Independence, and the New World of White-Collar Unemployment*. Ithaca, NY: Cornell University Press.

Lee, Nick. 2001. *Childhood and Society: Growing Up in an Age of Uncertainty*. Philadelphia, PA: Open University Press.

McCall, Leslie. 2004. "The Inequality Economy: How New Corporate Practices Redistribute Income to the Top." Demos Working Paper. December 6, 2004. Retrieved September 7, 2012, (http://www.demos.org/sites/default/files/publications/the_inequality_economy_final.pdf).

Miller, David W. 2007. *God at Work: The History and Promise of the Faith at Work Movement*. New York: Oxford University Press.

Muirhead, Russell. 2007. *Just Work*. Cambridge, MA: Harvard University Press.

Newman, Katherine S. 2012. *The Accordion Family: Boomerang Kids, Anxious Parents, and the Private Toll of Global Competition*. Boston: Beacon.

Ortner, Sherry. 2011. "On Neoliberalism." *Anthropology of This Century*. Issue 1. May 2011. http://aotcpress.com/articles/neoliberalism/. Accessed June 27, 2014.

Parker, Sophia. 2013. "Introduction." In *The Squeezed Middle: The Pressure on Ordinary Workers in America and Britain*, edited by Sophia Parker, 1–15. Bristol, UK: Policy Press.

Perlow, Leslie. 2012. *Sleeping with Your Smart Phone*. Cambridge, MA: Harvard Business Review Press.

Pew Research Center. April 27, 2014. "Characteristics of Single Mothers, 2012." http://www.pewsocialtrends.org/2014/04/08/after-decades-of-decline-a-rise-in-stay-at-home-mothers/sdt-2014-04_moms-at-home-1-02/. Accessed February 7, 2016.

Pugh, Allison J. 2013. "What Good Are Interviews for Thinking About Culture? Demystifying Interpretive Analysis." *American Journal of Cultural Sociology* 1(1):42–68.

Pugh, Allison J. 2015. *The Tumbleweed Society: Working and Caring in an Age of Insecurity*. New York: Oxford University Press.

Raley, Sara, Suzanne M. Bianchi, and Wendy Wang. 2012. "When Do Fathers Care? Mothers' Economic Contribution and Fathers' Involvement in Child Care." *American Journal of Sociology* 117(5):1422–1459.

Ritzer, George and Nathan Jurgenson. 2010. "Production, Consumption, Prosumption: The Nature of Capitalism in the Age of the Digital 'Prosumer.'" *Journal of Consumer Culture* 10(1):13–36.

Schneider, Daniel and Adam Reich. 2014. "Marrying Ain't Hard When You Got a Union Card? Labor Union Membership and First Marriage." *Social Problems* 61(4):625–643.

Sennett, Richard. 1998. *The Corrosion of Character*. New York: W.W. Norton.

Sharone, Ofer. 2014. *Flawed System, Flawed Self*. Chicago: University of Chicago Press.

Sherman, Jennifer. 2009. *Those Who Work and Those Who Don't: Poverty, Morality, and Family in Rural America*. Minneapolis: University of Minnesota Press.

Silva, Jennifer. 2013. *Coming Up Short: Working-Class Adulthood in an Age of Uncertainty*. New York: Oxford University Press.

Smith, Vicki. 2001. *Crossing the Great Divide: Worker Risk and Opportunity in the New Economy*. Ithaca, NY: Cornell University Press.

Stacey, Judith. 2011. *Unhitched: Love, Marriage and Family Values from West Hollywood to Western China*. New York: New York University Press.

Stearns, Peter. 1994. *American Cool: Constructing a Twentieth-Century Emotional Style*. New York: New York University Press.

Streeck, Wolfgang. November 2008. "Flexible Markets, Stable Societies?" Max Planck Institute Working Paper 08/6, http://www.mpifg.de/pu/workpap/wp08-6.pdf. Accessed March 10, 2015.

Sverke, Magnus, Johnny Helgren, and Katharina Naswall. 2002. "No Security: A Meta-Analysis and Review of Job Insecurity and Its Consequences." *Journal of Occupational Health Psychology* 7(3):242–264.

Thistle, Susan. 2006. *From Marriage to the Market: The Transformation of Women's Lives and Work*. Berkeley: University of California Press.

Twenge, Jean M. 2010. "A Review of the Empirical Evidence on Generational Differences in Work Attitudes." *Journal of Business and Psychology* 25(2):201–210.

Wallulis, Jerald. 1998. *The New Insecurity: The End of the Standard Job and Family*. Albany: SUNY Press.

West, Candace, and Don H. Zimmerman. 1987. "Doing Gender." *Gender & Society* 1(2):125–151.

West, Candace, and Don H. Zimmerman. 2009. "Accounting for Doing Gender." *Gender & Society* 23(1):111–122.

Williams, Joan C. 2000. *Unbending Gender: Why Family and Work Conflict and What To Do About It*. New York: Oxford University Press.

Williams, Joan C., Mary Blair-Loy, and Jennifer L Berdahl. 2013. "Cultural Schemas, Social Class, and the Flexibility Stigma." *Journal of Social Issues* 69(2):209–234.

Willis, Paul. 1977. *Learning to Labor: How Working-Class Kids Get Working-Class Jobs*. New York: Columbia University Press.

Young, Alford A. 2008. "The Work-Family Divide for Low-Income African Americans." In *The Changing Landscape of Work and Family in the American Middle Class: Reports from the Field*, edited by Elizabeth Rudd and Lara Descartes, 87–115. Lanham, MD: Lexington Books.

PART I

Culture, Emotions, and the Flexible Self

CHAPTER 1

<small>ᴄᴧᴏ</small>

The Making of a "Happy Worker"

Positive Psychology in Neoliberal Organizations

EDGAR CABANAS AND EVA ILLOUZ

Neoliberalism is more than a theory of political economic practices: it is a new stage of capitalism characterized by the rising conception of the free market exchange as "an ethic in itself" (Harvey 2007); by a renewed emphasis on utilitarian principles of choice, cost-benefit calculation, and profit maximization (Baudrillard 2004; Read 2009); by the exponential increase of labor uncertainty, economic instability, market competition, corporate risk-taking behavior, and organizational flexibilization and decentralization; and by the consolidation of a *therapeutic ethos* (Lasch 1978; Bellah et al. 1996; Nolan 1998) which sharpens the cultural expectation that individuals must strive and be responsible for their well-being, emotional health, and self-realization (Illouz 2007, 2008; Honneth 2004). More fundamentally, neoliberalism should be regarded as a dominant and pervasive anthropological vision of a universal human nature that conceives all individuals as free, strategic, responsible, and autonomous beings, able to govern their psychological states and their relationships with others in a way that allows them to best fulfill their interests and pursue what it is understood to be their inherent objective: the achievement of happiness.

Not surprisingly, the rapid expansion of neoliberalism since the midst of the last century, especially from the 1980s onwards, has been accompanied by an increasing interest in happiness—as an academic topic and as a *pratique of self*—to the extent that in the course of the last decade we could say we are currently witnessing a drastic "happiness turn" (Ahmed 2010), a "turn" in which happiness has become a sort of moral imperative (Ehrenreich 2009; Lipovetsky 2007; Cabanas 2013), as well a privileged psychological framework through which to understand and redefine economic and labor behavior.

This chapter is concerned with how and for what purposes the notion of happiness and its psychological techniques have become so valuable, useful, and extended in neoliberal societies in general and in the context of networking corporations in particular. The main claim is that positive psychologists have contributed to reshape both the meaning and the logic of construction of the worker's identity in order to adapt their behavioral patterns, self-image, and expectations to the emerging demands of organizational control and power distribution within networking corporations.

In the first section, we explore the growing importance of the new science of happiness. We claim that, contrary to the mainstream discourse, a socioeconomic explanation would better account for the academic rise and social influence of happiness studies in general and of positive psychology in particular.

In the second section, we will introduce the idea that Maslow's "Pyramid of Needs," on whose general principles managerial theory has relied in the last decades, is undergoing an inversion. In the current economic setting of labor uncertainty and insecurity it is increasingly assumed that workers no longer must satisfy certain needs of economic safety and social achievement before developing more and more complex levels of personal fulfillment; on the contrary, through continuous acts of consumption, choice, and investment in one's "human capital," workers now must first attain high levels of happiness and self-fulfillment as a prerequisite to success in a permanent changing workplace, to achieve some degree of economic stability and to increase the odds of climbing the social ladder.

In the third section, we examine the purposes behind positive psychologists' repertoires and techniques. How do positive psychologists apply these repertoires and techniques to enhance workers' autonomy; to help transfer the burden of the market and organizational uncertainty onto individuals; to identify workers' identities with corporate culture; and to increase individual flexibility, coping abilities, and resistance to stress, anger, and workplace setbacks?

THE GROWING IMPORTANCE
OF HAPPINESS: A SOCIOECONOMIC EXPLANATION

The scientific study of happiness has received a great deal of attention in the fields of economy and organizational theory in the past decades. On the one hand, drawing upon the "Easterlin paradox" (Easterlin 1974)—a notion whose validity has been lately contested (e.g., Stevenson and Wolfers 2008)—economists such as Richard Easterlin, Bruno Frey, Luigino Bruni, Pier Luigi Porta, and Richard Layard, to name a few, have become more and more interested in the use of the concept of happiness as a central criterion to measure economic utility and to qualify the assumption that individuals' choices reflect their tendency to maximize personal profit (e.g., Layard 2005). They have also become increasingly interested in the development of happiness as a universal, scientific, and objective criterion for political decision making as well as for measuring the impact and efficacy of national policies of all countries.

This research has exerted enormous influence on a macropolitical and economic level. For instance, in 2012 the United Nations declared March 20 the "International Day of Happiness," proclaiming "happiness and well-being as universal goals and aspirations in the lives of human beings around the world," and defending "the importance of their recognition in public policy objectives" of nations. Echoing this statement, the Organization of Economic Cooperation and Development (OECD)—an influential world-wide institution which issues global reports, advocates economic policies, and coordinates statistics between more than thirty of the wealthiest nations—recommended adopting well-being measures in the national accounting systems, something for which countries such as the United States, United Kingdom, Chile, Japan, Israel, Spain, and Australia, to name just a few, have already signed up. The purpose is to develop a "Gross National Happiness" (GNH) index which goes beyond Gross National Product (GNP) as a measure of social progress. The rendering of happiness as a quantitative, commensurable, and objective criterion to legitimize a wide array of governmental and institutional decisions and interventions should be regarded as a step forward in the increasing tendency to govern individuals and depoliticize politics by the use of numbers and statistics, a tendency which is characteristic of the technoscientific and neoutilitarian logic of neoliberal economies (Lamont 2012; Rose 1990, 1991).

On the other hand, the ubiquitous use of the modern notion of happiness in the labor sphere should be regarded as one step forward in the process of managing workers' behaviour in terms of their "psyche" (Cabanas and Illouz 2015; Illouz 2008). From the 1960s onwards, the psychological language of emotions, creativity, cognitive flexibility, self-control, etc., has progressively functioned as an effective way to palliate the structural deficits in recognition as well as the inherent paradoxes and contradictions that are characteristic of modern workplaces. Psychology has gradually made illegitimate the evaluation of workers' performance in terms of moral categories, providing instead a more neutral and scientific framework to reconceptualize workers' failures or successes in terms of their own "deficient" or "optimal" selves, and teaching people to cope with the burden of the risk of uncertain and competitive workplaces in terms of their personal autonomy and flexibility. In other words, the psychological language has made more and more possible the devolution to workers of individual responsibility for the structural deficits of the workplace. The modern notion of happiness takes this trend even further in encouraging the widespread assumption that if individuals work hard on themselves, they will overcome performance problems and find or make their way in the world of labor.

Thus besides economics and organizational theory psychology is the field in which the study of human happiness has drawn more attention in the last few decades, with "positive psychology" on the front line of happiness studies. Actually, research on happiness-related topics such as "subjective well-being," "positive emotions," "flourishing," "optimism," and "resilience" has quadrupled since positive psychology appeared in academia at the turn of the century (Schui and Krampen 2010), and the research is still growing. Positive psychologists have also quickly created a broad institutional network, widely disseminated through PhD programs in "Positive Psychology"; master's degrees programs in "Applied Positive Psychology"; courses and speeches addressed to human resources personnel, coaches, and popular audiences; frequent symposia and workshops all over the world; several websites from which they collect data and provide questionnaires; and numerous academic journals, such as the *Journal of Happiness Studies*, founded in 2000, the *Journal of Positive Psychology*, founded in 2006, and the *Journal of Applied Psychology: Health and Well-Being*, founded in 2008, to name a few.

The rather fast expansion of this network, founded in 2003 and mainly coordinated by Martin Seligman from the "Positive Psychology Center" at the University of Pennsylvania, has been economically backed by a wide array of institutions, corporations, foundations, agencies, and governments. Just to give some examples, the US government has invested $145 million in the "Comprehensive Soldier Fitness" program developed by positive psychologists with the intention of improving military motivation and soldiers' resilience to post-traumatic episodes (e.g., Reivich et al.

2011; Casey 2011; Seligman and Fowler 2011). Many corporations, such as Coca-Cola, have also invested in positive psychology, whose findings are claimed to provide cheaper and more efficient methods of increasing corporate productivity, enhancing workers' performance, and promoting "organizational citizenship behavior." In addition, institutions related to health care, such as the Robert Wood Johnson Foundation, have funded positive psychology's research, seeking methods to reduce health costs and to extend people's longevity (e.g., Seligman 2008). Even institutions such as the John Templeton Foundation have invested more than $8 million in a coordinated project on positive psychology to develop the field of "Positive Neuroscience" and to study the role of spirituality in successful living (e.g., Vaillant 2002).

Positive psychologists claim that both this academic proliferation and social interest in the field is due to its ability to provide a "new field" in psychology for "the scientific study of happiness and human flourishing," a topic that has been presumably marginalized by "traditional psycho-therapy" (Seligman and Csikszentmihalyi 2000; see also Seligman 2002, 2011; Peterson and Seligman 2004; Fredrickson 2001, 2009; Snyder and Lopez 2007; Catalino and Fredrickson 2011). Nevertheless, from the very moment of its foundation this claim has been disputed by many critics who have questioned its presumed novelty (Taylor 2001; Kristjánsson 2012); its ethnocentrism and universalist aspirations (Christopher and Hickinbottom 2008; Becker and Macerek 2008); its religious roots (Ehrenreich 2009); its resemblance to self-help literature (Cabanas and Sánchez 2012; Cabanas and Huertas 2014); its theoretical contradictions and weaknesses (Held 2004; Miller 2008; Pérez-Álvarez 2012); its methodological problems (Lazarus 2003; Simmons, Nelson, and Simonsohn 2011; Brown, Sokal, and Friedman 2013); its therapeutic efficacy (Mongrain and Anselmo-Matthews 2012; Pérez-Álvarez 2013); or its scientific utility (Fernández-Ríos and Novo 2012).

Yet perhaps a socioeconomic explanation would better account for the academic rise and social influence of positive psychology—as well as for the increase in happiness studies in general over the last decades. From this point of view, the rapid proliferation of the field would not be due to its accurate insights on the nature of happiness but to its ability to provide a specific model of human behavior that, founded upon a neoliberal anthro-pology, fully meets the ideological assumptions of consumer capitalism in general and the emerging economic demands of networking corporations in particular.

Positive psychology conceives happiness both as the *leitmotiv* of human action and as the main drive for autonomous and emotionally healthy and efficient behavior. This notion of happiness combines the modern romantic ideal of the emotional and affective inner life as a space that has to be cultivated and expanded, with the rational and utilitarian demand of self-control as the ability to discipline and be responsible for channeling emotions in terms of one's interests (Gergen 1991), with the notion of "emotional intelligence" a good example of this. Defined as "the ability to perceive and accurately express emotion, to use emotion to facilitate thought, to understand emotions, and to manage emotions for emotional growth" (Brackett, Mayer, and Warner 2004, 1389), a notion such as "emotional intelligence" is no longer considered oxymoronic, but rather a feature of a much wider social demand for emotional rationality, with emotions falling into the sphere of individual responsibility. Indeed emotions—and their management—are at the center of the self-care therapeutic ethos of contemporary societies: they are considered one of the principal sources of happiness, health, and social adaptation, but also the source of suffering, maladjustment, and disorders, and so individuals must strive for their correct regulation and management.

As Eva Illouz has pointed out, the demand of emotional self-control is a central feature of what she has called "emotional capitalism" (Illouz 2007, 2008), a broad cultural process that reaches its peak in neoliberal societies. In "emotional capitalism" the rationale of therapy and the rationale of economy progressively shape each other, with emotions becoming an essential aspect of economic behavior, and the logic of economic exchange and reciprocal relationships becoming crucial to influence and understand emotional life. Through complex choice mechanisms shaped by the logic of the market and flooded with the language of affect and emotions (Illouz 2012), individuals of neoliberal societies are demanded to make self-fulfilling, reflexive, and strategic elections among a highly plural and heterogeneous corpus of options (Giddens 1991; Rose 1998). In this system, since every choice made by individuals at any moment not only helps to define them, but also serves to improve or reduce their worth as persons (Feher 2009), positive psychology represents a further, more advanced stage (as well as a highly influential and authoritative field) in the intertwining of the spheres of emotional management and personal self-worth with the neoliberal ideology of success and the cost-benefit rationale of economics.

Positive psychologists render happiness or positive psychological states (e.g., "emotional intelligence," "positive affects," "optimism," "subjective well-being," etc.) as the main cause of an individual's successful choices and outcomes in life, and happy individuals as fully functioning citizens (e.g., Lyubomirsky, King, and Diener 2005; Judge and Hurst 2008; Diener and

Chan 2011; Luhmann et al. 2012). It is stated that happy people thrive in life because they "flourish"—that is, because they "do good by feeling good" (Fredrickson 2013), claiming that there exists a causal relationship between happiness and life success that endures mainly when happiness is not a temporary, fleeting, or passing state, but when individuals are consistently and frequently cultivating their positive emotions and cognitions (Seligman 2002, 2011). Thus from this perspective fully functioning citizens are those who persistently work on their own happiness.

As noted elsewhere (Cabanas and Illouz 2015; Cabanas 2013), this continuous self-cultivation of happiness is underpinned by the assumption that individuals are (and must be) "Self-Made Men and Women," albeit those whose "self" would never be completely or fully "made," because the "self" can always be fuller and better. This assumption enrolls individuals in a sort of endless project of continuously pursuing "the best part of themselves." This "fundamental incompleteness of the self," in the words of Beck and Beck-Gernsheim (2002), lies at the core an era in which neoliberal capitalism ascended, being undoubtedly useful for a market that links the ideal of self-improvement to the principles of consumption and productivity (see also Redden 2007). To this effect, an expanding "happiness industry" has arisen around the promise of leading people through the path of the constant "flourishing" of health and success (Davies 2015).

At work, positive psychologists offer a wide array of happiness-based repertoires and techniques aiming to help individuals enhance performance and autonomy in competitive workplaces, cope with organizational changes and multitasking demands, increase flexible behavior, manage emotional expressions, pursue newer and more challenging goals, recognize promising opportunities, build rich and extensive social networks, or rationalize failures in a positive and productive way.

HUMAN CAPITAL, WORKING IDENTITY, AND THE INVERSION OF THE "PYRAMID OF NEEDS"

From our point of view, few social agents have contributed to shape and institutionalize certain models of human behavior as much as corporations have. The market economy has changed remarkably within the last fifty years, and both the corporate setting and notions of "work" and "worker" have been transformed accordingly. The economic setting has moved from a bureaucratized, hierarchical, and rather static "industrial capitalism" to a constantly changing, risky and quite flexible "consumer capitalism" (Beck 2000; Bauman 2001; Honneth 2004; Brinkmann 2008). As the result of

the continuous organizational change cycle and the progressive dissolution in the past decades of the ideas of job security and stability, a new
"spirit of capitalism" (Boltanski and Chiapello 2005) has arisen, followed
by a renewed work ethic and a new managerial ideology. The previous work
contract between employers and employees has become a casualty (Stum
2001), so previous dominant expectations of the workforce are no longer
tenable within current economic and organizational life. As Bob Aubrey
observed:

> Organizations nowadays have to assimilate a new reality and treat each employee
> as if s/he were a firm. This change means that some of the suppositions that
> had dominated industrial society have to be abandoned, first and foremost, the
> idea that people are looking for job security. This is a 1950s concept born out
> of Abraham Maslow's famous "pyramid of needs," with its postulate that fun-
> damental needs must be satisfied before we can even begin to consider other
> types of fulfillment (. . .) [and that] the firm's first responsibility was to create a
> secure environment, with fulfillment only coming at a later stage (Aubrey 1994,
> as cited in Boltanski and Chiapello 2005, 185).

Regarding Aubrey's first sentence, one of the more characteristic changes
brought by the emergent neoliberal work ethic is the exceptional stress
on personal responsibility. According to Boltanski and Chiapello (2007),
the progressive transition from external control to self-control is one of
the hallmarks of the evolution of organizations and managerial theories within the last thirty years. This transition is well exemplified in the
replacement of the idea of "career" by the idea of a succession of working
"projects." Contrary to careers, projects are unstructured arrays of paths,
objectives, and risk-filled enterprises that demand flexibility, autonomy,
and creativity—demands that apply both to individuals and corporations
alike. Individuals can then decide for themselves which are the best skills,
means, and choices that allow them to adapt to a highly uncertain market, perform efficiently, grow as workers, and look for more promising and
challenging projects. The notion that best describes workers' subjectivity in
neoliberal capitalism is "human capital."

According to Feher (2009), one of the most profound changes that subjectivity has encountered in the transition from industrial to consumer capitalism stems from the development of the notion of human capital. As he points
outs, in industrial capitalism, subjectivity was split into two differentiated
parts: a labor power that was the property of the individual and that could
be rented out in the market, and a bigger, incommensurable and inalienable
inner part that was not subject to either the laws of economic exchange or

the consumption of commodities. It was broadly assumed that the individual could not grow personally in the same way as he grew materially, and that the spheres of production and consumption could be an impediment to developing the inner world. In consumer capitalism, on the contrary, subjectivity is not separated into these two different spheres; rather, the sphere of the self—authenticity, identity, personality—and the spheres of production and consumption mutually define each other, each sphere being a condition of possibility to develop the others (see also Du Gay 1996). Human capital is everything that individuals presumably obtain through their own acts and choices—identity, social status, salary, etc.—and that is hypothetically due to the investment in and the deployment of those features that seemingly define them as "unique"; "my human capital is me" (Feher 2009, 26). This notion should be regarded as the expression of an emergent neoliberal condition in which workers increasingly think of their occupations as fulfilling enterprises that requires both the autonomous application and the continuous improvement of all of their skills and abilities (Honneth 2012).

Aubrey maintains that that the expected "career itinerary" that grew from job security to personal self-realization has died out, and the ability of Maslow's "Pyramid of Needs" to provide a satisfactory model of human behavior has apparently vanished with it. As Luc Boltanski and Ève Chiapello (2007) pointed out, security formed an essential part of the implicit and distinctive definition of "career" and the "Pyramid of Needs" brought psychological evidence to buttress the belief that security needs were of crucial importance since they rested at the base of his hierarchy. According to Maslow (1970), certain needs of security and stability (ranging from the mere physiological to more emotional and interpersonal ones) had to be satisfied before the individual could consider developing higher personal tasks such as self-fulfillment. But an itinerary that starts from security and leads to personal self-realization is no longer suitable—rather, if there is any itinerary, its current logic seems to be the opposite: one must first attain self-fulfillment and well-being in order to achieve some economic security and personal and social success at any level. Thus while Maslow's theory of human motivation and personality (1970) has become less and less able to meet the demands of the emerging economic and corporate settings in the last decades, other movements and academic disciplines addressing the nature of human needs and happiness have promised to fill this gap. Positive psychology plays a fundamental role here, with its pledge to provide a wide set of happiness-based repertoires and techniques that will guide workers throughout "the pace of change, limited time, and scarce financial resources that characterize today's workplace" (Youssef and Luthans 2007, 776).

Positive psychologists claim that previous research on happiness has failed to grasp the "correct" causality between life success and happiness—namely, that the latter is not a consequence or a psychological state merely correlated with the former, but that happiness should be regarded one of the main causes of success in many important domains of everyday life. By alleging support on cross-sectional, longitudinal, and experimental studies, positive psychologists claim that since "happy people are more likely to acquire favorable life circumstances" (Lyubomirsky, King, and Diener 2005, 803), happiness brings up success in many valuable personal, social, and economic events (Luhmann et al. 2012). As they assert, happiness lies underneath the achievement of many desirable outcomes such as superior mental and physical health (Koivumaa-Honkanen et al. 2004; Seligman 2002, 2011); higher longevity (Seligman 2008; Diener and Chan 2011); less medication use (Gil et al. 2004); high-quality social relationships, greater prosocial behavior (Diener and Seligman 2002); and fulfilling marriages and more stable romantic relationships (Oishi, Diener, and Lucas 2007), to name just a few.

It is the world of labor, though, where happiness-based repertoires and techniques have made the most dramatic changes. Here positive psychologists claim to have demonstrated how "happiness is an important precursor and determinant of career success" (Boehm and Lyubomirsky 2008, 101). According to them, happy workers perform better, are more productive (Oishi 2012) and show greater "organizational citizenship behaviour" (Ilies, Scott, and Judge 2006). They are more committed to their jobs (Masten and Reed, 2002; Thoresen et al., 2003; Herrbach 2006); cope better with organizational changes and multitasking demands (Luthans, Vogelgesang, and Lester, 2006; Biswas-Diener and Dean 2007; Yousseff and Luthans 2007); show less burnout, emotional exhaustion, and job withdrawal (Thoresen et al. 2003; Gil et al. 2004); and are more employable (Roberts, Caspi, and Moffitt 2003).

Happy workers also seem to show more autonomy and flexibility (Peterson and Seligman 2004); engage riskier behaviors by entering novel situations and pursuing newer and more challenging goals (Carver 2003; Judge and Hurst 2008); make more creative and efficient decisions (Baron 2008); easily recognize promising opportunities (Luthans, Youssef, and Avolio 2007); and build richer and more extensive social networks (Lucas and Diener 2003), all of them valuable personal features that would increase the odds of achieving more secure jobs for those working under less secure occupations, and better jobs and positions for those seeking promotion (Lyubomirsky, King, and Diener 2005; Salmela-Aro and Nurmi 2007). These personal features would also increase the odds for all kind of workers to attain higher incomes in the future (Diener et al. 2002). In his latest review on happiness and well-being studies, Ed Diener concludes that all "these findings are compelling because they rule out reverse causality from good performance to job satisfaction" (Diener 2012, 593).

Besides drawing upon some cross-sectional, longitudinal, and experimental studies, positive psychologists also base their claim of the causal relation between happiness and work success on what they call the "upward spiral" of happiness (see, for example, Fredrickson 2001, 2009; Fredrickson and Joiner 2002). According to this idea, since happy people are more motivated, perform better, build more positive relationships, cope better with uncertainty and changing conditions, enjoy better health, etc., than others, the former would presumably achieve a wider number of early successes in life than the latter, resulting in a cumulative advantage that would increase the probability of achieving subsequent successes. Positive psychologists claim that, by triggering a sort of a "Matthew Effect," higher happiness levels lead to a series of short-term achievements that set the tone for long-run ones, explaining why some people end up better off than others, both in their lives in general and in their work projects in particular (Judge and Hurst 2008).

Having established a causal relation between happiness and life success, positive psychologists take it one step further by claiming that this relationship endures mainly when happiness is not a temporary, fleeting, or passing state. Presumably, happiness is much more a matter of frequency than of intensity, so low-grade but frequent positive emotions and feelings better define happiness than intense but rarer ones (Boehm and Lyubomirsky 2008, 101–102). They state that "chronically happy people" are in general more successful than temporarily happy people, and that "their success is in large part a consequence of their happiness" (Lyubomirsky, King, and Diener 2005, 804). Although during the past decade positive psychologists have discussed whether happiness is a trait-like (genetic) or a state-like (developmental) construct (see, for example Seligman 2002; Peterson and Seligman 2004; Linley and Joseph 2004); the most commonly accepted assumption amongst them is that happiness is something that can be trained to a great extent through a wide variety of positive psychological techniques. Thus from this point of view becoming a "chronically happy person" means frequently and constantly working on happiness.

Enhancing happiness—and related aspects such as positive affects, positive emotions, optimism, hope, resilience, etc.—thus becomes a *sine qua non* condition to attain success in almost every domain of life, especially at the workplace. Instead of requiring a secure background from which individuals can look for the satisfaction of those material and social needs that allow them to develop their authentic selves—as understood in Maslow's "Pyramid"—individuals now must first meet and develop that authenticity in order to do what they do best, reach certain degrees of economic stability, thrive in life, and cultivate their work projects. We claim that positive psychology is transforming the construction of workers' identity, in which both the requirements and the logic of working success are changing, with happiness being progressively understood as a sort of a *necessary psychological state* to thrive in the contemporary work world. We call this a process of "inversion of the Pyramid of Needs," which advances an emerging logic in the construction of workers' selfhood in the new century (Cabanas and Sánchez, 2016). This process is consistent with the reality posited by the assumptions and demands of neoliberal anthropology, and prompted by the powerful influence that happiness studies—with positive psychology at the forefront—have exerted in the world of labor over the past decades. Whereas more theoretical and empirical studies are required in this direction, we think that this process of "inversion of the Pyramid of Needs" is not limited to complementing previously existing models of subjectivity in the labor sphere, but it aims at progressively replacing them.

WOBBLY MARKETS, AUTONOMY, AND FLEXIBLE SELVES

Autonomy and flexibility are among the most valuable skills that workers must deploy to thrive in the interdependent and competitive logic of networking corporations. Happiness-based repertoires and techniques aim to construct self-regulated, resilient, and emotionally intelligent subjects—"happy workers"—capable of making their own decisions, managing working relationships, coping with uncertainty, adapting to unexpected changes, and reframing adversity in a positive and productive way. Indeed making "happy workers"—and not merely making workers happy—has become a first-order concern for many corporations, especially when Gallup estimated that, in the United States alone, the unhappiness of employees imposes a cost of "$500 billion a year in lost productivity, lost tax receipts, and health care costs" (Davies 2015, 9). Thus many corporations consult happiness professionals in order to cheer up their employees, restore their enthusiasm for work, help them to emotionally cope with layoffs, but, especially, to instruct employees in how to become more psychologically autonomous and more cognitively and emotionally flexible.

Autonomy and flexibility are paradoxical properties, though; while they offer a promise of self-fulfillment and emancipation from organizational control, they also provide an identity construction that compels workers to identify and to conform to corporate expectations. They pledge to provide workers with a high degree of individuality, autonomy, and initiative, even as a closer look at the organizational reality shows that far from fulfilling this promise, its application seems to produce quite contradictory outcomes (Marzano 2012). Happiness-based repertoires and techniques have become useful vehicles both to transfer external ways of control onto the internal locus of individual subjectivity, as well as to link workers' identity with the accomplishment of organizational objectives and "corporate culture."

Autonomy, organizational commitment, and personal strengths

The increasing transference from external control to self-control in the last thirty years has been mainly channeled through the notion of "corporate culture." This notion understands that the relation between the worker and the organization is no longer mediated by a working contract but by a moral bond of mutual trust and commitment through which the interests of the corporation and workers are not rendered as complementary, but as identical. In this regard, trust and commitment become the other face of self-control.

Although networking organizations no longer apply control mainly through explicit and external mechanisms or through promises of job security and career development, it is not that controlling mechanisms have disappeared within the organizational sphere. Rather, organizations draw upon mechanisms of individual recognition to make workers identify with the corporation's general principles, values, and productive criteria (Du Gay 1996; Rose 1998; Álvarez and Marín 2006; Pulido-Martínez 2010)— that is, with the "corporate culture."

Corporate culture takes the shape of a semidemocratic environment that helps workers create an affective and moral bond of commitment and trust with the corporation and with co-workers. On the one hand, by making the working environment more "home-like," distinctions between the worker's public and private spheres are blurred, thus increasing the worker's sense of belonging to the firm (Sointu 2005). On the other hand, workers are encouraged to find their own motivations and their own means for achievement. In both senses, networking organizations are rendered as highly personalized and seemingly democratic environments, and workers as indispensable and active units of the internalization, exemplification, and reproduction of corporative values. Google, Inc., among many others, is an archetypical example of this:

> Employees can show up to work anytime they want, can bring their dog, wear pajamas, eat gourmet food for free, enjoy a free fitness center and trainer, see the onsite doctor if sick, wash their clothes, and partake in free espresso at each corner of their "office". This relaxed, fun environment has worked well for Google, Inc. because it provides a psychological benefit to encourage employees to be more committed, more creative, and more productive. Google Inc.'s method of job design is staying away from monolithic hierarchies that stifle and distract creative ideas. When highly motivated and highly capable people have a common vision, they do not need to be micromanaged (. . .) Google, Inc. thrives in a "I think I can" culture, not the traditional "no you can't" bureaucracy (. . .) Talented people do not want to be told what to do; they want to interact in small intimate groups, they want feedback and challenging projects, they want time to work on their creative ideas, they want a genuine effort to promote improved personal life, they want a cool place to work in (Cook 2012).

In this vein, work should not be viewed as a necessity or a duty, so much as an opportunity. Workers are heartened to consider the workplace as a privileged site to "flourish," and positive psychology's repertoires and techniques are useful in shaping subjectivity in this direction. For instance, in their book *Positive Psychology Coaching: Putting the Science of Happiness to Work for your Clients*, Biswas-Diener and Dean claim that "so important is our work to our identity that we proudly claim our occupation as synonymous with who we are," with what makes us express our inner talents, needs, and interests (2007, 190). Individuals are most fulfilled, they argue, when they have a "calling-orientation" approach to work, meaning they work because they love to do it and because it makes them flourish, not because they "have to":

> People with a calling orientation typically love and value what they do in and of itself. They may be paid well for what they do but typically espouse the idea that they would "do this for free" . . .; these people like to think about their work, even when they are off the clock, and would be likely to take their work with them on vacation. It is important to note that these are not simply workaholics (although some may be) who are absorbed only with their jobs but are people who believe they are creating a better world (195).

To this effect, positive psychologists claim to provide scientific and objective instruments to "spot" and develop what they call individual's "strengths and virtues." According to them, individuals are naturally equipped with a certain set of inner psychological potential traits that entail "a particular way of behaving, thinking, or feeling that is authentic and energizing to the user, and enables optimal functioning, development and performance" (Linley and Burns 2010, 4), so the main reason why individuals achieve great outcomes in life is because they "focus on what they do best" (Hodges and Clifton 2004, 258). Thus it is by applying their authentic abilities to every task or challenge that individuals achieve an extraordinary sense of excitement, authenticity, and motivation (Peterson and Seligman 2004). To this regard, it is stated that the workplace provides both a highly demanding and rewarding site in which these strengths and virtues can be autonomously deployed, proved, and improved.

Autonomy is highly valuable in networking organizations because responsibility is no longer vertically distributed but horizontally spread and diffused. This means that individuals must assume a great deal of the contingencies of work, being completely responsible for their performance and having to autonomously manage their personal abilities, material means, and time to accomplish their objectives. Autonomy accompanies the expectation that workers adopt an active and creative self-organizing and self-directed role in the performance of their tasks. Sales agents are a good example of this: they have to develop their client portfolios, secure client loyalty, keep them satisfied, and come up with innovative ideas to increase productivity or to make their work more efficient, and the assumption is that the outcomes they obtain—whether successful or not—are mostly dependent of their own performance and effort.

Autonomy, which includes closely associated psychological concepts such as self-control, self-regulation, and self-efficacy, is one of the happiness-related keywords of positive psychology. According to the discipline, the development and deployment of autonomy is not only beneficial for the organization (e.g., insourcing of responsibility and less expenditure in external control and surveillance) but also fundamental for individual flourishing and success: as positive psychologists Christopher Peterson and Martin Seligman put it, those "who consistently exercise the muscle of self-control are happier, more productive, and more successful" (2004, 38). Thus taking the notion of autonomy as one of the primary variables explaining individual happiness and well-being, positive psychologists, as well as a multitude of self-help writers, counselors, motivational speakers, and coaches—where the latest trend is the so-called "self-coaching," a training aimed at turning workers into their own coaches—provide a multitude of happiness-based techniques for emotional and cognitive self-regulation. These techniques all promise workers that they will succeed in expanding their self-governing abilities in order to increase performance, build positive and profitable relationships, manage anger, develop healthy habits, cope with risk and uncertainty, rationalize everyday failures in a positive and productive manner, and so on.

There are multiple examples of these techniques, ranging from those consisting in changing emotional styles (defined as the way individuals rationalize the causes of their successes and failures—see Reivich and Gillham 2003); to those focused on making frequent positive self-affirmations (see Weis 2012); to training hope (defined as "goal-directed thinking in which people perceive that they can produce routes to desired goals [pathways thinking] and the requisite motivation to use those routes [agency thinking]"—see Lopez, Snyder, and Pedrotti 2003, 94); to practicing gratitude and forgiveness (presenting both as trait-like virtues and state-like abilities which individuals must develop in order to increase positive affect and to avoid focusing on defeatism and complaining—see Peterson and Seligman 2004); to cultivating optimism (defined as "an individual difference variable that reflects the extent to which people hold generalized favorable expectancies for their future"—see Carver, Scheier, and Segerstrom 2010, 1). Lately, one of the most popular happiness-based techniques is "mindfulness," which, like the previously mentioned techniques, has had a significant impact on the theoretical teachings of business studies and on managerial practices within organizations. Mindfulness training programs instruct individuals to focus intensely on their emotions and bodily signals, in order to reach full self-control and optimize their effects on personal well-being. Mixing spiritual counseling with positive science, mindfulness professionals promise to help workers reduce stress and anxiety, and offer organizations an effective service for increasing workforce performance, reducing absenteeism, and creating a more solid and emotionally healthy corporate culture. Although there is no clear evidence that mindfulness is as effective as it is claimed to be, many corporations such as Google, Inc., and institutions such as the US Marine Corps, have widely incorporated mindfulness services into their managerial policies (Cederström and Spicer 2015).

In contrast with this promise of success and satisfaction, however, autonomy actually poses a burden that might be too challenging for individuals to bear given the high levels of pressure and competition, multitasking and stressful demands, constant downsizing threats, etc., that really characterize networking organizations. Paradoxically, as Michela Marzano (2012) points out, the greater the anxiety and depression generated by this pressure on personal autonomy—and the less control that individuals have over their working lives—the more there are increases in the number of psychological techniques that promise to enhance self-control and self-directed behavior as the best solution to cope with all these stressful demands. These techniques often pledge to increase a sense of personal autonomy in a context in which the individuals generally lack of real control over their decisions, tasks, and objectives. But whereas this emphasis in workers' autonomy exerts contradictory effects over the workforce at the expense of higher benefits and adaptability for corporations, it also posits some dangers for corporations themselves, since their business activity becomes more and more dependent upon workers' engagement and commitment with the corporate culture in general and the organizational objectives in particular. Hence happiness-based techniques are not mere complementary tools for corporations to foster employees' sense of autonomy, but they stand out as central emotional resources for control and surveillance in the new labor setting.

Flexibility and resiliency

Another important feature that defines networking organization is paradoxically "permanent flexibility." Described as "the organization's ability to meet an increasing variety of consumer expectations while keeping costs, delays, organizational disruptions, and performance losses at or near zero" (Sánchez et al. 2007, 44; see also Zhang et al. 2002), flexibility depends much more on workers than on any technical factor. In this sense, an individual's ability to flexibly perform his tasks becomes a main source of corporative productivity, so psychological techniques aiming to enhance this kind of ability are highly valued and demanded.

Like autonomy, flexibility is a concept currently applied both to corporations (to their organizational structure) and individuals (to their cognitive and emotional structure) alike. Regarding corporations, the flexibilization of the organizational setting has produced low-cost and tangible benefits for corporations (Kokkaew and Koompai 2012; Mythen 2005; Allen and Henry 1997), but the risks and insecurities associated with employment and production have exponentially increased. A new employment regime based upon less secure jobs, more fragmented and varied tasks, and more precarious conditions prevails in networking organizations, which are subject to less and less regulation. As Uchitelle and Kleinfield pointed out (1996), "what companies do to make themselves secure is precisely what makes their workers feel insecure." With the number of casual, flexitime, part-time, and self-employed workers increasing dramatically in the last decades, corporations are freer to change the level of employment through hiring and firing, to make changes in working time by introducing flexible working hours and by making them coincide with highly productive periods, to increase job rotation and to require multitasking for the same wage (Sánchez et. al, 2007).

Regarding individuals, flexibility has also made possible the transfer of the burden of organizational uncertainty onto workers. Flexible workers are defined as those able to "change the number, scope, or type of job tasks," to "change the quality and amount of interactions with others on the job," or "to change cognitive task boundaries" (Biswas-Diener and Dean 2007, 198–199). One of the most popular concepts that positive psychologists use to define a flexible individual is that of "resiliency," defined as a psychological state-like capacity of adaptation and coping with adversity that the individual is able to cultivate and enhance in order to achieve higher levels of job satisfaction, work performance, and organizational commitment (Masten and Reed 2002). Presumably, resilient individuals do not let themselves be beset by problems and adversity, but they "bounce back and even beyond" to sustain effort and to attain success (Yousseff and Luthans 2007, 784), turning setbacks into stunning opportunities for self-development. According to positive psychologists, these kind of individuals are much more cognitively and behaviorally flexible; they cope better with multitasking demands, role restructuring, and job redesign; they are better able to improvise in changing situations; and they are more capable of using adverse experiences in their favor to increase performance on subsequent tasks than nonresilient employees (Luthans, Vogelgesang, and Lester 2006). In this sense, resilient workers are less prone to suffer from psychological problems such as depression, stress, "burnout," or emotional exhaustion (Linley and Joseph 2004).

Resiliency techniques range from identifying and discarding self-defeating and dysfunctional beliefs when facing challenges, so they can be replaced by more constructive and energizing ones, to imagining possible problematic situations and brainstorming solutions that would best work to solve them. They draw upon two principal tenets: prevention and a future-oriented behavior. Regarding the former, the idea of prevention suggests that resiliency and other positive psychological aspects such as optimism, positive emotions, positive thinking, and overall happiness provide a psychological "buffer" that protects individuals against setbacks, potential pathologies, stressful environments, burnout, and negative life events in general. Regarding the latter, resiliency techniques do not aim either to find profound psychological reasons that might be producing dysfunctional behaviors and thoughts or to deeply and structurally change the psyche, but to prompt individuals to always look ahead. Thus people must focus on the potentialities that have yet to be developed and deployed, on their abilities to create positive environments suitable to their needs and motivations, and on reframing problems and setbacks as new and promising opportunities to try harder and continue "flourishing."

CONCLUSION

In their book *The Wellness Syndrome*, Carl Cederström and André Spicer understand happiness as an emerging ideology that stresses the insourcing of responsibility; delineates a new moral regime that defines what is right and wrong; promises rewards for those who engage in psychic self-development; and punishes those who fail to conform to it (2015). Happiness pervades every sphere of everyday life, exerting a remarkable impact on all of them, especially in the realm of labor. As discussed in this chapter, the current socioeconomic setting of neoliberalism and positive psychology's notion of happiness are inherently entangled, with happiness-based techniques and measurements gearing the psychological and the emotional dimensions toward the new logic of productivity—more autonomous, more flexible, more interpersonal and emotionally saturated.

On the one hand, human happiness takes the shape of a model or schema that organizes a kind of subjectivity saturated with the neoliberal anthropology of the self-governed subject, defined as an autonomous, self-determined, and always incomplete individual who is responsible for choosing his own "worldview"; looking after himself in a highly competitive environment; and striving for authenticity, flourishing, and self-realization as the main causes of a successful and healthy life.

On the other hand, happiness-based repertoires and techniques articulate a new narrative and a new logic of identity construction that is tightly attached to the workplace, to a new work ethic, and to the new power distribution within networking organizations, bringing in the early 21st century profound transformations in the kind of subjectivity required to adapt to these changes. The most striking example of this is the phenomenon that we have called "the inversion of the Pyramid of Needs," a process by which both the requirements and the logic of working success are changing. Happiness—and related aspects such as positive affects, positive emotions, optimism, hope, resilience, etc.—is now a *necessary psychological state* to attain a wide array of material and social needs that are highly valuable, but scarce, arduous, and uncertain in current societies.

Within networking organizations, autonomy, flexibility, and commitment to the corporate culture are viewed as the main sources of corporate production and adaptation, and the primary means to elicit worker responsibility. This way, networking organizations transfer external mechanisms of control to internal and self-managed ones, delegate many of the contingencies of work to workers, and displace a great deal of burden of the market and organizational uncertainty onto individuals themselves. Happiness becomes a fundamental tool to manage worker subjectivity, with positive psychologists providing organizations with legitimate and scientific happiness models and instruments to account for their emergent needs of decentralization, competition, risk-taking, and control.

REFERENCES

Ahmed, Sara. 2010. *The Promise of Happiness*. Durham, NC: Duke University Press.

Allen, J., and N. Henry. 1997. "Ulrich Beck's Risk Society at Work: Labour and Employment in the Contract Service Industries." *Transactions of the Institute of British Geographers, New Series* 22(2):180–196.

Álvarez, C. M., and L. M. Marín. 2006. "Tecnologías Empresariales del Yo: La Construcción de Sujetos Laborales en el Contexto del Trabajo Inmaterial." *Universitas Psychologica* 6(1):49–58.

Baron, R. A. 2008. "The Role of Affect in the Entrepreneurial Process." *Academy of Management Review* 33(2):328–340.

Baudrillard, Jean. 2004. *The Consumer Society: Myths and Structures*. London: SAGE.

Bauman, Z. 2001. "Consuming Life." *Journal of Consumer Culture* 1(1):9–29.

Beck, Ulrich. 2000. *Risk Society: Towards a New Modernity*. London: SAGE.

Beck, Ulrich, and E. Beck-Gernsheim. 2002. *Individualization: Institutionalized Individualism and its Social and Political Consequences*. London: SAGE.

Becker, D., and J. Macerek. 2008. "Positive Psychology: History in the Remaking?" *Theory and Psychology* 18(5):591–604.

Bellah, R. N., R. Madsen, W. Sullivan, A. Swindler, and S. M. Tipton. 1996. *Habits of the Heart: Individualism and Commitment in American Life*. Berkeley: University of California Press.

Biswas-Diener, R., and B. Dean. 2007. *Positive Psychology Coaching. Putting the Science of Happiness to Work for Your Clients*. Hoboken, NJ: Wiley.

Boehm, J. K. and S. Lyubomirsky. 2008. "Does Happiness Promote Career Success?" *Journal of Career Assessment* 16(1):101–116. doi: 10.1177/1069072707308140

Boltanski, L., and E. Chiapello. 2005. "The New Spirit of Capitalism." *International Journal of Politics, Culture, and Society* 18(3–4):161–188.

Boltanski, L., and E. Chiapello. 2007. *The New Spirit of Capitalism*. London: Verso.

Brackett, Marc A., John D. Mayer, and Rebecca M. Warner. 2004. "Emotional Intelligence and Its Relation to Everyday Behaviour." *Personality and Individual Differences* 36(6):1387–1402.

Brinkmann, Svend. 2008. "Changing Psychologies in the Transition from Industrial Society to Consumer Society." *History of the Human Sciences* 21(2):85–110.

Brown, N. J. L., A. D. Sokal, and H. L. Friedman. 2013. "The Complex Dynamics of Wishful Thinking: The Critical Positivity Ratio." *American Psychologist*. Advance online publication. doi: 10.1037/a0032850.

Cabanas, Edgar. 2013. "La Felicidad como Imperativo Moral: Origen y Difusión del Individualismo 'Positivo' y sus Efectos en la Construcción de la Subjetividad." PhD diss., Departament of Basic Psychology, Universidad Autónoma de Madrid.

Cabanas, Edgar, and J. A. Huertas, 2014. "Psicología Positiva y Psicología Popular de la Autoayuda: un Romance Histórico, Psicológico y Cultural." *Anales de Psicología* 30(3):852–864.

Cabanas, Edgar, and Eva Illouz. 2015. "Fit Fürs Glück: Positive Psychologie Und Ihr Einfluss Auf Die Identität von Arbeitskräften in Neoliberalen Organisationen." *Verhaltenstherapie & psychosoziale Praxis* 47(3):563–578.

Cabanas, Edgar, and J. C. Sáchez. 2016. "Inverting the Pyramid of Needs: Positive Psychology's New Order for Labor Success." *Psicothema* 28(2):107–113.

Cabanas, Edgar, and J. C. Sánchez. 2012. "The Roots of Positive Psychology." *Papeles del Psicólogo* 33(3):172–182.

Carver, Charles S. 2003. "Pleasure As a Sign You Can Attend to Something Else: Placing Positive Feelings within a General Model of Affect." *Cognition and Emotion* 17(2):241–261.

Carver, Charles S., Michael F. Scheier, and Suzanne C. Segerstrom. 2010. "Optimism." *Clinical Psychology Review* 30(7):879–889.

Casey, G. W., Jr. 2011. "Comprehensive Soldier Fitness: A Vision for Psychological Resilience in the U.S. Army." *American Psychologist* 66(1):1–3.

Catalino, L. I., and B. L. Fredrickson. 2011. "A Tuesday in the Life of a Flourisher: The Role of Positive Emotional Reactivity in Optimal Mental Health." *Emotion* 11(4):938–950.

Cederström, Carl, and André Spicer. 2015. *The Wellness Syndrome.* Malden, MA: Polity.

Christopher, John, and Sarah Hickinbottom. 2008. "Positive Psychology, Ethnocentrism, and the Disguised Ideology of Individualism." *Theory and Psychology* 18(5):563–589.

Cook, J. 2012. "How Google Motivates their Employees with Rewards and Perks." HubPages. *www.ThinkingLeaders.com.* May 27. http://hubpages.com/business/How-Google-Motivates-their-Employees-with-Rewards-and-Perks

Davies, William. 2015. *The Happiness Industry: How the Government and Big Business Sold Us Well-Being.* London and New York: Verso.

Diener, Edward. 2012. "New Findings and Future Directions for Subjective Well-Being Research." *American Psychologist* 67(8):590–597.

Diener, Edarwd, C. Nickerson, R. E. Lucas, and E. Sandvik. 2002. "Dispositional Affect and Job Outcomes." *Social Indicators Research* 59(3):229–259.

Diener, Edward, and M. E. P. Seligman. 2002. "Very Happy People." *Psychological Science* 13(1):81–84.

Diener, Edward, and M. Y. Chan. 2011. "Happy People Live Longer: Subjective Well-Being Contributes to Health and Longevity." *Applied Psychology: Health and Well-Being* 3(1):1–43.

Du Gay, Paul. 1996. *Consumption and Identity at Work.* London: SAGE.

Easterlin, Richard A. 1974. "Does Economic Growth Improve the Human Lot? Some Empirical Evidence." In *Nations and Households in Economic Growth: Essays in Honor of Moses Abramovitz,* edited by Paul A. David and Melvin V. Reder, 89–125. New York: Academic.

Ehrenreich, Barbara. 2009. *Smile or Die: How Positive Thinking Fooled America and the World.* London: Granta.

Feher, M. 2009. "Self-Appreciation, or the Aspirations of Human Capital." *Public Culture* 21(1):21–41.

Fernández-Ríos, L., and M. Novo. 2012. "Positive Pychology: Zeigeist (or Spirit of the Times) or Ignorance (or Disinformation) of History?" *International Journal of Clinical and Health Psychology* 12(2):333–344.

Fredrickson, B. L. 2001. "The Role of Positive Emotions in Positive Psychology: The Broaden-And-Build Theory of Positive Emotions." *American Psychologist* 56(3): 218–226.

Fredrickson, B. L. 2009. *Positivity*. New York: Crown.

Fredrickson, B. L. 2013. "Updated Thinking on Positivity Ratios." *American Psychologist*. Advance online publication. doi: 10.1037/a0033584.

Fredrickson, B. L., and T. Joiner. 2002. "Positive Emotions." In *Handbook of Positive Psychology*, edited by C. R. Snyder and S. J. Lopez, 120–134. New York: Oxford University Press.

Gergen, Keneth. 1991. *The Saturated Self*. New York: Basic Books.

Giddens, Anthony. 1991. *Modernity and Self-Identity*. Cambridge, UK: Polity.

Gil, K. M., J. W. Carson, L. S. Porter, C. Scipio, S. M. Bediako, and E. Orringer. 2004. "Daily Mood and Stress Predict Pain, Health Care Use, and Work Activity in African American Adults with Sickle-Cell Disease." *Health Psychology* 23(3):267–274.

Harvey, David. 2007. *A Brief History of Neoliberalism*. New York: Oxford University Press.

Held, Barbara. 2004. "The Negative Side of Positive Psychology." *Journal of Humanistic Psychology* 44(1):9–46.

Herrbach, O. 2006. "A Matter of Feeling? The Affective Tone of Organizational Commitment and Identification." *Journal of Organizational Behavior* 27(5):629–643.

Hodges, T.D., and D. O. Clifton. 2004. "Strengths-Based Development in Practice." In *Positive Psychology in Practice*, edited by P. A. Linley and S. Joseph, 256–268. Hoboken, NJ: Wiley.

Honneth, Axel. 2004. "Organized Self-Realization: Some Paradoxes of Individualization." *European Journal of Social Theory* 7(4):463–478.

Honneth, Axel. 2012. *The I in We: Studies on the Theory of Recognition*. Cambridge, MA: Polity.

Ilies, R., B.A. Scott, and T. A. Judge. 2006. "The Interactive Effects of Personal Traits and Experienced States on Intraindividual Patterns of Citizenship Behaviour." *Academy of Management Journal* 49(3):561–575.

Illouz, Eva. 2007. *Cold Intimacies: The Making of Emotional Capitalism*. Cambridge, UK: Polity.

Illouz, Eva. 2008. *Saving the Modern Soul. Therapy, Emotions, and the Culture of Self-Help*. Berkeley: University of California Press.

Illouz, Eva. 2012. *Why Love Hurts: A Sociological Explanation*. Cambridge, UK: Polity.

Judge, T. A. and C. Hurst. 2008. "How the Rich and Happy Get Richer and Happier: Relationship of Core Self-Evaluations to Trajectories in Attaining Work Success." *Journal of Applied Psychology* 93(4):849–863.

Koivumaa-Honkanen, H., M. Koskenvuo, R.J. Honkanen, H. Viinamaki, K. Heikkila, and J. Kaprio. 2004. "Life Dissatisfaction and Subsequent Work Disability in an 11-Year Follow-Up." *Psychological Medicine* 34(2):221–228.

Kokkaew, N. and S. Koompai. 2012. "Current Practices of Human Resource Management HRM in Thai Construction Industry: A Risk and Opportunity Perspective." *Review of Integrative Business and Economic Research* 1(1):1–14.

Krisjánsson, Kristjan. 2012. "Positive Psychology and Positive Education: Old Wine in New Bottles?" *Educational Psychologist* 47(2):86–105.

Lamont, Michèle. 2012. "Toward a Comparative Sociology of Valuation and Evaluation." *Annual Review of Sociology* 38(1):201–221.

Lasch, Christopher. 1978. *The Culture of Narcissism: American Life in an Age of Diminishing Expectations.* New York: W.W. Norton.

Layard, Richard. 2005. *Happiness: Lessons from a New Science.* London: Allen.

Lazarus, Richard S. 2003. "Does the Positive Psychology Movement Have Legs?" *Psychological Inquiry* 14(2):93–109.

Lee, K., and N. J. Allen. 2002. "Organizational Citizenship Behavior and Workplace Deviance: The Role of Affect And Cognitions." *Journal of Applied Psychology* 87(1):131–142.

Linley, P. A. and G. W. Burns. 2010. "Strengthspotting: Finding and Developing Client Resources in the Management of Intense Anger." In *Happiness, Healing, Enhancement: Your Casebook Collection for Applying Positive Psychology in Therapy* edited by G.W. Burns, 3–14. Hoboken, NJ: Wiley.

Linley, A. and S. Joseph, eds. 2004. *Positive Psychology in Practice.* Hoboken, NJ: Wiley.

Lipovetsky, G. 2007. *La Felicidad Paradójica: Ensayo sobre la Sociedad de Hiperconsumo.* Barcelona: Anagrama.

Lopez, Shane J., C. R. Snyder, and Jennifer Teramoto Pedrotti. 2003. "Hope: Many Definitions, Many Measures." In *Positive Psychological Assessment: A Handbook of Models and Measures,* edited by Shane J Lopez and C. R. Snyder, 91–106. Washington, DC: American Psychological Association.

Lucas, R. E., and E. Diener. 2003. "The Happy Worker: Hypotheses About the Role of Positive Affect in Worker Productivity." In *Personality and Work,* edited by M. Barrick and A. M. Ryan, 30–59. San Francisco: Jossey-Bass.

Luhmann, M., R. E. Lucas, M. Eid, and E. Diener. 2012. "The Prospective Effect of Life Satisfaction on Life Events." *Social Psychological and Personality Science.* Advance online publication. doi:10.1177/1948550612440105

Luthans, F., C. M. Youssef, and B. J. Avolio. 2007. *Psychological Capital: Developing the Human Competitive Edge.* New York: Oxford University Press.

Luthans, F., G. R. Vogelgesang, and P. B. Lester. 2006. "Developing the Psychological Capital of Resiliency." *Human Resource Development Review* 5(1):25–44.

Lyubomirsky, S., L. King, and E. Diener. 2005. "The Benefits of Frequent Positive Affect: Does Happiness Lead to Success?" *Psychological Bulletin* 131(6):803–855.

Marzano, Michela. 2011. *Programados para Triunfar: Nuevo Capitalismo, Gestión Empresarial y Vida Privada.* Barcelona: Tusquets.

Maslow, Abraham H. 1970. *Motivation and Personality.* New York: Harper and Row.

Masten, A. S., and M. J. Reed. 2002. "Resilience in Development". In *Handbook of Positive Psychology,* edited by C. R. Snyder and S. Lopez, 74–88. Oxford: Oxford University Press.

Miller, Alistair. 2008. "A Critique of Positive Psychology –or 'The New Science of Happiness.'" *Journal of Philosophy of Education* 42(3–4):591–608.

Mongrain, M., and T. Anselmo-Mattews. 2012. "Do Positive Psychology Exercises Work? A Replication of Seligman et al. 2005." *Journal of Clinical Psychology* 68(4):382–389.

Mythen, G. 2005. "Employment, Individualization and Insecurity: Rethinking the Risk Society Perspective." *The Sociological Review* 53(1):129–149.

Nolan, J. L., Jr. 1998. *The Therapeutic State: Justifying Government at Century's End.* New York: New York University Press.

Oishi, Shigehiro. 2012. *The Psychological Wealth of Nations: Do Happy People Make a Happy Society?* Malden, MA: Wiley-Blackwell.

Oishi, Shigehiro, E. Diener, and R. E. Lucas. 2007. "The Optimal Level of Well-Being: Can People Be Too Happy?" *Perspectives on Psychological Science* 2(4):346–360.

Pérez-Álvarez, Marino. 2012. "La Psicología Positiva: Magia Simpática." *Papeles del Psicólogo* 33(3):183–201.

Pérez-Álvarez, Marino. 2013. "La Psicología Positiva y Sus Amigos: En Evidencia." *Papeles del Psicólogo* 34(3):208–226.

Peterson, Christopher, and M. E. P. Seligman. 2004. *Character Strengths and Virtues: A Handbook and Classification.* New York: Oxford University Press.

Pulido-Martínez, H.C. 2010. "Psychological Knowledge for the Governance of the South." *Critical Perspectives on International Businesses* 6(2–3):177–189.

Read, J. 2009. "A Genealogy of Homo-Economicus: Neoliberalism and the Production of Subjectivity." *Foucault Studies* 6:25–36.

Redden, Guy. 2007. "Makeover Morality and Consumer Culture." In *Reading Makeover Television: Realities Remodelled,* edited by D. Heller, 150–164. London: I. B. Tauris.

Reivich, K., and J. Gillham. 2003. "Learned Optimism: The Measurement of Explanatory Style." In *Positive Psychological Assessment: A Handbook of Models and Measures,* edited by C.R. Snyder and S.J. Lopez, 57–74. Washington, DC: American Psychological Association.

Reivich, K. J., M. Seligman, and S. McBride. 2011. "Master Resilience Training in the U.S. Army." *American Psychologist* 66(1):25–34.

Roberts, B. W., A. Caspi, and T. E. Moffitt. 2003. "Work Experiences and Personality Development in Young Adulthood." *Journal of Personality and Social Psychology* 84(3):582–593.

Rose, Nikolas. 1990. *Governing the Soul: The Shaping of the Private Self.* New York: Routledge.

Rose, Nikolas. 1991. "Governing by Numbers: Figuring out Democracy." *Accounting Organizations and Society* 16(7):673–692.

Rose, Nikolas. 1998. *Inventing Our Selves: Psychology, Power, and Personhood.* Cambridge, UK: Cambridge University Press.

Salmela-Aro, K., and J. Nurmi. 2007. "Self-Esteem During University Studies Predicts Career Characteristics 10 Years Later." *Journal of Vocational Behavior* 70(3):463–477.

Sánchez, A.M., M. Pérez, P. Carnicer, M. J. V. Jiménez. 2007. "Teleworking and Workplace Flexibility: a Study of Impact on Firm Performance." *Personnel Review* 36(1):42–64.

Schui, G., and G. Krampen. 2010. "Bibliometric Analyses on the Emergence and Present Growth of Positive Psychology." *Applied Psychology: Health and Well-Being* 2(1):52–64.

Scott, B. A., and T. A. Judge. 2006. "Insomnia, Emotions, and Job Satisfaction: A Multilevel Study." *Journal of Management* 32(5):622–645.

Seligman, M. E. P. 2002. *Authentic Happiness: Using the New Positive Psychology to Realize Your Potential for Lasting Fulfillment.* New York: Free Press.

Seligman, M. E. P. 2008. "Positive Health." *Applied Psychology: An International Review* 57, supp. 1:3–18.

Seligman, M. E. P. 2011. *Flourish: A New Understanding of Happiness and Well-Being— And How To Achieve Them.* London: Nicholas Brealey.

Seligman, M. E. P., and M. Csikszentmihalyi. 2000. "Positive Psychology. An Introduction." *American Psychologist* 55(1):5–14.

Seligman, M.E.P., and R. D. Fowler. 2011. "Comprehensive Soldier Fitness and the Future of Psychology." *American Psychologist* 66(1):82–86.

Simmons, J. P., L.D. Nelson, and U. Simonsohn. 2011. "False-Positive Psychology Undisclosed Flexibility in Data Collection and Analysis Allows Presenting Anything as Significant." *Psychological Science* 22(11):1359–1366.

Sointu, E. 2005. "The Rise of an Ideal: Tracing Changing Discourses of Well-Being." *Sociological Review* 53(2):255–274.

Snyder, C.R., and S. J. Lopez. 2007. *Positive Psychology: The Scientific and Practical Explorations of Human Strengths*. Thousand Oaks, CA: SAGE.

Stevenson, Betsey, and Justin Wolfers. 2008. "Economic Growth and Subjective Well-Being: Reassessing the Easterlin Paradox." *Brookings Papers on Economic Activity* 39(1):1–102.

Stum, D. L. 2001. "Maslow Revisited: Building the Employee Commitment Pyramid." *Strategy and Leadership* 29(4):4–9.

Taylor, Eugene. 2001. "Positive Psychology and Humanistic Psychology: A Reply to Seligman." *Journal of Humanistic Psychology* 41(1):13–29.

Thoresen, C. J., S. A. Kaplan, A. P. Barsky, C. R. Warren, and K. de Chermont. 2003. "The Affective Underpinnings of Job Perceptions and Attitudes: A Meta-Analytic Review and Integration." *Psychological Bulletin* 129(6):914–945.

Uchitelle, L., and N. R. Kleinfield. 1996. "On the Battlefields of Business, Millions of Casualties." *The New York Times*, March 3.

Vaillant, G. E. 2002. *Aging Well: Surprising Guideposts to a Happier Life from the Landmark Harvard Study of Adult Development*. Boston: Little, Brown.

Weis, Robert. 2012. "You Want Me to Fix It? Using Evidence-Based Interventions to Instill Hope in Parents and Children." In *Happiness, Healing, Enhancement: Your Casebook Collection for Applying Positive Psychology in Therapy*, edited by G.W. Burns, 64–75. Hoboken, NJ: Wiley.

Youssef, C. M. and F. Luthans. 2007. "Positive Organizational Behavior in the Workplace: The Impact of Hope, Optimism, and Resilience." *Journal of Management* 33(5):774–800.

Zhang, Q., M. Vonderembse, and J. Lim. 2002. "Value Chain Flexibility: A Dichotomy of Competence and Capability." *International Journal of Production Research* 40(3):561–583.

CHAPTER 2

⤫

Boomer and Gen X Managers and Employees at Risk

Evidence from the Work, Family, and Health Network Study

JACK LAM, PHYLLIS MOEN, SHI-RONG LEE, AND ORFEU M. BUXTON

Career and retirement paths are in considerable flux in light of uncertainties brought about by a turbulent global economy and the dismantling of the social contract between employers and employees, with resulting job insecurities a key risk factor for both mental and physical health (Burgard, Brand, and House 2009; Burgard, Kalousova, and Seefeldt 2012; Ferrie et al. 2003, 2005, 2013; László et al. 2010; Rugulies et al. 2008). How are these macro-level dislocations playing out in work environments to shape the emotional well-being of today's managers and nonsupervisory employees? Are members of the Boomer cohort (born 1946–1964) particularly at risk in organizational climates of uncertainty, given that they moved through most of their careers assuming that their jobs were secure? Or are workers at the same organization, regardless of age cohort membership, similarly affected by higher job insecurity and an impending organizational change?

We use two waves of survey data to investigate Boomers' and Gen X'ers' psychological well-being (including work-family conflict) as they come to terms with the "new economy," in the form of learning that their firm will be merged with another company, and, in fact, be absorbed by the other company (Moen et al. 2013). We expect that learning about the merger will result in a climate of uncertainty, coloring managers' and employees' lives beyond their cubicles and offices. However, it may be the case that even in this light of this organizational merger that some workers report feeling more secure than others (*see* Lam et al. 2015); therefore, we distinguish between *subjective job insecurity* (as perceived and reported by both employees and managers at baseline), and *objective job uncertainty*, in the form of learning about the impending merger over the two waves of data. Doing so allows us to tease apart which of the two forms of insecurity is most salient in terms of reducing workers' emotional well-being over a six-month period.

Since continued employment is key to making ends meet at home, a merger announcement and/or a sense of high job insecurity may affect workers and their families by increasing their stress and reducing life quality. We test whether this is the case for a unique sample of workers, building on the literature that has investigated how job insecurity affects workers' well-being (Burgard, Brand, and House 2009; Burgard, Kalousova, and Seefeldt 2012; Ferrie et al. 2003, 2005; Lau and Knardahl 2008; Wang et al. 2008).

For instance, there is considerable evidence of the deleterious effects of job insecurity (D'Souza et al. 2003, 2006; Ferrie et al. 2005; Lau and Knardahl 2008). Findings from these studies generally find job insecurity to be associated with adverse health outcomes, in terms of self-rated health (D'Souza et al. 2003; Ferrie et al. 2005; Lau and Knardahl 2008); minor psychiatric morbidity (Ferrie et al. 2005); depression (D'Souza et al. 2003; Ferrie et al. 2005); elevated odds of long-term sickness absence (D'Souza et al. 2006), and mental stress (Lau and Knardahl 2008). But are these changes more acute for managers or nonsupervisory employees? Are members of one age cohort more vulnerable than another? And do women or men experience similar changes in distress from job insecurity and/or upon learning about an upcoming merger?

Existing evidence

As the structure of paid employment changes, how might different generations of adults who entered the labor market at different time periods be affected? Life course scholars draw on various time-related conceptual tools—age, period, and cohort—to highlight and understand social forces that have varying impact on individuals (Elder 1999; Lynch 2006; Yang 2008). For instance, we may expect members of different age cohorts to be differentially emotionally affected by job insecurity and by the shock of learning about an impending merger. This suggests that Boomers might be especially at risk, given that they entered the labor force and pursued their career paths during a period when it was assumed that continuous employment was the pathway to job security, something that Gen X'ers have never taken for granted.

Older workers may face particularly complex challenges in the case of a merger, given the dismantling of company-specific career ladders (Cappelli 2008) that once awarded job security to those with long tenure, along with age discrimination limiting reemployment options (Roscigno et al. 2007) and pension risks in later life complicating the decision to retire in the face of potential layoffs (O'Rand 2011; O'Rand and Hamil-Luker 2011; Shuey and O'Rand 2004).

In support of this thesis, a study by Lippman (2008)—using the Displaced Workers, Job Tenure, and Occupational Mobility Supplements to the Current Population Survey, 1984 to 2004—finds that cohort is a better predictor than chronological age in considering how workers fare after displacement, reporting that Boomers suffer the most from displacement. As Lippman points out: "Those workers who were born, socialized, and entered the labor market during the previous period of employment stability appear to have more difficulty in responding to and recovering from displacement than those whose socialization and labor market experience began in the more flexible era" (Lippman 2008, 1285–1286). He also shows that Boomers do worse in terms of re-employment (Lippman 2008).

In addition, scholars (Rubin 2012; Rousseau 1990) have discussed paid employment in the form of a social and psychological contract between individuals, employing organizations, and institutions. However, there is scant evidence as to whether the links between job insecurity and well-being outcomes, much less the effects of an impending merger, might operate differently for Boomers and Gen X'ers or for different subgroups of employees. Nevertheless, we test whether these factors may have greater implications for Boomers, given their expectations of secure employment, conforming to the of "cycles of control" formulation suggesting individuals' sense of control declines and their stress increases when there is a gap between their expectations and reality (Elder 1985).

Conversely, it may be the case that all workers, regardless of cohort, have adjusted their expectations of the workplace. For instance, both qualitative and quantitative studies report that workers tend to emphasize the job rewards that they have (Johnson, Sage, and Mortimer 2012; Lindsay and

Knox 1984; Mortimer and Lorence 1979; Mortimer, Pimentel, Ryu, Nash, and Lee 1996; Smith 2001). This allows employees to view themselves in a positive light. In contrast, highlighting rewards (such as job security) in their absence may lead to a decline in self-esteem.

Further, the definition of a *cohort* is defined as individuals who have had similar experiences. According to Alwin (2012, 216): "members of a birth cohort share the experience of the life cycle at the same time, that is, they experience childhood, reach adolescence, grow into early adulthood, and mature into midlife and old age at the same period in history." While there's the idea of a birth cohort, defined by biological age, it may be the case that working at the same company regardless of age and age-cohort membership shapes their expectations of employment stability, rendering their views more similar than different.

Most studies of job insecurity, however, draw on survey data from large nationally representative samples (Burgard, Brand, and House 2009; László et al. 2010; Rugulies et al. 2008). Although these data sets are essential for capturing national trends, workers in national samples are employed in a variety of organizations, occupations, and environments across the country, making it difficult to drill down to the particular experiences of those working for a single employer sharing a common culture of insecurity. Accordingly, this chapter draws on data from a longitudinal, multilevel study of employees and managers in a single organization to describe the effects of an impending merger and perceived job insecurity in terms of changes in the emotional well-being of two different age-cohorts: older Boomers (born 1946–1964) and younger Gen X'ers (born 1965–1980).

Following a description of the study, we investigate how these two different age cohorts of managers and employees face the uncertainties associated with an impending merger, given their different ages as well as career and family life course stages. We examine whether managers or employees, as well as Boomers or Gen X'ers, are more at risk of having adverse psychosocial effects from learning about the merger. To do so, we estimate, using multivariate regression techniques, changes over six months in their work-to-family conflict, family-to-work conflict, psychological distress, and emotional exhaustion. Such factors permeate the lives of people on and off the job, crossing over to affect their families as well (Almeida and Davis 2011).

We address three research questions: 1) Does learning about an impending merger have a larger effect on the emotional well-being of Boomers than younger Gen X'ers, and do any effects differ for managers and non-supervisory employees within these age cohorts? 2) Does the learning about an impending merger have a greater effect than reported baseline job insecurity on work-family conflict and other well-being outcomes over the six months between surveys, and does this differ for Boomers as compared with their younger Gen X counterparts? 3) Which Boomers and Gen X'ers are most affected emotionally by the effects of the merger announcement, in terms of their gender, manager/employee status, and baseline insecurity? Specifically, do effects differ for men and women, managers and employees, or those with high or low insecurity at baseline, and are these subgroup effects more pronounced for members of the Boomer or Gen X age cohorts?

DESCRIPTION OF STUDY

Sample

Our sample consists of managers and nonsupervisory employees in the information technology (IT) division of a large Fortune 500 organization we call TOMO. The data were collected as part of a large, multilevel randomized field experiment, the Work, Family & Health Network Study (*see* King et al. 2012; Bray et al. 2013). Computer-assisted personal interviews lasting about sixty minutes were conducted by trained field interviewers at the workplace on company time. Note that 70 percent of invited non-supervisory employees (N = 823) and 86 percent of invited managers (N = 221) completed the baseline survey. Among the 1044 respondents, 51 percent (N = 537) were randomly assigned to a workplace initiative that served as the treatment in this larger experimental study (Bray et al. 2013; Kelly et al. 2014). To better understand and isolate the effects of an unexpected merger announcement (which was not part of the experiment) that occurred in the middle of data collection, we focus our analysis in this chapter on members of the control group, that is, the participants who did not receive the treatment but also were part of both baseline and six-month follow-up surveys. We do so to understand the ways the unexpected merger announcement might influence workers' emotional responses that extend beyond the workplace without simultaneously considering the effects of the intervention (Moen et al. 2013). The final sample includes 448 respondents, with about one in five being managers (N = 90, 20 percent). Women constitute over one third (35 percent) of the sample.

The impending merger (where TOMO would be folded into another organization) was announced during the period of data collection. This unexpected event permits us to investigate the emotional effects of a sharp escalation in the climate of uncertainty in terms of changes in managers' and employees' emotional well-being over the ensuing six months. Given that the merger was announced at one point in time even as employees, managers, and their work teams were staggered in their completion of the surveys (depending on when they were assigned to do so over a period of a year), several comparison groups emerged from this natural experiment based on the timing of when respondents were surveyed relative to learning about the upcoming merger.

Almost half (49 percent) of survey respondents in our analytic sample had already heard about the merger announcement before they were scheduled for the baseline interview, while most of the remainder (45 percent) learned about the merger between being interviewed at baseline and the six-month follow-up, and a few (6 percent) had already had their six-month interview before the merger was announced. The first group we call the "late study group," those already exposed to the shock of the merger before they took their baseline survey. Their baseline responses should already reflect the uncertainty associated with the impending merger as well as any short-term (by six months) adjustments to this new uncertainty in terms of possible habituation as they got used to the idea of their firm being bought out by another. The second group, the "early study group," learned about the merger only after having completed the baseline interview. Their resulting uncertainty would be reflected in changes in their responses between the baseline and the six-month follow-up surveys. It is the changes in the outcomes of this early study group that most clearly reflect the effects of the shock of the merger announcement. There remains a small third group of employees whose six-month interviews occurred before the merger announcement. In our multivariate models we control for this small group of twenty-eight employees/managers who did not know about the impending merger at either interview, consisting of approximately 6 percent of the sample.

Measures

We investigate how both the climate of uncertainty fostered by the merger announcement and job insecurity at baseline touches the lives of different age-cohorts (Boomers, Gen X'ers) in terms of their emotional well-being. We assess whether non-supervisory employees and managers feel insecure about their jobs (*Job insecurity*) with a question asking "Thinking about the next twelve months, how likely do you think it is that you will lose your job or be laid off?" on a 1 to 4 scale. We dichotomize the variable into "high job insecurity" (those reporting 3 *"fairly likely"* and 4 *"very likely"*) and "low job insecurity" (those reporting 1 *"not at all likely"* and 2 *"not too likely"*).

We examine changes over time in four well-being measures: 1) psychological distress, 2) emotional exhaustion, 3) work-to-family conflict, and 4) family-to-work conflict.

Psychological distress is measured by a six-item scale (K6) developed and validated by Kessler et al. (2003), which is a widely used mental health scale in the United States. Sample questions include "During the past thirty days, how much of the time did you feel so sad nothing could cheer you up?" and "During the past thirty days, how much of the time did you feel that everything was an effort?" on a 1 (*none of the time*) to 5 (*all of the time*) scale. Responses range from 6 to 30, with higher scores indicating higher level of distress.

Emotional exhaustion is captured by a three-item subscale of Maslach Burnout Inventory (MBI), which was developed by Christina Maslach (1986). The MBI defines burnout as "a state of exhaustion in which one is cynical about the value of one's occupation and doubtful of one's ability to perform." Of the twenty-two-item edition of MBI, emotional exhaustion, depersonalization, and reduced personal accomplishment are included and only the first subscale is adopted in the current study. A sample question includes "You feel emotionally drained from your work: How often do you feel this way?" and responses range from 1(*never*) to 7 (*every day*).

Work-to-family conflict and *family-to-work conflict* outcomes are assessed using scales developed and validated by Netemeyer, Boles, and McMurrian (1996). The two scales reflect the degree to which role responsibilities from one domain are incompatible with the other. Sample questions for the work-to-family conflict scale include: "The amount of time your job takes up makes it difficult to fulfill your family or personal responsibilities." and "Your job produces strain that makes it difficult to fulfill your family or personal duties." Sample questions for the family-to-work conflict scale are: "The demands of your family or personal relationships interfere with work-related activities." and "Family-related strain interferes with your ability to perform job-related duties." Response levels range from 1 (*Strongly Disagree*) to 5 (*Strongly Agree*), with a higher score indicating higher levels of conflict.

As presented in Table 2.1, we find differences in job insecurity by age cohort at baseline, with a greater percentage of Boomers reporting insecurity (42 percent), as compared to Gen X'ers (21 percent), among both employees and managers. However, such an age-cohort difference might be due to the timing of when members of each age cohort learned about the merger. It so happens that a higher percentage of Boomers (54 percent) were interviewed at baseline after the merger announcement as compared to Gen X'ers (44 percent); by contrast, a higher percentage of Gen

Table 2.1. DESCRIPTIVES OF OUR SAMPLE (N = 448)

	Full Sample (N = 448)						Boomers (N = 219)						Gen Xers (N = 229)						t-test
	N	Mean/ percent	Median	StdDev	Min	Max	N	Mean/ percent	Median	StdDev	Min	Max	N	Mean/ percent	Median	StdDev	Min	Max	
Predictors																			
Timing of Learning the Merger																			
Late Study Group	220	49.11					119	54.34					101	44.10					*
Early Study Group	200	44.64					86	39.27					114	49.78					*
Learners at 12 Months	28	6.25					14	6.39					14	6.11					ns
High Job Insecurity Baseline	140	31.25					91	41.55					49	21.40					***
Women (=1)	160	35.71					95	43.38					65	28.38					***
Manager Status (=1)	90	20.09					33	15.07					57	24.89					**
Dependent Variables																			
Baseline																			
Psychological Distress (6–30)	448	10.77	10	3.15	6	25	219	10.57	10	3.21	6	25	229	10.96	10	3.09	6	22	n.s.
Emotional Exhaustion (1–7)	448	4.25	4.33	1.48	1	7	219	4.21	4	1.54	1	7	229	4.28	4.33	1.44	1	7	n.s.

	Full Sample (N = 448)						Boomers (N = 219)						Gen X'ers (N = 229)						
	N	Mean/ percent	Median	StdDev	Min	Max	N	Mean/ percent	Median	StdDev	Min	Max	N	Mean/ percent	Median	StdDev	Min	Max	t-test
Work-to-Family Conflict (1–5)	448	3.08	3	0.93	1	5	219	2.99	2.8	0.95	1	5	229	3.17	3.2	0.90	1	5	*
Family-to-Work Conflict (1–5)	448	2.10	2	0.66	1	4.6	219	2.01	2	0.65	1	4.6	229	2.19	2	0.66	1	4.4	**
6-Months																			
Psychological Distress (6–30)	448	10.53	10	3.17	6	21	219	10.22	9	3.1	6	21	229	10.83	10	3.21	6	21	*
Emotional Exhaustion (1–7)	448	4.18	4	1.55	1	7	219	4.17	4	1.63	1	7	229	4.18	4	1.47	1	7	n.s.
Work-to-Family Conflict (1–5)	448	2.98	2.8	0.93	1	5	219	2.89	2.8	0.93	1	5	229	3.07	3	0.92	1	5	*
Family-to-Work Conflict (1–5)	448	2.1	2	0.63	1	4.4	219	2.00	2	0.59	1	4.4	229	2.20	2	0.65	1	4.2	***
Change (baseline to 6 months)																			
Psychological Distress (6–30)	448	−0.24	0	2.75	−10	12	219	−0.35	0	2.74	−9	12	229	−0.13	0	2.76	−10	9	n.s.
Emotional Exhaustion (1–7)	448	−0.07	0	1.16	−4.7	3.7	219	−0.04	0	1.18	−5	3.3	229	−0.10	0	1.14	−3	3.7	n.s.
Work-to-Family Conflict (1–5)	448	−0.10	0	0.75	−3	2.6	219	−0.10	0	0.73	−3	2	229	−0.10	0	0.76	−3	2.6	n.s.
Family-to-Work Conflict (1–5)	448	0.00	0	0.59	−2.2	2.2	219	−0.01	0	0.59	−2	2.2	229	0.01	0	0.59	−2	2	n.s.

Note: *p < 0.05; **p < 0.01; ***p < 0.001.

X'ers learned about the merger after the baseline survey but by the six-months survey wave (50 percent) compared to Boomers (39 percent). Thus Boomers' higher job insecurity at baseline might reflect the fact that many of them already knew about the merger, and were feeling more insecure about their jobs as a result.

There are other differences by age cohort as well. For example, a higher percentage of Boomers are women (43 percent) than Gen X'ers (28 percent), possibly because Gen X'ers are in the childrearing life stage, and may find the demands of the jobs in this organization incompatible with family care responsibilities, which fall disproportionately on women. There are also more managers among Gen X'ers (25 percent) than among Boomers (15 percent). Given these demographic differences, we examine below whether the relationships between insecurity and emotional stress as well as work-to-family strain vary across gender and managerial status, within each age cohort.

In terms of well-being outcomes, we see that at baseline, Gen X'ers report higher levels of work-to-family conflict on average (3.17 vs. 3, $p < 0.05$) and family-to-work conflict (2.19 vs. 2.01, $p < 0.01$) compared to Boomers. This could be expected, in that Gen X'ers are typically engaged in active parenting, while Boomers' children may be grown and gone. By the next survey wave, six months later, Gen X'ers continue to report higher family-to-work and work-to-family conflict, but also higher psychological distress than Boomers (10.83 vs. 10.22, $p < 0.05$). However, we see that on average, changes among individuals in well-being outcomes (within-person changes) do not differ by age cohort. In other words, respondents in our sample report on average generally better well-being over the six months, and this differs according to whether they are Boomers or Gen X'ers, with Gen X'ers reporting more conflict in the work-family interface and greater psychological distress. But when looking at change that each respondent experiences over the six months between surveys, the level of change doesn't vary by whether or not the respondent is a Boomer or Gen X'er. We next test whether there may be differences in factors driving workers' emotional health, specifically whether those exposed to job insecurity and/or the merger announcement are most at risk of greater conflict and emotional distress.

Table 2.2 presents descriptions of various subgroup differences in well-being outcomes at baseline—six months—as well as within-person changes by different groups of respondents. Here we only present statistically significant differences. We first show differences by the timing of knowledge about the impending merger. As a group, those who only learned about the merger *after* baseline, as compared to those who already knew about the

Table 2.2 DESCRIPTIVES OF OUR SAMPLE: SIGNIFICANT DIFFERENCES BY TIMING OF LEARNING ABOUT THE MERGER AND GENDER (N = 448)

Timing of Learning About the Merger	Early Study Group (N = 200)						Late Study Group (N = 220)						
	N	Mean	Median	StdDev	Min	Max	N	Mean	Median	StdDev	Min	Max	t-test
Baseline													
Emotional Exhaustion (1–7)	228	4.49	4.67	1.44	1	7	220	4.00	4	1.49	1	7	***
Work-to-Family Conflict (1–5)	228	3.28	3.3	0.91	1	5	220	2.87	2.7	0.91	1	5	***
6-Months													
Psychological Distress (6–30)	228	10.97	10	3.32	6	21	220	10.07	10	2.94	6	20	**
Emotional Exhaustion (1–7)	228	4.60	4.67	1.45	1	7	220	3.74	3.33	1.54	1	7	***
Work-to-Family Conflict (1–5)	228	3.18	3.2	0.91	1	5	220	2.77	2.6	0.9	1	5	***
Change (baseline to 6 months)													
Emotional Exhaustion (1–7)	228	0.11	0	1.2	–3.3	3.7	220	–0.26	–0.33	1.08	–5	2.7	***

Gender	Men (N = 288)						Women (N = 160)						
	N	Mean	Median	StdDev	Min	Max	N	Mean	Median	StdDev	Min	Max	t-test
Baseline													
Psychological Distress (6–30)	288	10.53	10	2.91	6	22	160	11.19	10	3.51	6	25	*

Note: $^{*}p < 0.05$; $^{**}p < 0.01$; $^{***}p < 0.001$.

merger prior to taking the baseline survey, had higher levels of emotional exhaustion (4.49 vs. 4.00; $p < 0.001$) and work-to-family conflict (3.28 vs. 2.7; $p < 0.001$). At six months, employees who learned about the merger continue to have higher emotional exhaustion and work-to-family conflict than those who already knew at baseline, but at this point also reported higher psychological distress (10.97 vs. 10.07, $p < 0.01$). On average, those who learned about the merger ("early study group") reported a mean increase of 0.11 in emotional exhaustion six months later, while those who already knew about the merger at baseline ("late study group") reported a decline of 0.26 in emotional exhaustion. This suggests that those who have known about the merger for a while may adjust to this new reality, while those just learning about it haven't yet had time to accommodate to its implications by the six-months interview.

Turning to gender differences, we see that, on average, women report higher psychological distress than men at baseline (11.19 vs. 10.53, $p < 0.05$). Comparisons of managers with employees on these outcomes show no statistically significant differences in well-being by whether or not respondents are managers or employees.

Does learning about a merger affect Boomers and Gen X'ers differently?

Next, we report findings from regression models. Given that the respondents are nested within work groups, we use hierarchical linear models to investigate the independent effects of the timing in learning about the merger as well as baseline job insecurity on changes in measures of emotional well-being over the six-month period between surveys. We also control for baseline measures of emotional well-being, so that what we are measuring is changes in these outcomes from baseline to six months. We estimated models separately for Boomers and Gen X'ers to examine whether the emotional effects of baseline insecurity and/or learning about the merger differ by age cohort.

What we find across outcomes, for Boomers as well as Gen X'ers, is that, net of job insecurity at baseline, it is *learning about the merger* that most predicts changes in respondents' emotional well-being. Thus this unexpected merger announcement that created a new climate of uncertainty, more than workers' baseline perceptions of job insecurity, is most consequential for the emotional well-being of employees and managers. Being a manager or nonsupervisory employee did not directly predict changes in these emotional outcomes from baseline to the six-month

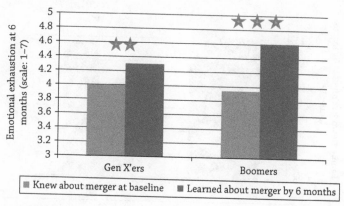

Figure 2.1: Predicted value for emotional exhaustion at 6 months, by knowledge of merger and age cohort.
**p < 0.01; ***p < 0.001.

interview, but we did find that managerial status moderated some of the effects of learning about the merger (which we discuss in a later section). For ease of interpretation, we present statistically significant results for Boomers and Gen X'ers in figures, enabling comparisons across age cohorts.

As shown in Figure 2.1, we find that, among Boomers, those who learned about the merger report higher emotional exhaustion at six months, as compared to those who were already aware of the merger at baseline (p < 0.001; see Figure 2.1). This suggests that the "late study group," those who already knew about the merger at baseline, might have become more acclimated (habituated) to the idea of the upcoming merger, but that those only just learning about it are adversely impacted by this shock. Among Gen X'ers, respondents who learned about the merger also report higher emotional exhaustion by six months, as compared to respondents who already knew about the merger before they were interviewed at baseline (p < 0.01). Thus, regardless of cohort, learning about the merger is associated with an increase in emotional exhaustion, feelings of depletion that invariably matter for life beyond work.

In Figure 2.2, we show a statistically significant association between learning about the merger and family-to-work conflict at six months for Boomers (p < 0.05). Compared to Boomers who already knew about the merger at baseline, those who learned about it after the baseline interview report a greater sense of conflict from the family environment spilling into the workplace by their six-months interview. This highlights the implications of moving into a climate of uncertainty at the workplace, with effects that extend beyond the cubicle in terms of changing Boomers' perceptions

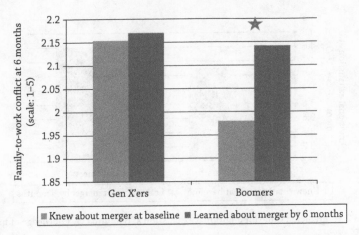

Figure 2.2: Predicted value for family-to-work conflict at 6 months, by knowledge of merger and age cohort.
*p < 0.05.

of their home environments and/or increases in the stress experienced by spouses who learn about this new uncertainty around their partners' work situation. While the merger announcement is an event occurring at work, our finding of the significant association of learning about the merger with family-to-work conflict suggests that the climate of uncertainty might intensify respondents' sense of family-related strain or actually increase family-to-work strain, possibly associated with concerns about future family financial security. There was no such effect for Gen X'ers, but recall that this younger age-cohort already had higher levels of family-to-work conflict at baseline (see Table 2.1).

Figure 2.3 reveals that, for Gen X'ers, learning about the merger is in fact associated with their experience of higher *work*-to-*family* conflict at six months, as compared to those who already knew about the merger at baseline (p < 0.05). This shows that in learning about an upcoming merger, Gen X'ers were more likely to feel greater strain associated with their jobs spilling over into their home lives than vice versa. Future research should further investigate the directionality of the work-family strain employees and managers perceive in light of uncertainties at the workplace, as well as mechanisms leading to each form of conflict. One possibility may be that workers are also working harder and longer hours in the months following learning about the merger, in order to shore up their position within the company prior to when the merger actually takes place, with greater impact on their perceived work-family strain. This suggests the need for future research chronicling changes in workers' behaviors in a climate of increasing uncertainty.

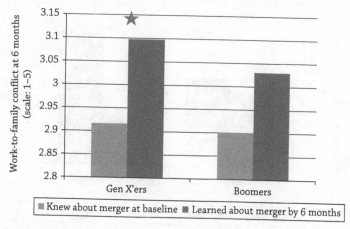

Figure 2.3 Predicted value for work-to-family conflict at 6 months, by knowledge of merger and age cohort.
$^*p < 0.05$.

Although we present results for these emotional well-being outcomes in terms of estimated levels at six months, as a test of robustness, we also modeled changes in well-being outcomes between baseline and six months as the outcome variables. We find a positive relationship between learning about the merger and adverse changes in terms of heightened emotional exhaustion (Boomers and Gen X'ers), providing support for the evidence in the figures we show here. This points to the importance of panel studies following respondents over time and in the face of changes in the climate of uncertainty to capture the dynamics of organizations and the impacts of changes (such as this merger announcement) on the life quality of employees and managers. To truly understand the effect of a sudden shift toward greater uncertainty it is essential to have panel data from both before and after these changes, as we were fortunate to have in this case.

Subgroup differences in changing emotional well-being

Next, we investigate subgroup differences within age cohorts to understand whether particular groups (e.g., men vs. women, or managers vs. employees) report greater changes in emotional well-being outcomes over six months in relation to perceived job insecurity or learning about the impending merger, as well as whether this is the case for Boomers, Gen X'ers, or both. We do so by testing interaction terms between gender and manager status and both job insecurity at baseline and objective uncertainty (indicated by learning about the impending merger between

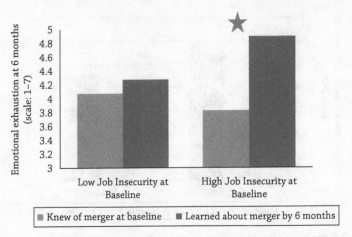

Figure 2.4: Predicted value for emotional exhaustion at 6 months, by knowledge of merger and job insecurity baseline, for Gen X'ers only.
*p < 0.05.

baseline and six-month interviews), including each interaction term separately in the final models (see previous section). We also examine whether the psychological effects of learning about the merger is greater for those with high job insecurity at baseline, adding this also as an interaction term.

We find important subgroup differences in the effects of learning about the forthcoming merger, including an interaction between learning about the merger and those with prior high job insecurity for Gen X'ers but not for Boomers. In fact, three out of the five statistically significant interactions show subgroup differences among Gen X'ers, suggesting the possibility of more heterogeneity in effects for Gen X'ers than for Boomers.

Figure 2.4 shows the interaction between subjective job insecurity at the baseline interview and subsequently learning about the merger on the Gen X'ers' feeling of emotional exhaustion. Specifically, Gen X'ers who had high job insecurity at baseline and then learned about the merger report higher levels of emotional exhaustion (p < 0.05) by the six-months interview, compared to those who were more secure at baseline. This suggests an accentuation effect, with already insecure Gen X'ers more vulnerable to the shock of learning that their firm is to be absorbed within another company.

We next examined potential differences between managers and employees. Figure 2.5 charts statistically significant differences in psychological distress among Gen X employees and managers who learned about the upcoming merger after the baseline interview. Gen X non-supervisory employees who learned about the merger after baseline reported greater psychological distress than those who had already heard the merger

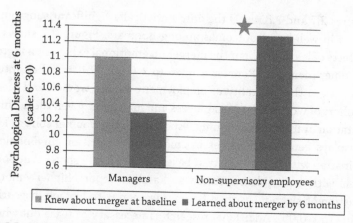

Figure 2.5: Predicted value for psychological distress at 6 months, by knowledge of merger and employee status, for Gen X'ers only.

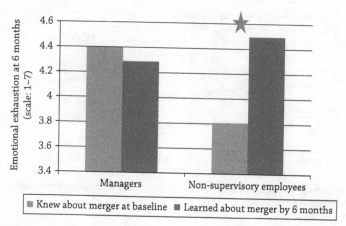

Figure 2.6: Predicted value for emotional exhaustion at 6 months, by knowledge of merger and employee status, for Gen X'ers only.

announcement prior to baseline ($p < 0.05$). Managers did not have such an adverse effect after finding out about the upcoming merger.

Figure 2.6 reveals a similar pattern for Gen X non-supervisory employees in terms of emotional exhaustion ($p < 0.05$). Both Figures 2.5 and 2.6 show that, as compared to Gen X managers, the effects of learning about the merger in terms of increases in exhaustion were higher for Gen X employees. Note, however, that managers report higher levels of emotional exhaustion overall, regardless of whether they already knew or had just learned about the merger, suggesting the chronic strain managers experience in their jobs.

Figures 2.7 and 2.8 reveal the only statistically significant subgroup differences in well-being outcomes among Boomers. Figure 2.7 shows that the effects of learning about the merger on emotional exhaustion is greater for Boomer men than Boomer women ($p < 0.05$). This may be capturing differences in the centrality of employment among women and men for this cohort of workers, both employees and managers, given the normative expectation of male breadwinning, especially in the Boomer cohort. Figure 2.8 displays gender differences in emotional exhaustion for Boomers in combination with job insecurity at baseline. This figure shows that Boomer women with high job insecurity at baseline report higher emotional exhaustion at six months than Boomer women with low job insecurity at baseline ($p < 0.05$). Additional research is necessary to tease out whether

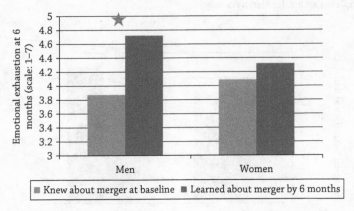

Figure 2.7: Predicted value for emotional exhaustion at 6 months, by knowledge of merger and gender, for Boomers only.
*$p < 0.05$.

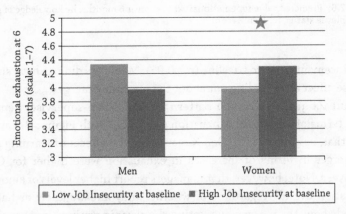

Figure 2.8: Predicted value for emotional exhaustion at 6 months, by baseline job insecurity and gender, for Boomers only.
*$p < 0.05$.

Boomer men are more vulnerable to an external shock (such as the merger announcement) and whether Boomer women are more vulnerable to ongoing feelings of job insecurity.

Discussion and conclusions

Risks and uncertainties are central tenets in modern life. Social scientists such as Richard Sennett (1998) and Anthony Giddens (1999) describe these dynamic forces as shifting value hierarchies and in the ways individuals perceive the world and respond to events. Learning about a company merger only deepens the culture of uncertainty within an IT workforce (*see* also Lam et al. 2015; Moen et al. 2013).

Our evidence on a sample of high-tech workers in a single firm followed over six months illuminates the challenges of a culture of uncertainty for both Boomers and Gen X'ers, managers and employees, women and men, and those with high and low job insecurity. While all workers are increasingly exposed to the uncertainty of a changing economy combined with a changing social contract, some are clearly more vulnerable than others.

Recall we had hypothesized that Boomers in particular would be more at risk of declines in their emotional well-being from both job insecurity and learning that their company is about to be absorbed by another. This is because if they do lose their jobs age discrimination may well prevent their finding another job. Thus Boomers have less of a possibility of "reinventing" themselves as easily as Gen X'ers in today's labor market. But our results show that both Boomers and Gen X'ers are affected by learning about the merger, though not always in the same ways, and, moreover, that different subgroups of Gen X'ers and Boomers experience different outcomes. Thus Boomers and Gen X'ers who learned about an upcoming merger report higher emotional exhaustion, while Boomers reported greater *family*-to-work conflict and Gen X'ers learning about the merger report greater *work*-to-family conflict. Taken together, these findings point to deleterious effects for both cohorts, effects that spill over into workers' family and personal lives. We also find that the dynamics of organizational change (in the form of an upcoming merger) matter more for changes in well-being than employees' perceptions of job insecurity, underscoring the need for longitudinal research examining continuity and change in organizations as factors that affect employees' and managers' lives both within and outside the cubicles and offices in which they work.

This study also points to the importance of investigating the emotional well-being of different age cohorts of employees and managers in response to changing conditions of work, rather than assuming all workers respond in similar ways, or simply controlling for age. We found both similarities and differences between Boomers' and Gen X'ers' well-being outcomes in the face of learning about an impending merger. But note that *changes* in well-being are not the same as age-cohort *differences* in levels of well-being. For example, Gen X'ers have higher levels of work-to-family and family-to-work conflict than do Boomers, regardless of when they learned about the merger. Nonetheless, Boomers learning about the merger reported higher family-to-work conflict compared to those in that age cohort who had had time to adjust to this new reality and Gen X learners reported higher work-to-family conflict.

Our evidence demonstrates the value of examining differences for various subgroups. We find Gen X'ers have different well-being outcomes depending on whether or not they are managers or whether they had previously high levels of subjective job insecurity. In particular, it appears to be Gen X nonsupervisory employees, not managers, who experience adverse effects in the form of greater psychological distress and emotional exhaustion following learning about the merger. While Gen X men and women do not differ in any statistically significant ways, gender does matter for Boomers. In particular, Boomer men and women respond differently, with learning about the merger related to higher emotional exhaustion for men, while baseline job insecurity is associated with greater emotional exhaustion for women. These gender differences among the Boomer cohort as well as the effects on nonsupervisory Gen X'ers both require additional research.

Finally, this study points to the importance of emotional exhaustion in particular as a key measure of well-being, one that seems especially responsive to changes in the culture of uncertainty at work. The findings here offer strong evidence that changes in organizational climates matter for the life quality of both managers and employees, with employees especially at risk of psychological distress and emotional exhaustion. An unexpected increase in uncertainty at the organizational level spills over into the work-to-family and family-to-work conflicts, emotional exhaustion, and psychological distress of different subgroups, affecting both Boomers and Gen X'ers lives at home as well as at work.

REFERENCES

Almedia, David M., and Kelly D. Davis. 2011. "Workplace Flexibility and Daily Stress Processes in Hotel Employees and Their Children." *Annals of the American Academy of Political and Social Science* 638(1):123–140.

Alwin, Duane F. 2012. "Integrating Varieties of Life Course Concepts." *The Journals of Gerontology, Series B: Psychological Sciences and Social Sciences* 67(2):206–220.

Bray, Jeremy W., Erin L. Kelly, Leslie B. Hammer, David M. Almeida, James W. Dearing, Rosalind B. King, and Orfeu Buxton. 2013. "An Integrative, Multilevel, and Transdisciplinary Research Approach to Challenges of Work, Family, and Health." RTI Press MR-0024-1303. http://www.rti.org/publications/rtipress.cfm?pubid=20777.

Burgard, Sarah A., Jennie E. Brand, and James S. House. 2009. "Perceived Job Insecurity and Worker Health in the United States." *Social Science and Medicine* 69(5):777–785.

Burgard, Sarah A., Lucie Kalousova, and Kristin S. Seefeldt. 2012. "Perceived Job Insecurity and Health." *Journal of Occupational and Environmental Medicine* 54(9):1101–1106.

Cappelli, Peter, ed. 2008. *Employment Relationships: New Models of White-Collar Work.* Cambridge, UK: Cambridge University Press.

D'Souza, Rennie M., Lyndall Strazdins, Dorothy Broom, Bryan Rodgers, and Helen L. Berry. 2006. "Work Demands, Job Insecurity and Sickness Absence from Work: How Productive is the New, Flexible Labour Force?" *Australian and New Zealand Journal of Public Health* 30(3):205–212.

D'Souza, Rennie M., Lyndall Strazdins, Lynette L-Y Lim, Dorothy Broom, and Bryan Rodgers. 2003. "Work and Health in a Contemporary Society: Demands, Control, and Insecurity." *Journal of Epidemology and Community Health* 57:849–854.

Elder, Glen H., Jr., ed. 1985. *Life Course Dynamics: Trajectories and Transitions, 1968–1980.* Ithaca, NY: Cornell University Press.

Elder, Glen H., Jr. 1999. *Children of the Great Depression: Social Change in Life Experience.* 25th Anniversary Edition. Boulder, CO: Westview. (Originally published in 1974, University of Chicago Press.)

Ferrie, Jane E., Mika Kivimäki, Martin J. Shipley, George Davey Smith, and Marianna Virtanen. 2013. "Job Insecurity and Incident Coronary Heart Disease: The Whitehall II Prospective Cohort Study." *Atherosclerosis* 227(1):178–181.

Ferrie, Jane E., Martin J. Shipley, Katherine Newman, Stephen A. Stansfeld, and Michael Marmot. 2005. "Self-Reported Job Insecurity and Health in the Whitehall II Study: Potential Explanations of the Relationship." *Social Science & Medicine* 60(7):1593–1602.

Ferrie, Jane E., Martin J. Shipley, S. A. Stansfeld, George Davey Smith, and Michael Marmot. 2003. "Future Uncertainty and Socioeconomic Inequalities in Health: The Whitehall II Study." *Social Science & Medicine* 57(4):637–646.

Giddens, Anthony. 1999. "Risk and Responsibility." *Modern Law Review* 62(1):1–10.

Johnson, Monica K., Rayna Sage, and Jeylan T. Mortimer. 2012. "Work Values, Early Career Difficulties, and the U.S. Economic Recession." *Social Psychology Quarterly* 75(3):242–267.

Kelly, Erin L., Phyllis Moen, J. Michael Oakes, Wen Fan, Cassandra Okechukwu, Kelly D. Davis, et al. 2014. "Changing Work and Work-Family Conflict: Evidence from the Work, Family, and Health Network." *American Sociological Review* 79(3):485–516.

Kessler, Ronald C., Peggy R. Barker, Lisa J. Colpe, Joan F. Epstein, Joseph C. Gfroerer, Eva Hiripi, et al. 2003. "Screening for Serious Mental Illness in the General Population." *Archives of General Psychiatry* 60(2):184–189.

King, Rosalind B., Georgia Karuntzos, Lynne M. Casper, Phyllis Moen, Kelly D. Davis, Lisa Berkman, et al. 2012. "Work-Family Balance Issues and Work-Leave

Policies." In *Handbook of Occupational Health and Wellness*, edited by R.J. Gatchel and I.Z. Schultz, 323–34. Springer Science and Business Media.

Lam, Jack, Kimberly Fox, Wen Fan, Phyllis Moen, Erin Kelly, Leslie Hammer, and Ellen Ernst Kossek. 2015. "Manager Characteristics and Employee Job Insecurity around a Merger Announcement: The Role of Status and Crossover." *The Sociological Quarterly* 56(3):558–580.

László, Krisztina D. et al. 2010. "Job Insecurity and Health: A Study of 16 European Countries." *Social Science & Medicine* 70(6):867–874.

Lau, Bjørn, and Stein Knardahl. 2008. "Perceived Job Insecurity, Job Predictability, Personality, and Health." *Journal of Occupational and Environmental Medicine* 50(2):172–181.

Lindsay, P., and W. E. Knox. (1984). "Continuity and Change in Work Values among Young Adults." *American Journal of Sociology* 89(4):918–931.

Lippman Stephen. 2008. "Rethinking Risk in the New Economy: Age and Cohort Effects on Unemployment and Re-Employment." In *Special Issue: Workers, Risk and the New Economy. Human Relations* 61(9):1259

Lynch, Scott. 2006. "Explaining Life Course and Cohort Variation in the Relationship Between Education and Health: The Role of Income." *Journal of Health and Social Behavior* 47(4):324–338.

Maslach, Christina, and Susan Jackson. 1986. *Maslach Burnout Inventory Manual*. 2nd ed. Palo Alto, CA: Consulting Psychologists Press.

Moen, Phyllis, Erin Kelly, Jeremy Bray, David Almeida, Leslie Hammer, J Michael Oakes, et al. 2013. "Job Insecurity, Job Satisfaction and Turnover Intentions in Changing Organizational Contexts: Results from the Work, Family and Health Network Study." Unpublished Draft.

Mortimer, Jeylan T., and Jon Lorence. 1979. "Work Experience and Occupational Value Socialization: A Longitudinal Study." *American Journal of Sociology*, 84(6):1361–1385.

Mortimer, J. T., E. E. Pimentel, S. Ryu, K. Nash, and C. Lee. 1996. "Part-Time Work and Occupational Value Formation in Adolescence." *Social Forces* 74(4):1405–1418.

Netemeyer, Richard G., James S. Boles, and Robert McMurrian. 1996. "Development and Validation of Work-Family Conflict and Family-Work Conflict Scales." *Journal of Applied Psychology* 81(4):400–410.

O'Rand, Angela M. 2011. "2010 SSS Presidential Address: The Devolution of Risk and the Changing Life Course in the United States." *Social Forces* 90(1):1–16.

O'Rand, Angela M., and Jenifer Hamil-Luker. 2011. "Late Employment Careers, Transitions To Retirement, and Retirement Income in the United States." In *Aging Populations, Globalization, and the Labor Market: Comparing Late Working Life and Retirement in Modern Societies*, edited by Hans-Peter Blossfeld, Sandra Buchholz, and Karin Kurz, 283–305. Edward Elgar.

Roscigno, Vincent J., Sherry Mong, Reginald Byron, and Griff Tester. 2007. "Age Discrimination, Social Closure, and Employment." *Social Forces* 86(1):313–334.

Rousseau, Denise. 1990. "New Hire Expectations of Their Own and Their Employer's Obligations: A Study of Psychological Contracts." *Journal of Organizational Behavior* 11(5):389–400.

Rubin, Beth A. 2012. "Shifting Social Contracts and the Sociological Imagination." *Social Forces* 91(2):327–346.

Rugulies, R., B. Aust, H. Burr, and U. Bültmann. 2008. "Job Insecurity, Chances on the Labour Market and Decline in Self-Rated Health in a Representative

Sample of the Danish Workforce." *Journal of Epidemiology and Community Health* 62(3):245–250.

Sennett, Richard. 1998. *The Corrosion of Character: The Personal Consequences of Work in the New Capitalism.* New York: W.W. Norton.

Shuey, K. M., and A. M. O'Rand. 2004. "New Risks for Workers: Pensions, Labor Markets, and Gender." *Annual Review of Sociology* 30:453–77.

Smith, Vicki. 2001. *Crossing the Great Divide: Worker Risk and Opportunity in the New Economy.* Ithaca, NY: Cornell University/ILR Press.

Wang, Jianli, Alain Lesage, Norbert Schmitz, and Aline Drapeau. 2008. "The Relationship between Work Stress and Mental Disorders in Men and Women: Findings from a Population-Based Study." *Journal of Epidemiology and Community Health* 62(1):42–47.

Yang, Yang. 2008. "Social Inequalities in Happiness in the US 1972–2004: An Age-Period-Cohort Analysis." *American Sociological Review* 73(2):204–226.

CHAPTER 3

✧

Unemployed Tech Workers' Ambivalent Embrace of the Flexible Ideal

CARRIE M. LANE

In an editorial titled "The Start-Up of You," published in 2011, *New York Times* editorialist Thomas Friedman informed new college grads that today's employers "are all looking for the same kind of people—people who not only have the critical thinking skills to do the value-adding jobs that technology can't, but also people who can invent, adapt, and reinvent their jobs every day, in a market that changes faster than ever." The article warned young readers, "this is not your parents' job market. ... You can't just say," as graduates' parents' generation allegedly did, "'I have a college degree, I have a right to a job, now someone else should figure out how to hire and train me.'" Instead, graduates were urged to shirk off this passive approach and adopt "an entirely new mind-set," one in which they "approach career strategy the same way an entrepreneur approaches starting a business" (Friedman 2011).

Friedman's advice was neither new nor especially distinctive. The entrepreneurial approach to career planning has been advocated since at least 1976, when management expert Douglas T. Hall first predicted the rise of "protean careers," professional trajectories guided not by organizational objectives but by an individual's own choices and priorities (Hall 1976). By the time of Friedman's editorial, the version of the ideal worker he extolled could be found in in myriad forms and forums—op-ed columns, advice manuals and self-help books (McGee 2005), college graduation speeches, business school courses, job-search clubs (Lane 2011, 99–102; Torres 1996), and even reality television programs about job loss and downward mobility (Rosenblum 2010).[1] Specifics vary by industry, firm, and nation (as Alexy, Frenkel, and Utrata demonstrate in this volume), but these narratives tend to share the presumption that flexibility, creativity, and self-direction are the hallmarks of a good job candidate, at least for the sought-after middle- to upper-income full-time positions that have become especially scarce of late.[2] Loyalty, once a prized attribute among both employers and employ- ees, is now seen as something of an albatross, signaling not solid moral fiber but a dependent mindset and inclination toward inertia and entitlement (Korkki 2011; Lane 2011, 45–48). In this new context, mutability and con- stant self-monitoring and self-improvement have replaced steadfastness as the "only reliable insurance against economic insecurity" (McGee 2005, 13; see also Sennett 1998). Job-seekers today are thus urged to position themselves not as employees with a specific set of skills and experience to offer, but as independent-minded entrepreneurs who, if hired (whether part time, full time, or on contract), will reinvent themselves continuously, and on their own dime, to meet the ever-changing needs of their employ- ers, until, of course, that employer no longer needs them, at which point they will quietly and amiably depart, eager for new opportunities to dem- onstrate their skillfulness and flexibililty.

Friedman's editorial suggests this approach has yet to be widely embraced among American workers, especially the older generations he claims are wedded to outdated expectations of their employers. Indeed, as other chapters in this volume demonstrate (Lam et al., Schulz and Robinson, Whitaker), there are many different ways of thinking about and responding to changing expectations of work and workers in the contemporary United States. And yet there are some groups of American workers, and not just young ones, who have embraced the entrepreneurial approach Friedman describes, and they did so long before his editorial hit the presses. Their stories and perspectives demonstrate what this ideology looks like on the ground, rather than in its prescriptive, idealized form. They reveal how much work, emotional and sometimes physical, is required to live up the ideal of the flexible, entrepreneurial worker, and how heavy the costs can be, both of achieving that goal and falling short of it.

In 2001, I began a study of unemployed high-technology workers laid off during the turbulent period following the crashes of the dot.com and tele- com industries, terrorist attacks of September 11, and subsequent reces- sion. For more than three years, I joined job-seekers at job fairs, job search seminars, and networking events designed for the unemployed in Dallas, Texas, a city that housed a mix of high-tech fields, including budding

Internet start-ups, long-standing computing firms, major telecommunications companies, and myriad related industries. I spoke informally with hundreds of job-seekers and conducted open-ended interviews with seventy-five of them, some as many as five times; in 2009 I reinterviewed a group of primary informants to see how they had fared in the five years since I left the field. Interviewees ranged in age from their early twenties to mid-seventies; a majority were white men, which was representative of the Dallas high-tech workforce at the time. I consciously sought out the perspective and experiences of women, who made up about one-third of interviewees, and racial minorities (11% of interviewees were Asian American, 4% were Mexican American, and 3% were African American). The vast majority of study participants were middle and upper class, with pre-layoff incomes ranging from $40,000–$100,000 per year. With one exception the positions they had worked in would be described as white-collar office (or home office) jobs. Nearly all had college degrees and many had graduate or professional degrees (MAs, MBAs, JDs, and PhDs). This group therefore enjoyed many privileges not available to most American job-seekers, including actual capital in the form of savings and retirement accounts and easy access to credit, and social and cultural capital in the form of strong professional networks and the ability to present themselves in the manner valued and expected in the professional workplace. These advantages cushioned some of the harsher aspects of job loss and prolonged unemployment but by no means eradicated them (see Corse and Silva, this volume).

COMPANIES OF ONE

Over the course of my research, in interview after interview, I heard exactly the attitude Friedman was touting as "new" a decade later, usually from people who could easily be the parents, or even the grandparents, of the college grads to whom his editorial was directed. As early as 2001, these job-seekers were describing themselves as entrepreneurial companies of one, hence the title of my book, *A Company of One* (2011). They believed it was folly to expect long-term employment in an era characterized by downsizing, outsourcing, and the rise of contingent employment, and thought of themselves as independent contractors rather than dependent employees. They expected equally little from government agencies and political leaders; although most accepted unemployment benefits when they were eligible, in general, regardless of party affiliation, job-seekers saw government intervention as ineffective, if not counterproductive.[3] Instead, they were adamant that each individual should take responsibility for his or her own fate in this increasingly global and volatile labor market, staying alert to industry and market trends, retraining as necessary on one's own dime to avoid obsolescence, and constantly networking to be well-positioned for the inevitable job change to come.

These declarations were not just a matter of toeing the party line. Unemployed men and women were exceptionally clear about what was expected of them as "good job-seekers," and they worked hard to live up to the flexible ideals they espoused. They attended dozens of different networking groups, tailored and tweaked their resumes for each new position, learned new coding languages, obtained professional certifications and advanced degrees, and rehearsed and revised their "commercials," a condensed version of one's professional experience and objectives that can be smoothly delivered at a moment's notice.[4] They reached out to friends, family, and former colleagues, and volunteered at schools, nonprofits, and as-yet-unfunded start-ups. They worked out, dressed up, and, like the "happy workers" Cabanas and Illouz describe in this volume, stayed positive, because they knew those things helped stave off depression and discouragement, dangerous emotions that might lead one to underperform in interviews and networking interactions.[5] They offered unemotional, level-headed explanations for why their layoffs were understandable, even necessary, and optimistic, forward-thinking narratives of how they'd keep their skills and professional networks up to date even once they found a new job. In today's market, they believed, security was not about keeping your current job, but about being ready to move to the next job as soon as, if not before, this job disappeared.

In general, job-seekers were remarkably faithful to the tenets of this flexible ideal, even when their loyal adherence did not necessarily translate into success on the job market. A few interviewees found reemployment in their chosen fields at similar or even higher levels of pay and status, although usually only after a prolonged period of joblessness (average unemployment duration for tech workers in this region was 13.6 months at that point [Virick 2004]). For others, the rewards of constant reinvention and strategic self-promotion were more elusive. Most interviewees ended up changing industries, taking sizable pay cuts, relocating to less desirable areas (see Whitaker, this volume), or dropping multiple rungs down the corporate ladder. To pay the bills and keep busy while continuing their search, others found low-paid "interim" positions, such as selling electronics or waiting tables, some of which eventually became permanent when new tech jobs failed to materialize. And despite the many tangible and cultural advantages available to educated, middle-class workers, even the most objectively successful among the job-seekers (those who found good jobs relatively quickly) faced significant hardships during the job search, from anxiety, depression, and self-doubt, to financial setbacks and marital strife.[6]

Yet my focus in this essay is not on the challenges presented by prolonged unemployment, although those will be touched upon herein, but on the human costs of trying to live up to the flexible ideal itself. The question is not whether middle-class US workers have embraced the entrepreneurial approach Friedman and others continue to tout as a "new mind-set"— clearly many of them already have. Nor is my purpose to determine whether this approach to looking for work is an especially effective one, although readers interested in that question will certainly find fodder for thought in the stories presented here. Instead I use close readings of interview excerpts to analyze moments when unemployed white-collar workers invoked this flexible ideal, as well as moments in which they diverged from it. For as often as interviewees articulated the importance of autonomy and flexibility, even evangelized about them to other job-seekers, there were also times when they questioned and contradicted the very perspectives they so fervently espoused. These moments of disjuncture, however brief, provide important glimpses into the work—emotional, cognitive, and even sometimes physical work—involved in trying to live up to the ideal of the flexible, entrepreneurial worker. And in these moments we can see other less popular but equally if not more compelling ways of responding to the ongoing challenges of both unemployment and the increasingly insecure nature of contemporary work.

EXPLORING INCONSISTENCIES
THROUGH ETHNOGRAPHIC INTERVIEWS

Ethnographic research is exceptionally well-suited to the task of getting at the infinitely complex ways people think and behave in everyday life. In my own research, the meandering nature and long duration of ethnographic interviews—mine tend to range from one to four hours—created opportunities to touch on the same topic multiple times over the course of an interview, or across multiple interviews with the same person. When asked about his financial situation, for instance, a job-seeker might say money is not a problem, as he has ample savings on which to draw. An hour later, when I ask about his health, he might note he's started taking anxiety medication because he's been obsessing over what will happen when his money runs out. These two statements do not exactly contradict one another, but they offer very different perspectives on the interviewee's sense of financial security and the emotional impact of his layoff. Such asymmetries should not automatically be taken as evidence of duplicity or confusion on the part of the interviewee (although certainly there are occasions when interviewees are either confused by or less than completely honest with their interviewers). As Katherine Newman has argued, "We like to think that people try to make sense, if not to the scholars they speak to, then at least to themselves. But it is in the nature of our culture, and no doubt of most cultures, to live with incoherence and contradiction" (1993, 169–170). It is hardly surprising, then, that inconsistencies and paradoxes occasionally emerge over the course of an ethnographic interview or over multiple interviews with the same individual. It would be a mistake, however, to dismiss these instances as indicative of nothing more than the human capacity for internal contradiction. Instead it is at such moments, not only when interviewees contradict themselves but also when they struggle to articulate themselves or dismiss their own responses as somehow foolish or flawed, that we are able to glimpse the complicated mental and cultural processes at work behind their accounts.[7] In my own research, exploring such moments within the context of both individual lives and broader cultural forces reveals powerful tensions between how job-seekers experience unemployment and how they believe they *should* experience unemployment, and the heavy if sometimes intangible costs of their efforts to reconcile those competing perspectives.

"THIS IS NOTHING PERSONAL": JOB LOSS AND SELF-BLAME

As noted above, most interviewees were understanding, although rarely pleased, about the company's decision to lay them off. Nearly all knew or at least suspected a layoff was coming, and most actually sympathized with their employer's need to cut workers in the face of a recession and, for dot-com and telecom companies, industry-wide crisis. Despite having lost his job nearly six months earlier, Amit Mehta, an Indian-American man in his twenties, still assumed his former employer's perspective when discussing his layoff, even using the term "we" to include himself in the company's decision to terminate him: "[Revenue streams] kind of dried off after the September 11th attacks, and so the only way to cut costs was to let go of people. And so after that we had a 10 percent reduction in workforce and my job was eliminated." His was a common response. With a few notable exceptions, such as when companies engaged in fraudulent labor practices or reneged on promised severance packages, interviewees rarely offered direct criticisms of their former employers or the layoff process; some even praised companies for handling the layoffs so well. Yet within these measured, matter-of-fact accounts, we can find moments, however brief, in which laid-off workers balk or bristle at their former employers, when they question the expectation that, as flexible agents in a free-market system, they should experience as "nothing personal" terminations that in fact felt deeply personal, and sometimes deeply unfair.

On the morning after the company-wide conference call in which the CEO announced impending layoffs, thirty-five-year-old engineer and project manager Enrique Vivar arrived to work at his usual 8:00am. Before he was even settled at his desk, he was called into his manager's office. "I need to see you," said his supervisor, a likable guy with whom Enrique regularly lunched. Not missing a beat, Enrique replied with a knowing laugh, "I don't want to see you." "He knew that I knew," Enrique explained, "and so I just walked into his office and he said 'I'm really sorry to tell you, but ...'" Despite his manager's reassurance that, "You know, this is nothing personal," Enrique had a few theories as to why he'd been selected for termination. "I knew," he said, "that the things that I was doing were not horribly essential to the team." He also knew his manager wanted him to work far more than his usual 45–50 hours a week, something Enrique was unwilling to do with a wife and two young children at home and MBA classes at night.

By 8:10am, Enrique's layoff was official. By 9:10am, he says, "I was out of there. No [company ID] badge, no nothing." Accompanied by uniformed escorts, he was permitted to say goodbye to his coworkers and collect his personal belongings, although not the company laptop on which he'd stored his MBA coursework. None of this was a surprise to Enrique. "Of course they had police officers making sure that safety was [maintained]. I knew that it was going to be that way. I had heard about it, I had seen it previously because we had had layoffs before twice. I had seen it, I knew that it was the way to do it, but I felt like a piece of furniture, or a piece of hardware."

In most respects, Enrique accepted his layoff and how it was carried out. He expressed no antagonism for his former employer; later in the same interview, which occurred five months after the layoff, he even praised them for giving him valuable experience in the telecommunications field, which he'd been new to when he took the job two years before. He also noted that the six months' severance and two weeks' vacation he received were more generous than he'd had in a previous layoff. He felt duly warned of the impending layoff and considered himself "fortunate" to have received the news from someone he considered a friend. Enrique's gallows humor— "I don't want to see you"—suggests the level of comfort he felt with his supervisor, as well as his willingness to dissipate some of the tension for them both. Even the messy business of the security escort is couched as an unfortunate necessity. Positioning himself as an experienced employee who knows the policies and accepts their rationale, "I knew that it was going to be that way. . . . I knew that it was the way to do it," Enrique suggests there was no alternative and therefore no blame to be laid for the negative emotions he experienced at his abrupt and chaperoned departure.

And yet in his description of that day we can find equally compelling evidence that Enrique was *not* entirely at peace with his layoff experience, not at the time it occurred, and not months later when he first told me about it. Despite his laughing delivery, the blunt statement "I don't want to see you" might also be read as reflecting Enrique's true feelings at that moment. He did not want to walk into that office, did not want to be laid off, did not want to pack his things and go. The joke was a small show of resistance, but a show nonetheless.[8]

Enrique's comments about the "police officers" who oversaw his departure are equally complicated. The uniformed men were more likely private security guards, but the fact that Enrique described them as police officers conveys something of how he felt as they followed him on his final trip through the office. At that moment, despite his embrace of the flexible ideal, Enrique did not feel like a freelancer at the end of a contract. Suddenly he was the potential threat to public safety, the one who could not be trusted without constant monitoring. Although he still insisted this was the right way to do a layoff, he still felt mistreated, discarded without ceremony like a chair, a desk, or an outdated computer.

When I asked Enrique what came next, what he did after receiving the bad news, he described driving straight to the career center at the university where he was working on his MBA. He met with their director, borrowed some books on resume writing, and sent an email to his entire MBA cohort asking for leads and contacts. In short, he did exactly what a good, self-directed job-seeker is supposed to do. Yet immediately after ticking off the list of what he'd done and the positive responses he'd received to his email, Enrique paused, then revealed another reason he'd decided to go to the career center:

> I was afraid to go home. It was a very rough time for me. But at the same time I knew I hadn't done anything about it [to deserve the layoff]. Financially-wise, I felt a little vulnerable. And at the same time I felt like I had done something wrong. Even though I knew I hadn't done it. Was it the MBA? . . . Was it the fact that I wasn't working seventy hours a week? What is it, you know?

Just as Enrique's manager assured him, these days layoffs are not supposed to be personal. They are the result of market forces, global competition, national recessions, and technological innovations, forces well beyond any individual worker's control. Enrique knew this was true, or knew it was supposed to be true, and yet it did not *feel* that way to him. We hear his ambivalence as he wavers between reassuring himself he'd done nothing wrong and running through a list of possible sins that might have brought this tragedy down upon him. He believes these two contradictory things simultaneously—that this layoff was not his fault, and that he must have done something to deserve it.

"I'M IRRATIONALLY ANGRY": EMOTION MANAGEMENT AMONG THE LONG-TERM UNEMPLOYED

I encountered similarly ambivalent responses in other interviews. Job-seekers confidently stated that their layoff was not personal, that they had done nothing to deserve it, an easy claim to make when tens of thousands of tech workers were losing their jobs each week. Yet as our conversations progressed, more complicated emotions inevitably emerged.

When I first asked Ed Donnelly, a programmer in his mid-50s, about his layoff, he explained he'd been working at a telecommunications company. "And if you've been tracking IT [the Information Technology sector]," he said, "which you obviously have, you realize that telecom was not a good place to be in the last year, and they laid me off." After that succinct explanation of his layoff, Ed went on to describe how he and his family (he had a wife and teenaged son) had been managing since he lost his job seven months before. "Financially," he explained, "we're quite well off. We've always lived fairly conservatively." His wife, who'd also recently lost a job in high tech, was now working full-time at a real estate firm, and Ed had found a part-time job selling gardening supplies while he learned new and more in-demand programming languages. He was regularly attending networking meetings, which he found to be "a very positive experience, motivating and so on. So far I haven't gotten really that many hard leads from them, but I haven't gotten them anywhere else either, so I can't really hold that against them." He was surprised his search was taking so long, but hopeful things were turning around and he'd soon be reemployed as a programmer, a job he loved and was eager to return to. "To me," he said, "a computer is a toy, and when I found out that people were actually willing to pay you good money to do that, it was 'lead me to it!'"

A year and a half later, when we spoke again, Ed was still working at the gardening store. He continued to periodically look for jobs in high tech, but admitted he was not as motivated as he'd once been:

> Sitting down for an hour or two hours a day, going through the job postings one by one in detail, seeing if there's anything that I even remotely resemble, shooting out a resume, hitting every contact I can. I did that as long as I could and basically got tired of getting doors slammed in my face. So when I start seeing signs that things really are turning around, then I'll try to get serious about it again. Until then, all I can do is keep my ear to the ground because I don't have the psychic energy to keep beating my head against the wall.

Since we'd last spoken, Ed had started taking medication to combat the depression and low self-esteem he'd experienced since his layoff. He had also become more critical about his own role in his layoff, although he still had few complaints about his previous employer. "They did what they had to do," he said, accepting as natural that companies should privilege profit over employee well-being or the social good. "If I had been at all aware of what was going on I would have seen it coming. But, I just sat there at my desk coding, fat, dumb, and happy and the world came crashing down around my ears." The company might have been "a little bit too greedy," he said, but "I didn't feel like they treated me badly. Actually, I survived several waves of layoffs and I was glad I made it as long as I did." Although in many ways consistent with his original statement, Ed's narrative had shifted slightly from one in which his layoff could be explained away by the economic meltdown and related telecom crash to one where Ed himself bore the blame for having sat "fat, dumb, and happy." His employer, in contrast, still received just a sliver of responsibility.

When I recontacted him five years later, eight years after his layoff and seven since our initial interview, Ed was sixty-two, making nine dollars an hour at the gardening store, and "hanging on teeth and toenails" trying to pay expenses. The work was enjoyable but physically demanding, and Ed hoped his body would hold out until his Social Security benefits kicked in and he could retire. Although programming was still his dream job, he no longer expected he'd ever work as a programmer again. When I asked how he felt about his current situation, Ed replied with a sigh: "Resigned. A little angry. It bothers me that I let myself get into this situation. There are any number of things I could have done, but hindsight is 20/20. And once I was in this situation there was no way to get out of it. So I've just had to accept it." The self-blame and resignation had surfaced in our previous conversations, but the anger was new, and I asked Ed at what, or whom, he was angry:

> Myself, the IT world, the world in general, you know. Something goes wrong, you get angry. You don't have to have a rational reason for it. It bothers me that I didn't see it coming and take steps to avoid it. I'm irrationally angry that other people, having used me in the past, now refuse to find a use for me and have discarded me without what I, emotionally, at least, feel like is full return for the work I did. Intellectually I know that I got paid well for what I was doing and it's my own fault that I didn't leave myself an out.

Like Enrique, Ed struggles with two competing ways of feeling about his layoff. There is what he describes as the rational, intellectual view, in which he has only himself to blame for not keeping his programming job or finding a new one, and the irrational, emotional one, in which he feels angry at the company that laid him off and the many others that have refused to hire him, to "use" him in a manner befitting his skills and experience. (Even in the latter view, it is worth noting, Ed accepts that his purpose is to add value to an employer, to be used for their ends.) Arguably, these two ways of seeing are equally valid, and yet the former—the so-called rational one—is so widely endorsed in the contemporary United States that it has come to stand in as the "real" way of seeing things, rather than just one perspective among many.

Ed works remarkably hard to "feel the right feelings," as Utrata puts it in this volume, to force himself into alignment with the prevailing view that he has no right to blame or make demands on his former employer, or any employer, for that matter, even as it becomes clear that thinking this way has taken a huge emotional and psychological toll on him. And yet it turns out Ed works equally hard to convince himself he is not entirely to blame for his downward mobility. Ed is plagued by some of the same questions that torment Enrique: "What's wrong with me that I can't hold down a good job like I used to? I still feel the same inside, but nobody else agrees that I'm worth it." When those feelings threaten to overwhelm him, he struggles to assert, as he did in our initial interview, that his layoff was the result of forces beyond his control. "It's hard," he says, "to keep telling myself that there's nothing wrong with me, it's the outside world that's changed." And yet, he continues, "I just have to shake myself by the ears, so to speak, and say, 'Look, that's not really the way things are. Get over it.' But emotionally it's still there in the background."

Over the course of these interviews, we can actually watch Ed "try[ing] on alternative belief systems," to borrow Allison Pugh's term (2009, 63), none of which adequately encompass how he thinks and feels about what's happened to his career. Blaming anyone other than himself feels irrational, even petulant, but blaming himself alone feels equally untrue, not to mention incredibly painful. Thus Ed finds himself trapped between two interpretations of job loss—layoffs happen to people who deserve them, or layoffs are the fault of uncontrollable economic forces—neither of which offers him consistent comfort.

ITCHING FOR SECURITY: THE ANXIETY OF EMBRACING INDEPENDENCE

One might conclude that Ed's crisis, if we can call it that, is a product of his starting his career in one ideological era and ending it, or being on the verge of ending it, in an entirely different one. When Ed entered the workforce forty years ago, he expected his college degree and then-cutting-edge programming skills would be enough to secure him lifelong employment. His was not quite the era of the Organization Man—that short-lived moment of cradle-to-grave employment for middle-class white men was already winding to a close when Ed began working in the 1970s—but it was not far from it, at least not for educated men like Ed. He might not have expected to stay with a single company for life, working as he did in the volatile field of high tech, but he did expect he'd always be able to find a new job if the old one disappeared. Yet over his career, Ed watched his industry change, as secure jobs grew increasingly rare, and even insecure ones became harder to land, especially for older workers. It was, he said, "like the rules got changed on me in mid-game and I didn't have any choice in helping decide what the rules were." Ed does not necessarily object to the new rules—he later said the shift had probably been a good thing overall, as it allowed people, although of course not himself, more flexibility in building their own careers—but he resented the bait and switch he felt had been pulled on his generation.

Ed's failure to thrive in this new era of flexible employment might be explained away by his age (and, as he sometimes suggests, by age discrimination, which is especially common in high tech). In this volume Lam and his co-authors demonstrate that generational differences can play a significant role in shaping experiences of job loss and job insecurity. As Ed said, he started work under one set of rules and was expected to automatically adjust to a new one, an experience that could understandably lead to the high levels of stress and ambivalence he experienced. Yet when I spoke with younger workers—those who came of age when insecurity was already the

norm for corporate employment, who had watched their own parents negotiate multiple layoffs and job searches—I encountered similarly ambivalent
responses to the new emphasis on flexible work and the commensurate
expectation that individuals are responsible for managing their own careers.

When we first spoke in 2004, twenty-six-year-old Daniel Klein could
have been the poster boy for the new world of white-collar work. He'd been
laid off the year before from a dot-com consulting firm in New York but,
after relocating to Dallas to be near his fiancé, quickly found a new position at a small software company. At that time, a lot of tech companies,
including his own, were beginning to offshore some of their manufacturing and programming work, sending it overseas to be performed for less
by foreign workers with commensurate skills. Although this made Daniel
a bit nervous about his own job, he saw the potential threat of offshoring
as a catalyst for making him think more strategically about his own career.
He told me about an article he'd recently read in *Wired* magazine which
pointed out the positive effects of offshoring. "It was kind of talking about
the fact that this isn't necessarily a bad thing. I guess my responsibility to
my career or to myself is to always evolve, to take care of my own career
progression and growth." In contrast, he pointed to some of his coworkers,
who complain that their employer does little to help employees manage
their career growth. "That annoys me," he says, "because I feel like, you guys
aren't children. You need to manage your own careers. We can help you, but
if you don't take responsibility for your career growth then you're hurting
yourself. Why should a company have to do that for you?"

By the time I interviewed Daniel again five years later, in 2009, he'd gotten married and his wife had taken a break from her own high-tech career
to stay home with their two young children (making them "contemporary
traditionalists," as defined by Gerson in this volume). He had left one job
for a better opportunity elsewhere, only to be laid off just a few months
after his arrival. His description of that layoff included echoes of Enrique
Vivar's experience years earlier: "So when I got called into my new boss's
office, I knew right away, because he called me at my desk and he never did
that. And he said, 'Would you come into my office?' And I was like, oh, okay.
And I walked in there and the head of HR [Human Resources] was there, so
I knew right away what was going on. So it wasn't a surprise in that sense."
Daniel's main concern was that he get a good severance package, which he
did. "So I wasn't pissed off about it. It was, to me, understandable. . . . I'm
a very logical person. I have that attitude of understanding business, like
why those decisions are made. They're not personal, so I wasn't just pissed
off about it, it was really to me just finally an opportunity for me to get off
my ass and do something different."

As Daniel described the two months he spent looking for reemployment, however, it becomes clear that despite the generous severance package and his openness to doing "something different," the experience was by no means easy for him. "As the provider, it was definitely stressful to not have a job and to kind have this nervousness about, 'Okay, am I going to be bringing in money soon?' kind of a thing." The couple's financial security eased those fears a bit, but Daniel's anxiety began to manifest itself physically. "I actually wound up developing these weird itch attacks. All of a sudden I'd get . . . my whole body would just instantly start totally itching. It was really weird." The itching receded when Daniel found a new job at another small software company. Although he'd always seen himself as on the track to upper management, his new role as sole provider and the experience of yet another layoff had readjusted Daniel's career expectations. He'd decided to focus on more technical jobs which, although offering less money and fewer advancement opportunities than his previous managerial positions, were more numerous and, he believed, less likely to be eliminated in the face of cost-cutting.

Although he had no reason to believe his current job was at risk, Daniel told me he wanted to avoid growing complacent. "The key for me," he explained, "is to just decide to go update my resume . . . that's the first step, and just start looking around a little bit and interviewing just for the heck of it, just to see what's out there. Because I've always believed that it's never a mistake to leave a place you're at. Things can only go better if you choose it that way." In the next breath, however, he admitted he hadn't been practicing what he was preaching. He recalled a conversation with his wife the weekend before. He'd mentioned, not for the first time, that he needed to work on his resume. He laughed as he imitated her exasperated reply: "Well then, do it! You keep saying you're going to do that and you never do!" Reflecting on why he had not yet done so, Daniel said, "It isn't because it's hard to work on a resume. I'm actually very, very good at resume writing and stuff like that, but it's the thought of, is there really anything there that's going to match what I have?" His hesitation, then, was less about the challenge of finding time to work on a resume with a full-time job and two young children than it was about the lurking fear that, even if he were to update his resume and start applying, there still might not be companies willing to hire him.

In most respects, Daniel was the ideal flexible worker. He had consciously managed his own career, making strategic choices based on his knowledge of the industry and where he thought it was headed. He was neither beholden to not dependent upon his employer, and was perfectly willing to reinvent himself to remain marketable to potential employers. Yet even for optimistic, self-reliant Daniel, being out of work was, he said, "a brutal experience." Not only did it trigger bodily discomfort in the form of itch attacks, but the fear of finding himself out of work and without prospects had prompted Daniel to scale back his career ambitions. Rather than fly too high and risk plummeting, he'd decided to take a more middling path, one less volatile but also less financially rewarding than he'd imagined for himself as a younger man with fewer responsibilities. Even after these concessions, Daniel remained anxious enough about his career prospects that he was avoiding taking the very actions (updating his resume and continuously applying for new positions) he perceived as most likely to protect his future career prospects.

"IT'S LIKE A PIECE OF ART": THE LABOR OF REINVENTION AND SELF-PRESENTATION

It is especially interesting that the thought of revising his resume had triggered Daniel's anxiety, as resume preparation had proved equally stressful for Enrique Vivar, whose layoff I described earlier in this chapter. Enrique shared Daniel's commitment to keeping his resume always up to date. Even before his layoff Enrique had prepared three different versions of his resume, each emphasizing a different aspect of his previous experience. In the course of his job search, Enrique, like most job-seekers, had sent out hundreds of resumes, usually submitted through online job boards such as Monster.com, each carefully tailored to a specific opening.[9] After a year of unsuccessful job searching, Enrique began to worry there was something wrong with his resume. He attended resume workshops and asked friends and associates to look it over for him. As each reviewer suggested a different set of changes, most of which contradicted each other, Enrique grew frustrated, and became increasingly convinced his flawed resume was what had been keeping him back all along:

> I don't know. I don't know if [my job search methods] work or not. It's kind of like you plant your seeds and you wait for the corn to grow. Right now I've planted a lot of seeds and I've got a good networking background, but at the same time I haven't seen the fruits of that hard work, fruits of the hard labor. The one thing is, I don't know, maybe my resume didn't work. I went to [my school's] career center, they checked it out, and then I gave it to somebody else and they said it stinks, and then I rewrote it and gave it to somebody else and he says it stinks. I mean, I have people rewriting it for me. I've gone every single route with my resume short of hiring a professional to write my resume. And

every time I give it to someone new, he says it stinks. I guess what I'm trying to think of is that it's like a piece of art. Some people are going to say "I love it," and some people are going to say "That's a piece of junk." So I don't know. At this point it kind of undermines your confidence, too, on what your writing abilities are. And I am just frustrated, and that's the only bog, when I think, in hindsight, I should have gone and hired someone and paid $350–$400 to get my resume done professionally and then this wouldn't have happened.[10]

His realization that a resume, "like a piece of art," is subjective and will never appeal equally to all readers, would seem to offer Enrique a way out of his endless cycle of self-criticism. If no resume is perfect, the fact that his own is imperfect can hardly be taken as evidence of personal failure. Accepting that logic, however, would mean surrendering one of the few aspects of the job search over which job-seekers are able to exert some control. What would it mean to be responsible for your own career if you concede that unpredictable forces beyond your control shape your chances as much as, or more than, your own actions do? Confronted with a choice between having no clear path to reemployment and having chosen the wrong path, Enrique opts for the latter, ignoring his own insight and continuing to seek out the fatal flaw in his resume-crafting process.

As both Daniel's and Enrique's experiences attest, the pressure to constantly revise one's resume can prove both exhausting and anxiety-inducing, as job seekers place an almost talismanic faith in a single document to shield them from the perils of joblessness.[11] In this sense, resume preparation stands in as a concrete representation of the larger task required of all job-seekers today. Like writing a resume, constantly re-inventing oneself is a Sisyphean feat, always in process and never quite complete. The human costs of this unremitting pressure are evident in the accounts above, but they are for the most part absent from the laudatory accounts of flexible work circulating in American culture today.

THE HIGH COSTS OF FLEXIBILITY

When Douglas T. Hall (1976) first introduced the idea of the protean career, he foresaw an empowering opportunity for workers to continually reinvent themselves while pursuing self-fulfillment. At that time, in the 1970s, white-collar workers were still generally insulated from the threat of mass layoffs, and, for this privileged group of educated workers, most job changes were voluntary. In the decades since, the social contract of employment that had once provided white-collar workers with secure jobs and steady upward mobility in return for loyalty and hard work has been broken, and white-collar workers have accounted for an increasing share of layoffs in each of the last four recessions (Mishel, Bernstein, and Boushey 2003; Stettner and Wenger 2003; Shierholz and Mishel 2009). In this new landscape, even protean careers' original champion now recognizes the immense burden being shouldered by individuals attempting to successfully manage their professional fates in increasingly insecure work environments. In a 2001 interview, Hall offered a more nuanced assessment of the protean career and the mutability it entails:

> Now that I can see the "protean career" up-close I can see both sides—the upside . . . and the not-so-positive elements. It can certainly be very stressful, when people suddenly find themselves out of job. They've tried to build something in a particular line of work or a particular organization and suddenly, they are looking for something different. It puts much more stress on people. In the face of all the adaptation people need to make, it is really hard to maintain your sense of identity, of who you are. If you are constantly coping with major loss or change, you don't think about higher-level ideas. It is hard to maintain a sense of identity. The lack of security makes it difficult. (Quoted in Harrington 2001)

Hall's assertion that flexibility is now as much a burden as an opportunity makes infinitely more sense than the prevailing narrative that insecurity imbues individuals with divine power over their own fates. Yet in a culture obsessed with unfettered individualism and heroic self-reliance, it can be difficult to acknowledge these burdens or to conceptualize viable, positive alternatives to the flexible, entrepreneurial self being celebrated as the only logical response to insecure employment.[12]

In the current neoliberal climate, any resistance on the part of job-seekers, any lingering expectation that the reward for hard work should be some form of job security, is dismissed as the sour grapes of entitled and outmoded loafers. According to the logic of the flexible ideal, the very experience of feeling angry, frustrated, or sad about one's professional situation is evidence of a failure to think "right," a refusal to become the "happy worker" neoliberal organizations require (Cabanas and Illouz, this volume), and therefore an explanation for why one's job search has been going so poorly.[13] (A similar logic is used to dismiss those who participate in more overt, collective forms of resistance, such as the Occupy Movement, whose demand for more and better employment opportunities was met with the directive, as vitriolic as it was ironic, to "stop whining, take a bath and get a job" [Wyler 2011]). Rather than calling into question the soundness of the original tenet that constant reinvention is the key to career success, this cyclical reasoning prevents that question from ever being called. Those who fail to achieve professional success—such as the tens of millions currently out of work in the United States—are simply dismissed as not having reinvented themselves frequently or enthusiastically enough, just like the benighted parental generation that functions so effectively as a straw man in Friedman's editorial.

Thus job-seekers were left struggling to shoehorn their experiences into a framework that fails to fully encompass their experiences and emotions. They tried on alternative belief systems—it's not my fault, it's no one's fault but mine—unable to settle on a single explanation that felt both rational and true, and not too excruciatingly painful. As the quotations above demonstrate, the logic job-seekers most often articulated was, in fact, the same one employers and management experts do. They endeavored, in myriad ways, to maintain a consistently flexible sense of self—an oxymoron if there ever was one. They modified their resumes, crafted new commercials for themselves, and spent scare resources retraining in new fields.[14] They did so despite the heavy toll it took on themselves and their families, marching valiantly ahead toward the satisfying futures that, on the good days, they were confident awaited them. If, as Friedman and so many others claim, the key to solving high unemployment lies in changing individual workers' behaviors and attitudes, the crises facing both the nation and these job-seekers should have been short-lived. Yet in the decade since my initial fieldwork began, the United States has weathered another serious recession and seen unemployment leap to more than 10%. And while some of the job-seekers I interviewed have been more successful than others in their quest for reemployment, none made it through their job search unscathed.

Enrique's frustration and self-recrimination; Ed's anger, depression, and financial straits; Daniel's itch attacks and diminished aspirations, all are a direct result of their efforts to bear the mantle of flexibility. Some of these losses are more traumatic than others, but all are losses nonetheless. Yet each of these men remains tied to the logic that brought him to this point, aligning himself with the flexible ideal even as it explains away his suffering as the result of his own flawed choices and failed efforts. Ed, who has given up hope of his own return to high tech, still thinks the shift to insecure employment is a good thing for most people, even though it's been a terrible thing for him. Daniel and Enrique strive to continually remake themselves in the guise of the ideal employee, even though their efforts, like all best-laid plans, may still not protect them from again experiencing the brutal anxiety of joblessness. And that, of course, is the flaw in the flexible ideal. Today's job-seekers—like the job-seekers of a decade ago—can be as flexible, entrepreneurial, and creative as they like, and still have no guarantee of gainful reemployment. Those fortunate enough to find new jobs may lose them just as quickly. And now that commitment has been reframed as complacency, not even those with relatively secure positions are exempt from the neverending job search that is the flexible career.

CONCLUSIONS AND POSSIBILITIES

It is time we stop proclaiming the flexible ideal something new and noteworthy. For nearly four decades, American workers have become increasingly responsible for their own professional fates. Some have resisted this shift, but far more have embraced it, however reluctantly, revising their resumes, rethinking their career plans, and reinventing themselves as needed to woo potential hiring managers. They have asked less of their employers, less of their government, and more and more of themselves. Their reward has come not, as promised, in the form of more exciting and fulfilling careers, but in escorted departures, downward mobility, and the nagging persistence of self-recrimination. In and of itself, there is nothing wrong with flexibility, nothing objectionable about change and choice and reinvention. But enacted as it is within an unequal framework where employers reap the benefits of flexibility while workers bear its burdens, the flexible ideal has become a Potemkin village behind which hide the painful realities of insecure employment and its effects on American workers.

What, then, *should* we be telling new college graduates, or, for that matter, anyone who is looking for work or suspects they one day might be? We should tell them to go ahead and take Friedman's advice while rejecting the implicit self-blame that goes along with it. Educate yourself about trends in and around your industry, and do be creative in envisioning and pitching the kind of jobs to which your skills and experience would be especially well-suited. It is by no means a bad thing to be optimistic about your own future, to believe that through hard work, innovation, and sheer moxie you have the chance to build a professional life that will be both satisfying and financially sustaining. But as anthropologist Claudia Strauss (2016) has noted, in a work environment as insecure as the one job candidates face today, positive thinking has become less a job search strategy than a magical incantation to ward off fear and failure, a desperate effort to wrest control back from the forces that have radically reconfigured the labor market to the disadvantage of individual workers. Thus even as job-seekers work to advance their interests in a volatile labor market, they need to recognize the limits of their own abilities.

Both individually and as a society, we need to identify and draw attention to the structural barriers to full, or even close to full, employment that have been conveniently concealed behind the guise of meritocratic individualism. In today's labor market, arguably in any labor market, people do not sink or swim solely by their own devices, and it is time we publicly reject that fallacy. We also need to recognize that the legal protections currently enjoyed by workers and employers alike are the product of specific historical and political events; what are generally now considered to be rights (a minimum wage; safe work environs; freedom from discrimination in hiring, firing, and promotion) were hard-won by previous generations of workers and their advocates. The status quo is neither natural nor immutable. Rather than valiantly trying to survive within a world of work characterized by insecurity, dwindling benefits, and persistently high levels of unemployment, we need to push back against those trends, to press— individually and collectively—for changes that would improve the lot of working and unemployed Americans alike.

To invert Kennedy's classic injunction to the American people, the time has come to ask what, exactly, your country—and its corporations—are willing to do for you. There are many directions reform efforts might take, but the most pressing ones concern how local, state, and federal governments can better meet the needs of those who are currently unemployed. For example, jobless workers might demand more generous and long-lasting unemployment benefits designed to encourage, not preclude, the taking of low-paid or part-time interim positions.[15] Other activists might enter the ongoing fray around President Obama's Health Care for America Plan (also known as ObamaCare) to agitate specifically for the provision of free or affordable health care to the unemployed, many of whom go without health insurance or purchase policies only for their children.[16] Americans might also call for the expansion of government-funded counseling programs for jobless workers, both career counseling designed to help job-seekers assess their skills and plan their job search strategies and individual and family therapy to help manage the emotional, psychological, and social challenges of job loss and unemployment.

Of course it is not only the government who might be pressed to be more responsive to the needs of the unemployed and insecurely employed. Employers benefit immensely from the widespread supposition that joblessness is an individual issue, rather than a social ill. Much could be gained from demanding greater corporate responsibility to both current and former employees and the community at large. Employees could call for greater job security; more long-term and worker-friendly employment contracts;

better, more consistent severance packages; guaranteed employer-funded retraining and transition assistance; and a halt to the gradual disappearance of once-common benefits such as health insurance, paid vacation, and pensions. Recruiters and hiring managers might also be incentivized to hire applicants from among the pool of long-term unemployed, rather than trying to poach already employed individuals from their current jobs. Conversely, companies who lay off employees during periods of growth and high profits or offshore jobs to foreign countries might be penalized by forfeiting all tax breaks and government subsidies.

More radically, people might advocate a fundamental rethinking of the relationship between work, income, and security in the United States. They might push for a basic income guarantees, a standard yearly income provided to all citizens or residents regardless of whether or at what they work (Graeber 2011; Standing 2012), or follow the Nordic model of "flexicurity" in which the challenges of a flexible (i.e., insecure) labor market are buttressed by high minimum wages, lifelong job training and placement assistance, and generous income support during job transitions (Schulze-Cleven 2015).

Of course, none of these changes will happen unless the American people agitate for them, loudly and in unison. A decade ago, I might have felt less optimistic about this possibility, but recent examples of collective grassroots activism—the Occupy Movement, most notably, but also legal and social reform efforts around gay marriage, immigration, and the cost and quality of public education—suggest the era of political apathy and defeatism that has reigned since the 1970s may be coming to a close. Thus as new graduates go about looking for that first job, and so many others start looking for the next one, I hope they will think not just about who employers want them to be, but also about who they want to be, and what sort of nation they want to live in. The flexible ideal is a powerful myth; it shapes both the minds of individual workers and the labor market in which they find themselves struggling. Yet the burdens of that flexibility have been unequally distributed. Employees are expected to become infinitely mutable while employers become increasingly rigid, demanding that workers ask nothing more than a paycheck—no benefits, no training, no personal accommodations, no promise of security or upward mobility. It is time that we rebalance that burden, shifting some of it off the shoulders of individual workers and onto the companies that employ them and the government that is supposed to support and protect them. Only then will the real rewards of flexibility and hard work start to resemble the idealized versions we have been promised for so long.

NOTES

1. An especially popular example of this ideology is found in the bestselling *Who Moved My Cheese?* (Johnson 1998), a parable chronicling a group of mice who come to embrace change in their search for a peripatetic pile of cheese.

2. Not only has job growth been exceptionally slow since the "Great Recession" of 2007, but most of the new jobs being created are clustered in low-wage occupations (National Employment Law Project 2012).

3. In this, job seekers follow the tenets of a generalized American "culture of anti-politics" (Giroux 2001, 2), in which social change and collective action are dismissed as futile. High-tech job seekers were equally skeptical of organized labor, which they saw as obsolete and ill-suited to the needs of professional workers. They felt unions had served an important role in American history and could provide useful protections for the working class, but saw themselves as better able to negotiate for themselves than any union ever could. For an extended discussion of job seekers' attitudes to government intervention and unions, see Lane 2011, 52–61.

4. Once termed "elevator speeches," the new moniker "commercial" is representative of the self-commodifying language so ubiquitous in today's market-obsessed culture. On the encroachment of market ideology into conceptions of the self, especially for job seekers, see Ehrenreich 2005 and Illouz 2010, 87–89.

5. On the roots and impact of positive thinking in the United States, see also Ehrenreich 2009, and Strauss 2016.

6. On the negative impact of prolonged unemployment and insecure work on US jobseekers' marital relationships, see Lane 2009; 2010; and 2011, 103–130, 150–151 as well as Gerson's and Whitaker's chapters in this volume.

7. To be certain, such exchanges do not provide unfettered access to interviewees' deepest thoughts—as William Shakespeare and Erving Goffman (1959) agree, all the world's a stage, every interaction a performance of some kind—yet they can offer us access to unpolished, or less polished responses, and to other, more nuanced sorts of data than might be gathered by alternative means.

8. The obvious and important reference here is to "weapons of the weak," or the subtle but nonetheless significant forms of resistance exercised by those in subaltern positions (Scott 1987).

9. While a few dozen copies of a single resume printed on high-quality paper used to suffice in a job search, the new expectation is that every job-seeker maintain a variety of resumes for different types of jobs, and each resume must be custom-tailored to the job at hand before it goes out for consideration. These resumes, in addition to business cards and a profile on the business networking website LinkedIn, are now considered key components of the "marketing materials" job seekers are expected to have at the ready. During my fieldwork, online job boards were touted as the futuristic alternative to paper resumes and newspaper want ads, but now, job boards themselves are considered antiquated. "No good software engineer puts his resume on Monster," a recent article alleged. Recruiters now prefer to scour social networking sites such as Facebook and LinkedIn for potential candidates, most of whom are not actively looking for work (Kharif 2012). Those who submit their resumes through job boards, rather than through personal contacts, are disparagingly referred to by recruiters as "Homers," after the lazy and oafish Homer Simpson (Schwartz 2013).

10. Most job-seekers saw professional resume writing services as unnecessary—nearly every networking event and job fair offered free resume workshops—and many condemned them as predatory attempts to take advantage of the desperation of the unemployed.

11. Although job-seekers unanimously cite networking as the single most effective job search strategy, submitting a resume—whether paper or electronic—is still a required part of nearly every application process.

12. The neoliberal context that allows for such narratives to dominate public discourse is well-documented in the works of Henry Giroux (2001, 2008) and David Harvey (2005), among others.

13. This catch-22 resembles the "prosperity gospel," a Christian religious doctrine that financial blessings are the will of God. According to this tenet, increasingly popular among Christian megachurches, wealth is evidence of having earned God's blessing, while poverty is evidence of not having lived according to Christian principles. See, for example, Harrison 2005.

14. Other workers took the challenge of re-inventing themselves more literally. Having been told he looked "too nice" for the "dirty work" of helping tech companies go international, one executive in his 40s shaved his head and grew a beard, hoping the tougher image would appeal to employers.

15. Although participants in my research were grateful for the multiple extensions of unemployment benefits offered by the Bush administration (and renewed by the Obama administration), the increasingly long duration of unemployment, especially for older workers and those in high-level positions, meant that many job seekers were eventually left with no benefits at all. Others had to give up part-time or low-paid interim jobs because their income, although a fraction of their former earnings, disqualified them from receiving benefits. Although job-seekers enjoyed the emotional and physical benefits of having a job to go to, however low paid, those jobs were generally insecure and offered little chance of promotion, and so when forced to choose, job-seekers usually quit rather than sacrifice their more reliable unemployment benefits.

16. Many interviewees noted that most supplemental health insurance policies available to unemployed persons were prohibitively expensive. Yet rather than expecting the government to provide a more affordable alternative (these interviews took place before President Obama passed the Health Care for American Act designed to provide affordable health insurance for all Americans), job-seekers expected insurance companies would soon start to compete for the business of the growing number of unemployed or insecurely employed workers, and the ensuing price war would drive costs down for everyone.

REFERENCES

Ehrenreich, Barbara. 2005. *Bait and Switch: The (Futile) Pursuit of the American Dream.* New York: Metropolitan Books.

Ehrenreich, Barbara. 2009. *Bright-Sided: How the Relentless Promotion of Positive Thinking Has Undermined America.* New York: Metropolitan Books.

Friedman, Thomas. 2011. "The Start-Up of You," *New York Times*, July 12.

Giroux, Henry. 2001. *Public Spaces, Private Lives: Beyond the Culture of Cynicism.* Lanham, MD: Rowman and Littlefield.

Giroux, Henry. 2008. *Against the Terror of Neoliberalism: Politics Beyond the Age of Greed*. Boulder, CO: Paradigm.

Goffman, Erving. 1959. *The Presentation of Self in Everyday Life*. New York: Anchor.

Graeber, David. 2011. *Debt: The First 5,000 Years*. Brooklyn, NY: Melville House.

Hall, Douglas T. 1976. *Careers in Organizations*. Glenview, IL: Scott, Foresman.

Harrington, Brad. 2001. "Protean Career: A Conversation with Tim Hall." *Sloan Work and Family Research Network Newsletter* 3(2):5, 7.

Harrison, Milmon. 2005. *Righteous Riches: The Word of Faith Movement in Contemporary African American Religion*. New York: Oxford University Press.

Harvey, David. 2005. *A Brief History of Neoliberalism*. Oxford: Oxford University Press.

Illouz, Eva. 2010 [2007]. *Cold Intimacies: The Making of Emotional Capitalism*. Malden, MA: Polity.

Johnson, Spencer. 1998. *Who Moved My Cheese? An Amazing Way to Deal with Change in Your Work and in Your Life*. New York: Putnam.

Kharif, Olga. 2012. "Finding Job Candidates Who Aren't Looking." *St. Louis Post-Dispatch*, December 21. http://www.stltoday.com/business/local/finding-job-candidates-who-aren-t-looking/article_33602dac-229a-5b10-baa5-2bf6365bfaab.html.

Korkki, Phyllis. 2011. "The Shifting Definition of Worker Loyalty," *New York Times*, April 23.

Lane, Carrie. 2009. "Man Enough to Let My Wife Support Me: How Changing Models of Career and Gender Are Reshaping the Experience of Unemployment." *American Ethnologist* 36(4):681–692.

Lane, Carrie. 2010. "'If The Shoe Ain't Your Size, It Ain't Gonna Fit': Ideologies of Professional and Marital Instability among US White-Collar Workers." *Iowa Journal of Cultural Studies* 12(1):37–54.

Lane, Carrie. 2011. *A Company of One: Insecurity, Independence, and the New World of White-Collar Unemployment*. Ithaca, NY: Cornell University Press.

McGee, Micki. 2005. *Self-Help, Inc.: Makeover Culture in American Life*. Oxford: Oxford University Press.

Mishel, Lawrence, Jared Bernstein, and Heather Boushey. 2003. *The State of Working America 2002–03*. Washington, DC: Economic Policy Institute.

National Employment Law Project. 2012. "The Low-Wage Recovery and Growing Inequality." August. http://www.nelp.org/page/-/Job_Creation/LowWageRecovery2012.pdf?nocdn=1.

Newman, Katherine. 1993. *Declining Fortunes: The Withering of the American Dream*. New York: BasicBooks.

Pugh, Allison. 2009. *Longing and Belonging: Parents, Children, and Consumer Culture*. Berkeley: University of California Press.

Rosenblum, Constance. 2010. "On Hard-Times TV, Dumpster Diving and Résumé Rehab," *New York Times*, October 29.

Scott, James. 1987. *Weapons of the Weak: Everyday Forms of Peasant Resistance*. New Haven, CT: Yale University Press.

Schulze-Cleven, Tobias. 2015. "Labor Market Policy: Toward a 'Flexicurity' Model in the United States?" In *Lessons from Europe? What Americans Can Learn from European Public Policies*, edited by R. Daniel Kelemen, 77–96. Thousand Oaks, CA: SAGE/CQ Press.

Schwartz, Nelson. 2013. "In Hiring, a Friend in Need Is a Prospect, Indeed," *New York Times*, January 27.

Sennett, Richard. 1998. *The Corrosion of Character: The Personal Consequences of Work in the New Capitalism*. New York: W.W. Norton.

Shierholz, Heidi, and Lawrence Mishel. 2009. "Highest Unemployment Rate since 1983." Economic Policy Institute Jobs Picture Preview. June 16. http://www.epi.org/publications/entry/jobspict_2009_july_preview/.

Standing, Guy. 2012. "The Precariat: From Denizens to Citizens?" *Polity* 44(4):588–608.

Stettner, Andrew, and Jeffrey Wenger. 2003. "The Broad Reach of Long-Term Unemployment." Economic Policy Institute. Issue Brief #194. May 15. http://www.epi.org/publication/issuebriefs_ib194/.

Strauss, Claudia. 2016. "Positive Thinking about Being out of Work in Southern California during the Great Recession." In *Anthropologies of Unemployment: New Perspectives on Work and Its Absence*, edited by Jong Bum Kwon and Carrie Lane, 171–190. Ithaca, NY: Cornell University Press.

Torres, Alicia. 1996. "When Weak Ties Fail: Shame, Reciprocity, and Unemployed Professionals." MA diss., University of California, Santa Barbara.

Virick, Meghna. 2004. "Research Report: Follow-Up Survey on the Effects of Layoffs in the North Texas Region." Dallas: North Texas Technology Council and University of Texas at Arlington.

Wyler, Grace. 2011. "Newt Gingrich Slams Occupy Wall Street: 'Take a Bath' and 'Get a Job'." *Business Insider*. November 21. http://www.businessinsider.com/newt-gingrich-occupy-wall-street-video-2011-11.

CHAPTER 4

༄

Laboring Heroes, Security, and the Political Economy of Intimacy in Postwar Japan

ALLISON ALEXY

Mariko Ando had been dating her boyfriend for four years when he first asked her to get married. They had met in college, when they both attended an elite university, and after graduation began jobs in the Tokyo financial sector. Although they didn't work in the same firm, they had similar jobs and experienced the requirements that come with such positions—lots of stressful work, long hours, evenings and nights socializing with coworkers and clients. As they approached their mid-twenties, Mariko's boyfriend thought it was time for them to get married. She wasn't against it, exactly, but she did take time to think about what she would want from a marriage. She finally agreed to get married if her boyfriend would consent to two requests. First, she wanted to be able to live close to her mother, to help as she got older. Second, she wanted to be able to keep working. Throughout the postwar period, the statistically common pattern has been for Japanese women to leave full-time paid work either when they get married or at the birth of their first child. Although the majority of women eventually return to the labor market, usually after children are in school, by that point they are likely to hold part-time or underpaid positions (Brinton 1993; Broadbent 2003; White 2002). Mariko liked her job, and had worked very hard to get it, and wasn't interested in quitting. Her boyfriend agreed to both requests and they got married in 2000, when they were both twenty-five years old.

Despite Mariko's forthright attempt to build a style of marriage that would fit her needs and plans, it didn't take long for serious problems to creep into her relationship. Although her husband kept his promises, and had no problem with her staying at her job, he also had firm expectations about the division of labor within their new home. It became readily apparent that he expected her to be responsible for all the housework, from cleaning to laundry to preparing meals. Because she was still working a demanding job, Mariko found herself devoting her entire weekends to frantically accomplishing household duties. In between cleaning and doing laundry, she made and froze a week's worth of meals, so that they would have something home-cooked when they came home exhausted. She kept up this blistering schedule for about a year before she had an epiphany: her husband hadn't *lied* when he agreed to let her keep working after they got married. He'd meant it. But he'd also assumed that her paid work wouldn't reduce her responsibilities for the housework. When she had asked permission to keep working, he understood that as permission to *add* paid labor to the automatic roster of household tasks that he imagined as her responsibility. Their eventual divorce was the result of this misunderstanding coupled with his unwillingness to learn to share domestic responsibilities. They split a few years after marriage, and Mariko says they're still friendly enough. Her key insight, which she imparted to me in a tone reflective of a hard-won life lesson, was: don't marry the son of a housewife. No matter what such a man says, he will always expect his wife to act like a housewife.

Mariko's experiences are remarkably reflective of recent patterns in Japanese society in that they demonstrate the relationship between constructions of intimacy and labor. While her elite educational background and particular job make her far from average, Mariko is a member of a generation increasingly likely to divorce and her reasons for divorce reflect increasingly common explanations. The divorce rate in Japan hit a postwar peak in 2002 and now suggests that between one-third and one-fourth of marriages will end in divorce (Statistical Yearbook 2013). Beyond broad statistical and demographic patterns, common reasons for divorce have shifted in two key ways since the 1980s: who is requesting divorces, and the reasons they give to justify it. First, through the late 1980s, husbands were more commonly initiating divorce, while according to current common knowledge divorce is now something that Japanese women want and men have to work to avoid. Second, earlier divorces were explained either as a method for a husband to be with another woman (formalizing what was probably an extramarital affair) or for a wife to escape extreme domestic violence. In the current moment, as Mariko's case demonstrates, divorce in Japan is much more likely to reflect both spouses' sense that a marriage is not enabling them to be the people they want to be. Such a focus on subjectivity, and understanding relationships as tools that inhibit or enable particular senses of self, mirrors intimate transitions in other cultural contexts (Giddens 1993; Pugh 2015; Simpson 1998).

For much of the postwar period, there has been a clear economic hero in Japan: the salaryman worker. Stereotypical salarymen were white-collar employees working hard for their families and the nation by regularly toiling from early morning until very late at night, often capping busy days with mandatory nighttime socializing with clients or coworkers. Staring in the 1970s, in Japanese popular media and international representations, the salaryman became a popular synecdoche for the nation's new economic muscle. Although there has always been a range of laborers in Japan—from part-time agricultural workers to working women—such diversity failed to reduce the symbolic importance of salarymen in the postwar Japanese political economy. Men in such positions led arduous, but highly predictable, work lives that led to personal financial security and national economic recovery. Their reward came in the "lifetime employment system" that guaranteed employment from high school or college graduation to retirement. Yet salarymen were only made possible by particular forms of domestic intimacy. Working such long hours, augmented by obligatory late-night drinking, a salaryman rarely had time for anything else. For requirements of basic living—food, clean clothes, paid bills—a salaryman relied on his wife, who often accomplished all tasks surrounding the household and children. According to research conducted in the 1970s and 1980s, spouses rarely socialized together and instead found freedom by building emotional bonds with other people, often of the same gender (Lebra 1984). Conforming to patterns most typically surrounding "arranged" marriages, many Japanese people at that time were reluctant to place their spouse at the center of their emotional lives. I label these patterns of relationality "salaryman intimacies."

In the recessionary decades since the Japanese economic bubble burst in the early 1990's, the salaryman's primacy has been increasingly challenged in both economic and intimate realms. In an effort to downsize, Japanese companies are less willing to hire so-called "lifetime" workers and instead now build business models on legions of "contract" workers who can easily be laid off. Simultaneously, the Japanese divorce rate's increase is driven partially by people ending marriages that conform to the "salaryman intimacies" popular a generation before. In contrast to previous norms, now people of all ages speak about ideal intimacies based on emotional connections and shared activities (Hayashi 2005; Ikeuchi 2005; TBS Programming Staff 2006). Especially frightening to older workers, even wives in their 60s and older—the very same wives who supported their salaryman husbands decades before—are increasingly likely to divorce men who maintain these "salaryman intimacies." It is not uncommon to hear such retired salarymen complaining that they are now being punished for doing exactly what they were asked to do a few years before.

This chapter analyzes contemporary Japanese theories and practices connecting employment with intimate possibilities. Given the recent history linking categories of employment with marital forms, many Japanese people attempt to balance security and flexibility in work and intimate realms, finding it especially difficult to sustain security in both at the same time. Based on ethnographic fieldwork in the mid- and late-2000s with single, married, and divorcing men and women, this chapter examines discourse and practice to analyze how contemporary Japanese people relate intimacy, security, and employment. I argue that although they might first seem to be separate, experiences and idealizations of intimacy have long been mutually constituted in relation to labor patterns and that this dynamic now has particular resonance given recent calls to search for a spouse as if one is searching for a job.

THE POSTWAR ECONOMIC MIRACLE

At the end of World War II, few people predicted that the Japanese economy would ever become one of the largest in the world. The defeated nation lay in ruins, not only from two atomic bombs, but also from the extensive firebombing of Tokyo and the cost of decades of extensive colonial expansion (Allen 2013 [1946]; Cohen 1948, 279; Dower 1999, 45; Young 1998). But the Japanese economy began to grow for a number of reasons, not the least of which was the Cold War proxy war fought on the Korean peninsula (Ikeda 2002, 111; Bestor 2002, 31). Between 1950 and 1973, the Japanese economy doubled every seven years (Blomström, Gangnes, and La Croix 2001, 2; Ikeda 2002); and between 1946 and 1976, the economy increased fifty-five-fold (Johnson 1982, 6). By the early 1990s, the Japanese economy was the second largest in the world and astronomical prices for land in Tokyo led to giddy media coverage about how the land under Tokyo's Imperial Palace was supposedly worth more than the entire state of California (Epstein 2009). The bursting of the economic bubble—which had been built on an extremely strong yen, mistaken assumptions that land would always increase in value, and business practices premised on these two facts—pushed the Japanese economy into two long recessionary decades, short-handed as "the Lost Decades" because of their negative or neutral economic growth. In the mid-2010s, this economic malaise still lingers, and in 2010 China's economy surpassed Japan's as the second largest in the world, although the Japanese per capita GDP remains substantially higher (McCurry and Kollewe 2011; World Bank 2014).

Although there were meaningful variations in labor patterns throughout the long postwar period, in this chapter I divide these decades into three extended moments: first, the immediate postwar period characterized by high unemployment and a recovering economy (1945–1955); second, the economic miracle characterized by a labor shortage, rapid GDP growth, and eventual creation of the bubble economy (1955–1991); third, the bursting of the economic bubble and extended recessions (1992 to present). Focusing here on the latter two periods, I concentrate on the way labor in those moments was made possible by, and idealized in relation to, particular forms of intimacy.

LABOR AT THE CORE OF A MIRACLE

Despite a diverse set of employment possibilities for Japanese men and women, popular imagination in Japan and elsewhere often pinpointed the postwar "miracle" economy on a particular character: the "salaryman." Although the English term might suggest any man who earns a salary, the meaning in Japanese is quite specific[1]. The quintessential salaryman is an overworked white-collar man in a relatively anonymous suit, with a conservative haircut and boring tie. He goes to work early in the morning and works long hours that are extended even further by mandatory socializing either with coworkers to build "team spirit," or with clients to improve business. He might get home very late at night, too late to see his children awake, only to wake up early the next morning to start the whole process again (Dasgupta 2013). Significant scholarly and ethnographic attention has been focused on the salaryman as a key social character in Japan's long "miracle" economic boom. While doing research about urban communities in the 1980s, Theodore Bestor found salarymen to be ascendant compared to formerly elite labor categories (Bestor 1989, 263). Doing research a few years later, Anne Allison worked in a hostess bar and described the salaryman customers as crudely aggressive and sexist, but also largely controlled by their employers, who coopted their lives as much outside work as within it (Allison 1994). In Yoko Ogasawara's research in a Tokyo bank branch, salarymen have the potential for promotion—a path largely unavailable to female workers—but are also feel stuck in particular tracks or dependent on underlings (Ogasawara 1998). In the many comic books (*manga*) and films representing salarymen, their relatively privileged white-collar position belies the brutality of a daily grind keeping them from almost everything but work (Matanle, McCann, and Ashmore 2008; Skinner 1979).[2] Although many people identified with salarymen, wanted to become one, or wished the same for their sons, simultaneous media coverage commented on the difficulties of the salaryman lifestyle, especially the long hours away from family and the daily requirements for work. As early as the 1970s, Crawcour was describing the salaryman as "once the object of envy but now increasingly a figure to be pitied" (Crawcour 1978, 245).

Almost from the moment of the creation of the term "salaryman," men who fall into this category have been simultaneously envied for their regular salary, pitied for the requirements that come with their job, and constructed as a synecdoche of the nation—a pinnacle of masculine power in a nation constitutionally forbidden to raise a military.[3] The salaryman was such a common representation of Japanese men, that when Roberson and Suzuki assembled a volume concerning Japanese masculinity, they subtitled it "Dislocating the Salaryman Doxa." In their introduction they describe the centrality of the image of this particular worker:

> "The salaryman as dominant (self-)image, model and representation of men and masculinity in Japan indexes overlapping discourses of gender, sexuality, class, and nation: the middle-class, heterosexual, married salaryman considered as responsible for and representative of 'Japan'" (Roberson and Suzuki 2003, 1; see also Tokuhiro 2009).

Both within and beyond Japan, salarymen have been deployed as powerful and popular symbols of the postwar recovery, economic power, or Japaneseness in general.

For most of the postwar being a salaryman indexed a particular, and particularly predictable, system of employment. First, unlike most other workers in Japan, salarymen were offered so-called "lifetime employment," an implicit guarantee from employers that any man hired as a salaryman would have a position at the company until his retirement. Although such a policy might seem to breed inefficiency, for many workers it instead partially justified the loyalty due employers. Popular rhetoric, during the "economic miracle" period especially, described companies as families, and suggested employees owed loyalty to their employers much as family members should honor their relatives and lineage (Abegglen 1958, 11; Cole 1971, 52; Kelly 1986, 603; Rohlen 1979). The lifetime guarantee helps support such a claim of an employee-employer relationship maintained by more than "just" extraction of labor value; Chalmers Johnson calls this Japan's "all in the family" (*uchiwa*) economic system (Johnson 1982, 11). Salarymen might not have always believed such claims, but for most of the postwar period Japanese male employees changed jobs with less frequency than American workers (Aoki 1988, 61; Levine 1983; Mincer and Higuchi 1988).

The implicit promise of lifetime employment provided employees and their families with the sense of security that comes with predictability. This predictability was largely a result of a second characteristic of this employment structure: the majority of a salaryman's salary was calculated based on years of service in the company, rather than on merit or company revenue. Aware of such a formula, salarymen could literally predict, with significant accuracy, how much money they would be making in the future (Holzhausen 2000; Rohlen 1979). Other ethnographic examples describe salarymen positively reflecting on this predictability, and the comforting links between labor lives and the general lifecourse. For instance, Anne Allison describes how salary and employment security made salarymen an extremely attractive option:

> "This new class is the class of the *sarariiman*: the white-collar worker whose position in a large company is the standard goal of youths whose parents are, or wish their next generation to become, comfortably middle-class. The security and status offered by big companies—for example, lifetime employment and a wage structure based on seniority (*nenkō joretsu*)—are greatly desired" (Allison 1994, 92).

Throughout the postwar period until the early 2000s, salarymen's lives were represented as predictable, possibly a little boring, but intensely secure.

Despite the image of being intensely predictable, cultural understandings of "predictability" in this postwar moment often centered on salary rather than other characteristics of employment. In addition to the promise of lifetime employment and predictable salary increases, salarymen's work lives were shaped by frequent transfers within a company and between branch offices. While salarymen could predict a large portion of their salaries, they couldn't easily predict their division within the company or where, geographically, they would be working. Lifetime employees were regularly required to accept transfers to other divisions within the same company, often every few years. The logic behind this strategy suggested that employees who had firsthand knowledge about more than just one particular specialty would be more well-rounded and better prepared to fulfill the company's needs (Rebick 2005, 124). Thus salarymen were typically trained as generalists, and it was common for one worker to be placed in radically different divisions over the course of his career, especially if he were trying to move up the corporate ladder. In addition to these internal transfers and the requisite (re)training, salarymen were similarly required to transfer to different branch offices within the same company, sometimes elsewhere within Japan or to overseas branches. As with the transfers between divisions, accepting these transfers and succeeding in the newer situation were measures used to judge potential promotions. So as not to interrupt children's schooling, salarymen often moved alone and left their families behind. One typical image is of a solitary salaryman, transferred away from his family but within Japan, commuting home on Friday evenings for a weekend visit. This regularity of transfers, despite a lack of predictability about their details, formed the third common characteristic of salaryman employment[4].

BECOMING A SALARYMAN

For most of the postwar period, the regularized process of becoming a salaryman formed another pillar of Japanese labor practices. Like lifetime employment, seniority pay, and frequent internal transfers, the hiring process came to be understood as an integral part of how business was accomplished in Japan (Brinton 1993). In this process, recruitment, interviewing, and hiring were done once a year on a very regular schedule, annually producing a new crop of employees[5]. Rather than a year-round job market, employment opportunities at elite companies opened up only once a year with precise deadlines—akin to the American college application process—and created distinct cohorts of employees.

To become a salaryman, or get hired in any other white-collar position in most companies, applicants needed to go through a process called *shūshoku katsudo*, literally meaning "job hunting." In regular Japanese speech, the term is often shortened to *shūkatsu*, which takes the first syllable of each word. Although there was always some variation between companies, the general pattern of *shūkatsu* remained similar. Students attended information sessions offered by potential employers, first probably at their school and later possibly at the company's headquarters. Rather than submitting an application for a particular position or division, applicants instead applied to join the company in the most general terms. Although an applicant's background or education might be taken into account, he was being hired not for specific skills he might already hold but based on evidence that he might be able to become a good employee. In this process, companies were looking for potential employees that had the right attitude, who could fit into the company culture, who were, in short, train*able* instead of already trained. Because job rotation and internal training were regular parts of employment at this level, potential recruits were judged on their abilities to work within this system, not on particular knowledge. For much of the postwar and continuing in some ways today, this preference for the "right kind" of applicant often perpetuated stigmas and discrimination. For instance, it was common for applications to request a copy of each applicant's household registry (*koseki*), a government record detailing all the births, deaths, marriages, and divorces in an extended family. By looking at such a document, anyone could see potentially stigmatized anomalies, such as a divorce, births out of wedlock, or a family living in a "bad" neighborhood, which a company could take as evidence that an applicant wasn't the "right kind" of person for the job[6] (Chapman and Krogness 2014).

Throughout the process, applicants were expected to perform and exhibit particular comportments, backgrounds, and attitudes. In addition to submitting the formal record of family history, applicants might be asked to write a short essay or take an exam. Missing the job hunting season or failing to be hired meant that an applicant would have to wait another year to retry. The scheduling of *shūkastu* events were as visible in Japanese cities as the changing of the seasons. When *shūkastu* began, suddenly trains and buses were crowded with young people wearing almost identical black suits. The suits are of a single style with almost no variation: they are black with no hint of additional color or pattern, and are worn over equally plain white shirts (Nikkei HR 2004; Takashima 2013). In this self-presentation, young applicants are striving to seem like the "right kind" of person that companies would want to hire, while avoiding or hiding anything that would make them seem less a team-player or company man. Many people took out piercings or toned down makeup to fit into an idealized model of normalcy.

Shūkastu is a regularized set of hiring practices that immediately connote a regimented schedule of required steps to get the most elite jobs. Although applicants for blue collar or service positions certainly go through an application process, the term *shūkastu* most commonly refers only to what is required to get a white-collar job, and a job at one of the best companies at that. For applicants, *shūkastu* represents a series of hoops that are no easier to get through for being so predictable. For companies, *shūkastu* helps produce a cluster of new employees who clearly recognize themselves as a defined group (for example, the Dupont entering cohort of 1985). This discrete group goes through welcome ceremonies and company retreats together, thereby creating and strengthening a sense of their bonds to each other and the company (Kondo 1990). Having a large group of new employees means that they can be trained at the same time. Mary Brinton sums up the social and economic effects of this recruitment process to suggest it as a *sine qua non* of Japanese employment (Brinton 1993, 101). Although a similar schedule might occur for other, less elite positions, *shūkastu* most typically is associated with the steps required to get the best jobs.

Although salarymen regularly stood for Japan, the postwar economic recovery, or the average working man, their symbolic importance was never matched by actual employment statistics. Salarymen were, and to some extent still are, ubiquitous as symbols but relatively few Japanese people ever experienced work lives in this form. Throughout the postwar period, various studies have suggested that about 30% of employees were in "lifetime" positions with the attendant guarantees, seniority pay, and regular transfers (Aoki 1988, 87; Tachibanaki 1987, 669). The actual number of salarymen is difficult to calculate because although "salaryman" has long been an incredibly recognizable and powerful social category, it is not one that can be used explicitly in surveys. The promise of lifetime employment for certain male workers was always an implicit promise, a sense that came with particular jobs, rather than a contracted guarantee. Salarymen fell within the categories of "regular" employees (as opposed to part-time or contract employees), but that category also included workers who will not stay with the company for the course of their careers. Writing in the early 1970s, Cole summarized this statistical uncertainty as: "At present, it is difficult to delimit exactly the number of workers covered by the practice of permanent employment. Government statistics are ill-suited for this purpose with their more nebulous category of regular workers" (Cole 1971, 47). Twenty years later, Brinton added that "No explicit contractual agreement exists, either for the employer not to dismiss the employee or for the employee not to quit and seek employment elsewhere" (Brinton 1993, 131). The majority of Japanese workers found employment as white-collar workers without lifetime employment, in blue-collar positions such as in manufacturing, or in service, agricultural, or part-time jobs. Thus although images of salarymen overwhelm many discussions of Japanese employment, both within and beyond Japan, in actual practice these positions were more aspirational than typical.

Most specifically, as the gendered terminology might suggest, the secure trajectories associated with salarymen were entirely foreclosed for female workers. Despite the popular image of Japanese women as "only" housewives, in practice, throughout the postwar period, Japanese women have labored for pay with incredible regularity. But these patterns of women's labor are marked by a few key characteristics that demonstrate why women were unlikely to become salarymen or, perhaps, 'salarywomen,' a term which doesn't exist in Japanese (Roberts 2011). First, although a majority of women work for pay, many quit either when they marry or when they have their first child (Brinton 1993; White 2002). The causality in these decisions is difficult to figure out—do women quit because they want to, or does the demonstrable lack of promotional opportunities for female employees reinforce social incentives to leave paid employment? After having left a job because of family needs (or perceived family needs), parallel needs push women back into the labor market. Partially to cover the high costs of children's education and other needs, many women return to the workforce as part-time employees after their children are in school. Until 2007 it was legal for job advertisements to limit available positions by applicant's age, and even though it is no longer legal to include gender preferences in most job ads, there remains a strong sense that certain jobs are better for men or women (Buckley 1993, 349; Lawler and Bae 1998). Even after it became illegal to advertise such gender or age preferences, companies are still able to hire based on them; it is the explicit advertising for applicants limited by gender or age that's prohibited, not the underlying preference in hiring.

SALARYMAN INTIMACIES

Especially for generations of Japanese people building families in the 1970s, 1980s, and early 1990s, strong social norms dictated a gendered division between spheres of influence. In an archetypal family, fathers were associated with paid labor outside the home, and mothers were associated with domestic work inside the home. Even though women regularly left their homes, and often worked part-time at various points in their lives, older generations can still articulate a standard that women should be home as much as possible. A more recent magazine quiz for husbands trying to avoid divorce, for instance, asks men if they expect women to be home most of the time—implying that an affirmative answer would be evidence of old-fashioned chauvinism that also increases the likelihood of divorce in the mid-2000s (Itō 2006). Although this kind of belief in highly gendered, and separated, spheres of influence might serve as a negative example in the mid-2000s, it was a standard cultural norm throughout the previous decades. Men, laboring as salarymen or otherwise, were responsible for the paid income coming into a family, and were associated with outside-ness. Women, even if they worked outside the home, were still idealized as people better suited to, and more reflective of, inside-ness. These separate spheres were reflected in friendship groups and socializing practices. Ishii-Kuntz and Maryanski found that married couples tended to socialize in same-gender groups without spouses present (Ishii-Kuntz and Maryanski 2003). Husbands would spend their leisure time with friends or colleagues from work; wives would socialize with other women they knew from the neighborhood, children's activities, or work. Neither group, especially within older generations, would be inclined to socialize with spouses in mixed-gender groups. These patterns of socializing echoed the dominant understandings of gender division.

Despite such overwhelming ideologies separating men and women in labor and socializing, in practice these spheres were fundamentally connected. Men who were responsible only for outside labor were dependent on their wives to provide all domestic needs, even the most basic. In ideology, labor realms, and patterns of socializing, spouses were largely disconnected. But deep connections underlay these dynamics, and both spouses were supported, in social terms, by the other's complementary set of responsibilities. Writing in the 1980s, Walter Edwards created an evocative phrase to capture the particularities of this relationship: complementary incompetence (Edwards 1990). This term describes the simultaneous need and separation between Japanese spouses. Because labor norms often discriminated against married women or mothers to push women out of full-time labor, the average woman was unable to find a career that enabled her to support herself. Men, on the other hand, were not taught basic domestic necessities like how to do laundry or cook nutritious meals. Even if a particular man had domestic skills or knowledge, the demands of his work schedule would likely make it impossible for him to feed and clothe himself. Thus, Edwards convincingly argues, Japanese spouses in the 1970s and 1980s were linked together partially through their complementary needs and abilities—her need for a financially viable salary, and his for the domestic assistance required to earn such a salary.

Although marriages built on such linkages might not seem particularly romantic to an American audience, Japanese cultural norms in the 1970s and 1980s are replete with representations of such relationships as ideally romantic. In those representations, a husband/father who sacrifices himself for his family—indeed, who sacrifices himself so much to his work that he barely has time to see his family—is held up as a beautiful example of mature love. In contrast to an immature or childish "puppy love," for instance, Lebra's interlocutors in the 1970s describe mature love as occurring between spouses who live largely separate lives, but do so for the benefit of each other (Lebra 1984). Glenda Roberts describes how assumptions about gendered labor also suggest particular ways that men could demonstrate their commitment to family only as wage laborers:

> "From Azumi [Company]'s regular-status male employees, as for men in other large firms, total commitment to the firm is expected, taken for granted. Furthermore, a man's commitment to his firm also signifies and stands as a measure of his commitment to his family: the harder he works for the firm, the higher he climbs, the greater are his household's income and social status" (Roberts 1994, 3).

Thus in discourse in the 1970s, 1980s, and early 1990s—the period between the growth of the economic miracle and the bubble bursting in 1991—Japanese men were represented as better fathers if they concentrate on paid labor, rather than domestic responsibilities. In the contemporary moment, such emotionally disconnected models for paternity are increasingly offered as negative examples. In the course of my research in the mid-2000s, many men and women told me clearly that they were trying to build families in opposition to such examples provided by their parents.

Within this dynamic of some intense (financial) connections and other (emotional) disconnections between spouses, in archetypal form salaryman sexual intimacies were directed in two different directions. First, starting soon after marriage, marital sexuality was directed at reproduction. Married couples were expected to have children, so much so that it was not uncommon for new wives to be symbolically discussed as protomothers (Ivry 2009; Lebra 1984). Second, in addition to facing such pressures to have and support children, salarymen were also associated with substantial, if not flagrant, extramarital sexuality. Especially during the economic boom of the 1980s, later to be labeled a bubble, salaryman customers supported the sex trade economies euphemistically labeled the "water business" (mizu shobai). Water business activities could range from a bar hostess paid to flirt with customers to a sex worker paid to engage in sexual acts. The common expectation was that salarymen would have sexual relationships outside of marriage. For instance, in her fieldwork as a bar hostess at the height of the economic bubble, Anne Allison talked with both the salaryman customers that patronized the club where she worked and wives of salarymen. In the club, which was demonstrably high-end, Allison witnessed (and experienced) groping and sexual banter initiated by the salaryman workers who would often enter the club as office groups. Although no sex was permitted between hostesses and clients, the atmosphere was absolutely sexualized, and one common refrain was that customers wanted to be, or would tease other men for being, "lecherous" (sukebe). The wives of salarymen with whom Allison talked had a general sense that something sexual might be going on between their husbands and other women, possibly hostesses, but they really weren't interested in the details. As long as their husbands continued to demonstrate their paternal responsibilities through their salaries, these wives, at least, weren't concerned with extramarital sexuality. I once heard a similar point of view expressed by a woman I'll call Mizuno-san who was in her 50s in 2003. After hearing about my friend's crisis over her husband's affair, Mizuno-san asked, "Did he have one mistress or many?" She asked this question, she explained to me, because the former scenario seemed much worst to her than the latter. Only one mistress would mean that the husband had an emotional connection with another woman; lots of mistresses meant that he just had a lot of sex, and the latter was much preferable. In this conversation Mizuno-san wasn't talking about her own husband but her preferences also represent the ways in which certain forms of extramarital sexuality were predictable, if not accepted, for salarymen[7].

In both these arenas for sexual relationships, salarymen's intimate relationships were constructed on and through labor practices. As described above, when wives got married and had children, typically they became increasingly dependent on their husbands for the stable, predictable salary that was most available to men. The complementary incompetence described by Edwards as an ideal was only made possible by the salary earned by a male spouse. The additional sexual relationships that men had outside of marriage were similarly dependent on men's employment patterns. As Allison describes, the hostess bar in which she conducted research was so expensive as to be only accessible for men using company expense accounts. Certainly there were cheaper venues to pay for sexual contact, and extramarital sexual contact was not limited to that between salarymen and paid sex workers, but the regular company visit to a hostess bar was, and to some degree still remains, a characteristic associated with salaryman labor. In those instances, salarymen's employment—literally their status as an employee of a company willing to cover the costs of visiting a hostess bar, or their responsibilities to entertain clients in those venues—enabled these intimate relationships.

POST-BUBBLE LABOR AND SELF-RESPONSIBILITY

Despite the terminology now used, the bursting of the economic bubble did not happen in a single moment, nor was the shift immediately identified as the beginning of an economic crisis. Between 1989 and 1992, yen became less cheaply available, making inflation of housing prices and land evident, and corporations were left underwater with mortgages for high prices that properties would never be able to reach again. As Grimes describes it, "borrowers became unable to pay back loans collateralized with land and securities whose value was plummeting" (Grimes 2001, xvii). After the bubble's burst, as a result of ineffective policies, the Japanese economy hovered around recessionary levels for more than a decade, a period labeled the "lost decade" or "the Heisei recessions" after the era's name in Japanese. From 1992 to 1999, average real GDP growth was one percent (Mori, Shiratsuka, and Taguchi 2001, 54). As the government and the private sector attempted to spring the nation out of recession, they instantiated substantially new ways of organizing, legislating, and encouraging labor. While millions of people lost wages or work altogether, the Japanese labor market was radically reformed.

The recent antecedents to contemporary labor patterns grew from governmental and private responses to the recessionary decades and largely revolve around changing employment opportunities, especially for younger people. As described by Brinton, when Japanese companies were faced with dramatic profit loss in the mid-1990s, they decided to protect their lifetime employees by retaining benefits for those older workers and offering many fewer options for younger workers (Brinton 2011). Rather than laying off, or reducing the benefits of, lifetimes employees, companies instead kept supporting those older generations of male workers and significantly reduced hiring new lifetime employees. These decisions to continue supporting older male workers reflect the continuing expectation that such men were breadwinners or, in a figurative Japanese term, the central pillar that holds up a whole house (Hidaka 2011, 112). Instead of hiring a new generation of employees through the process of *shūshoku katsudo*, as typical in previous decades, companies instead increased positions for temporary contract workers (*haken*) or part-time workers (*pāto*). Younger workers, men and women alike, faced job prospects akin to those common for women in previous generations—perpetual part-time work with few benefits or predictability—and new categories of "contract" labor. In this latter type, workers were hired to complete work that had previous been done by full-time and lifetime employees, but were paid a fraction of the salary (Driscoll 2009, 300). These changes in practice were both codified and expanded in 2004 with passage of a renewed Dispatch Workers law, allowing companies leeway to convert more full-time positions to contract jobs, while also allowing them to hire contract workers for a longer continuous period (three years, increased from one year) before being legally required to offer them full-time employment (Araki 2007, 277).

In the midst of such changes in practice and discourse, the 2000s brought a new popular consciousness surrounding "self-responsibility." The term (*jiko sekinin* in Japanese) was popularized by Prime Minister Junichiro Koizumi when he suggested that the Japanese economy would never recover from recession unless individual citizens began to take responsibility for themselves. Elected in 2001, Prime Minister Koizumi undertook a massive program of privatization, emphasizing particularly the Japanese Postal Bank. The publicly owned bank of the Japanese Post Office system was, at the time, the world's largest financial institution, with 240 trillion yen in holdings as of July 2002 (Scher and Yoshino 2004, 121). This accounts for approximately 30% of all Japanese household savings and, combined with the life insurance also offered, the Post Office held "a quarter of Japan's personal financial assets" (Porges and Leong 2006, 386) and "virtually every" Japanese citizen had a postal savings account (Imai 2009, 139). In a nation with comparatively high savings rates (Garon 2002), these patterns created a large supply of capital sitting, as it were, in the Postal Bank's coffers. Although Koizumi justified his call to privatize this bank as a necessary step to recover from the still-lingering recession, scholars and commentators also described it as bowing to international pressure, particularly from the United States. Because it was a public company, foreign capital was unable to access the Postal Bank's funds; if the bank were privatized, it would also be open to international speculation (Porges and Leong 2006).

After Koizumi dissolved parliament and called a new national election, the summer of 2005 was full of campaigning targeted at creating popular support for the privatization of the Postal Bank (Nemoto, Krauss, and Pekkanen 2008; Maclachlan 2006). In the midst of this campaign, in attempts to explain and popularize a movement to private sector ownership, Koizumi emphasized ideals related to independence and individuality. Specifically, he argued that truly mature people had "self-responsibility" (*jiko sekinin*) and relied on themselves rather than their families, communities, or government to achieve what they needed (Takeda 2008; Thorsten 2009). In Japan in the mid-2000s, newly articulated ethics of "self-responsibility" were linked with the promise of economic recovery, particularly through a privatized Postal Bank. Koizumi's plebiscite election on the possible privatization was a fantastic success for him, and even members of his own party who had voted against earlier version of the law changed their votes. Although a law was passed in October 2005 to privatize the postal system into four separate companies, this process is not scheduled to be finished until 2017 (Maclachlan 2006). In everyday terms, one result of this election is a continuing discursive focus on self-responsibility.

FREETERS AS NEW HEROES

Although the post-bubble job market included a higher percentage of workers laboring without predictable stability, many of the categories of worker had existed in earlier moments, as smaller percentages of the total labor force. *Freeters* were the exception to this pattern, and represent a new category of experience in the labor market. Since the early 1990s, tremendous popular and academic attention has been directed at counting, representing, analyzing, and attempting to diagnose the motivations of freeters.

The term "freeter"[8] is a Japanese neologism created in the early 1980s but only popularized in the 1990s (Kosugi 2008). The root words are both "loan" words: "free" from English and "aribater," meaning "part-time worker," from German.[9] A "free part-time worker" originally described a person who worked one or many part-time jobs while their real focus was on another project, often an artistic or otherwise creative work. In the 1990s, for instance, common images of freeters in popular media and academic work describe them as creative, slightly flighty dreamers who worked only the bare minimum needed to survive and fund their true callings, be those rock bands or local theater. In this earlier discourse, freeters, and young people more generally, were often represented as choosing such irregular work because they were either lazy or committed to other, non-work, projects. For instance, the sociologist Yamada Masahiro famously labeled the population of young workers as "parasite singles," describing them as unmarried young adults who effectively mooch off their parents while still living at home. Because it is incredibly common for even adult children to continue to live with their parents until marriage, the population Yamada was describing was quite large and, until he labeled them differently, considered normal. He suggested that by living at home and spending any extra income on frivolous luxury goods, young people were further damning the Japanese economy. Instead of taking vacations or buying fancy bags, he said, what would really help the economy is if they bought houses, cars, or practical things like washing machines (Yamada 1999). Although he was not talking specifically about freeters, such characterizations of young workers as frivolous painted all people in that category with a broad, and condemnatory, brush.

The common picture of freeters in the 2000s is substantially different and instead describes them as potentially hard workers who are unable to find the full-time, permanent employment they seek. Common explanations have shifted from explaining new labor patterns through personal preferences or laziness, to linking such shifts with larger structural changes, particularly the kinds of employment available to contemporary Japanese people (Cook 2013, 2014, 2016; Kusugi 2008; Genda 2007; Honda 2005).

For instance, Mae-san is a woman in her late 30's who graduated from high school but never attended college. She earned a stylist's license and worked as much as possible in hair salons. However, because those jobs were often unsteady and she was dependent on salon owners to give her a space in their shops, she found she had to augment her income with other part-time jobs. To be clear, if she could have found full-time work, she would have gladly taken it. As it was she applied for multiple full-time jobs, including one as a test stylist for a company producing hair dye. In that case, she was told by the interviewer that she was simply too old for the position, and if she were hired, she would be older than her supervisor. Because the employers understood such a dynamic—a younger worker supervising an older worker—to be ripe for conflict, Mae-san was not hired. Instead she supplemented her catch-as-catch-can salon work with an early morning shift in a bakery, door-to-door sales of hairpieces for men, and irregular work at a convenience store. None of these many jobs provided dependable income or a sense of security, though she was certainly "free" relative to the constricted and scheduled lives of salarymen. She had the time to meet for coffee in the middle of the day, but rarely the extra money to pay for it.

New popular awareness of the category of "freeter" reflected, but did not fully acknowledge, the tremendous shifts that occurred in the Japanese labor market over the course of the Heisei recessions. Although the freeter became a symbol of new ways of working—both new ways of wanting to work, and newly restricted opportunities for being hired—labor market shifts occurred well beyond this single category of worker. Like the salary-man of earlier generations, the freeter came to represent Japanese labor, although actual practices are more diverse and include other patterns of work. Broadly speaking, in popular discourse and private conversations people actively questioned the benefits of the security that came with older-style employment—trading one's free time for an implicit promise to always have a job and predictably increasing income. Younger Japanese people fall at all points along this spectrum, from freeters who desperately want a full-time job and the security that comes with it, to those who might dream of work but be unwilling to accept the requirements that come with such a position, to those who have largely given up hope (Cook 2013, 2014, 2016; Driscoll 2007).

INTIMACY IN AN AGE OF NEW LABOR

The romantic and intimate appeal of a new kind of male worker was the central lesson of a hugely popular entertainment franchise in mid-2000s

Japan. The story, told in various media forms including a movie, a television show, a manga series, and online bulletin board systems, is collectively titled "Train Man" (Nakano 2004; Nakano 2007; Takeuchi, Masaki, and Kazuhiro 2005; Murakami 2005). The narrative began on March 14th, 2004, on the popular online bulletin board system called "Channel Two," which is akin perhaps to Reddit in sheer numbers of users and rapidly updated content. On that day, in a post, a person using the handle "train_ man" (*densha otoko*)[10] told a story and asked for advice. An extreme and antisocial nerd (*otaku*), train_man was riding home from buying geeky figurines when a drunken salaryman began to harass and threaten women in his train car. Gathering his courage, train_man finally got brave enough to step up to the man when he harassed a young woman that train_man found to be quite beautiful. Train_man didn't accomplish much but, after the police arrived and stopped the harasser, the women were so grateful to train_man that they asked for his mailing address to send him thank you cards. On the bulletin board post, train_man asks his unknown readership for advice about how to respond to this, and how to possibly make himself attractive enough to win the heart of the beautiful young woman. The rest of the narrative plays out his attempts to enact the advice he gets from his online audience and, depending on the media iteration, he either succeeds in winning the girl or imagines the whole thing.

This story, told and retold in various media forms, occupied a central segment of mainstream popular culture in 2005. It is a remarkably warm-hearted story suggesting, among other things, that even Internet connections with strangers can produce lasting and meaningful relationships. Although there is no evidence to suggest that the original events ever took place—that they were "real" instead of imaginary or staged—the story broadly suggests that real human connection (*ningen kankei*) is possible even through the Internet[11]. Moreover, for our purposes, the story also represents a sea change in idealized forms of Japanese masculinity. The entire narrative is prompted by a drunken, threatening salaryman harassing random women. In this moment, the former hero of the Japanese economic miracle has become a belligerent, entitled drunk who does nothing apparently productive. Throughout the film, all representations of salarymen are equally negative: they are either drunk, rude, or in crisis because the pornography they've downloaded on their office computer has prompted a bug. Conversely, although train_man is not a freeter—we see him working IT support in a company full of useless and lecherous salarymen—his style of labor is much closer to that of a freeter than of a salaryman. In contrast with the generalist salarymen, train_man appears to be a specialist with a tremendous amount of computer knowledge and no obligation to join any of the obligatory drinking sessions that are typical for salarymen. And yet, importantly, he is the romantic hero of the film. After a makeover prompted by suggestions from his online friends, and after he learns to still be himself to win the girl he likes, train_man does exactly that. In contrast to the myriad salarymen represented in the story, train_man wins the girl. Such a representation was one of many that suggested a different kind of man was newly attractive, at least to some people, in mid-2000s Japan.[12]

While I was doing ethnographic research about divorce in mid-2000s Japan, many people told me that they worked hard to create marriages that were the diametric opposite of their parents' relationship. Although a few people mentioned their own families as ideal forms they tried to emulate, many described typical salaryman families as typologies that might have made sense at one time, but are no longer attractive or good for the people involved. Although there are many highly debated and debatable tips for how to create a good marriage—ranging from how to speak to your spouse, to sharing housework—Japanese people are likely to describe employment as a vital element in creating a "good" relationship. What counts as good, for whom, and in what context, are actively debated in the current moment on daily television talks shows, within newspaper articles, by policymakers, and in private conversations, a process I've described in other publications (Alexy 2007, 2011). But within these thoroughly heterogeneous conversations that often include radically different conclusions about how to improve relationships, how people work almost always figures into the equation.

CONCLUSIONS

In this chapter, I have argued that economic development and patterns of employment in postwar Japan have not just responded to, but fundamentally require, particular forms of intimate relationships. The unmarked links between labor and intimacy were reinforced in the late 2000s when the neologism "*konkatsu*" was suddenly everywhere in Japan. It competed as a nominee for the most important word of 2009, was discussed regularly on talk shows and in private conversations, and became a trendy term highlighted in a television drama title (Fuji TV 2009; Yamada and Shirakawa 2008). Coined by a prominent public intellectual and sociologist, Yamada Masahiro,[13] *konkatsu* describes a new attitude and energy around marriage. The term both reflected behavior the authors already witnessed and modeled potential actions that, they suggested, could improve Japanese marriages, families, and the nation-state. Since Yamada popularized the term, it has become a standard term people use to describe relationships, even if they refuse to participate in what they understand to be its requirements.

Konkatsu defines a self-conscious search for a marriage partner that intentionally mimics the market ideology surrounding employment: the term asks people to search for spouses like they search for jobs. To Japanese speakers, the link between marriage and employment is made obvious through the phrasing. *Konkatsu* is an abbreviation for "marriage hunting" *kekkon katsudou* (the shortened term takes the middle two syllables) which itself refers to the long-standing term describing "job hunting" *shūshoku katsudou,* often abbreviated to *shūkatsu.* In both phrases, "hunting" or "searching" is described with the same word, and only the object of that hunt varies. As examined in earlier sections of this chapter, "job hunting" *(shūshoku katsudou)* connotes more than just a search for employment, and instead describes the highly regularized pattern of events required to land the most elite types of jobs. In both employment and intimate realms, the term "search" *(katsudo)* immediately signals a tight, formal schedule of required activities targeted toward a goal, and a vast wealth of self-help goods marketed to those hoping to be successful. It also suggests a difficult process that few people probably enjoy but everyone who wants the "good" outcome knows they need to push themselves through. It is a difficult rite of passage, a key step on the way to becoming a social adult *(shakaijin).* To look for a marriage as if it's a job means, in this context, to take it seriously and do what needs to be done: make oneself physically attractive, buy the right clothes, attend the required meetings (dates or parties), and do it all performing a particular kind of seriousness with a constant presence of mind focused on the end goal. Such a model for finding a spouse is radically different from arranged marriages and casual dating, both of which have been typical methods for finding a spouse in postwar Japan (Applbaum 1995; Lebra 1984). The quick and sustained popularity of this term—if not the practices it purports to recommend—demonstrates the ways in which employment and intimacy were already linked in Japanese popular consciousness.

Looking back on what we might retrospectively describe as the salaryman epoch, "job searching" *(shūkatsu)* guaranteed participants social and economic security. If a young man was able to participate in this standardized recruitment process—if he was in the minority of men who had the educational and class backgrounds required to enter the pool of potential employees—he was practically guaranteed lifelong employment. Difficult as the process might have been, stepping into "job searching" was a foot on a steady escalator, a social contract promising employment security to the relatively few men who were included. Although many people are now quick to question the ways such "lifetime" employment positions impeded intimate and family relationships, the jobs certainly brought employment security.

In the mid-2000s, during the moment when such job security evaporated, the terminology and associations used to describe employment security were transferred into the intimate realm. By replacing "job" with "marriage," the new terminology suggests marriage as a goal that will produce the lifelong security no longer commonly available through lifetime employment. In actual practice, given the rising divorce rate, marriages are statistically less likely to provide what might be traditionally thought of as security—lifelong predictability. Although this might at first seem like a contradiction, it also prompts an expanding definition of "security." Rather than measuring security in terms of time, some people understand it as a depth of emotional support and commitment. A secure marriage, or an intimate relationship that provides security for one or both partners, could be judged by the affective ties and emotional support it includes, rather than how long it sustains. Judging by this standard, the typical long-term salaryman marriage wasn't secure at all, a fact rendered more publicly obvious by recent media frenzies documenting how hard some retired men are working to keep their wives from leaving them (Alexy 2007). In these unfolding dynamics, security might still be a prominent goal, but its referent could be radically shifting. As people look to intimate relationships to provide the promise of security previously available from the labor market, they are also reimagining what "security" means. Moving away from the long-term financial connection and emotional separation described by Edwards as "complementary incompetence" to a more integrated emotional ideal, many people are still interested in finding security for themselves. But they do so in a moment when the definition of what counts as security, let alone how to get and keep it, is fundamentally unsteady.

ACKNOWLEDGEMENTS

The research on which this chapter is based was generously funded by the Fulbright IIE program and the Japan Foundation. My thanks to Allison Pugh for her extremely helpful comments on drafts and her work creating this volume, and to Glenda Roberts for helping me find and understand the details of Japanese labor law.

NOTES

1. The term in Japanese is pronounced as a "loan" word from English, and written in the *katakana* characters that explicitly mark it as a "foreign" word, although it probably won't make sense to any English speakers who don't also speak Japanese.

The term can be glossed as *sarariiman, sararīman,* or *salaryman.* In this chapter, I choose to use the latter.

2. For instance, the series "Salaryman Kintaro," which tells the story of a reformed hooligan (*bōsōzoku*) who becomes a tough, nonconformist salaryman. The story was first published as a serialized comic (Motomiya 1994) and then was also made into a film (Miike 1999), live-action television drama (Morita, Tomita, and Kuranuki 1999), and animated television series (Katsumata 2001).

3. For more on the complex relationship between masculinity and militarism in a nation with a constitutional prohibition against any military other than self-defense forces, see Frühstück 2007. As of this writing, in fall 2015, the Japanese Diet is beginning to make changes to military policy that might allow Japanese forces to participate in more than just self-defense, but it remains a developing story.

4. Trade unionism is another important characteristic of the Japanese employment system, but I do not have the space to expand on it here. For more on the topic, see Gerteis 2011; Gordon 1998; and Tsuru and Rebitzer 1995.

5. This description of the recruitment process most accurately reflects the experience for people applying to work in the largest companies with over one thousand employees. For more on how firm size impacts employees, see Aoki 1988; Hazama 1976; Koike 1988; and Plath 1983.

6. Location of residence can enable discrimination because Japan's historically stigmatized underclass, *Burakumin* or *Eta,* were often restricted to particular neighborhoods. If a job applicant, or one of his relatives, ever lived in such a neighborhood, the applicant could be refused because of this association. In this case, residence—present or previous, personal or within the extended family—is a key mechanism of ongoing discrimination (Hah and Lapp 1978, 498; Hankins 2014; Neary 1997).

7. For more on attitudes and experiences with extramarital affairs, see Ho 2012; Moore 2010.

8. There are a few different ways to gloss this term into English. The original Japanese term, フリーター, is transliterated as *furiitaa,* or *furītā.* Many scholars now use "freeter" which conveys a meaning to English speakers that perhaps better reflects what it sounds like in Japanese (e.g., Cook 2013). I will use the latter spelling in this chapter. I will also add an –s to the word to designate a plural, conforming to English language conventions rather than Japanese.

9. This latter term was already in regular use in Japanese. To have a part-time job is described as having an *arubaito* or *baito* for short. This kind of position is most typically associated with a student worker who is trying to make a little money on the side while going to school, not an older worker who is trying to make enough money to live.

10. Japanese language doesn't have space between words as does English so "Train Man" is written with three characters written together: 電車男. Various people have translated the term with slightly different punctuation and TrainMan or Train-Man could both be accurate. I use "train_man" because it is the gloss used in the film version (Murakami 2005), which includes impressive techniques for visually representing digital text on screen—let alone with subtitles.

11. Indeed if the story was faked—if the initial narration of what happened on the train doesn't reflect real events—the creator/author nevertheless did a fantastic job of guessing a topic and creating a character that many people would find compelling. The significance of the story doesn't hinge on its veracity but on its

popularity as an interactive exchange (people posting on a bulletin board) and a narrative successful across various media forms.

12. Since then, it has become common to characterize such supposedly "weak" men as "herbivores"—as opposed to carnivores—because they enact masculinity in ways that disrupt or refuse earlier models for masculine silence, emotional distance, and patriarchal control (Slater and Galbraith 2011; Deacon 2013). In derogatory terms, they are wimpy. This label could be an insult or a new badge of pride, and it's equally possible to find people who relish the distinction from older performances of masculinity or those identify such a "loss" of masculinity as evidence of Japan's decline.

13. He had also coined the term "parasite single" (*parasaito singuru*) to describe supposedly problematic young adults who mooch off their parents, as mentioned earlier in this chapter.

REFERENCES

Abegglen, James. 1958. *The Japanese Factory: Aspects of Its Social Organization*. Glencoe, IL: The Free Press.

Alexy, Allison. 2007. "Deferred Benefits, Romance, and the Specter of Later-Life Divorce." *Contemporary Japan [Japanstudien]* 19:169–188.

Alexy, Allison. 2011. "Intimate Dependence and Its Risks in Neoliberal Japan." *Anthropological Quarterly* 84(4):895–917.

Allen, George Cyril. 2013. *A Short Economic History of Modern Japan*. London: Routledge.

Allison, Anne. 1994. *Nightwork: Sexuality, Pleasure, and Corporate Masculinity in a Tokyo Hostess Club*. Chicago: University of Chicago Press.

Aoki, Masahiko. 1988. *Information, Incentives and Bargaining in the Japanese Economy: A Microtheory of the Japanese Economy*. Cambridge, UK: Cambridge University Press.

Applbaum, Kalman D. 1995. "Marriage with the Proper Stranger: Arranged Marriage in Metropolitan Japan." *Ethnology* 34(1):37–51.

Araki, Takashi. 2007. "Changing Employment Practices, Corporate Governance, and the Role of Labor Law in Japan." *Comparative Labor Law and Policy Journal* 28(2):251–282.

Bestor, Theodore C. 1989. *Neighborhood Tokyo*. Stanford, CA: Stanford University Press.

Bestor, Victoria L. 2002. "Toward a Cultural Biography of Civil Society in Japan." In *Family and Social Policy in Japan: Anthropological Approaches*, edited by Roger Goodman, 29–53. Cambridge, UK: Cambridge University Press.

Blomström, Magnus, Byron Gangnes, and Sumner La Croix, eds. 2001. *Japan's New Economy: Continuity and Change in the Twenty-First Century*. Oxford and New York: Oxford University Press.

Brinton, Mary. 1993. *Women and the Economic Miracle: Gender and Work in Postwar Japan*. Berkeley: University of California Press.

Brinton, Mary. 2011. *Lost in Transition: Youth, Work, and Instability in Postindustrial Japan*. Cambridge, MA: Cambridge University Press.

Broadbent, Kaye. 2003. *Women's Employment in Japan: The Experience of Part-Time Workers*. London and New York: RoutledgeCurzon.

Buckley, Sandra. 1993. "Altered States: The Body Politics of 'Being-Woman.'" In *Postwar Japan as History*, edited by Andrew Gordon, 347–372. Berkeley: University of California Press.

Chapman, David, and Karl Jakob Krogness, eds. 2014. *Japan's Household Registration System and Citizenship: Koseki, Identification, and Documentation.* London and New York: Routledge.

Cohen, Jerome B. 1948. "Japan's Economy on the Road Back." *Pacific Affairs* 21(3):264–279.

Cole, Robert E. 1971. "The Theory of Institutionalization: Permanent Employment and Tradition in Japan." *Economic Development and Cultural Change* 20(1):47–70.

Cook, Emma. 2013. "Expectations of Failure: Maturity and Masculinity for Freeters in Contemporary Japan." *Social Science Japan Journal* 16(1):29–43.

Cook, Emma. 2014. "Intimate Expectations and Practices: Freeter Relationships and Marriage in Contemporary Japan." *Asian Anthropology* 13(1):1–16.

Cook, Emma E. 2016. *Reconstructing Adult Masculinitites: Part-time Work in Contemporary Japan.* Oxford: Routledge Press.

Crawcour, Sydney. 1978. "The Japanese Employment System." *Journal of Japanese Studies* 4(2):225–245.

Dasgupta, Romit. 2013. *Re-Reading the Salaryman in Japan: Crafting Masculinities.* London and New York: Routledge.

Deacon, Chris. 2013. "All the World's a Stage: Herbivore Boys and the Performance of Masculinity in Contemporary Japan." In *Manga Girl Seeks Herbivore Boy: Studying Japanese Gender at Cambridge*, edited by Brigitte Steger and Angelika Koch, 129–176. Zurich, Switzerland: LIT.

Dower, John W. 1999. *Embracing Defeat: Japan in the Wake of World War II.* New York: W.W. Norton.

Driscoll, Mark. 2007. "Debt and Denunciation in Post-Bubble Japan: On the Two Freeters." *Cultural Critique* 65(1):164–187.

Edwards, Walter. 1990. *Modern Japan through Its Weddings: Gender, Person, and Society in Ritual Portrayal.* Stanford, CA: Stanford University Press.

Epstein, Edward Jay. 2009. "What Was Lost (and Found) in Japan's Lost Decade." *Vanity Fair*, February 17. Available online: http://www.vanityfair.com/online/daily/2009/02/what-was-lost-and-found-in-japans-lost-decade.

Frühstück, Sabine. 2007. *Uneasy Warriors: Gender, Memory, and Popular Culture in the Japanese Army.* Berkeley: University of California Press.

Garon, Sheldon. 2002. "Saving for 'My Own Good and the Good of the Nation': Economic Nationalism in Modern Japan." In *Nation and Nationalism in Japan*, edited by Sandra Wilson, 97–114. London: RoutledgeCurzon.

Genda, Yūji. 2007. "Jobless Youths and the NEET Problem in Japan." *Social Science Japan Journal* 10(1):23–40.

Gerteis, Christopher. 2011. "Losing the Union Man: Class and Gender in the Postwar Labor Movement." In *Recreating Japanese Men*, edited by Sabine Frühstück and Ann Walthall, 135–153. Berkeley: University of California Press.

Giddens, Anthony. 1993. *The Transformation of Intimacy: Sexuality, Love, and Eroticism in Modern Societies.* Stanford, CA: Stanford University Press.

Gordon, Andrew. 1998. *The Wages of Affluence: Labor and Management in Postwar Japan.* Cambridge, MA: Harvard University Press.

Grimes, William W. 2001. *Unmaking the Japanese Miracle: Macroeconomic Politics, 1985–2000.* Ithaca, NY: Cornell University Press.

Hah, Chong-do, and Christopher C. Lapp. 1978. "Japanese Politics of Equality in Transition: The Case of the Burakumin." *Asian Survey* 18(5):487–504.

Hankins, Joseph D. 2014. *Working Skin: Making Leather, Making Multicultural Japan.* Berkeley: University of California Press.

林 恭弘 [Hayahi, Yasuhiro]. 2005. ちょっとした一言で相手が動く夫婦の心理テクニック—ここちいい関係になれる14のルール *[Easy Verbal Techniques to Improve Your Marriage: Build a Good Relationship with 14 Rules]*. Tokyo: Sogo horei shuppan.

Hazama, Hiroshi. 1976. "Historical Changes in the Life Style of Industrial Workers." In *Japanese Industrialization and Its Social Consequences*, edited by Hugh Patrick and Larry Meissner, 21–51. Berkeley: University of California Press.

Hidaka, Tomoko. 2011. "Masculinity and the Family System: The Ideology of the 'Salaryman' across Three Generations." In *Home and Family in Japan: Continuity and Transformation*, edited by Richard Ronald and Allison Alexy, 112–130. London and New York: Routledge.

Ho, Swee Lin. 2012. "'Playing Like Men': The Extramarital Experiences of Women in Contemporary Japan." *Ethnos* 77(3): 321–343.

Holzhausen, Arne. 2000. "Japanese Employment Practices in Transition: Promotion Policy and Compensation Systems in the 1990s." *Social Science Japan Journal* 3(2):221–235.

Honda, Yuki. 2005. "Freeters: Young Atypical Workers in Japan." *Japan Labor Review* 2(3):5–25.

Ikeda, Satoshi. 2002. *The Trifurcating Miracle: Corporations, Workers, Bureaucrats, and the Erosion of Japan's National Economy*. New York: Routledge.

池内ひろ美[Ikeuchi,Hiromi].2005.いい夫婦になるいたってシンプルな30のヒント *[Thirty Simple Hints for Becoming a "Good Couple"]*. Tokyo: Seishun shinso.

Imai, Masami. 2009. "Ideologies, Vested Interest Groups, and Postal Saving Privatization in Japan." *Public Choice* 138(1–2):137–160.

Ishii-Kuntz, Masako, and A.R. Maryanski. 2003. "Conjugal Roles and Social Networks in Japanese Families." *Journal of Family Issues* 24(3):352–380.

[伊藤武彦].Itō, Takehiko. 2006. 熟年離婚したいのはオレだ [Men Who Want to Divorce in Later Life]. *Aera* 19(5): 34–36.

Ivry, Tsipy. 2009. *Embodying Culture: Pregnancy in Japan and Israel*. Newark, NJ: Rutgers University Press.

Johnson, Chalmers. 1982. *MITI and the Japanese Miracle: The Growth of Industrial Policy: 1925–1975*. Stanford, CA: Stanford University Press.

Katsumata, Tomoharu, directors. 2001. "サラリーマン金太郎 [Salaryman Kintaro]". Tokyo: BS-i. Available online: http://www.barnesandnoble.com/w/dvd-salaryman-kintaro-1/9640322.

Kelly, William W. 1986. "Rationalization and Nostalgia: Cultural Dynamics of New Middle-Class Japan." *American Ethnologist* 13(4):603–618.

Koike, Kazuo. 1988. *Understanding Industrial Relations in Modern Japan*. Translated by Mary Saso. New York: St. Martin's.

Kondo, Dorinne K. 1990. *Crafting Selves: Power, Gender, and Discourses of Identity in a Japanese Workplace*. Chicago: University of Chicago Press.

Kosugi, Reiko. 2008. *Escape from Work: Freelancing Youth and the Challenge to Corporate Japan*. Translated by Ross Mouer. Melbourne, Australia: TransPacific.

Lawler, John J, and Johngseok Bae. 1998. "Overt Employment Discrimination by Multinational Firms: Cultural and Economic Influences in a Developing Country." *Industrial Relations: A Journal of Economy and Society* 37(2):126–152.

Lebra, Takie Sugiyama. 1984. *Japanese Women: Constraint and Fulfillment*. Honolulu: University of Hawaii Press.

Levine, Solomon B. 1983. "Careers and Mobility in Japan's Labor Markets." In *Work and Lifecourse in Japan*, edited by David Plath, 18–33. Albany: State University of New York Press.

Maclachlan, Patricia L. 2006. "Storming the Castle: The Battle for Postal Reform in Japan." *Social Science Japan Journal* 9(1):1–18.

Matanle, Peter, Leo McCann, and Darren Ashmore. 2008. "Men under Pressure: Representations of the 'Salaryman' and His Organization in Japanese Manga." *Organization* 15(5):639–664.

McCurry, Justin, and Julia Kollewe. 2011. "China Overtakes Japan as World's Second-Largest Economy." *The Guardian*, February 14.

Miike, Takashi. 2001. サラリーマン金太郎 *[Salaryman Kintarō]*. Tokyo: Toho.

Mincer, Jacob, and Yoshio Higuchi. 1988. "Wage Structures and Labor Turnover in the United States and Japan." *Journal of the Japanese and International Economies* 2(2):97–133.

Moore, Katrina L. 2010. "Sexuality and Sense of Self in Later Life: Japanese Men's and Women's Reflections on Sex and Aging." *Journal of Cross-Cultural Gerontology* 25(2): 149–163.

Mori, Naruki, Shigenori Shiratsuka, and Hiroo Taguchi. 2001. "Policy Responses to the Post-Bubble Adjustments in Japan: A Tentative Review." *Monetary and Economic Studies* 19(supp. 1):53–102.

Morita, Mitsunori, Katsunori Tomita, and Kenjiro Kuranuki, directors. 1999. サラリーマン金太郎 *[Salaryman Kintarō]*. Tokyo: TBS. Available online at: http://wiki.d-addicts.com/Salaryman_Kintaro.

Motomiya, Hiroshi. 1994. サラリーマン金太郎 *[Salaryman Kintarō]*. Tokyo: Shueisha.

Murakami, Shosuke, director. 2005. 電車男 *[Train Man]*. Tokyo: Toho.

Nakano, Hitori. 2004. 電車男 *[Train Man]*. Tokyo: Shinchosha.

Nakano, Hitori. 2007. *Train Man*. New York: Del Ray Books.

Neary, Ian. 1997. "Burakumin in Contemporary Japan." In *Japan's Minorities: The Illusion of Homogeneity*, edited by Michael Weiner, 50–78. London and New York: Routledge.

Nemoto, Kuniaki, Ellis Krauss, and Robert Pekkanen. 2008. "Policy Dissension and Party Discipline: The July 2005 Vote on Postal Privatization in Japan." *British Journal of Political Science* 38(3):499–525.

日系HR編集部 [Nikkei HR Department]. 2004. 就職活動ナビゲーション *[Navigating A Job Search]*. Tokyo: Nikkei.

Ogasawara, Yuko. 1998. *Office Ladies and Salaried Men: Power, Gender, and Work in Japanese Companies*. Berkeley: University of California Press.

Plath, David, ed. 1983. *Work and Lifecourse in Japan*. Albany: State University of New York Press.

Porges, Amelia, and Joy M Leong. 2006. "The Privatization of Japan Post." In *Progress toward Liberalization of the Postal and Delivery Sector*, edited by Michael Crew and Paul Kleindorfer, 385–400. New York: Springer.

Pugh, Allison. 2015. *The Tumbleweed Society: Working and Caring in an Age of Insecurity*. Oxford: Oxford University Press.

Rebick, Marcus. 2005. *The Japanese Employment System: Adapting to a New Economic Environment*. Oxford: Oxford University Press.

Roberson, James E, and Nobue Suzuki. 2005. *Men and Masculinities in Contemporary Japan: Dislocating the Salaryman Doxa*. London and New York: Routledge.

Roberts, Glenda. 1994. *Staying on the Line: Blue-Collar Women in Contemporary Japan*. Honolulu: University of Hawaii Press.

Roberts, Glenda S. 2011. "Salary Women and Family Well-Being in Urban Japan." *Marriage & Family Review* 47(8):571–589.

Rohlen, Thomas P. 1979. *For Harmony and Strength: Japanese White-Collar Organization in Anthropological Perspective*. Berkeley and Los Angeles: University of California Press.

Scher, Mark J, and Naoyuki Yoshino. 2004. "Policy Challenges and the Reform of Postal Savings in Japan." In *Small Savings Mobilization and Asian Economic Development: The Role of Postal Financial Services*, edited by Mark J Scher and Naoyuki Yoshino, 121–146. Armonk, NY: M.E. Sharpe.

Simpson, Bob. 1998. *Changing Families: An Ethnographic Approach to Divorce and Separation*. Oxford: Berg.

Skinner, Kenneth. 1979. "Salaryman Comics in Japan: Images of Self-Perception." *The Journal of Popular Culture* 13(1):141–151.

Slater, David, and Patrick W Galbraith. 2011. "Re-Narrating Social Class and Masculinity in Neoliberal Japan: An Examination of the Media Coverage of the 'Akihabara Incident' of 2008." *Electronic Journal of Contemporary Japanese Studies* 7. September 30. Available online: http://www.japanesestudies.org.uk/articles/2011/SlaterGalbraith.html.

Statistical Yearbook. 2013. Available online: http://www.stat.go.jp/english/data/nen-kan/back62/index.htm.

Tachibanaki, Toshiaki. 1987. "Labour Market Flexibility in Japan in Comparison with Europe and the US." *European Economic Review* 31(3):647–678.

高島 悠人 [Takashima, Yūto]. 2013. こう動く！就職活動オールガイド *"15年版 [Let"s Go! The Complete Guide to Job Searching for 2015]*. Tokyo: Seibido shuppan.

Takeda, Hiroko. 2008. "Structural Reform of the Family and the Neoliberalisation of Everyday Life in Japan." *New Political Economy* 13(2):153–172.

Takeuchi, Hideki, Nishiura Masaki, and Kobayashi Kazuhiro, directors. 2005. 電車男 [Train Man]. Produced by Fuji Television, Tokyo.

TBS 番組制作スタッフ [TBS Programming Staff]. 2006. 熟年離婚の理由100 [100 Reasons for Later-Life Divorce]. Tokyo: Junkudo. Available online at: http://www.amazon.co.jp/熟年離婚の理由100-TBS番組制作スタッフ/dp/4862340369.

Thorsten, Marie. 2009. "The Homecoming of Japanese Hostages from Iraq: Culturalism or Japan in America's Embrace?" *The Asia-Pacific Journal* 22(4). Available online: http://www.japanfocus.org/-marie-thorsten/3157.

Tokuhiro, Yoko. 2009. *Marriage in Contemporary Japan*. London and New York: Routledge.

Tsuru, Tsuyoshi, and James B Rebitzer. 1995. "The Limits of Enterprise Unionism: Prospects for Continuing Union Decline in Japan." *British Journal of Industrial Relations* 33(3):459–492.

White, Merry I. 2002. *Perfectly Japanese: Making Families in an Era of Upheaval*. Berkeley and Los Angeles: University of California Press.

World Bank. 2014. "GDP per Capita (current US$)." The World Bank. Accessed May 25. http://data.worldbank.org/indicator/NY.GDP.PCAP.CD.

Young, Louise. 1998. *Japan's Total Empire: Manchuria and the Culture of Wartime Imperialism*. Berkeley: University of California Press.

山田 昌弘 [Yamada, Masahiro]. 1999. パラサイトシングルの時代 *[The Age of Parasite Singles]*. Tokyo: Chikumashobō.

山田 昌弘 [Yamada, Masahiro] and 白河桃子 [Tōko Shirakawa]. 2008. 「婚活」時代 *[The Age of "Konkatsu"]*. Tokyo: Disukavātuentiwan.

CHAPTER 5

∽

"Relying on Myself Alone"

Single Mothers Forging Socially Necessary Selves in Neoliberal Russia

JENNIFER UTRATA

Although the transformation of the US economy has been profound in recent years, few changes have been as momentous in scope as the transition from state socialist to market capitalist workplaces in Russia. In the years following the collapse of the Soviet Union in late 1991, American and other Western advisors preached a neoliberal global gospel which led to the rapid privatization of formerly state-owned property and an accompanying retrenchment of the socialist state. Over the past couple of decades Russians have endured a wide range of crises, from the financial to the political and demographic. The "global policy" (Calhoun 2006) of the privatization of risk, with its "preference for private property over public institutions" is especially stark in Russia.

Ordinary Russians have gone from having guaranteed employment and a range of state protections during the Soviet era to navigating competitive, insecure workplaces with few supports today. People have experienced insecurity in multiple spheres, but insecure workplaces are a critical part of Russia's broader transition to a society of heightened insecurity and inequality. We have much to learn from the dramatic post-Soviet Russian case, in terms of understanding how ordinary people adapt to systemic changes and refashion the kind of selves newly capitalist work-places demand of them.

The dominance of neoliberalism in Russia (Zigon 2011) is shaping new forms of personhood, involving both discourses of self-reliance and efforts to improve one's life chances in insecure workplaces. Unlike in the West, where neoliberal subjects have emerged gradually (Yurchak 2003), in Russia discourses of neoliberalism have become dominant with remark-able speed. New ideologies, after all, may be even more appealing to people, and more visible as "culture" during times when people feel adrift and their lives are unsettled (Swidler 1986). The neoliberal worldview promotes the idea that independent individuals should exploit opportunities in the mar-ket, without depending on the state or anyone else. Personal responsibility for one's actions serves as the main "moral disposition" of neoliberalism, along with "ethical practices of work on the self" (Zigon 2011, 13–14). Due to the growth of neoliberal market capitalism and accompanying ideolo-gies of independent self-reliance, Russians are working to transform their thoughts, feelings, actions, and selves to not only survive but to "make it" in spite of the rampant insecurities surrounding them.

Individuals and families of all kinds face risks in Russia's new economy. But as Cooper (2008, 1252) demonstrates in her study of insecurity and inequality in Silicon Valley, "individuals live in different types of risk soci-eties in which they are more or less vulnerable and more or less on their own." As Russians remake their selves to cope with increasingly insecure workplaces, neoliberalism shapes the self in gendered ways. Though not a homogenous group, many single mothers are in an exceptionally vul-nerable position with minimal supports from men, the state, or employ-ers as they juggle paid work and parenting (Thistle 2006). In the United States, for instance, Warren (2006) has argued that "two-parent families are struggling to swallow the risk" but their "single-parent counterparts are choking." While Russia's single mothers similarly face intensified chal-lenges relative to two-parent families, they are also navigating a double transition: to market capitalism's neoliberal model of work organization (Williams 2013) and to motherhood on their own.

Single mothers with whom I spoke are nearly unanimous in proclaim-ing that they rely on themselves alone. But single mothers must work to transform their selves, and their feelings, according to what newly insecure workplaces require of them. Compounding the extremely low levels of trust most Russians have in institutions, especially since the collapse of state socialism (Shlapentokh 2006), there is a vacuum left by the shrinking state and a perceived critical mass of unreliable men. And as other authors in this

volume have shown, wherever instability and insecurity become normalized there will likely be a dearth of trust in institutions and intimate relationships (Corse and Silva, this volume). This lack of trust is exacerbated in
Russia during the postsocialist transition to capitalism. Rather than focus
on changing state policies or even finding a good man to help support
their burdens, most single mothers instead accept the need to "make it on
their own," fatalistic about existing alternatives to the new market system.
Rather than being "freer" under market capitalism, Russian single mothers, disappointed in both men and the state, are constrained to accept a
dominant neoliberal discourse of "relying on myself alone." I describe more
fully in my book this process of conforming to "practical realism," a gendered form of neoliberal ideology (Utrata 2015). During the transition to
capitalism, Russian single mothers feel compelled to present themselves as
autonomous, competent, and self-reliant—for the sake of their own dignity. Of course, discourses and strategies of self-reliance in the face of insecure, neoliberal workplaces are hardly unique to Russia. Self-reliance is part
of how many other women adapting to a world of insecure work describe
their efforts to forge new paths in the face of insecurities (Edin and Kefalas
2005; Gerson 2010; Hertz 2006; Nelson 2005). But even though discourses
of self-reliance are "private responses to social dilemmas" (Gerson 2010,
135) in multiple contexts, these discourses are particularly noteworthy in
Russia. After all, a previous generation of Russian women, the mothers of
the contemporary single mothers I interviewed, had many more protections and social guarantees they could count on. Disillusioned with both
men and the state, many of today's Russian women make a virtue out of
necessity by demonstrating their ability to cope with insecure workplaces
and provide for their families against the odds.

FROM STATE SUPPORT TO MARKET "FREEDOMS"

The Soviet system was hardly a utopia for women, but citizens had many
more state supports and guarantees. These supports have been reduced
dramatically since the 1990s. Although women's liberation under state
socialism was a common mantra, the Soviet state upheld mostly a veneer
of gender equality. Requiring women's participation in paid labor markets,
the state nonetheless naturalized women's "second shift" (Hochschild and
Machung 1989) responsibilities as mothers. Russian women did (and still
do) most of the unpaid work of caring for a home, raising children, making
meals, shopping for a variety of goods in conditions of frequent shortages,

and other housework (Ashwin 2000; Ashwin and Lytkina 2004). So although women had to work toward building state socialism, at the same time they bore primary responsibility for carework in their families. The state did strive to support women as "worker-mothers" (Berdahl 1999), but it did not encourage men to do their share at home and with children. Instead, men were expected to prioritize paid work and service to the state.

In light of these contrasting messages of women's formal equality in their "right" to work combined with their naturalized responsibilities at home and with children, Soviet women were frequently considered second-order breadwinners (Ashwin 2000; Ashwin and Lytkina 2004). Women's secondary status in labor markets was reinforced by a gender wage gap where women earned roughly 65 percent to 70 percent of men's wages in Soviet times (Lapidus 1988). At the same time, then as now, Russian women were responsible for ensuring their household's survival (Burawoy, Krotov, and Lytkina 2000), typically managing the family's household budget.

Russian women are on the front lines of managing the new economy's insecurities. But since 1991 major cutbacks have affected women's opportunities. The Russian state has been concerned primarily with the decline of the Russian population, often described as the "demographic crisis," since the fall of the Soviet Union. Thus, although initial reports are skeptical about its success, the Russian state since 2007 began offering the largest baby bonus in the world to encourage women to bear a second child (Rivkin-Fish 2010; Zavisca 2012). Although this "maternity capital" policy shows that the Russian state still has some interest in influencing family life, the post-Soviet state has at the same time cut back significantly in its supports for women combining work and home responsibilities.

Institutions that once supported women as mothers and as workers no longer function adequately (Zdravomyslova 2010). Women feel they have no choice but to try their best to make up for these institutional problems, doing more with less. Recent research based on survey data has shown that "Women are disadvantaged on the labor market to the extent that, relative to men, they have *higher* rates of layoff and voluntary employment exit, *lower* rates of employment entry and job mobility, *higher* odds that their new jobs are low-quality positions, and *lower* odds that they are high-quality" (Gerber and Mayorova 2006). Child care centers are much fewer in number than during the late-Soviet period (Teplova 2007) and there is dramatically reduced enforcement of child support laws since the 1990s (Utrata 2008). Discrimination against women in employment, especially women as mothers, is widespread, regardless of laws upholding the illegality of such discrimination (Sperling 2015; Utrata 2015, 2011).

INSECURITY AS THE NEW NORMAL: GENDERED IMPLICATIONS

Given the many changes Russians have experienced over the past two decades, most people are trying to create a sense of normalcy in their lives, turning inward toward their families. Indeed, the very idea of "crisis" has become normalized in everyday life and in speech in recent years. Many Russians demonstrate their autonomy and personal competence in navigating insecure workplaces, as well as their competence in navigating a society in flux during the transition to market capitalism, by embracing the idea that crisis itself is an expected part of Russian life (Shevchenko 2009). According to many Russians, the key to navigating crises is developing the proper positive outlook as well as a flexible and adaptable self.

Yet flexible selves are gendered, as is the transition to capitalism itself (Gal and Kligman 2000). Most Russians feel that flexibility is more important for women, and that women are "naturally" better at mustering the flexibility needed to adapt to new challenges. Of course, marital status, class, age, race/ethnicity, levels of social support, and other salient axes of inequality likewise affect how Russians cope with insecurities. But gender is especially important given that Russian women have long been stereotyped as remarkably strong and adaptable, whether having to compensate for men's heavy drinking or for the state's inefficiencies. Since Russian women have had virtually no choice but to juggle home and work responsibilities since Soviet times, the idea that women must be strong, flexible, and adaptable is not entirely brand new. But further demands are made on women in the post-Soviet era, constraining women to conform to neoliberal discourses.

Buttressing the idea of women's strength and adaptability is an entrenched cultural discourse asserting that Russian men, in contrast, are often weak and unreliable. Men as well as women frequently refer to this negative discourse as they make sense of social changes and challenges to gender relations (Utrata 2008; 2015). While women are often credited for being adaptable in the face of new insecurities, women's strength in this regard is all too frequently naturalized as simply how Russian women *are*.

Yet the kind of selves women are actively forging to meet the demands of insecurity culture under capitalism requires greater attention. Even though Russian women have long been required to adapt, so much more is expected of women today. In a market capitalist system with reduced state support for citizens, the stakes for success are much higher and the costs of failure more dire. Women's purported strength is far from natural, and rendering it so erases the cultural work that women engage in to adapt to newly insecure workplaces.

Besides the greater magnitude and risks inherent in the challenges women face, in Soviet times women could at least complain to others about their many burdens and problems. In the late-Soviet period, Ries (1997) documented this speech genre as a kind of feminine litany or lament. But today's Russians are more apt to proclaim that they are "masters of their own lives and destinies" (Ries 1997, 162). Complaining about one's problems, or even confiding in others about them, is seen as much less legitimate, if not stigmatizing, today. This represents a major cultural shift. A married mother acquaintance explained: "It is no longer proper to admit that you have problems. It's personally embarrassing to have problems nowadays. Before connections and who you knew mattered a lot more. Today if you are not making it, most people think you only have yourself to blame." Many women responsible for their household's survival, but especially single mothers, are expected to step up, without complaint, to compensate for systemic weaknesses and structural inequalities in labor markets (Utrata 2015). Even though many of my single-mother respondents end up embracing this necessity to rely on oneself, they describe having to do a great deal of emotion work (Hochschild 1983) in the process of trying to feel the "right" feelings.

Current statistics also corroborate this picture of women's endless adaptability in the face of structural gender inequality in workplaces and in homes. Russia has the largest gender gap in life expectancy in the world at twelve years, with men's life expectancy now sixty-two (up from a low of fifty-nine years in the mid-1990s), and women's seventy-four (Bobrova, West, Malyutina, Malyutina, and Bobak 2010; Shkolnikov, Field, and Andreev 2001). Heavy drinking among men as well as a high incidence of accidents, violent deaths, and stress-related illnesses are some of the problems contributing to men's lower life expectancy (Utrata, Ispa, and Ispa-Landa 2013). Although alcohol has long been an important part of Russian culture, the practice of binge drinking is also highly gendered. Men's drinking has worsened in the post-Soviet period, with alcohol available in more contexts and with fewer social sanctions. Indeed Russia is also distinctive for having the world's largest gender gap in drinking (WHO 2011). Women have long tried to reduce the effects of men's drinking on the family unit, and women do drink more now than they did under state socialism. But overall, drinking heavily is still much more closely associated with men and masculinity (Hinote and Webber 2012). Due to their many responsibilities at home and with children, in addition to paid work, most women simply cannot allow themselves to drink in the way in which men can (Pietilä and Rytkönen 2008).

While it is clear that the rules of the game have changed since Soviet times, in my research I also witnessed the extent to which Russian women are now expected to summon new reserves of strength. They engage in much cultural work to transform themselves, including stifling their feelings and downscaling their notions of security (Cooper 2011). Furthermore, women often experience newly capitalist workplaces as masculine, with no room for accommodating the many family obligations shouldered mostly by women. Many workplaces have adopted ideal-worker norms that are gendered masculine (Williams 2000), assuming unencumbered males with no caregiving responsibilities as prototypical workers. Under these circumstances, single mothers must be unusually flexible and adaptable. Even though Russian women still predominate in more stable state sectors like culture, health care, and education, where the pay is much lower, these jobs seldom pay enough to make ends meet. Women routinely leave these positions to take on better-paying jobs, or at least extra jobs, in the newer but more insecure sectors of the emerging market economy (Utrata 2015). Women also comprised forty-one percent of entrepreneurs in Russia as recently as 2007 (Salmenniemi, Karhunen, and Kosonen 2011).

SINGLE MOTHERS FORGING SOCIALLY NECESSARY SELVES

The data in this chapter are drawn from ninety in-depth interviews I conducted myself, in Russian and without the use of interpreters, with all kinds of single mothers, whether divorced, unmarried, or separated from partners.[1] Most interviews took place in the mid-sized provincial city of Kaluga, but about twenty percent of them took place in Russia's capital city of Moscow. Through focusing most of my time in Kaluga, I was better able to immerse myself in families and in social networks, allowing me to develop a broader and deeper portrait of family life. These ninety interviews form part of a larger project (n=151) in which I also interviewed grandmothers, Soviet-era single mothers, nonresident fathers, and married mothers. Interviews were important for building trust and developing rapport, but I primarily sought to engage in what Mitchell Duneier calls "in-depth, context-driven fieldwork," participating in single mothers' and their family members' lives as fully as possible, taking notes over time. I became enmeshed in several networks of single mothers with varied class backgrounds, watching their kids, joining families for evenings around the kitchen table, celebrating birthdays and holidays at home, and visiting parks and cafes.

In a country where social networks have long been critical for establishing trust and getting work accomplished, I relied on snowball sampling. My sample of informants was purposefully very diverse. I included representatives across the spectrum of single mothers in the general population, stratifying by income, education, age, marital status, employment, and living arrangement. Respondents ranged from twenty-three to fifty-four years of age and slightly over half had higher education. Reflecting national trends, most single mothers are divorced and have one (63%) or two (24%) children, though one in four had never been married. I use the stories and words of single mothers to illuminate the cultural and emotion work on the self in which diverse kinds of women engage as they adapt to insecure workplaces and fewer state protections than their own mothers had.

The remainder of this chapter introduces Sveta, a working-class single mother focused on remaking herself and improving her life chances in spite of the losses of security she has experienced since the early 1990s. I then draw on a wider group of single-mother respondents to further elaborate how disillusioned most single mothers are with both men and the state, describing how hard women work at transforming themselves to become even stronger and more flexible than their own mothers were during Soviet times, a necessity in navigating insecure workplaces. In the final section I reflect on the implications of the new economy's demand for gendered, flexible selves, both in the Russian case and across the globe.

When I first met her, Sveta was cleaning several houses all over the city to make ends meet. Besides cleaning she spent much of her time "running around" the city due to inefficient public transportation and an insecure and unpredictable work schedule. Indeed because of the interview's length we nearly missed the crowded *marshrutka* (shared fixed-route minibus) back to the city center, a form of transport which cost her a few more rubles than the regular bus but got her to her daughter's school at a more predictable time. I was appreciative of her time and treated her and her daughter to some ice cream in the city center while they waited for the bus home. Sveta could not get over this "generosity," and said she could not remember the last time someone had done something nice for her, explaining that Russians have become more "mercenary" in recent years. "One must somehow adapt to this selfish place that Russia has become. There's no other way. These days people look out only for their own," Sveta reflected.

A thirty-five-year-old former factory worker and single mother of a seven-year-old girl, Sveta lives in a dormitory room with a shared kitchen and bathroom on the outskirts of Kaluga, a mid-sized city in northwest Russia.[2] Several months after our first meeting she was excited to report that she had found a new job as a nanny for a well-to-do family in the city center. She could bring her daughter to work in a pinch since her employer seemed to understand her predicament as the single mother of a young child. With the rise of this kind of informal work, Sveta and many other mothers are acutely aware that much depends on the willingness of individual employers to empathize with and accommodate workers' constraints. Those employers who are unwilling to compromise can exploit workers' precarious positions in the new economy. "I really got lucky with this family," Sveta declared, showing me a refrigerator her employer had given to her when they opted to upgrade their own. Sveta appreciates being able to access more amenities and appliances formerly in scarce supply. But at the same time she used to have more rights as a worker: "Back in Soviet times, workers were respected as experts and we had a voice. Now only those with money are respected." Few single-mother informants believe that their rights matter much anymore as either employees or as citizens. They have better access to consumer goods, which women are very happy about, but alongside this increased access their rights as workers and as citizens have diminished. And in Sveta's case, even acquiring the refrigerator was made possible by an individual employer's kindness and Sveta's "luck" with this family.

Like many single mothers, Sveta attributes her affinity for constant movement to her personality at first. She exclaimed: "I'm the kind of person who is constantly on the move. I can't sit still! I'm constantly moving. I've always got something to do, some problems to solve." She explained that while some people like to relax, she enjoys being on the go. She glosses over her lack of alternatives in getting around in a city with overcrowded public transportation as well as the lack of jobs in her technical specialty paying a living wage. But later on in the interview, she emphasizes that she is simply used to this way of living where she must keep moving and cannot count on others much: "I've been on the go for so long and I've gotten so used to it that I don't really consider anything difficult. . ... Besides, I know that I can't count on anyone else. I'm alone, you know? No one is going to do my laundry, make me something to eat, or look after my child. *I'm relying on myself alone*, my own strength." Single mothers frequently describe relying on themselves alone. Importantly, many single mothers actually depend heavily upon their own mothers for support of various kinds, from child care and housework to material and emotional support (Utrata 2011). Yet single mothers of all kinds still *feel* alone given the retrenchment of the state in recent years and their disillusionment concerning most men.

Most single mothers I spoke to, regardless of their specific economic circumstances, feel "unprotected" as workers but also, significantly, as mothers. Most have little trust in other people, especially men, a finding consistent with wider survey research on low levels of trust in Russian society (Shlapentokh 2006). Sveta notes that just as her material situation is improving, more suitors have taken an interest in her. She finds this worrisome. One guy recently had the nerve to suggest they move in together. "He wants to be supported in style, with me taking over his cooking and cleaning!" She laughs at the very idea of pooling resources with a man who has "no apartment of his own and no decent job." Men do not help out much with housework or child care in Russia even compared to men in other industrialized countries. Second shift inequalities prominent in other Western countries are intensified in Russia, where women still do the majority of housework (Perelli-Harris and Isupova 2103; see also Ashwin 2000). Single mothers feel that it is harder than ever to find a reliable man who can bring at least something useful, typically defined as a decent paycheck or a place to live, to a relationship.

For the most part single mothers I interviewed are convinced that the good men are already married. They also argue that they are well aware that the state no longer has any need for their children, in contrast to a Soviet state where children were needed and motherhood was a public duty rather than a private choice (Issoupova 2000).[3] This atmosphere of distrust and disappointment regarding most men and the state only reinforces the convictions of Sveta, and those of many other single mothers, that they can ultimately rely mainly on themselves. Thus single mothers work hard to become stronger and more flexible, trying to steel themselves in order to better cope with the insecurities surrounding them.

In contrast to Soviet Russia where every citizen was guaranteed a job, according to my informants life in the New Russia demands a different, more flexible kind of self. For instance, Sveta believes learning to think differently, and more positively, can turn her life around. The idea that "everything depends on you" is new in Russia. Sveta was one of many to argue that "in Soviet times people like my mom just went to work and came home and no one had to worry about the future. Some lived better than others, but everyone could get by. Everyone was needed. Today there are none of those guarantees."

But while my single-mother informants generally wish there were more guarantees for mothers today, most accept that the rules of the game are completely different. Some appreciate new opportunities to be more successful, at least in theory, than their own mothers could be. Today, relying on oneself, and working to transform oneself to become even stronger, is the main strategy for Russian mothers fatalistic about the chances of any man, much less the state, coming to their aid. Sveta reads self-help books every evening, absorbing the translated works of Andrew Carnegie and

Joseph Murphy. She sells Amway products and finds the business meetings each month inspirational. Cutting her neighbors' hair for extra money, she is proud to have managed to save enough for her daughter's eye operation. She is putting away a little money each month to buy an apartment of her own eventually, but this process will take at least ten to fifteen years. In the meantime, she keeps moving. Whether lighting the candles illuminating icons at a nearby Russian Orthodox church, or drinking with a few friends on a weekend night, Sveta is open to whatever will give her the added strength she needs to make it in a world where old certainties have dissolved.

She used to take pride in her technical expertise at work, back when she was a factory worker. But those jobs are gone. At least in the new world of work, she tells herself—and repeats to others in an effort to convince herself of it—she really controls her own destiny. At a gathering of a few friends one evening, Sveta's friend Alyona started complaining about the fact that her husband had abandoned her and her hearing-impaired daughter. She worried that maybe she would never find a life partner again considering her age and circumstances. But the others present admonished her for giving in to feeling sorry for herself and urged her to focus on transforming herself, which could potentially transform her life. Sveta advised: "You need to think differently. I can give you some psychological books that will help you to think differently about your life and work and help you to make things different. It's all up to you. You need to think, 'I am worthy. I have the best, prettiest, most charming daughter and any man in his right mind would be lucky to have me as his wife.'" Women discipline one another to remain within this discursive frame embedded in neoliberal ideology, making other frames for women's thoughts and actions almost unimaginable. Speech genres, according to Ries (1997, 110), are " ... not merely a way of speaking about the world but also a way of *acting* in the world." While multiple discourses are found in Russia, the idea that one can create the kind of self who can better make it in the world is dominant among single mothers, enforced among them as a way of demonstrating competence under the new rules of market capitalism.

During my fieldwork, many discussions with single mothers began with the idea that Russian women are strong without much conscious effort. It was only over time, and often in informal conversations with single mothers, that it became clear that new reserves of strength are demanded of women today. Women worked to present themselves as self-reliant and competent, even when some confessed to not always feeling especially strong. Russia, after all, is in a state of not only insecure workplaces, but a state of normalized crisis (Shevchenko 2009) in institutions, social relations, and even the gender order itself (Utrata 2015).

DISILLUSIONMENT WITH MEN AND THE STATE

Russian single mothers become savvy postsocialist subjects, demonstrating their competence to others, in part by allowing themselves to be somewhat fatalistic about the chances of a man or the state coming to their aid soon. Women argue that they will not be taken in by men's promises or the state's proclamations, even though they might have moments when they are tempted to believe in both. But because women have to become stronger in order to take care of themselves, they can hardly permit themselves to succumb to fatalism completely. Their general stance is a "blend of self-reliance and fatalism" (Shevchenko 2009, 75).

Women's negative discourses on men and the state most frequently overlap, producing a kind of double disillusionment. For instance, many women worry about how to raise their kids well due to a state which can no longer be counted on to enforce men's support or to adequately support women. The state no longer ties men to their families as it once did through discouraging divorce and mandating child support, and it provides fewer protections than it once did. Due to this double disillusionment, many single mothers feel they must personally embody the strength necessary to teach their children to survive in a harsher Russia. Mothers of sons worry about how to shape their sons into "real men" who will later become responsible for their own families rather than letting women shoulder most of life's burdens. "So many of our men let women do everything," Masha noted, "But I want my son to learn to be responsible. Teaching this is hard in Russia." Even though mothers want their sons to both respect women and be responsible, there is a sense that there is only so much mothers can do with sons given a dearth of male role models.

However, mothers of daughters are adamant that they must teach their daughters how to survive by becoming stronger in the face of adversity. Some wish their daughters could be traditional, family-oriented women in intact marriages, but counting on this scenario strikes most as unwise given what most perceive as the chances of finding a good man. Reflecting on raising her five-year-old daughter, Yelena, a twenty-six-year-old divorced bookkeeper, emphasized that many women have to work very hard to become stronger, to control their emotions, and to avoid dependence:

> I want my daughter to be independent, and strong. Psychologically strong. All kinds of things can happen in life. We women are very emotional, our hearts are vulnerable. But all the same in this life we have to work on becoming stronger. So that everything doesn't affect you. Or at least you cannot show how much things affect you. I will do all I can to make sure that she can survive on her own in any situation. She can't be dependent on anyone.

Although Yelena began by suggesting that becoming dependent on a man would be a mistake, she went on to say that women were "more protected" during the Soviet period, so women didn't have to steel themselves in the same way that they do today. In contrast to what Yelena perceives as women's "natural" (involving emotion and vulnerability) state of being, life under market capitalism requires distance from these feminine characteristics. "Women cannot count on any man, nor on the state," Yelena added. "Before there were more guarantees and the state supported families." In today's Russia, whatever their desires, women must manage their feelings and work to cultivate strength since being weak or unwilling to adapt to new modes of work under market capitalism can have dire consequences for one's family, including ending up "on the street."

Blurred boundaries in the form of a double disillusionment with men and state is typical, yet overall women had much less to say about the idea of the state once more providing protections for mothers with children. The idea of state support has become almost unthinkable, or at least a sign of naiveté. Most women I interviewed found the idea of the state doing much to help them alternatively laughable, insulting, or humiliating. They tended to dismiss the idea of state support, eager to talk about other more important aspects of their lives. Rimma, a divorced thirty-six-year-old mother of three who is officially unemployed but makes traditional dolls and folk crafts to sell at local festivals, needs additional money. Yet she finds it too humiliating to prove it to the state that she is in need: "My husband will want an official divorce only when he decides to marry that woman, but basically for now he just left me. I don't have any certificates showing what he earns. ... Collecting all those papers is hard, all those certificates ... oh dear! All of that to get only seventy rubles for each child! I think that I'm healthy enough to work and earn that money myself rather than running around everywhere humiliating myself. And then those awful lines. The whole situation makes me jittery."

Women expressed their disillusionment with men much more frequently and openly, often in a ritualistic manner, especially in groups of women. I encountered this fatalism so often that it started to seem "normal" to me. Once I accompanied a group of girlfriends, mostly single mothers, to the local *banya* (Russian sauna) to celebrate Margarita's birthday. While lying around in the steamy room, a few of them gently teased me about how hard, and indeed boring, it must be for me to be alone in Russia for so long, mainly talking to women. "Zhenya, are you spending time talking to our Russian *men* too, I hope?" one woman queried with a smile, while others giggled. I started to launch into my interview plans, but one woman interrupted me. She warned me that I'd have to be prepared to find only a few good men in Russia. Another woman cut in with: "No wonder her husband back in America isn't jealous! After all, we hardly have men to speak of, especially in Kaluga!" Everyone laughed.

The discourse on weak men, of course, is not a statement of fact; instead it is a discourse of gender relations in a state of normalized crisis. At the same time, Russia does have alarming statistics on male alcoholism and premature male mortality, and intimate partner violence and male infidelity are normalized in everyday life. The negative discourse on men and the state appears useful for many single mothers in making sense of their lives. These rituals of referring to the negative discourses on men strengthen women's feelings that they can only count on themselves or on other women.

The prevalence of this negative discourse is also noteworthy because today newer discourses, in which men are competent breadwinners, are more widespread. After all, many Russian men are reliable enough to hold most positions of leadership in politics and business, with President Putin cited by women occasionally as embodying a decent man's sober reliability. The Russian media, along with the Russian Orthodox Church, have also been idealizing nuclear families in which men earn enough money to support stay-at-home wives and children while still remaining strong leaders and fathers in their families. Nevertheless, " . . . the new family ideal in which the man plays a key role does not as yet match reality" (Issoupova 2000, 50). Women describe a critical mass of men who should be reliable but are not. Among single mothers, the Soviet-era negative discourse on weak, irresponsible men is dominant and has been infused with new meaning.

The negative discourse on men only reinforces the unreliability and weakness of men as the societal status quo. Lada, a thirty-year-old factory worker with a four-year-old daughter, wishes she earned more money and hates being so dependent on her own mother. Yet she still feels proud of doing her best as a single mother, and hardly feels at fault in this regard given the state of Russia's men: "Today everyone knows that women simply cannot rely on men. When a woman can't count on a man to take care of the family she goes it alone. . . . . We have very few men who are really reliable, men you can count on. Men now depend on women. People know this!" The idea that men live at the expense of women and depend on them is derided as shameful. Because some women have a better chance than before of earning good money, women feel there are more men than ever seeking to free-ride on women's work. The Soviet state compelled men and women to work. But now people are "free" to refrain from working, if they can find adequate support.

Even class differences among women tended to blur when women reflected on their disillusionment with men. Lida, a professor in Moscow who earns more money through her political consulting side jobs than most women could ever manage to earn in Kaluga, shares the views of many lower-income women. Despite her relative advantage, Lida references a broader context of intimacy insecurity in Russia when she notes that a job—any kind of job—feels like a decent prospect relative to other options. Lida explained: "A man can decide to support you in the manner that you've become accustomed. Or he can decide that for one reason or another he no longer wants to support you. I mean, who knows? He might fall in love with another woman, or just find himself a lover. Whatever he likes really. Therefore a stable job is much better than the dubious support of a man."

Of course, given that stable jobs are much more scarce than they were under state socialism, when everyone was guaranteed work and there was less social inequality, most women are adapting instead to insecure, low-paid jobs. However, most single mothers with whom I spoke found their workplace prospects more hopeful, even in the absence of stable jobs, because so many mothers distrust the state and find most men unreliable. Even when their class circumstances differ, most single mothers I interviewed agree with Lida: they continue to speak of relying on themselves alone, as if self-reliance is the main strategy they can trust, or the main discourse which allows their actions as single mothers to make sense to others.

STRENGTHENING THE SELF, NAVIGATING INSECURE WORKPLACES

As much as women may be trying to adapt to insecure workplaces, these workplaces are far from friendly toward women. Nearly every woman interviewed described how hard it is for mothers to find employment when they are either of childbearing age, have young children, or are over forty. Mothers bristle at this limited window of opportunity, even as they try to strategize around it. Evgenia, grateful to have a job even though she feels capable of more than the work she does repairing meters, explained: "At first women aren't needed because they might soon have children. If the girl is young employers say, 'you're going to get married and have children soon' and that's a problem. Then later a woman is raising her children and employers say: 'You've got kids and they're going to get sick, so why should we hire you?' And then after women turn forty they are old and no longer needed."[4] Should women fail to become strong enough, they risk falling into the pitied category of Russians who are "needed by nobody" (Höjdestrand 2009). In a society where people are increasingly defined by how much they earn, and what kind of career they have built, especially in the case of single mothers where it is assumed that their "personal lives haven't worked out," most women work hard to create the kind of selves which can adapt and withstand pressures. Even though Evgenia wishes conditions were otherwise, she and other mothers see few alternatives to trying to become even stronger.

As women try to summon strength and change their outlook on life, they are simultaneously adapting to what they perceive as a world made by and for men. Their perceptions are based in the gendered world of paid work where women's jobs pay systematically less. Women routinely comment on their salaries in gendered terms, arguing "it's not that bad for a woman's salary in Kaluga." Jobs have only become more sex-segregated since state socialism's collapse (Gerber and Mayorova 2006).[5] As Lena put it: "Of course, a woman and her child should be more protected in our rather tough world. It is a man's world right now. Women have no choice but to acquire more masculine qualities in order to make their way in this world." Yet in trying to conform to standards of masculine ideal workers who have no caregiving responsibilities, women describe feeling alienated from themselves.

New gendered feeling rules of post-Soviet single motherhood require suppressing one's emotions, an alienation from one's self and one's feelings that is also a result of the gendered forms that the privatization of risk takes in insecure workplaces. Recall Yelena's statement that women "have to work on becoming stronger. So that everything doesn't affect you. Or at least you cannot show how much things affect you." Larissa, a lawyer in a private firm and mother of a seven-year-old, was one of several mothers who described an inability to cry, at least when facing real-life troubles:

> I have a masculine character . . . what I mean is that I don't give up no matter what, I will find a way out of any situation no matter how terrible the circumstances might be. I never lose heart and I never cry. I can watch TV and start to cry, read a book and start to cry, but when I face real-life troubles I will never cry. Of course, probably a real woman should cry. When she has an argument with her husband she should let her tears fall, and then her husband should feel sorry for her. But I can't.

Other women argue that their femininity is undermined by the very masculine qualities to which women such as Larissa attribute their relative success. These mothers argue that women should be able to occasionally cry, and should have "strong shoulders" to lean on. But because many women feel Russia lacks "real men," as the widespread negative cultural discourse on men's weakness maintains, it is also difficult for women to become what they see as "real women." Single mothers have become inured to controlling their emotions, becoming estranged from the part of themselves that might want a good cry now and then. Although women must be flexible in adapting to a man's world of work, in doing so they no longer know what to feel.

Besides suppressing feelings, women actively try to reduce what they feel entitled to or need. I repeatedly heard women work on reducing their needs by developing exceptional abilities to go without sleep, to never get sick, to enjoy moving constantly (as we saw with Sveta earlier) whenever circumstances demand it. They develop what Hochschild (1989, 195–196) describes in a very different context as a ". . . conception of themselves as 'on-the-go, organized, competent,' as women without personal needs." Anya, a divorced mother of two teenaged sons, was one of a handful of women who tried for a time to earn more money by working at a job coded as masculine. Her boss had been reluctant to hire her due to the physical labor outdoors, but Anya surprised him by becoming "more like a man," proud that she had developed the ability—indeed, the flexibility—to ignore things that other women might complain about:

> In our society we don't exactly have equality between women and men. Let's just say that equality is a somewhat relative term here! Employers prefer men.... People believe women are sufficiently capricious, that they demand all kinds of special conditions. So men cannot be themselves, they can't relax, they can't use foul language, and so on. But I let them know that I wouldn't tire anyone with my demands. They could swear and say anything to me. I wouldn't mind at all.

Whether or not Anya actually minded the extensive daily use of *mat* (obscene language), for her becoming stronger meant accommodating an all-male collective while stifling any demands of her own. Even when it comes to such basics as a safe work environment, women are doubtful about what they can manage to get given the insecure and discriminatory conditions of labor markets in Russia. Flexible femininities, and not just flexible selves, are required to conform to masculine workplace norms which offer scant protection from harassment, and fewer real workplace protections than were available in Soviet times.

When Anya and I discussed the issue of juggling paid work and motherhood on another occasion, she explained that women, if only they worked hard enough on it, could think their way out of many problems including the "invented problem" of combining work and motherhood. If women would only think differently, she argued, their "problem" would disappear. "If someone complains, 'Oh, look at you, you're poor and unhappy,' you will start to believe them. You know what I mean? But I don't consider myself unfortunate.... I've always been lucky in work, and I'm very fortunate in terms of my children," Anya concluded.

During the time I knew her, Anya described doing all she could to keep her family together prior to her divorce, including finding her former husband work and taking jobs she considered beneath her status. But she also draws on newer discourses of self-reliance and making one's own life, trying to transform her thinking and maintain a positive attitude. Divorce too, Anya emphasizes, can bring good fortune like increased personal time, and insecure workplaces might even inspire creativity and self-fulfillment, she argues at other times. In any case, Anya explained, people mainly need to keep their chins up and be willing to work—regardless of the kinds of workplaces they might confront. Anya cannot afford to let herself be weak. Her husband is in another country, an alcoholic who has given up on the world, and she receives no child support. She must support both sons on her own.

Overall, most Russian single mothers describe becoming stronger matter-of-factly, as if a tendency to refrain from complaint was also a personality characteristic rather than an issue of having to conform to a new "self-reliant" kind of self under neoliberal capitalist work conditions. Aleftina, a divorced nurse with no family support, working two cleaning shifts after hours in order to make ends meet, stated: "I don't really need moral support. I don't like to complain or ask for help. Some other people don't mind, but I prefer to just manage on my own, with my own strength." Even when mothers touch on moments of weakness and vulnerability in their lives, they quickly move on to describe "getting a hold of themselves" and feeling more appropriate feelings. Luba, a taxi driver trying to pay back a huge debt she incurred as a result of a pyramid marketing scheme, paused before replying to my question about what she has found hardest during the transition to capitalism: "Is it hard to be alone? Only sometimes. When I start to feel frustrated, when I start thinking and feeling sorry for myself. But it soon passes. I calm down and get a hold of myself." Through "getting a hold of themselves," single mothers work to summon the strength necessary to deal with multiple levels of insecurity.

It is likely no accident that the qualities that single mothers say come naturally to them, or those qualities they most prefer—being constantly in motion, never needing to cry, never getting sick, relying on themselves, and so on—are also precisely what is demanded of them in neoliberal Russia. Many mothers feel constrained by this pressure to appear self-reliant and strong in a society with few supports for parenting and working single-handedly (Utrata 2015). Single mothers have little control over whether they will find a good man and they have little faith that they will get more help from the state. In contrast, in spite of insecure and discriminatory workplaces, many mothers believe improving their material situation is at least within their grasp, as long as they find a way to control their very selves, or at least the way they present themselves to others.

Of course, women do vary in how much confidence they are able to claim for themselves. A handful of women I interviewed were unable to present themselves as savvy postsocialist subjects. Inna, a divorced mother of two freelancing as a children's book writer, feels lost by the insecurity all around her. She confided: "A good mother should be even-tempered, calm, confident, and probably strong as well. This is especially so if the mother is raising her children alone! Unfortunately my kids are growing up without this sense of confidence. If I were stronger they would feel differently." Failing to summon the proper way of being in the world means more than failing as a breadwinner. For single mothers, it means feeling like a failed mother.

But for many women, forging the socially necessary selves capable of dealing with insecure workplaces allows them to garner respect as single mothers in neoliberal Russia. Single mothers are more respected by other Russians now than they were in Soviet times, but this respect is conditional. Single mothers are respected mainly if they can manage to provide well for their families, maintaining a positive attitude rather than complaining about their challenges (Utrata 2015).

IMPLICATIONS OF INSECURE WORK AND FLEXIBLE SELVES

Despite the odds stacked against them as mothers, and the insecurities of work in the New Russia, most single mothers place great hope in their chances of getting by, if not making it, in the workplace. This is not to say that women's jobs, on average (with the exception of Lida's job described above), are secure or fulfilling. Most jobs in the newly capitalist economy are far from it. But Russian mothers perceive few other realistic alternatives. Neoliberal ideology and policy has spread around the globe, even to places where most women still wish they had the state protections their own mothers had. Russian women believe mothers should be treated differently due to their caregiving work which benefits society—indeed they feel both the state and men should step up to do more on behalf of mothers and the contributions they make to their families—but most women do not see this happening any time soon.

Even though women had more supports as mothers in the late-Soviet period, most single mothers believe that today it is at least possible for women to earn more than men, and to really improve their own family's material situation considerably. Of course, what is possible is not necessarily probable, but the belief in women's ability to not only get by, but to succeed, is alive and well. When I spoke with Lilya, a forty-nine-year-old unmarried librarian, about why it seemed to her that women have more freedoms today, she explained: "Well, women, of course, always earned less than men back then. It's somewhat different now . . . but back then women definitely always earned less." Many single mothers value this chance for a better life, however unstable the better life might be, and however slim the chance for achieving it.

Overall, the extent to which single mothers support a new ideology of hard work and potential success under market capitalism is striking. This does not mean that women do not still want plenty of socialism in terms of subsidized housing, education, health care, and childcare. Yet many also want more capitalism. Ksenia, a thirty-nine-year-old factory worker who was raised in a Soviet "boarding school" after her mother died during her childhood and her father abandoned her and her siblings, believes people need to focus more on loving their children than on earning more money. However, she has no sympathy for women who earn only 1500 rubles a month (US$50) and complain about their situation rather than taking it upon themselves to find a second job. They might instead work on transforming their thinking and take a job which might seem "beneath" them temporarily. Opportunities exist now in Russia, which did not exist before:

> Before there was that "iron curtain" and if you didn't have connections and ties then you couldn't get anything or make your way anywhere or get out. Now, in principle, every person can climb up from the bottom if they wish. There is already such an opportunity, whereas before it didn't seem to be the case . . . There were more limitations before . . . Now I'm dependent on my job and on other people, my employer. But I would like to be fully independent. Then I would really be successful, if I had my own business where I could be my own boss.

Because Ksenia had spent time doing some of the most insecure and unglamorous of jobs, she believes others should seize "opportunities." She dislikes being so dependent on her employer, but the promise of being her own boss, one day, is an alluring prospect. Even though women do not like feeling "unprotected" with inadequate state support, many conform to newer discourses of self-reliance, hard work, and market success.

Through espousing an ideology of hard work and marketplace success, planning their next career moves, and saving for their next major purchases, mothers are also putting their faith in themselves, and their ability to make it in the workplace, rather than in men or the state. Women work on transforming themselves to better cope with what they see as the somewhat inevitable insecurities of neoliberal market capitalism. In the context of the proliferation of insecure forms of work under market capitalism, Russian women, perhaps, are not really exceptional. Even in the relatively more stable context of the contemporary United States, Gerson (2010) describes women of the unfinished gender revolution for whom self-reliance is paramount. "Self-reliant women look to the workplace as the most straightforward route to gaining financial security, social status, and personal identity" (Gerson 2010, 135). In neoliberal Russia, too, women like Zoya routinely declare, in spite of challenging circumstances: "I don't need anyone else. I can handle anything that comes my way." As single mothers cope with the cultural dominance of neoliberal capitalist ideologies, most work on forging socially necessary selves needed by workplaces, in hopes that they will get "lucky." Moreover, Russian single mothers suggest that this ability to forge new selves—endlessly flexible and adaptable selves accepting of a world marked by crisis and insecure work, all while refraining from complaint—might also be deserving of a badge of honor.

NOTES

1. Fieldwork was conducted in 2003 and 2004, in two separate six-month trips.
2. Kaluga is a medium-sized city of 330,000 located approximately 110 miles southwest of Moscow. Most Russians live in mid-sized cities outside of the more cosmopolitan centers of Moscow and St. Petersburg.
3. The state may want Russian women to have "more children" for the state's benefit but women still feel that the state is unwilling to invest in children and in the challenges of caring for children, at least relative to the kinds of supports available in Soviet times.
4. While men also face ageism as well, women tend to face a harsher version of it given the emphasis on youthful beauty in many female-dominated service jobs as well as in male-dominated private sector firms.
5. In the 1990s, especially, job advertisements were blatantly sexist, advertising for secretaries with long legs and "without complexes" (i.e., those open to intimate relations beyond the job). These have diminished somewhat, but Sperling (2015) notes that even in 2009, "27 percent of want ads specified the sex of the desired applicant." Overall, gender inequalities persist at the level of hiring, pay, and promotion.

REFERENCES

Ashwin, Sarah, ed. 2000. *Gender, State, and Society in Soviet and Post-Soviet Russia*. London: Routledge.

Ashwin, Sarah, and Tatyana Lytkina. 2004. "Men in Crisis in Russia: The Role of Domestic Marginalization." *Gender & Society* 18(2):189–206.

Berdahl, Daphne. 1999. *Where the World Ended: Re-Unification and Identity in the German Borderland*. Berkeley: University of California Press.

Bobrova, N., R. West, D. Malyutina, S. Malyutina, and M. Bobak. 2010. "Gender Differences in Drinking Practices in Middle-Aged and Older Russians. *Alcohol and Alcoholism* 45(6):573–580.

Burawoy, Michael, Pavel Krotov, and Tatyana Lytkina. 2000. "Involution and Destitution in Capitalist Russia: Russia's Gendered Transition to Capitalism." *Ethnography* 1(1):43–65.

Calhoun, Craig. 2006. "The Privatization of Risk." SSRC. Retrieved on February 20, 2013. Available at: http://privatizationofrisk.ssrc.org.

Cooper, Marianne. 2008. "The Inequality of Security: Winners and Losers in the Risk Society." *Human Relations* 61(9):1229–1258.

Edin, Kathryn, and Maria Kefalas. 2005. *Promises I Can Keep: Why Poor Women Put Motherhood Before Marriage*. Berkeley: University of California Press.

Gal, Susan, and Gail Kligman. 2000. *The Politics of Gender After Socialism: A Comparative-Historical Essay*. Princeton, NJ: Princeton University Press.

Gerber, Theodore P., and Olga Mayorova. 2006. "Dynamic Gender Differences in a Post-Socialist Labor Market: Russia, 1991–1997." *Social Forces* 84(4):2047–2075.

Gerson, Kathleen. 2010. *The Unfinished Revolution: Coming of Age in a New Era of Gender, Work, and Family*. New York: Oxford University Press.

Hertz, Rosanna. 2006. *Single by Chance, Mothers by Choice*. New York: Oxford University Press.

Hinote, Brian P., and Gretchen R. Webber. 2012. "Drinking toward Manhood: Masculinity and Alcohol in the Former USSR." *Men and Masculinities* 15(3):292–310.

Hochschild, Arlie Russell. 1983. *The Managed Heart: Commercialization of Human Feeling*. Berkeley: University of California Press.

Hochschild, Arlie Russell, and Anne Machung. 1989. *The Second Shift*. New York: Viking.

Höjdestrand, Tova. 2009. *Needed by Nobody: Homelessness and Humanness in Post-Socialist Russia*. Ithaca, NY: Cornell University Press.

Issoupova, Olga. 2000. "From Duty to Pleasure? Motherhood in Soviet and Post-Soviet Russia." In *Gender, State and Society in Soviet and Post-Soviet Russia*, edited by Sarah Ashwin, 30–54. London: Routledge.

Lapidus, Gail. 1988. "The Interaction of Women's Work and Family Roles in the USSR." *Women and Work: An Annual Review* 3:87–121.

Mudge, Stephanie Lee. 2008. "What is Neo-Liberalism?" *Socioeconomic Review* 6(4):703–731.

Nelson, Margaret K. 2005. *The Social Economy of Single Motherhood: Raising Children in Rural America*. New York: Routledge.

Perelli-Harris, Brienna, and Olga Isupova. 2013. "Crisis and Control: Russia's Dramatic Fertility Decline and Efforts to Increase It." In *Fertility Rates and Population Decline: No Time For Children?* edited by Ann Buchanan and Anna Rotkirch, 141–156. New York: Palgrave Macmillan.

Pietilä, Ilkka, and Marja Rytkönen. 2008. "'Health is Not a Man's Domain': Lay Accounts of Gender Difference in Life-Expectancy in Russia." *Sociology of Health & Illness* 30(7):1070–1085.

Ries, Nancy. 1997. *Russian Talk: Culture and Conversation During Perestroika*. Ithaca, NY: Cornell University Press.

Rivkin-Fish, Michele. 2010. "Pronatalism, Gender Politics, and the Renewal of Family Support in Russia: Towards a Feminist Anthropology of 'Maternity Capital.'" *Slavic Review* 69(3):701–724.

Salmenniemi, Suvi, Paivi Karhunen, and Riitta Kosonen. 2011. "Between Business and Byt: Experiences of Women Entrepreneurs in Contemporary Russia." *Europe-Asia Studies* 63(1):77–98.

Shevchenko, Olga. 2009. *Crisis and the Everyday in Postsocialist Moscow*. Bloomington: Indiana University Press.

Shkolnikov, V. M., M. G. Field, and E. M. Andreev. 2001. "Russia: Socioeconomic Dimensions of the Gender Gap in Mortality." In *Challenging Inequalities in Health: From Ethics to Action*, edited by T. Evans, M. Whitehead, F. Diderichsen, A. Bhuiya, and M. Wirth, 139–155. New York: Oxford University Press.

Shlapentokh, Vladimir. 2006. "Trust in Public Institutions in Russia: The Lowest in the World." *Communist and Post-Communist Studies* 39(2):153–174.

Sperling, Valerie. 2015. *Sex, Politics, & Putin: Political Legitimacy in Russia*. New York: Oxford University Press.

Swidler, Ann. 1986. "Culture in Action: Symbols and Strategies." *American Sociological Review* 51(2):273–286.

Teplova, Tatyana. 2007. "Welfare State Transformation, Childcare, and Women's Work in Russia." *Social Politics* 14:284–322.

Thistle, Susan. 2006. *From Marriage to the Market: The Transformation of Women's Lives and Work*. Berkeley: University of California Press.

Utrata, Jennifer. 2008. "Keeping the Bar Low: Why Russia's Nonresident Fathers Accept Narrow Fatherhood Ideals." *Journal of Marriage and Family* 70(5):1297–1310.

Utrata, Jennifer. 2011. "Youth Privilege: Doing Age and Gender in Russia's Single-Mother Families." *Gender & Society* 25(5):616–641.

Utrata, Jennifer. 2015. *Women without Men: Single Mothers and Family Change in the New Russia*. Ithaca, NY: Cornell University Press.

Utrata, Jennifer, Jean Ispa, and Simone Ispa-Landa. 2013. "Men on the Margins of Family Life: Fathers in Russia." In *Fathers in Cultural Context*, edited by D.W. Shwalb, B. Shwalb, and M. E. Lamb, 279–302. New York: Routledge.

Warren, Elizabeth. 2006. "Rewriting the Rules: Families, Money, and Risk." SSRC. Retrieved on February 20, 2013. Available at: http://privatizationofrisk.ssrc.org/Warren/.

Williams, Christine L. 2013. "The Glass Escalator, Revisited: Gender Inequality in Neoliberal Times, SWS Feminist Lecturer." *Gender & Society* 27(5):609–629.

Williams, Joan. 2000. *Unbending Gender: Why Work and Family Conflict and What to Do About It*. New York: Oxford University Press.

World Health Organization. 2011. *Global Status Report on Alcohol and Health*. Geneva, Switzerland.

Yurchak, Alexei. 2003. "Russian Neoliberal: The Entrepreneurial Ethic and the Spirit of 'True Careerism.'" *The Russian Review* 62(1):72–90.

Zavisca, Jane. 2012. *Housing the New Russia*. Ithaca, NY: Cornell University Press.

Zdravomyslova, Elena. 2010. "Working Mothers and Nannies: Commercialization of Childcare and Modifications in the Gender Contract (A Sociological Essay)." *Anthropology of East Europe Review* 28(2):200–225.

Zigon, Jarrett. 2011. *"HIV is God's Blessing": Rehabilitating Morality in Neoliberal Russia*. Berkeley: University of California Press.

PART II

Insecurity and Inequalities

CHAPTER 6

c>∿⊃

Different Ways of *Not* Having It All

Work, Care, and Shifting Gender Arrangements in the New Economy

KATHLEEN GERSON

Just as the industrial revolution created a new way of life by separating earning an income from domestic caretaking, the rise of a new economy is again reshaping the ways people organize work and care. This new economic revolution, however, is undoing the clear division that once assigned women and men to different physical, social, and economic spheres. At the height of this period, in the mid-20th century, three out of five US households consisted of a breadwinning husband and homemaking wife. While this option was never available to everyone, structured career ladders and secure unionized jobs made it possible for the majority of middle- and working-class men to become their household's primary provider, while stable marital bonds gave most women access to men's earnings. Even among the large proportions of working-class and minority families who were unable to attain this ideal, the norm itself held great sway.

Since that period, however, widespread and deeply anchored economic and social shifts have eroded the institutional underpinnings of this gender-divided arrangement.[1] The rise of what is often termed a "new economy" (characterized by the dominance of technological, information, and service-based economic activity) has included a decline in stable jobs and a rise in insecure work, creating unpredictable occupational prospects for all but the most privileged men and women.[2] In a parallel shift, the decline of stable marriages and the rise of more fluid intimate partnerships have created similarly uncertain interpersonal prospects. The rise in interpersonal uncertainties has implications for women and men of all class backgrounds, with the more educated more likely to postpone marriage and the less educated more likely to see marriage as a "luxury" they cannot afford.[3] However diverse the consequences, the rise in financial and interpersonal uncertainty has undermined the institutions and blurred the boundaries that once demarcated a clear division between work and care as well as distinct pathways for American women and men.

Although a system of separate spheres neither meets the needs nor reflects the aspirations of most twenty-first century adults, the contours of a new system—and its implications for gender arrangements—remain unsettled and contested.[4] Some argue that the gender revolution has stalled (England 2010) and may have reached its end (Cotter, Hermsen, and Vanneman 2011). There is certainly considerable evidence to support this view, including a plateau in women's labor force participation, a continuing gender gap in earnings and occupational attainment, an intensification of cultural pressures to practice "intensive mothering" (Hays 1996), and the decision among some professional women to "opt out" (Belkin 2003; Stone 2007).

Others posit a countervailing trend. Pointing to evidence that women are outpacing men in educational attainment and men are falling behind in earnings and ambition (Rosin 2012; DiPrete and Buchmann 2013), these analysts see women's aspirations on the upswing and men becoming increasingly adrift as opportunities to secure stable blue- and white-collar jobs contract. For some, these shifts in the fortunes and outlooks of women and men represent not just a declining gender gap but a growing gender reversal. Others see related developments—such as the rise of cohabitation, postponed marriage, single motherhood, and single adults living alone—as a troubling trend toward unmoored individualism and away from enduring commitments to work or care (Wilcox 2010; Beck and Beck-Gernsheim 2001).

There are elements of truth in both arguments, but they are partial truths. Like the proverbial blind men who touch different parts of the elephant, those looking at only parts of the whole are likely to reach different conclusions that are misleading if taken alone. Uncertain, uneven change may prompt even the most careful analysts to reach different conclusions, but this unevenness should also make us wary of unilinear views about the direction of change. Whether the stress is on a return to tradition or a new world of disconnected adults, neither scenario represents the only way forward. It is more accurate—and, I argue, more useful—to consider the full range of patterns emerging in response to the fundamental economic and social shifts that are dissolving the boundaries between home and work and creating new insecurities at work and in relationships.

CHARTING THE NEW LANDSCAPE OF WORK AND CARE

To understand how today's adults are navigating the increasingly uncertain occupational and family waters wrought by the new economy, I conducted in-depth interviews with a randomly selected sample of women and men currently residing in the area in and around Silicon Valley. As home to the high-tech economy and its ancillary occupations, this location offers a high concentration of cutting-edge jobs that form the core of the new economy. Since the area contains a mix of both old and new occupational niches, as well as what Kalleberg terms "good" and "bad" jobs (Kalleberg 2011), it provides fertile ground for examining how new jobs and occupational trajectories compare with more traditional ones as well as how the growth of new workplace and career structures is shaping the social and economic options for everyone.

To discover the work-care strategies emerging in this context, I interviewed women and men between the ages of thirty and forty-five, when pressures to build a family life and establish an occupational career are most intense. Finally, to explore the ways that class and financial resources shape options and strategies, people were selected from areas containing a diverse mix of educational and economic backgrounds (excluding the very affluent who are insulated from many of the challenges facing others).

Using these sampling criteria yielded a sample that includes an equal number of women and men from a range of backgrounds who are currently working at a variety of jobs—including service, technical, managerial, and professional occupations—and currently living in an array of family situations—including singles, childless couples, and couples with children.[5] Despite these differences, each respondent resides in a climate of "boom and bust" opportunities, increasingly blurred boundaries between home and work, and unpredictable work and family options.

How are these women and men experiencing and responding to the new challenges of earning a living and caring for others? And what are the implications for gender—and class—inequality? Amid the diversity of my respondents' lives, four general patterns emerge. One, which I call "neo-traditionalism," conforms to the images of a stalled revolution in which the arrival of children prompts parents to divide paid work and caretaking in gender-specific ways, usually despite their preferences.

Another, which can be described as "on one's own," embodies the concerns of those who see a trend away from marital commitment.[6] This pattern encompasses a variety of situations, from those who are single parents rearing children without the help of a partner to those single, childless adults living on their own. (Although most single parents are mothers, Gretchen Livingston [2013] reports that the proportion of single-parent households headed by a father has risen to 24 percent, which accounts for 8 percent of all US households). Despite the differences between singles who are childless and those rearing children, both circumstances contain the challenges posed by living outside the context of a stable intimate relationship.[7]

These two patterns are well represented in my sample, with slightly more than a third of my interviewees living on their own or as a single parent and another third in a relationship with a clear gender division in earning and caretaking. Taken together, they exemplify the dual, if divergent, concerns of those who argue we are either in the midst of a stalled revolution or a rise in uncommitted individualism. Yet these patterns do not tell the whole story, since another third are neither on their own nor pursuing a traditional strategy. These individuals, instead, are transgressing historic gender divisions in a variety of ways, including some who are reversing work and care domains and others who are taking conscious steps to share these domains as equally as possible. About 15 percent are "reversers," who are in relationships that divide primary responsibility for earning and caretaking, but not in a way that conforms to stereotypic gender assignments. Although the gender arrangements in these households differ from those in more traditional ones, the reversed pattern reflects a different response to similar work-family conflicts. The basic economic changes that have produced both time-demanding jobs and insecure work requires many households to assign work and caregiving in a way that leaves each partner mainly responsible for one, even though reversed couples find themselves relying primarily on a woman's earnings.[8]

The final 15 percent are "egalitarians" who are taking extraordinary steps to resist gender divisions and share the work of earning and caretaking in a relationship. These women and men are determined to seek a more equal balance between work and care, but usually find themselves, in the words of one respondent, "swimming against the tide." For some, this means a heavy load of caretaking in addition to working, while others have concluded that equality means forgoing parenthood to preserve equal commitments to work.

From a longer-term historical perspective, reversers and egalitarians are more innovative and thus easier to overlook, yet they are also on the rise. A recent Pew study reports, for example, that among households with children younger than eighteen, the share consisting of married mothers who out-earn their husbands and are considered the breadwinner now hovers around 15 percent, compared to just 4 percent in 1960 (Wang, Parker, and Taylor 2013).[9]

Each of these patterns illustrates diversity in how people cope with the conflicts and tradeoffs between work and care (as the examples below will amply illustrate), and the distinctions among them can become blurry as some people move from one category to another in response to changes in their economic and interpersonal fortunes. Taken together, however, they provide a framework for charting the options people face today and the strategies individuals are developing as they build life paths amid the contradictions and conflicts of today's uncertain economic and interpersonal landscape.

BECOMING TRADITIONAL, LIKE IT OR NOT:

About one-third of my interviewees—of whom 45 percent are women and 55 percent men—are engaged in what we have come to call traditional strategies for dividing work and caretaking.[10] Rearing children in committed marriages, they have adopted a clear division between who is responsible for breadwinning and who for caretaking. Yet even these couples rarely conform to the classic image of a satisfied stay-at-home caretaker and securely employed breadwinner. While a minority depended on one income, most were in a relationship where the primary caretaking partner either worked to some extent or wished to do so. These "neo-traditionals," including both husbands and wives, more often moved toward specializing in either work or care despite an earlier and often enduring preference for a more balanced, flexible, and equal arrangement. Why and how did these reluctant traditionals become so? Some clues can be found in the experiences of two respondents—not married to each other—who found themselves in a gender-traditional situation. Neither Kyra, currently a stay-at-home parent, nor Tim, a primary earner, had foreseen or preferred their current positions. First, Kyra's story:

> Reared primarily by her mother after her father died when she was a preschooler, Kyra assumed she would support herself. She managed to work her way through a small local college near her home in Michigan, although strained finances left

her juggling the demands of school with a series of part-time jobs. After finishing her degree, she found full-time work in a small public relations firm in Detroit, where her energy, managerial skills, and outgoing personality helped propel her up the ladder and on to a series of increasingly influential and better paying positions. A decade later, Kyra was committed to her career, optimistic about her future prospects, and comfortable living on her own.

Around this time, Kyra met Tony, an industrial engineer who dreamed of designing cars. Having weathered a series of unhappy relationships, she was surprised to see her relationship with Tony grow deeper and stronger. After a year of dating, she surrendered her skepticism and agreed to cement their status as a couple by living together. Several years later, they married and made plans to start a family. Two years later, they had their first child.

Kyra continued to work full-time and helped to support Tony as he moved from job to job in the unpredictable world of design consultancies. With the car industry in free fall, however, his prospects looked bleak and his spirits were plummeting. At the tensions in their marriage mounted, two unexpected developments converged: Kyra became pregnant again, and Tony was offered the chance to work at a small startup design firm in California. With another baby was on the way, Kyra feared the time to make a career change could not be worse. But despite the toll a move might take on her own hard-won success, she could not ask Tony to relinquish what seemed like a once-in-a-lifetime opportunity to follow his dream. With decidedly mixed feelings, she joined Tony in California.

Today, Kyra is at home with two young children and working as a part-time freelance instructor teaching an online course for very little money. She has applied for dozens of full-time positions—some well below her qualifications—and lost count of the number of in-person interviews, but none has produced an offer. Despite her experience, past achievements, and glowing recommendations, employers have hinted—and, in some cases, explicitly stated—that they are wary of hiring a mother with young children who might not be able or willing to put in the long hours they expect.[11]

Kyra notes, with a mix of cynicism and irony, that no one seems concerned about Tony's status as a father. To the contrary, his employer has made it clear that he is expected to spend long days at the office and be on call 24/7. The company cannot survive, he is told, unless everyone works from early morning into the night and is available to answer emails and phone calls that arrive on weekends and even after midnight.

In Kyra's distilled account, a series of unforeseeable events left her out of work and caring almost singlehandedly for their two young children, an arrangement she did not seek and does not prefer. In a mirror image to Kyra's conundrum, Tim finds himself on the other side of the work-care divide, feeling frustrated that the pressure to work long hours has left him unable to carve out enough time for caretaking:

As far back as he can remember, Tim has been committed to building a relationship of equal sharing with his wife, Margaret. Married in their twenties, they have fostered each other's work aspirations from the outset. For his part, that has meant supporting Margaret through the many years she worked toward her medical degree and post-medical school training in family practice.

Margaret has been equally supportive of Tim, but his aspirations have not followed such an organized track. Born in the Midwest to parents of modest means, he felt lucky to attend college and gave little thought to his future plans. Looking for a job after college, he stumbled into public relations when offered a job in a local firm. When Margaret's medical training brought them to the West Coast, he landed a series of jobs with a variety of small companies whose fortunes rose and fell in the fast-changing technology sector. For most of their married life, this arrangement has served Tim and Margaret well. Margaret's career has offered economic security and stable earnings, which has allowed Tim to work at jobs with less certain prospects.

As they entered their thirties and decided it was the time to start a family, they began to realize that their long work weeks, once an acceptable fact of life, had become a big drawback. With a child on the way, they both sought ways to cut back but soon discovered that only Margaret had the option. As part of a large practice, her partners agreed share the patient workload. Tim's employers, however, did not welcome any decision that would let his new family responsibilities come before his "loyalty" to the job.

Now the father of a six-month-old, Tim worries that his marriage and his career are both teetering. For the first time in their long relationship, Margaret is expressing sustained anger. While she is content to work fewer days a week to care for their son, she resents his lack of involvement. For his part, Tim wants to spend more time with both of them, but he feels even greater pressure to prove his worth by working as much as possible. Amid the pressures of an uncertain local economy, he does not believe he can afford to pull back without risking the loss of his job to "someone in India or Russia who will work for a third of what they're paying me."

A constellation of work pressures, gendered obstacles, and economic forces have left both Kyra and Tim contending with a division of work and care that neither intended nor finds satisfying. Not all couples in traditional situations would prefer another arrangement, but over half of those I interviewed do.[12] Their stories are instructive not just because they demonstrate that behavior cannot be assumed to reflect preferences. Equally important, they illustrate how and why institutions that reinforce a strict division of work and care along gender lines are out of sync with the needs and desires of a large proportion of contemporary workers.

ON THEIR OWN, BUT NOT ALIKE

If traditional strategies sit at one end of the work-care spectrum, the other end is inhabited by those who—at a similar age—remain single and on their own. This includes people living alone who have decided to forgo parenthood as well as single parents raising children without the help of a committed partner. Though diverse, this group is united by the single status of its members. On the surface, Michelle, a single mother, and Jason, a bachelor with no children, may appear to have little in common, but both of their lives illuminate the social forces that are prompting a growing number to go it alone:

Although Michelle always expected to have at least one child, she never imagined she would do it on her own. Growing up in the Midwest, she was reared by parents who had a long and apparently happy marriage. Her dad earned a stable income as a mid-level manager and family breadwinner. She did not excel at school, but she knew it was important to attend college and be able to support herself.

After graduation, she worked at a few uninspiring sales jobs and then decided to move to the West Coast, where she could live with an aunt until she found work and could pay her own bills. A series of dead-end jobs made it possible for Michelle to find her own place, but they left her feeling bored and adrift. Hoping to find more challenging, meaningful work, she took some night courses in business, which led to an entry-level position at a small nonprofit that provided services for the poor and disabled.

To her own surprise, Michelle proved to be a gifted administrator and moved steadily up the organization's ladder. After several years, the director retired and she landed the top spot. Being responsible for the survival and smooth running of the organization left little time for life outside the office and often pushed her beyond her "comfort zone," but the payoff in self-esteem and a sense of making a difference in people's lives made the hard work worthwhile.

In contrast to her work life, Michelle's personal life did not proceed so smoothly. As she entered her mid-thirties, a series of ill-fated relationships left her wondering if she would ever find a life partner. Then, on a business trip to Arizona, she met Gary and began a whirlwind courtship. Though separated by many miles, they took turns visiting each other and began to consider ways to be together. Michelle pondered a move, even though that would require giving up her job and starting over in another city.

Just as the Michelle was weighing these options, she discovered—to her surprise—that she was pregnant. Though unplanned, the pregnancy provided one more reason to leave her life and start a new one with Gary. But when Michelle shared the news on her next visit, Gary reacted with anger and dismay, making it clear he did not want a child or any involvement as a father. She returned in a "state of shock," knowing the relationship was over.

After much soul-searching, Michelle decided that she would not let her single status prevent her from having a child. Although the circumstances were far from ideal, she concluded this might be her "last chance." If Gary had greeted the news of her pregnancy with enthusiasm, Michelle might have found herself in Kyra's shoes—moving to a new city with a young child, limited employment options, and a partner too busy to share caretaking. Instead she became a single mother.

Today Michelle is rearing her two-year daughter, Courtney, with the help of a dedicated paid caretaker and a network of close friends, but no financial support or involvement from Gary. She remains single, although she recently began dating someone who is divorced and shares custody of his son. Courtney appears to be thriving and Michelle has no regrets about her decision, but being a single mother has required a change in her work situation. Though continuing to work full-time, she has reluctantly relinquished her nonprofit directorship to take a more secure if less inspiring job in the human resources division of a well-established research institute (where, not coincidentally, women at her company are concentrated). Her new position offers neither the influence nor challenges she once enjoyed, but it provides a steady income, demands less time, and has a predictable schedule, all of which make it easier to juggle the twin responsibilities of supporting and caring for Courtney.

While Michelle must shoulder the load of both work and care without a life partner, Jason is coping with a deficit of each. If she is "doing it all" and ultimately responsible for it all, he is largely on his own. As Eric Klinenberg (2012) has documented, "going solo" is an increasingly common choice for women and men of all ages, but the thirty- and forty-somethings in this category are doing so at an age when most people are forging family bonds of some kind. By rejecting commitments to marriage and children, Jason stands at the far end of the singles spectrum:

Growing up in a suburban neighborhood of tract housing in southern California, Jason felt shy and reticent in most social situations. Good at math, he won a scholarship to a local college, where he learned the language of computer coding.

Several years later, when a teacher recommended him for a job at a nearby small company, he left school without a degree to make his way in the growing high-tech world. When a Silicon Valley employer made an offer in his late twenties, he jumped at the opportunity to move there.

Over the last decade, Jason has moved through a series of jobs, as the companies he joined have either downsized, gone out of business, or simply changed direction with no further need for his skills. In parallel fashion, he has had a series of relationships that he describes as "not serious" and has never felt comfortable making a permanent commitment. Although he lived briefly with his last girlfriend, it felt more like an arrangement of convenience until she was able to find a job and pay her own rent.

Now thirty-nine, Jason lives alone with his cat. During the day, he goes to local coffee house, where he works on his laptop amid a scattering of similarly occupied coffee drinkers. Single again, after his last girlfriend moved out, and laid off a year ago from his last job as a programmer, he spends most of his time in the solitary pursuit of a new computer code, with occasional breaks to hang out with other nonemployed aspiring coders and go to dinner with his new girlfriend.

Considering his disappointments in love and thwarted opportunities at work, Jason has concluded that his marginal employment and modest social skills leave him ill positioned either to find a stable job or to settle down with a life partner. He hopes to live off his savings until he is able to "get back in the game" or, even better, make it big on his own. In the meantime, the coffee house will remain his workplace and his second home.

Although Michelle is a single mother raising a child on her own and Jason lives alone without close family ties of any kind, they are both coping without the support—or demands—of a committed partner. Like their traditional counterparts, neither Michelle nor Jason anticipated being where they are now. Yet work options and personal circumstances converged to leave them in a state of sustained singlehood. Though wistful about their single status, they also take solace—and a degree of pride—in their own self-reliance.

UNEASY REVERSALS

A small, but telling group of respondents are in relationships that reverse the classic gender division between earning and caring.[13] Not surprisingly, none of these women or men had sought or planned for this arrangement, which still contradicts deeply ingrained and widely held beliefs about who should be responsible for what. Yet a reversal of economic fortunes, with wives able to find more secure employment, made gender reversal not just the most sensible option, but often the only one. Dolores, a medical researcher, and Adam, a self-employed website developer, illustrate this dynamic:

Dolores grew up in southern California in a modest working-class neighborhood. Reared mostly by her mother after her parents divorced, she helped care for her younger sisters and felt fortunate to attend a nearby community college. Choosing a biology class because it fit with her work schedule, she discovered a love for the subject and decided to major in it. This decision proved fortunate in two ways: she found a calling and also met her husband-to-be, Steve. Also a biology major, he shared her interests and fully supported her growing desire to become a scientist.

At the urging of her favorite professor, Dolores applied and earned a fellowship to continue her studies at a four-year university. Around the same time, she also married Steve, who took a job working in a lab at a pharmaceutical company. Between Steve's job and her fellowship, they were able to make ends meet, and when she became pregnant unexpectedly, they decided to start a family. Despite the challenges of school, work, and limited finances, their past experiences overcoming financial hardship had left them feeling confident about handling the extra load.

As her graduation approached, Dolores faced a crossroads. Dolores received a generous fellowship to attend graduate school in Oregon just as Steve began to worry that his job was imperiled by impending layoffs. Knowing Steve would need to find another position in any case, they decided to move. In the beginning, all went well. Dolores made steady progress through her program, while Steve found another, albeit less promising, job as a lab technician. With fewer demands—or challenges—at work, Steve was able to take on the bulk of childcare, and they decided to have another child. Then matters took a downward turn. As Dolores approached the completion of her graduate degree, Steve lost his job. Unable to find another one, he grew increasingly withdrawn and depressed. Dolores hoped his prospects—and spirits—would improve when she received an offer to move back to California to join a research project at a medical school.

Now resettled again, Steve has still not been able to find a job and has become not just the family's primary caretaker, but a stay-at-home dad. Dolores continues to love her work, but she has become demoralized about the state of her marriage. Steve's emotional state continues to slide, and she feels torn between gratitude for his support at home and a mixture of worry and anger that their marital tensions signal a breakup to come.

As Dolores's career blossomed and her husband's job prospects shriveled, Dolores became her family's primary breadwinner. Adam, in contrast, became his family's primary caretaker when his wife's steady paycheck made it possible for him to follow a riskier work path:

> As far back as Adam can remember, he has preferred what he called "adventure." Estranged from his largely absent father and raised almost singlehandedly by his mother, he could hardly wait to leave school and join the military, which he did right after high school graduation. Rather than joining the infantry, however, he was assigned to data processing, where he discovered an interest and facility for computing.
>
> After several stints in the Army, Adam returned to his hometown, Kansas City, where he took a job at a local computer company. Several years later, however, the business began to falter and his job disappeared. He moved on to a new Internet venture that had just been started by a friend and coworker. Even if his earnings fluctuated with the ups and downs of a business whose future was unknown, he enjoyed working on a risky venture with a small group of friends.
>
> At about the same time, Adam met Tatiana. Because she shared his sense of adventure, he began to relax his doubts about settling down and several months later moved in with her. Living together allowed them to pool their incomes, and Tatiana's steady job as an administrative assistant in a well-established national corporation provided a measure of financial security (albeit at the modest level typically found in women-dominated office jobs) that they had never known. Several years later, when Tatiana was offered a transfer to California, they decided to marry and move to the heart of high-tech innovation.
>
> Today, Adam and Tatiana are living in a small apartment with their young son, Ethan. As the main breadwinner, Tatiana earns just enough to pay the family's bills but not enough to afford more spacious quarters, to save for the future, or even to afford childcare. She goes to work every day and relies on Adam to look after Ethan. Adam is affiliated with a "computer cooperative" that houses a self-styled group of hackers who share the rent on a small building. Every afternoon, Adam takes Ethan to his "office," where he works on his projects alongside other self-styled "nerds." He has some misgivings about depending on Tatiana's earnings, but he enjoys being a hands-on dad and believes his dream of making it big will eventually pay off for everyone. In the meantime, he does his best to ignore the looks and comments that sometimes come his way from neighbors and others who do not entirely approve.

Dolores and Adam are members of a small, but growing group of couples who have reversed the traditional division between breadwinning and caretaking. Given the persisting pressures on men to be "good providers"

(Bernard 1981; Townsend 2002), it is not surprising that these arrangements prompt varying degrees of discomfort. While Adam welcomed the opportunity to rely on his wife's paycheck so that he could work in a riskier but more satisfying way, he nevertheless could not escape the subtle and overt expressions of curiosity and skepticism when he tried to explain his situation to neighbors, acquaintances, and even friends. Dolores, too, appreciated the support of her husband, which made it possible for her to succeed beyond her anything she had dared to expect; but watching her husband fall into a chronic state of depression and disillusionment seemed a heavy price for both of them to pay. These diverse reactions reflect the cultural ambivalence that persists despite the growing changes in gender arrangements. Persisting cultural norms—especially those that stress the importance of paid work in measuring a man's worth in a market economy—exert a powerful force on people's emotional responses, even when their own preferences do not align with these values. It is not possible to escape the cultural context, even when one is not able or willing to conform.

It would be a mistake, however, to presume that only couples who trade places experience frustration. Most traditional couples also express disappointment about having to divide earning and caretaking.[14] Although the gender assignments differ, both arrangements stem from economic forces that are fueling the rise of both excessively time-demanding jobs and insecure work. In reversed cases, husbands face uncertain job prospects and financial insecurity while wives are able to find more secure employment with a steady income stream. Whether reversed or traditional, a similar set of economic pushes and pulls prompts couples to divide rather than share work and care.

PRACTICING EQUALITY

Whether traditional, reversed, or on their own, most of the women and men I interviewed sought to find meaning and satisfaction in their work-care arrangements. Yet most also hoped for a more integrated and equal balance than they had been able to achieve. A small group, however, did more than hope. About 15 percent had managed, usually against the odds and with great effort, to share work and care more or less equally. I use the modifier "more or less" because it is not easy either to define what equality means or to achieve it. All of these cases involve committed couples in which both partners are committed to sharing work and care, but their strategies for accomplishing these goals take varied—and not altogether satisfying—forms. Danny, for example, is determined to share everything with his wife, but he feels "like a salmon swimming upstream":

Danny grew up in a Latino community near San Francisco with his parents and three siblings. His father worked hard in construction to "keep a roof over our heads," and his mother devoted herself to the care and feeding of the family. Then, just as Danny finished high school, his father died suddenly of a heart attack.

Danny had always known he would need to work to put himself through college, but his father's death meant postponing college as well as plans to move out on his own. After several years of working in construction, Danny was able to save enough money to move out and enroll in a two-year college. Even though he continued to work full-time to support himself and pay for his educational expenses, he was able to perform well enough in his classes to transfer to a four-year college several hours away. Finally, he was able to live on his savings and devote his time to school.

After graduating with a major in business and finance, Danny took a job at a large brokerage firm. He liked the work, and his disciplined work habits and outgoing personality served him well. But the best part of this job was meeting Francesca, who worked on the same floor, several aisles over. After years of "playing the field," he realized he had found his "soulmate." As their relationship grew closer, they both moved onto jobs at different firms, which eased the discomfort of dating a coworker.

Describing himself as "old-fashioned," Danny did not live with Francesca until they were ready to marry. By then, Danny had set out on his own as a financial management consultant, while Francesca continued her work at an investment firm. When they realized a baby was on the way, they agreed it was important to raise their daughter, Alyssa, together. Neither felt comfortable hiring someone else to care for Alyssa, nor did they find it possible or desirable for either to quit work altogether.

Today Danny and Francesca are doing their best to share Alyssa's care and juggle it with their equally demanding jobs. Danny works at home every morning and hands the childcare off to Francesca in the afternoon, when she returns early from the office. Danny is convinced that parents are the best caretakers and is determined to do everything without hiring anyone else, even though he feels chronically exhausted. He worries that the meager childcare available in his community is both too expensive and not of high quality. He is eager to have another child, but wonders how they will manage and if they have the time, money, or energy to try.

Like Danny, Carmen also shares work and care with her spouse, Julio. In her case, however, they are caring for nieces and nephews who have become their "surrogate kids" even though they chose not to have their own biological children:

Carmen grew up in Colorado in a large, close-knit family, overseen by her father, the child of Mexican immigrants, and her mother, who emigrated from the Philippines. Without the funds to go to college, she joined the military after high school, where she spent the next decade living in different parts of the country, working in a variety of office jobs, and taking college-level courses. By the time she decided to return to civilian life, she was living in Northern California and decided to stay. She had also gained enough experience to land a job as an office manager in a small start-up.

Carmen proved to be an inspired and inspiring administrator. Her ability to oversee and motivate others more than compensated for her lack of technical acumen, and she soon became a valued member of the work team. After a few years, however, the company floundered and went out of business. Carmen, like most of her coworkers, moved to another startup. This pattern repeated itself with unnerving regularity as one company after another went out of business. But changing jobs also brought a network of contacts, which finally led her to a startup filled with past coworkers and friends. This time, instead of failing, the company was purchased by a major firm with a global presence, where Carmen now works as the division's administrative head.

In the midst of this dizzying series of job changes, Carmen met and married Jose, the "love of my life." Unlike the unpredictable nature of her work life, Carmen's marriage has proved strong and stable. They are, in Carmen's words, "a team." As a construction worker and small contractor, Jose has never been able to match Carmen's earnings; but he has worked steadily, and together, they have been able to buy a small house. Their home has become the center of a large extended family and a refuge for relatives who have fallen on hard times, including a niece and nephew who live with them because their own parents could not provide the stability they needed. They make every effort to share the load amid their frenetic schedules. With more flexibility during weekdays, Jose gets the kids to school and prepares evening dinners, while Carmen steps in on the weekends.

Today, Carmen marvels at how far she has come, but she nevertheless is prepared to move on, aware that her new employer could decide at any time to "take a different direction and leave us out on the street." At home, she takes pleasure and pride in her "adopted" children, which offset the wistfulness that her busy life with Jose did not leave time for them to have children of their own.

Carmen and Danny are both in stable relationships marked by a commitment to sharing work and care. Compared to their traditional, single, and reversed peers, they have come closer to achieving their aspirations. Yet they also feel, as Danny put it, "like I'm swimming against the tide." As a result, Danny is struggling to find the time to share care or to have another child, while Carmen has opted to care for other people's children rather than having her own. They both know their financial fortunes could change at any time, knowledge which adds to their worries about meeting the care obligations they now shoulder whether or not they dare to take on new ones. Practicing equality is not the same as "having it all." To the contrary, it is an insecure position that requires hard work, concerted effort, and countless sacrifices, and it may be lost at any time with little warning.

EXPLAINING DIVERGENT STRATEGIES: SHARED DILEMMAS, DIFFERENT COMPROMISES

Contemporary adults are fashioning a variety of strategies to meet the challenges of earning a living and caring for others in a transforming economic and social landscape. This diversity includes couples who are recreating separate gender spheres and singles who are living without support from or obligations to a committed partner, but it also includes women and men who find themselves in gender-reversed relationships and those who are dividing work and care more equally. Why did people fashion such divergent strategies?

Individual preferences and desires cannot explain the differences among traditionalists, reversers, egalitarians, and do-it-on-their-owners. To the contrary, most women and men aspired to a better balance and integration of work and care than they were able to achieve. Neither gender identity nor individual personal preferences can thus account for the shape of a person's work-care strategy. Instead, a set of factors in the workplace and the domestic sphere converged in different combinations to prompt diverse reactions to work-care conflicts.

In the case of traditional and reversed couples, the partner with the more stable, but also more time-demanding job became the main breadwinner, leaving the partner with less promising work options to take on the lion's share of caretaking. In most instances, men enjoyed the best prospects at work but also faced the highest work demands and pressures; but when a woman's job offered more security, income, and/or advancement opportunities, she became the primary financial provider despite the cultural injunction that places this responsibility on men. Whether the job of breadwinning fell to a man or a woman, the need for one person to hold onto a job and build a career by working long hours without letup placed stringent limits on the options of the other. As the default, if not preferred, arrangement became leaving responsibility for caretaking to the person with fewer opportunities at work, the process of dividing work and care became self-sustaining.

In contrast, many people were unable to establish a stable, enduring intimate relationship, although this situation had different implications for men and women. When men were unable or (in some cases) unmotivated to find secure work, they often became wary of making a long-term commitment as well. Accepting the traditional view that a married man should provide for his family, many concluded they were therefore "unmarriageable." Among those who were able to find secure work, marriage appeared to entail the loss of too much autonomy in choosing a work path that did not offer a sufficiently large or steady paycheck. Yet the freedom from the pressure to be a family provider also left these men searching for ways to create close ties to others amid a dearth of commitments to work or care.

Single women were more likely to face a different dilemma. While some women opted to remain childless (and thus faced challenges similar to those of single, childless men), most were rearing children without the help or support of an intimate partner. Far from having too few commitments or responsibilities, these single mothers were the primary providers of both income and care. While they looked to others to help with care, they also had to scale back work commitments—and often ambitions. More often than not, it meant shifting to less time-demanding work that also offered fewer financial rewards and less potential for advancement.

Finally, egalitarians confronted a different set of options than their traditional, reversed, or single peers. They were able to find jobs they found satisfying and to create relationships with partners who were equally committed to work. Some concluded that this equal commitment to work left little room for having a child and taking on care responsibilities without risking the strength of their relationship as well as their own mental and physical health. Yet other egalitarians endeavored to share work and care despite the obstacles. They chose work that offered some degree of flexibility as well as a partner who was also willing to do the same, even if it meant sacrificing some degree of work security. Yet these egalitarian parents could rely on few supports—either at work or in their communities—to help sustain a shared arrangement. Pulling back from work, even temporarily, threatened their long-term financial security, while working long hours threatened their relationship and emotional well-being. Like single parents, egalitarian parents found that doing it all did not mean having it all. Whether they opted to remain childless or to share caretaking, all egalitarian partnerships faced a distinct, if different, set of pressures and trade-offs.

Stepping back to survey the entire landscape, it is clear that changes in both the nature of jobs and the shape of relationships are generating a diverse set of work-care strategies. The growth in economic insecurity and job uncertainty makes change inevitable and unavoidable, but the shape that change assumes also depends on how people navigate their personal lives in this new economic context. These two domains—that is, access (or lack of access) to secure work and the ability (or inability) to establish a stable relationship—can converge in different ways for individuals. And for those with partners, her or his partner's work options are added to the complex mix that is generating a mosaic of strategies.

Despite their differences, all these strategies represent efforts to fashion a coherent life path amid rising job uncertainty, increasingly fragile relationships, and mounting work-family conflicts. In an earlier era, gender offered a resolution to the institutional conflicts between work and care; for better or worse, men specialized in market work and women in the nonmarket activities of caretaking. Today, the rise of both unpredictable work paths and optional relationships has undermined this once strong link between gender, work, and care. Yet work and parenting structures and norms forged in an earlier era have actually intensified in this new one, not just continuing to presume that the "ideal worker" always puts work first (Williams 2000) and the ideal parent practices "intensive" caretaking (Hays 1996) but even raising the standard for how much time should be devoted to both. The traditional bargain between breadwinning husbands and caretaking wives is increasingly unappealing and out of reach, but the cultural and structural supports for more balanced and egalitarian resolutions have yet to emerge. This context of incomplete change creates intractable dilemmas. It is not surprising that these dilemmas prompt diverse strategies, each unsatisfactory in its own way.

BEYOND "HAVING IT ALL"

Despite an almost universally expressed desire to strike a more equal and integrated balance between earning and caring, my respondents developed a range of strategies that nevertheless fall far short of this aspiration. Even those who strove for equal sharing faced exhausting schedules and strains in their relationships. The new economy has irreversibly eroded a system of strict gender differences, with secure work available to most men and secure marriages available to most women; but it has not replaced this once-entrenched order with newly institutionalized and satisfying ways to resolve the dilemmas and conflicts between paid work and private care.

In this context, "having it all" is a misleading and even dangerous meta-phor that obscures the institutional roots of everyone's difficulties. Most often used to assert that no one can have it all, the phrase implies that those who try—especially if they are women—are selfish, greedy, and doomed to fail. Yet there is no necessary conflict between work and care. This conflict is rooted, instead, in institutional arrangements that continue to separate private caretaking from paid work, to devalue and privatize carework of any kind, to presume that market activities should always take precedence, and to assume that households can depend on a family breadwinner (pre-sumably, a man) with access to a secure, well-paying job. Amid the new job and relationship uncertainties facing women and men alike, the wish to combine paid work and caretaking is anything but selfish. To the contrary, secure work and gender-neutral options for integrating work and care are now key requirements for insuring the well-being of children, the stability of relationships, and the economic health of societies. Freud once declared that the ability to work and love are the twin hallmarks of a healthy per-son (Erikson 1963). In the context of the new economy, a healthy society depends on creating institutions that allow women and men to integrate and balance work and care.

What form can and should these institutions take? What policies would ease the hardships that contradictory change has produced? And what are the political possibilities in the US context? A policy approach that stresses both equality and care offers the most effective and just response to the work-care conflicts wrought by the new economy. Achieving these goals means creating policies that provide equal opportunities for women at work, for men in caregiving, and for families to weather unpredictable changes in their economic fortunes and household composition. Though no society has fully attained these outcomes, the Scandinavian model comes closest by providing all citizens with a minimum economic floor, universal childcare (along with healthcare and education), and "use it or lose it" paid parental leave policies that encourage men's caregiving and lesson the penalties for taking time out from work. As a package, such poli-cies provide greater economic security, lessen work-care conflicts, and con-strain inequality within and between families. They also begin to redress the imbalance that places a higher social and economic value on market work than on caregiving in its many forms.

The possibilities for creating such a work-care policy package—and the steps needed to achieve it—depend on political context, and the American political context poses daunting obstacles. Americans tend to possess a well-known distrust of broad-based government policies that many per-ceive as "interfering" unduly in the realm of private life, and the rise of family diversity has generated a strong backlash from those who wish to restore an earlier work-family order. Ironically, the rise of work-care conflicts also drains the time and energy of workers and parents who need new social supports, leaving them ill positioned to actively fight for policies that might ease their plight (Putnam 2000).

Despite these roadblocks, however, we have seen a marked increase in support for gender flexibility and work-family integration, especially among younger generations (Pedulla and Thebaud 2015). The growing support for paid family leave, nationally subsidized health insurance, and a higher minimum wage suggests that most Americans are ready to entertain transformative social policies. If the moment has arrived to overcome past political stalemates, then the first step in this process is to distinguish between the social changes that are unavoidable and the options available to shape social arrangements through collective choices. Economic uncertainty and relationship fragility, along with diversity and fluidity in family forms, are integral aspects of inexorable economic and demographic shifts and thus not likely to reverse. These forces will continue, whether or not some pockets of American society wish it were not so. Yet the decline of secure jobs and stable traditional marriages does not determine the shape of the future. That depends on how—and if—social actors develop policies to address the new tensions these changes create between work and care.

As demographic and economic shifts integral to the new economy continue to transform the lives of successive generations, the conflicts between work and care will only become more apparent. Change is inescapable, and going back is not an option. Going forward, the choice is between new forms of inequality and insecurity or the creation of new supports for equalizing and integrating responsibility for work and care. The good news is that, alongside new insecurities and inequalities, the revolutionary shifts now taking place have created an unprecedented opportunity to achieve greater gender equality within families and to reverse the growing economic inequality between families. In a society as diverse and divided as the United States, the political challenge is to find common ground to forge a new social contract that realigns our work and caregiving structures so that workers and parents may pursue the work-care strategy they prefer without fear of falling down or falling apart.

NOTES

1. I use the term "institutional" to refer both to structural arrangements, such as the family wage that made it possible for an employed father to support a household

on his income, and to cultural norms, such as the ideal of the "good provider" father and the "stay-at-home" mother.

2. In today's environment, women are almost as likely as men to hold a paid job and consequently face job insecurity. Job insecurity is on the rise at all class levels, but is especially high among wage workers in the service sector, where women are especially likely to find employment. (See, for example, Hacker 2008, 2011).

3. Rates of divorce and single parenthood are higher among the less affluent, but these rates have risen among all classes and economic levels. Cherlin (2014) provides an in-depth analysis of changes in the economic prospects of working-class families that make stable marriage difficult to obtain or sustain.

4. Recent research has confirmed my findings that aspirations for more egalitarian relationships and a more equal personal balance between work and family life are rising, especially among younger generations of women and men (Gerson 2011; Pedulla and Thebaud 2015).

5. The sample includes forty women, forty men, and one male-to-female transsexual, for a total of eighty-one respondents. The interviews gathered in-depth information about everyone's past and current relationships, but none of the interviewees are in a relationship with another respondent. All of the names are pseudonyms.

6. A recent cover of *Time Magazine*, for example, showcased a young woman lounging on the floor with a cell phone in her hand and a headline above her that proclaimed, "The Me, Me, Me Generation" (Stein 2013).

7. My rationale for combining singles who are childless with those who are rearing children is to highlight the options and dilemmas contemporary adults face if and when they cannot look to a partner (whether or not that partner is a legal spouse) to share the responsibilities of breadwinning or caretaking. By doing so, I do not mean to imply that being married—or in a committed relationship—is "better." To the contrary, many adults, as my interviews show, face good reasons to remain single and perceive notable advantages in light of their other options. In this sense, I disagree with those who argue that marriage is an inherently preferable state. (See, for example, Waite and Gallagher 2000.)

8. Jerry Jacobs and I considered the simultaneous rise of both time-demanding jobs and underemployment in *The Time Divide* (2004).

9. According to the Wang, Parker, and Taylor (2013), "breadwinner moms," including mothers who are the sole or the primary source of their family's income, now make up 40 percent of all households with children under age 18 (compared to 11 percent in 1960). Among this group, 37 percent are married mothers who earn more than their husbands, and 63 percent are single mothers.

10. In an important sense, "traditional" is a misnomer for the homemaker-breadwinner pattern, which emerged in the 19th century, reached its peak in the mid-20th century, and is now in steep decline. Yet the term has become so ubiquitous that it is difficult to avoid. Based on my findings in *The Unfinished Revolution*, I refer to a "neo-traditional" pattern that continues to stress women's responsibility for care and men's for earning an income, even if the woman holds a paid job (Gerson, 2011).

11. This is a clear example of "the motherhood penalty" that has been well documented in experimental and other quantitative studies (Correll et al. 2007; Budig and England 2001).

12. Recent studies show that fathers are likely to experience as much or more work-family conflict as mothers. A survey conducted by the Families and Work Institute reports, for example, that 60 percent of fathers in dual-earner couples report

experiencing work-family conflict, compared to 47 percent of men (Aumann et al. 2011). This discrepancy is likely due to the pressure on fathers to work longer hours.

13. This percentage corresponds to the Wang, Parker, and Taylor's estimate that about 15 percent of households with children under eighteen contain a married couple in which the wife earns more.

14. Recent research continues to provide evidence that sustained stay-at-home motherhood holds longer-term perils. Frech and Damaske (2012) find, for example, that continuously employed mothers report better health at forty than mothers who were full-time homemakers and even those who worked part-time or intermittently.

REFERENCES

Aumann, Kerstin, Ellen Galinsky, and Kenneth Matos. 2011. The New Male Mystique. National Study of the Changing Workforce. New York: Families and Work Institute. http://familiesandwork.org/downloads/NewMaleMystique.pdf.

Beck, Ulrich, and Elisabeth Beck-Gernsheim. 2001. Translated by Patrick Camiller. *Individualization: Institutionalized Individualism and its Social and Political Consequences.* London: SAGE.

Belkin, Lisa. 2003. "The Opt-Out Revolution." *New York Times Magazine*, October 26.

Bernard, Jessie. 1981. "The Good Provider Role: Its Rise and Fall." *American Psychologist* 36(1):1–12.

Budig, Michelle J., and Paula England. 2001. "The Wage Penalty for Motherhood." *American Sociological Review* 66(2):204–225.

Cherlin, Andrew J. 2014. *Labor's Love Lost: The Rise and Fall of the Working-Class Family in America.* New York: Russell Sage Foundation.

Correll, Shelley J., Stephen Benard, and In Paik. 2007. "Getting a Job: Is There a Motherhood Penalty?" *American Journal of Sociology* 112(5):1297–1338.

Cotter, David A., Joan M. Hermsen, and Reeve Vanneman. 2011. "The End of the Gender Revolution? Gender Role Attitudes from 1977 to 2008." *American Journal of Sociology* 117(1): 259–289.

DiPrete, Thomas A., and Claudia Buchmann. 2013. *The Rise of Women: The Growing Gender Gap in Education and What It Means for American Schools.* New York: Russell Sage Foundation.

England, Paula. 2010. "The Gender Revolution: Uneven and Stalled." *Gender & Society* 24(2):149–166.

Erikson, Erik. 1963. *Childhood and Society.* New York: W.W. Norton.

Frech, Adrianne, and Sarah A. Damaske. 2012. "The Relationships Between Mothers' Work Pathways and Physical and Mental Health." *Journal of Health and Social Behavior* 53(4):369–412.

Gerson, Kathleen. 2011. *The Unfinished Revolution: Coming of Age in a New Era of Gender, Work, and Family.* New York: Oxford University Press.

Hacker, Jacob S. 2008. *The Great Risk Shift: The New Economic Insecurity and the Decline of the American Dream.* New York: Oxford University Press.

Hacker, Jacob S. 2011. "Working Families at Risk: Understanding and Confronting the New Economic Insecurity." In *Old Assumptions, New Realities: Economic Security for Working Families in the 21st Century*, edited by Robert D. Plotnick,

Marcia K. Meyers, Jennifer Romich, and Steven Rathgeb Smith, 31–70. New York: Russell Sage Foundation.

Hays, Sharon. 1996. *The Cultural Contradictions of Motherhood*. New Haven, CT: Yale University Press.

Jacobs, Jerry A., and Kathleen Gerson. 2004. *The Time Divide: Work, Family, and Gender Inequality*. Cambridge, MA: Harvard University Press.

Kalleberg, Arne L. 2011. *Good Jobs, Bad Jobs: The Rise of Polarized and Precarious Employment Systems in the United States, 1970s to 2000s*. New York: Russell Sage Foundation.

Klinenberg, Eric. 2012. *Going Solo: The Extraordinary Rise and Surprising Appeal of Living Alone*. New York: Penguin.

Lang, Molly Monahan, and Barbara J. Risman. 2010. "A 'Stalled' Revolution or a Still Unfolding One?" In *Families as They Really Are*, edited by Barbara J. Risman, 408–412. New York: W.W. Norton.

Livingston, Gretchen. 2013. "The Rise of Single Fathers: A Ninefold Increase Since 1960." Washington, DC: Pew Research Center. July 2.

Pedulla, David, and Sarah Thebaud. 2015. "Can We Finish the Revolution? Gender, Work-Family Ideals, and Institutional Constraint." *American Sociological Review* 80(1):116–139.

Putnam, Robert D. 2000. *Bowling Alone: The Collapse and Revival of American Community*. New York: Simon & Schuster.

Rosin, Hanna. 2012. *The End of Men and the Rise of Women*. New York: Riverhead.

Stein, Joel. 2013. "The Me, Me, Me Generation: Millennials are Lazy, Entitled Narcissists Who Still Live with Their Parents." *Time*, May 20.

Stone, Pamela. 2007. *Opting Out? Why Women Really Quit Careers and Head Home*. Berkeley: University of California Press.

Townsend, Nicholas W. 2002. *The Package Deal: Marriage, Work, and Fatherhood in Men's Lives*. Philadelphia: Temple University Press.

Waite, Linda J., and Maggie Gallagher. 2000. *The Case for Marriage: Why Married People Are Happier, Healthier, and Better Off Financially*. New York: Broadway.

Wang, Wendy, Kim Parker, and Paul Taylor. 2013. "Breadwinner Moms." Washington, DC: Pew Research Center. May 29.

Wilcox, W. Bradford. 2010. "When Marriage Disappears: The Retreat from Marriage in Middle America." Institute for American Values, University of Virginia. Charlottesville, VA: The National Marriage Project.

Williams, Joan. 2000. *Unbending Gender: Why Family and Work Conflict and What To Do About It*. New York: Oxford University Press.

CHAPTER 7

✧

Racialized Family Ideals

Breadwinning, Domesticity, and the Negotiation of Insecurity

ENOBONG HANNAH BRANCH

The basic outlines of postindustrial employment restructuring in the United States are, by now, familiar: Globalization, the rise of the service sector, increasing returns to higher education, and a political environment that favors capital over labor have each contributed to a polarized employment structure with fewer stable jobs for the middle and working classes (Kalleberg 2009). To some degree insecurity was always expected among low and semiskilled workers in the secondary labor market, but the extension of the trend to skilled workers in the primary labor market as well during the 2000s marked the transition to broad labor market employment insecurity.

Scholarly accounts of rising employment insecurity have developed without close examination of its racialized and gendered implications (Andersen 2001). The Great Recession, for instance, was commonly referred to as the "mancession," due to the disproportionate loss of men's job in the construction and manufacturing sectors of the economy (Bukszpan 2012). The number of stay-at-home dads, Pew researchers found "reached its highest point—2.2 million—in 2010, just after the official end of the recession" (Livingston 2014). Nearly a quarter of stay-at-home dads reported that they were home because they could not find work. While men were being laid off and women's jobs seemed more secure during the initial period of the recession, women suffered disproportionate job losses during the recovery (Boushey 2011).

The gendered impact of the Great Recession and its aftermath are markers of the US institutional arrangement as a flexible labor market and the "fluctuation ... [in] men's breadwinning status," Cha and Thébaud argue, "matters for men's gender ideology." Fluctuation permits men to maintain a "normative perception that a man's earnings are primary, whereas his spouse's are secondary, even when men earn less than their partners" (Cha and Thébaud 2009, 237). Men's gender ideology, they argue, "is distinctly related to their individual breadwinning experiences," and is, "negotiated through the private experience of norm contestation and resolution within the family." Flexible labor market arrangements are a hallmark of rising employment insecurity with clear consequences for the family. How are women negotiating men's job insecurity in the context of gendered expectations?

While access to secure jobs and the ability to provide for one's family has traditionally been central to conceptions of hegemonic masculinity, the ability of men to meet the ideal, historically, was fundamentally raced and classed (Connell 1993; Mutari, Power, and Figart 2002). Conceptions of black and white femininity were also defined in opposition to one other. Black femininity was defined by the expectation (and often necessity) to work on behalf of the family and white femininity was defined by cultural norms that discouraged work upon marriage in order to care for the family (Hill 2004; Barnes 2015). While the feminist movement certainly challenged this notion, white married women are relatively recent entrants into the labor market, and whites' relatively more secure economic base may have facilitated the maintenance of traditional gender roles (Damaske 2011). Hence, the very meaning of rising employment insecurity and desirability of work for women may vary by racial, gender, and class position.

What is the influence of uncertainty and fear of downward mobility in an insecure economy on conceptions of masculinity, specifically the breadwinning role? Insomuch as the rise of insecure work has undermined white men's historical capacity to fulfill the traditional breadwinner role and live up to the cultural dictates of masculinity, what are the implications for the family? How are black and white women making sense of the rise of insecure work and its implications for the necessity of their own labor, and how are their experiences informed by their economic realities and historical expectations drawn from experiences of economic privilege or exploitation? Tackling these questions requires situating contemporary negotiations of insecurity in a historical frame.

RACIALIZED FAMILY IDEALS

The rise of the gendered division of labor in the nineteenth century, which separated work into public and private spheres and relegated women's labor to the latter, created the now normative gender ideals of the male breadwinner and the female homemaker. The "cult of true womanhood" and the cultural support for gender norms, however, excluded black women (Barnes 2015; Connell 1993; Jones 1986). The industrial revolution birthed and the Jim Crow era nurtured distinct racialized family ideals. Indeed the attempts of black women and their husbands to redefine their family roles post-slavery was met with intense resistance as the economic recovery of the South was dependent on their labor (Landry 2000). At the same time that white women were encouraged to hearken to hearth and home, black women's own familial needs were to be secondary to the demands of their employer (Jones 1986).

Social reformers whose organizing led to the passage of minimum wage legislation at the state level between 1912–1923 aimed to establish "protective legislation" for working immigrant women to "promulgate American values, specifically a male-breadwinner family in which wives did not work for pay" (Mutari, Power, and Figart 2002, 38). The ultimate passage of the Fair Labor Standards Act, which set the federal minimum wage in 1938, largely abandoned the protective aim for working women and instead focused on securing a minimum wage floor for nonunion affiliated men, which effectively "reinforced the male breadwinner family as a marker of whiteness during this period" (Mutari, Power, and Figart 2002, 54). Black women's labor, however, was culturally accepted and economically necessary, thus the occupations and industries that employed the majority of black men (and women) were excluded (Palmer 1995; Mink 1996).

The 'traditional' family was an aspirational ideal that was an uneasy fit for the majority of Americans who lacked the economic means to subsist on one income, but it was also a white ideal. Magazines in the mid-1950s, such as *Esquire* and *Life*, disparaged working wives as a "menace" and considered their employment a "disease" (Landry 2000, 14–15). Television portrayed the iconic postwar family in *Leave it to Beaver*; June was the perfect housewife and Ward, the breadwinner, always came home in time for dinner (Coontz 1993). Black women stood outside of this cultural ideal and were judged harshly as a result as "less than a moral, 'true' woman" (Giddings 1984, 47; Jones 1986).

Black women forged an alternate model of femininity, a "co-breadwinner" model that aimed to reconcile the constraint of black men's depressed wages with a valuation of women's contribution to the household and to the community (Landry 2000, 73). Yet even this alternate image was debated among black women and at times resisted by black men (Franklin 2000, 83). The relationship between domesticity, breadwinning, and race was irreconcilable inasmuch as black families' desire for autonomy to independently determine the 'right' roles for themselves was constrained in an economic climate and racial era that overtly limited their choices (Branch 2011). Widespread racial discrimination limited black men's earnings, requiring black women to work (Hill 2004; Baca Zinn 1990). The pursuit and advancement of the co-breadwinner model was by middle class black women, especially activists, who willingly merged the public and private spheres juggling work and family responsibilities to further racial uplift (Franklin 2000, 83).

EXPECTATIONS AND THE RISE OF INSECURE WORK

The rise of insecure work after 1980 was most disruptive of white men's employment experiences, as women and racial minorities had often been confined to insecure employment conditions until that period (Branch 2011; Stainback and Tomaskovic-Devey, 2012). Women, especially white women, have responded to increased economic vulnerability of their families by increasing their financial contribution to the household. The 2000s witnessed a dramatic growth in female breadwinners; Pew Researchers found "40% of all households with children under the age of 18 include mothers who are either the sole or primary source of income for the family" (Wang, Parker, and Taylor 2013).

The inability of men to meet the expectations of the traditional breadwinner role impacts familial expectations leading them to resist egalitarian relationships and insist on traditional gender roles (Gerson 1993; Zuo 1997; Crompton 1999). Gerson (2011) found that even men who embrace egalitarian ideals fall back on a "neotraditional model" when pressed. Yet Baca Zinn (1990) critiques the normative focus on the arrangements of the traditional white family, and argues that what appears new for whites now (e.g., a rise in female breadwinners or egalitarian relationships) has been common among blacks for years. Differences in "family lifestyles," Baca Zinn argues, reflect differences in "structural patterns . . . because social and economic conditions produce and may even require diverse family arrangements" (1990, 73).

The historically disparate economic and cultural realities of black and white women inform their expectations of men and employment security (Baca Zinn 1990). More than just structuring their worldview, the expectations of black and white women act as "empty shapes" whose contours are defined, in part, I argue, by history and are the lens through which they make sense of the present and "demand personal accountability" or perhaps structural recourse. (Pugh 2015, 30). Pugh (2015) argues that expectations do the work of shaping our emotions, "generating what we feel and also restricting what we are allowed to feel. Expectations tell us who exceeded their obligations and who fell short, and thus about whom we might feel resentful, grateful, or impressed" (30).

The rise of insecure work and the erasure of the distinction between the primary and secondary labor market, which left all workers vulnerable to uncertainty, stands in stark contrast to a labor market history and white women's expectations for security procured by their husband's breadwinning (Newman 1993). What are the emotions generated by the disjuncture between expectations and economic reality? Does black women's distinct racial history with economic insecurity differently shape their expectations of and emotions about black men? Is economic struggle understood as individual failure or is there recognition of the structural barriers to success (Newman 1999b)?

DATA

To understand black and white women's expectations of masculinity, particularly, breadwinning in an age of insecurity, my research team conducted forty-two in-depth interviews with twenty-three Black women and nineteen white women in the summer of 2015.[1] The majority of white women were married (twelve), divorced and cohabitating (two), or partnered (one); only three out of nineteen were single-never married.[2] The majority of black women were single-never married (eleven), although a substantial number were married (six), partnered (four), or divorced (two). The interviews took place in a medium-sized diverse city in New England. This city has a diversified economy anchored in healthcare and education, as well as manufacturing. While it experienced a decline in manufacturing jobs in the 1980s and thereafter, the city also includes job sectors that experienced growth.

Interviews ranged from 1.5 to 3.5 hours and gathered information on their employment experiences and perceptions of insecurity, as well as their influence on men, the family, and chances for getting ahead in America. Participants were between the ages of thirty-five and fifty-five, when individuals are generally expected to have attained stable jobs. All except one had at least some college education and many had advanced degrees. Given their age and educational level, these women likely anticipated attaining relative security yet are grappling with the actual experience of or risk of insecurity that all workers today must contend with. The vast majority had household incomes over $40,000 and those with lower incomes were currently unemployed or underemployed, and thus earning less than they would have had they been employed in their previous occupations.

How did my participants make sense of rising employment insecurity? Did white and black women have different expectations of men given their historical experiences with economic privilege and exploitation? Five key and related themes emerged out of black and white women's narratives: 1) the persistent breadwinner ideal; 2) cracks in the armor of masculinity; 3) racialized expectations; 4) the tyranny of gender norms; and 5) resisting gender roles.

IDEALIZING THE TRADITIONAL FAMILY

The male breadwinner exists as a persistent ideal among black and white women despite its increasing economic and practical obsolescence. The majority of black and white women held traditional expectations of the male breadwinning role, or thought men did. Often it was not clear where women themselves fell between simply acknowledging a widely accepted cultural ideal and buying into it. What was clear was the near unanimous influence of the ideal on naturalizing the gendered division of labor. Take for example, Kelly, a forty-seven-year-old white woman, who said, "I think it's through prehistoric time that the man is the one that's supposed to be giving the bread on the table, this and that. I think that's what they're feeling." Keisha, a fifty-four-year-old black woman largely echoed her sentiment:

> If you think about it from a historical [perspective], men were providers, and
> I think probably deep down, though they may not have been ... sometimes
> I think that was how we evolved. You know, they were the hunters, the survivors
> and the providers, and we were supposed to be taking care of the kids. I mean,
> that was how we were—if you think about way back when, that's how the family
> structure was. Things have changed so much since then, but I still think men
> ultimately want to provide for their kids and their family.

Both Kelly and Keisha reference a notion of the historical past that shapes their understanding of the present.

For Kelly it's "prehistoric," for Keisha it's "historical," but both do not question the expectation that the man should provide, and both idealize a vision of the traditional family that is historically inaccurate (Coontz 1993). White women in preindustrial times were central to the functioning of their households; the rise of domesticity, many argue, robbed them of their formerly productive household role and made them dependent on their spouses (Cowan 1985). Black women's role in the economic survival of the household is also well documented; only black middle-class men were able to meet the cultural dictates of provision and most of their wives resisted the domestic role and insisted on the value of their paid labor (Franklin 2000; Baca Zinn 1990). Both Keisha and Kelly's odes to a "prehistoric," or "hunter/survivor" past romanticize a gendered model of provision and illustrate the lasting impact and effectiveness of the cultural messages of the nineteenth and twentieth centuries. This is all the more salient, since Keisha and Kelly faced distinct economic realities. Keisha is a single-never-married therapist with an advanced degree, whereas Kelly is a married medical assistant with an Associate's degree. Yet both convey similar expectations of what men believe about male provision.

Lacy, a forty-six-year-old white married woman, was underemployed by choice at the time of our interview (given her college degree and work experience) because she was frustrated in previous positions that matched her skills. Her perspective on male breadwinning focused on the family and men's responsibility. "Well, if the man has a family," she said, "you need to be a provider, you provide safety and security to your family." Her emphasis on provision was how she defined "the job" of manhood: "He is the breadwinner, he is the main support, he is going to be the only supporter of our family." Lacy offers a fascinating perspective on male breadwinning that stands in stark contrast to women's responsibility. Although she is college-educated and able to earn more money if she could tolerate unfulfilling jobs she does not have to:

> So, when I come to him and say, "What would you think about me quitting my job? Do you think we could do it?" I'm honestly asking him because I have no idea. In some respects, I feel like that's wrong of me. I think I should be more involved, know more, be a contributor to that ... And I don't want to. I don't want to. And I have that freedom because my job pays so much less than his, I have that freedom where he doesn't. And so, he's here, so okay, so a man in America is a provider and, um ...

It was his "job" to provide and her low wages gave her "freedom." Her care-free and cavalier approach to work and financial responsibility did not begin in marriage but has crystallized within it, as she stopped doing the things that she "didn't handle that well," such as manage her finances. Although Lacy feels some guilt about the burden this places on her husband and even acknowledges that it may be unfair, she does not want to change. In the end, for Lacy, breadwinning is the man's responsibility.

Lacy's point of view is steeped in a traditional ideal of male breadwinning. Unlike Keisha and Kelly who reference a historical ideal of provision for men that departed from their present economic circumstances, Lacy anchored her breadwinning ideal in the present. For Lacy, the male bread-winner was not just a historical model but also a contemporary goal. While Lacy's view was in some ways unusual, she was not alone. Rhonda, a forty-two-year-old single black woman, described a good man as a "hard worker," who "wants to provide for his . . . kids or he has a family, this is what your life is." While Rhonda's life does not match the ideal, her perception of what that ideal should be is clear, "You're really trying to work to keep them safe, to keep them happy, to keep them financially stable. All of that. To try and provide a good life for them."

Rhonda, like Lacy, is advocating for a traditional family ideal, where it is the man's responsibility to provide. For black women, the majority of whom were single, the adherence to this ideal seems contradictory to their desire for a mate, given black men's earnings. Ashley, a forty-eight-year-old single-never-married black woman, says "Now, to be quite honest with you, I got my girlfriends, and we get together and we be like, I don't want nobody if he ain't making $100,000." This salary is 40 percent more than she makes, despite this stated ideal shared among girlfriends, Ashley is more undecided than she appears. "I can work with a guy that's only bringing $40,000 home and I'm making $80,000. I can work with that . . . so I'm not one of those, you know, women that [says to men] you're the breadwinner."

Where does Ashley really fall? At first it appears that she is resolutely in the traditional camp and desires a man that can provide for her despite her high earnings, yet she doubles back and expresses a contrary view where she can work with whatever the man earns; "he can be a trash man," she says. Ashley shares a story of a friend that seems to guard her expectations: "I think that's what's really yielded her a lot of her issues, because she believes that a man is supposed to take care of the house." For Ashley, this cautionary tale (Hochschild 1989) leads her to adjust her expectations, "My philosophy is while I don't need you to take care of me, I can take care of myself, but whatever you have, let's put it together." While Ashley began with the stated ideal adhering to a male primary breadwinner norm, in the end Ashley is conflicted, between acknowledging the ideal as a powerful cultural trope and buying into it.

IT'S "HARD" FOR MEN: CRACKS IN THE ARMOR OF MASCULINITY

Despite the persistence of the male breadwinner as an idealized target, black and white women know that men are struggling; this knowledge creates cracks in the armor of masculinity. Unlike the ideal of the male breadwinner, which was grounded primarily in a false perception of history and sometimes a desire to return to that, black and white women's understanding of the hardship the breadwinner role poses came from reflections on the challenges in their present relationships (Coontz 1993). Phoebe, a fifty-four-year-old married white woman, bluntly described the challenge of men who fell short: "How are you going to be satisfied with your life if you can't at least provide?" She describes this need to provide as being "very caveman" and connected to men's "sense of self." "I know it was hard for my husband when I made more money consistently because I was a salaried person," Phoebe recalled. "There was a part of him that was like, 'wait a minute I'm supposed to earn more money than you.'"

Claire, a forty-one-year-old married white woman, reflects on the response of multiple men in her life to not fulfilling traditionally masculine roles. "It's been really hard on my husband," she says, but "I mean, I have known a large number of men who've ended up doing like either splitting care taking or being out of the labor force and being that home caretaker. I mean I have one friend who loves it." This friend she describes as a "grasshopper," a free spirit who is comfortable going against the grain. His wife has a solid professional career that frees them from financial concerns and he is "devastatingly handsome" and "totally happy ... greeting his wife with an apron on and like kissing her." But for most men, Claire's view is less sanguine, "I think that for many men, it's profoundly destabilizing to feel like they're not fulfilling these older ideas about like (deepens voice) 'what it means to be a man.'"

Callie, a fifty-year-old married white lesbian women, opined that men's "ego" was "tied up" when the woman is supporting the family. She recalled an old male friend who lost his job and never "recaptured his former glory." Callie continued "his wife who was always working in a medical field got a very good job at the corporate level. Ultimately they divorced and he committed suicide." While Callie's story may seem extreme, Kelly, the aforementioned forty-seven-year-old white woman, described men's inability to earn money and contribute in similar terms, "It's horrible for them, it's like death." Both Kelly and Callie suggest that the pressures of the breadwinner role are suffocating many men. Kelly again remarks, "I think for men it's so much harder. I think women snap out of it much more quickly than men."

Black men face a similar fate, some women acknowledged. When asked how men are coping with the mounting challenge to provide, Keisha answered:

> I think they're probably angry. They may, you know, check out, you know? If you're not—you know, if you're not happy in your job, and—or just the pressure, you walk away. You may walk away from your family. You may turn to drugs, turn to alcohol, turn to, whatever other things, just because you can't do what you feel you need to do for your family, or other things. You may feel like, well, I'm going to get it some kind of way, and then it leads to trouble. So I think it makes it hard. . . . You know, they don't just want to, not do right, but either it's education, or just the struggles, or the temptations, or all of those things lead them to do something else, you know?

Ashley, a forty-eight-year-old single black woman said, "I know it's hard. It's hard, and you know what, I didn't realize that. It's—I think it's extra hard for men than it is for women—black men more so than black women. It's very hard." Black and white women both perceived cracks in the armor of masculinity; while the breadwinner ideal persisted, most women could and did point to instances where it harmed men themselves or stunted relationships.

RACIALIZED EXPECTATIONS AND THE STABILITY OF THE BREADWINNER IDEAL

Race, however differently, shaped the expectations black and white women had for their lives and, by extension, the expectations that they had of men. Stephanie, for example, a forty-eight-year-old married white woman, compared her life to her mother's. "Well my mom is a stay-at-home mom. She quit her job after she had my brother and then she stopped working." Hence, the male breadwinner model was not simply a traditional ideal for Stephanie but a childhood reality that she measured her current family situation by. Being a stay-at-home mother was "something I always would like to do, because [my mother] had that, I would like that . . . So I feel like

my daughter ... we're missing out on some things because I'm at work."
While Stephanie is resigned to the fact that "everybody around us is doing
the same thing" and "the norm has changed" she would welcome a return
to not-too-distant familial past of economic security that limited her role
to caring in the home.

Betsy, a forty-four-year-old married white woman, also drew on history
to situate the expectations and desires of contemporary women:

> Because, if you think back to the 50s and 60s, the husband went to work, the
> woman stayed home, you had your two point two children, you had your dog and
> your cat and, you had your little lot of land with your
>   house .... But now ... families are changing and there's more same-sex cou-
> ples, there's more people having babies on their own without a partner, or—it's
> hard to not bring it all back to babies and love because that's what I do but, and
> that's what I see too. You know what I mean?

While families are indeed changing, Betsy's construction of the past is a
racially exclusive one, exemplified by the idealized suburban white family,
the Cleavers, in *Leave it to Beaver*. Its almost as if Betsy is drawing on that
fictional family to describe her historical memory of "two point two children ... with a little lot of land ... with your house." For a subset of white
families, the stay-at home-mom and breadwinner dad was a reality, albeit
a now distant one, that continues to shape the contours of white women's
expectations for themselves and for men. Although Betsy implores us to
"bring it back to babies and love," it is not clear where that leaves us, and
her jumbled syntax suggests that she too was not sure. She ventures to
consider an alternate future motivated by changing families in the present,
yet that is constrained by historical family forms of the past. Babies still
require care and the unanswered question is who should do it.

Black women, in contrast, largely cannot reference this version of a
historical past. Although one black women (out of 23) said she wanted
to stay home and did, it was motivated by a desire to combat educational
inequality for her children by homeschooling as opposed to solely pursuing
a gendered homemaker ideal. Culturally the expectation and, often, economic need for black women's work shaped their narratives. Unlike white
women, whose expectations drew on a storied past that created conflicts
and frustrations with the demands of the present, black women's expectations of black men incorporated historical and present-day acknowledge-
ment of the constraints on their ability to provide. For example, Trisha, a
forty-two-year-old married black woman, said, "There's plenty of African

American households where the woman brings home all the money and sometimes the men are there to help care for the kids." Trisha's report that many black women are primary breadwinners is a statement of fact that reflects, in her view, the myriad of individual and structural reasons that prevent black men from being breadwinners. She continues:

> It's not their fault all the time, it may just be their spotty work history because they don't know how to keep a job, it could also be that they may have a drug addiction or they may have gone to jail, which makes it harder for you to get a job. These are things that are bigger factors in the African American household than in other households. I'm on the fence on what this crisis [the Great Recession] did. It gave people certain options and it took away other options for others.

Unlike white women who harbor expectations that conflict with contemporary economic needs, black women's expectations account for structural constraints. They struggle instead with black men's conception of themselves, Trisha mentioned above says, "sometimes they have that thought in their head that they have to be the breadwinner, and they can't." Falling short of their own expectations is hard for black men. Angelique, a fifty-two-year-old single black woman, says "Actually . . . they can't deal with it. Most men can't deal with it" (i.e., not being the breadwinner). Black men's inability to cope, in Angelique's view, is tied to their adherence to the breadwinner role despite its infeasibility. "Because at first when you're the man of the house, you're the father and you're the one that's bringing all the money in. And if you can't bring it in what's the first thing you do?" Black men, she says, try to figure it out on their own, but she maintained they don't have to. "I mean it's sad that we put that limitation on them like that because you have a partner," she said.

Angelique, like Trisha, modeled an expectation of black men that was collaborative: the "co-breadwinner model" that middle-class black women historically espoused (Landry 2000). "You both do [have a partner], you both should be able to bring the money in, not just men," she argued. Yet, their accounts suggest that these women see the resistance not from black women but from black men. "Most men don't like women to be the breadwinner of the house because they want to bring it all in. But if you can't do it, you got to work together . . . " Angelique ends where Trisha began: Black women are primary or co-breadwinners and that's okay. She goes on to reference structural constraints, the "statistics on you as a black man" that make getting ahead harder. Her expectation is not tied to male provision, but rather, as she put it, "if you can't make it, let's get it together."

Some black women described a reality of non-traditional labor market roles, but nonetheless maintained a spoken aspiration to the traditional familial ideal. Shena, a thirty-eight-year-old single-never-married black woman, told of a friend whose husband was not the primary breadwinner but was still the "head of the household." "He's very type A," she says, "he's very traditional in those roles like men do this, women do this." Although, the man is not the primary breadwinner, she continues, "he wants to be, and he's going to work to be that but he still acts in the home as if he's the head of the household because he is." While the breadwinner is often assumed to be a man and the head of the household, these black women (and their men) are separating these roles.

Simone, a forty-four-year-old married black woman, clarifies this further, "Breadwinner does not mean financially, 'cause when I say he's the head of the home I don't mean financially the head of the home, not in a financial way. He's just the man of the house, 'cause he is the dad." For Simone, this was related to religious norms of the man as the head of the house. Women, in Simone's view, can be breadwinners and her mother was for a long time but "that didn't mean she was the man or she liked to feel that she's the man of the house. But, um . . . She was the one who had the job."

This separation of the ideals of breadwinning (i.e., financial provision) and the reward of breadwinning (i.e. respect and household position) made it possible for these black families to reconcile the conflict between the cultural ideal and structural realities. They honored the ideal with their spoken word and household actions, even as their everyday lives of co-breadwinning or woman as breadwinner stood in contradiction. In doing so, however, black women themselves lost as the balance of power; the gendered division of labor and patriarchy were reaffirmed (Hill 2004).[3] Yet, it seems they were making a trade to enable their men to be "men" despite economic constraint. Simone's words again are instructive:

> My brother right now in New York, he's not working, because he got laid off, not that he was not employed or was a bum. Economy's hard, so he got laid off. His wife is who is working right now, so she's the one making the money, but he's still the head of the home. You know, his daughters and his wife still respect him.

Simone draws a distinction among men that it seems would be less deserving of respect, those who are "not employed" or a "bum" versus her brother who was "laid off." Men do not deserve respect in families because they are always able to financially provide, but because they are men and they are trying (Franklin 2001).

TYRANNY OF GENDER NORMS

Despite black and white women's recognizing and sometimes embracing the need for alternative models to account for the hardship the breadwinner ideal places on men, they recognize the constraints of societal pressures for men to conform. Their attempts at familial negotiation and redefinition bump up against the tyranny of cultural gender norms. Claire, the forty-one-year-old white woman mentioned earlier, aptly summarizes the stranglehold of gender norms (Williams 2000):

> Heteronormative masculinity just sucks for everybody. You know? It means that men are supposed to be like macho and manly. And it creates a gender ideal that's as impossible to live up to as like female heteronormative gender roles. Like heterogender roles and this really extreme masculine, feminine bifurcation is really—it's damaging to everybody, because it means that you have to be constantly making this facade of being like a man enough or being feminine enough. And I, I don't know. Maybe I say this apparently as somebody who's just like never been good at woman drag. I think that man drag is probably also really hard to wear all the time. You know? And especially if you're in a generation of people for whom you can't find a good job, you can't find a good enough job. You just, like you, suck as a man because you've been unemployed for two years.

The power of gender norms is in the general consensus that there are "specific behaviors and personal attributes deemed socially desirable for members of each sex" (Chafetz 1991, 78; Butler 1989). "Lack of conformity," Chafetz (1991) argues, "is defined as deviance," and deviant behavior has consequences. Men and women who fail to live up to gender norms can endure disciplinary censure from themselves and others, Claire maintains, as in "you suck as a man."

Paula, a forty-eight-year-old married white woman, describes this tension for stay-at-home dads who are not living up to gendered expectations to provide, but who she argues are "certainly providing and doing a great job of it … " Paula is redefining what providing means but immediately interjects "I've met men who do that who really struggle with it," recognizing that cultural support does not exists for her alternate definition. She continues:

> I had a patient on the unit recently who was having a very hard time with that and just raising kids at home and feeling like he was getting a lot of negative sort of commentary I guess from people. And we kind of helped him find some support groups or like meetup groups for other fathers who had kids, because he's like, "I don't know anybody else doing this in my area," and he felt very kind of

alone in that decision, even though he was like I'm doing—I feel like I'm doing a great job with it. He's like, "I'm great with my kids and I,"—you know? "I like actually being at home and cooking." He's like, "I don't mind, you know, I don't mind all the tasks," but he said, "I feel, you know, kind of bad about myself, like I'm not doing enough." And so, I think that he was sort of speaking to—and I remember in the group that a lot of the men were like, "Yeah, I can relate to that, I can—I would have a hard time with that too," or you know, people definitely were agreeing with him that that's hard being a man and trying to do a nontraditional role.

Yet while the cultural support might be missing, men who are active caregivers can still fulfill those tasks well, she argued. "So I don't think it's totally supported in our society but more so . . . I think most men do well with it, you know," she said. "I think most men just—are just kind of plugging away and doing the best that they can and embracing all the different roles so they can have more so."

Economic insecurity for many men and women seemed to be the nudge they needed to consider whether the historically defined gender roles made sense for their family lives. However, the decisions men and women made about how to organize their family lives were judged by societies' rigid gender expectations (Stone 2007). Black and white women described this tension for men as destructive. Trisha referenced a 2015 sociological study by Christin Munsch (Munsch 2015), which was widely covered in the press, that found men with breadwinning spouses were more likely to cheat. In her words:

> Stay-at-home dads are the ones that are cheating now because they feel degraded by the fact that they are stay-at-home dads, even though they love being stay-at-home dads, they want to be the ones that support their family.

Trisha viewed this finding as evidence of the societal constraint on men and women's ability to "choose" gender roles in accordance with familial needs (Milkie and Peltola 1999; Cha and Thébaud 2009). Munsch largely concurs stating, "Infidelity may allow economically dependent men to engage in compensatory behavior while simultaneously distancing themselves from breadwinning spouses (2015: 469).

When I asked Trisha how she thought men were dealing with the fact that "it isn't as easy as it used to be for men to find jobs that allow them to be stable breadwinners of a family," she said, "Some men turn to the bottle, some men turn to drugs, some men dig deep down into themselves and figure out a way to make it work out."

RESISTING TRADITIONAL GENDER ROLES

Despite the persistent influence of historical models of breadwinning on contemporary relationships, whether held by white women or black men, changing economic times are enabling (and at times forcing) men and women to reconsider what the right familial roles are. Trisha, a black woman, said, "I think this [economic] crisis has made it where it's a little bit easier for you to look at what works best for you and your household." Claire, the white married woman who we heard from earlier, agrees, "You know, you need to have money to make your household run," but she points immediately to the stubbornness of traditional gender roles. "And then, there's all of the domestic labor which historically has been women's work. But that really, it's not women's work. It's just work that needs to be done." Claire articulates the same view as Trisha—there is work that needs to be done but families don't have to be tied to historical norms of who "should" do it. Claire continues, listing the tasks and eschewing the pronoun "he" or "she" and instead invoking "somebody" to illustrate the yet undetermined person who gets assigned the task:

> Somebody needs to do the dishes. Somebody needs to mow the lawn. Somebody needs to help the kids with their homework. Somebody needs to force them to brush their teeth. You know, um, somebody needs to pay the car insurance every six months, like and it doesn't matter who does it, but somebody needs to do it.

For Claire the needs of a functioning household are clear: you need money and "somebody" needs to do the endless tasks, but there is no gender assignment or clear separation of roles. She feels, "if you're going to be the primary breadwinner or you're going to be co-breadwinners or you're going to be the primary domestic person or you're going to share it, like it doesn't matter."

The problem in her view is history and its infiltration into prevalent expectations in the present. While for her the "stuff has to get done by somebody," history dictates exactly who should do it. She observes:

> Historically, because the domestic labor has been unpaid and has been women's labor, I think that many men do not like to have that role because it, it feels emasculating and that they don't take any pride in it and they, they see it as like bitch work, which like, in my household at least, this has been a perennial problem that like if I've been at work forty hours a week and I'm breastfeeding a baby all night long and I come home at 5:00 PM and the baby wants to nurse, like why is there not fucking food in the crock pot? Like, you know?

Despite Claire's progressive and clear articulation of how a household should function separate from gender roles, at the end of the day stubborn gender roles still governed how her house functioned.

Kate, a fifty-two-year-old divorced white woman, echoes Claire's frustration, "My ex-husband didn't want to do anything. He wasn't going to vacuum, do a load of laundry, nothing." However, she also recognizes changes among some men, "Today, I see a lot more men taking a lot more responsibility in the household and with the kids than years ago." She recalls a former employer, a lawyer, whom she described as the "mommy-daddy," whose wife commuted to an "excellent" job far away. Even though "he was a partner in the firm" he performed a lot of the care duties for his daughter, "He'd take her to school, pick her up after work, make her dinner." For Kate, this stood in stark contrast to her husband and the men "of her day," who she says, "weren't doing any of that." Yet, Claire is more than ten years younger than Kate, and her husband, theoretically of a different "day," resembles Kate's ex-husband rather than her former employer. Raley, Bianchi, and Wang (2012) find that men, indeed, are willing to do more primary care for children as opposed to other household tasks when their wives work outside the home, and men do more childcare when women earn more. At the same time, men's household labor continues to lag considerably behind women's, even in dual-income households (Bianchi, Robinson, and Milkie 2007).

Thus the white women in this study report they are attempting to resist traditional gender roles but are bumping up against stubborn norms, finding themselves partnered to men who either relinquish and redefine themselves accordingly or insist on tradition to the ultimate demise of the family. Leslie, a forty-year-old single-never-married white woman, said, "He can provide in other ways than bringing home the money. I wouldn't pigeonhole a man into just being a sole breadwinner. He's also a father if he had kids and he's staying home with the kids, he's a father." For Leslie, the right thing to do was whatever was in the best interests of the family; gender norms should have nothing to do with it. "Traditional," she says, "it's a word we like to use but sometimes it's like whatever and the traditional stuff doesn't work."

In contrast, black women are pursuing more flexible gender ideals, as well, but for them it is a continuation of a flexible past that recognizes the impact of rising economic insecurity. Ashanti, a thirty-eight-year-old black married woman, spoke of the need for flexibility with the "shifting of the economy" that doesn't tie men's worth to breadwinning. "Your husband loses a job and then you're working, it doesn't make him any less of a good person." While she acknowledges that "ideally that's kind of what we have in our mind in terms of a good man ... realistically especially with the economy changing, it doesn't always work out that way." Ashanti then reconceptualizes the worth of a man around effort rather than financial contribution, "If there's effort being made by that man and nothing is coming through then, I think that's okay."

Shirley, a forty-seven-year-old black woman, described a coworker who sounds very much like Kate's former employer, the "mommy daddy." The man earns a good salary, but his wife is more highly educated and successful, so "he does a lot of the regular domestic stuff because his wife doesn't have time to . . . he takes the daughter to daycare, he picks the daughter up from daycare," and is in Shirley's view "happy as a lark."

Brenda, a forty-year-old partnered black woman, thinks its "okay to have two people in a household bringing in the money, you know, um, whether it be the male or the female," but acknowledges that "it's still a reputation that the male is the breadwinner, the primary breadwinner." Given the historical challenges to breadwinning for black men, the pervasiveness of the norm is striking, but my informants also point to the acceptance in the black community of black women's need to work (Hill 2004).

Yet Brenda thinks this is changing in the younger generation, much like Gerson (2011) found in her interviews with younger men and women, who want to be in committed relationships where responsibility for paid work and care work was equally shared:

> I don't think a lot of males in this day and age, that's their expectation anymore that a woman must be at home, barefoot and pregnant, and the homemakers. They want someone who is on their same level with them who is really willing to go out there and make money and bring home money to help the family to be successful overall.

Who made more was not important, in Brenda's opinion, but contributing to the household having "a good lifestyle together" was key; each partner had to "bring something to the table." This is an important shift, given Brenda's belief that the "reputation" at least for her generation is the "male is breadwinner, the primary breadwinner." Brenda's inkling of what the next generation thinks, reflects shifts in the cultural beliefs about gender that Jacobs and Gerson (2016) argue are "more complex and conditional than the hegemonic male breadwinner model presumes" (23).

GENDER PERSISTENCE AND RESISTANCE

Given the rapidly changing reality of women working outside of the home, it is somewhat surprising that the notion of the male provider and the woman as caregiver persists, especially given the increasing economic inability of men to provide. Even the older women in this study came of age in the 1970s (ages 35–55) a time of resistance to traditional gender roles when white mothers were increasingly entering the labor force. While some women expressed a desire to work and "keep their minds busy," others viewed the changing economic reality where women were working out of economic need as a loss for them and their children.

Despite broad cultural resistance to (and the financial inability of black families to attain) norms of masculinity and the breadwinning role, many black women in this study either subscribed to it or strongly believed black men did. This finding is surprising given the persistent claim that poor and nonwhite populations adhere to different views than more advantaged groups (Bourdieu 1984; Branch and Scherer 2013). How can black men and women prize or honor ideals that are, for them, particularly unattainable, the very ideals that have historically positioned their families as failed or problem families?

Nonetheless, this study's findings are buttressed by other scholars who have found important congruence in cultural ideals across class and race, such as Katherine Newman's study of the inner-city working poor (1999a); Sharon Hays (2004) analysis of welfare recipients; or Edin and Kefalas's (2011) research on unmarried low-income mothers. Indeed we can see the full extent of the power of those mainstream cultural messages that denigrate some families while uplifting others, when the very people whom those ideas castigate accept them, even partially. In sum, cultural norms are pernicious, in that even those who do not possess the structural means to attain their ideals buy into them and often judge themselves sharply as a result.

Part of the explanation for the persistence of cultural norms in the face of changing economic reality and labor force participation of women is the paradoxical combination I found in some black women's households, where they would attest to traditional ideals while at the same time maintaining a nontraditional division of paid labor (i.e. woman as breadwinner [Hill 2004; Barnes 2015]). For them, the traditional family rests on the man as "head of the household," which often assumes financial provision; but they focus instead on respect, enabling their men to "feel like men." Finally, white women and black women were measuring their contemporary reality against two very different pasts. Their variation in the experience of economic privilege versus economic exploitation shaped their perception of masculinity and the flexibility of the breadwinner role. While both white and black women insisted that men did not have be the primary breadwinner and there could be sharing of responsibility for both financial and household duties, this conclusion reflected an accounting of different expectations for how their lives would proceed. For some white women, there was the understanding "we knew we would not get married right out of high school" (like the previous generation) that set them both up to be earners and work. For others the desire to stay home and the primary responsibility they felt (or their husbands felt) for the care of the home posed challenges. Both of these instances reference a historical ideal for white women for "the care of hearth and home" and the loss or shift in the present that did not exist for black women and as a result did not shape their perceptions of breadwinning to the same extent.

For black women, the past of economic necessities requiring flexibility in gender roles came through clearly (Baca Zinn 1990). While black women expressed a desire for the cultural ideal of the man as the provider, they almost immediately accounted for the racialized obstacles that prevented men from achieving it and how "hard" it was for black men as a result. Their reference to the male provider role was an expression for some of desire for the ideal, but for most it seemed to be context for how they made sense of the struggle of black men with the reality of not earning more.

Many referred to their own households or that of friends where the women earned more as normative, resulting from higher levels of education and salaried work that provided consistency. They also made reference to drug use, felony status, etc., as reasons it was more difficult for men to provide and especially to be primary breadwinners, which led them to offer alternatives for how they could still "be men." Yet even for black women, if men did not provide, the consequences were great if they were not "flexible in their manhood," demonstrating the tyranny of gender norms whether stemming from pressures from their peers or family.

Both black and white women spoke at length of the pressures men put on themselves and how "destabilizing" and "depressing" it was when the ideals of manhood and provisioning work conflicted with the economic reality (Townsend 2002). Given the fundamental shifts in the economy and the erasure of a path free from economic insecurity for all but the most advantaged workers, men and women facing the pressure of traditional ideals are at an impasse (Hacker 2008; Hollister 2011). They can resist normative gender roles in their nuclear family but must contend with the judgment from others (Coltrane 1996; Lane 2009). We need a cultural shift that corresponds to the economic shift that values paid and unpaid labor— something feminists have long sought (Thistle 2006). Given the harm to men as well as women, to whites as well as blacks, perhaps the twenty-first century will bring about sufficient buy-in for true social change.

ACKNOWLEDGEMENT:

Supported by NSF #1424140, "The Rise of Insecure Work and Changes in Durable Inequality." I would also like to acknowledge the extensive support provided by several graduate students: Armanthia Duncan, Kyla Walters, Lucius Couloute, Kelly Giles, and Jackie Stein as well as three undergraduate students: Lajeanesse Harris, Sarah Lilley, and Darriel Alicea. I would also like to acknowledge the contribution of Amy Schalet and Emmanuel Harris to the research design and data collection. Finally, I would like to thank Joya Misra, Katherine Newman, and Allison Pugh for their feedback on earlier drafts.

NOTES

1. The larger study also includes men, but I focus only on women in this analysis.
2. Two of the white participants were lesbian, one married and the other partnered.
3. Black women are not alone in this gendered compensatory practice, Economists Bertrand, Kamenica, and Pan (2015) found that when women earn more than their husbands they take on more household responsibility, spending more time on household chores perhaps to compensate and reaffirm their gender roles (see also Hochschild 1989).

REFERENCES

Andersen, Margaret L. 2001. "Restructuring for Whom? Race, Class, Gender and the Ideology of Invisibility." *Sociological Forum* 16(2):181–200.

Baca Zinn, Maxine. 1990. "Family, Feminism, and Race in America." *Gender & Society* 4(1):68–82.

Barnes, Riche' J. Daniel. 2015. *Raising the Race: Black Career Women Redefine Marriage, Motherhood, and Community*. New Brunswick, NJ: Rutgers University Press.

Bertrand, Marianne, Emir Kamenica, and Jessica Pan. 2015. "Gender Identity and Relative Income within Households." *The Quarterly Journal of Economics* 130(2):571–614.

Bianchi, Suzanne M., John P. Robinson, and Melissa A. Milkie. 2007. *Changing Rhythms of American Family Life*. New York: Russell Sage Foundation.

Bourdieu, Pierre. 1984. *Distinction: A Social Critique of the Judgement of Taste*. London: Routledge.

Boushey, Heather. "The End of the Mancession: Now It's Women Who Are the Economy's Big Losers." *Slate*, January 25, 2011.http://www.slate.com/articles/double_x/doublex/2011/01/the_end_of_the_mancession.html

Branch, Enobong Hannah. 2011. *Opportunity Denied: Limiting Black Women to Devalued Work*. New Brunswick, NJ: Rutgers University Press.

Branch, Enobong Hannah, and Mary Larue Scherer. 2013. "Mapping the Intersections in the Resurgence of the Culture of Poverty." *Race, Gender, and Class* 20(3–4):346–358.

Bukszpan, Daniel. "Economy: The Man-cession and the He-covery." *USA Today*, January 17, 2012. Retrieved on December 21, 2015. http://usatoday30.usatoday.com/money/economy/story/2012-01-29/cnbc-mancession/52826370/1

Butler, Judith. 1989. *Gender Trouble: Feminism and the Subversion of Identity*. New York: Routledge.

Cha, Youngjoo, and Sarah Thébaud. 2009. "Labor Markets, Breadwinning, and Beliefs: How Economic Context Shapes Men's Gender Ideology." *Gender & Society* 23(2):215–243.*

Chaftez, Janet Saltzman. 1991. "The Gender Division of Labor and the Reproduction of Female Disadvantage". In *Gender, Family, and Economy: The Triple Overlap*, edited by Rae Lesser Blumberg, 74–97. Newbury Park, CA: SAGE.

Coltrane, Scott. 1996. *Family Man: Fatherhood, Housework and Gender Equity*. New York: Oxford University Press.

Connell, R. W. 1993. "The Big Picture: Masculinities in Recent World History." *Theory and Society* 22(5):597–623.

Coontz, Stephanie. 1993. *The Way We Never Were: American Families and the Nostaligia Trap*. New York: Basic Books.

Cowan, Ruth Schwartz. 1985. *More Work for Mother: The Ironies of Household Technology from the Open Hearth to the Microwave*. New York: Basic Books.

Crompton, Rosemary. 1999. *Restructuring Gender Relations and Employment: The Decline of the Male Breadwinner*. New York: Oxford University Press.

Damaske, Sarah. 2011. *For the Family? How Class and Gender Shape Women's Work*. New York: Oxford University Press.

Edin, Kathryn, and Maria Kefalas. 2011. *Promises I Can Keep: Why Poor Women Put Motherhood Before Marriage*. Berkeley: University of California Press.

Franklin, Donna. 2000. *What's Love Got to Do With It? Understanding and Healing the Rift Between Black Men and Black Women*. New York: Simon & Schuster.

Gerson, Kathleen. 1993. *No Man's Land: Men's Changing Commitments to Family and Work*. New York: Basic Books.

Gerson, Kathleen. 2011. *The Unfinished Revolution: Coming of Age in a New Era of Gender, Work and Family*. New York: Oxford University Press.

Giddings, Paula. 1984. *When and Where I Enter: The Impact of Black Women on Race and Sex in America*. New York: William Morrow.

Hacker, Jacob S. 2008. *The Great Risk Shift: The New Economic Insecurity and the Decline of the American Dream*. New York: Oxford University Press.

Hays, Sharon. 2004. *Flat Broke With Children: Women in the Age of Welfare Reform*. New York: Oxford University Press.

Hill, Shirley. 2004. *Black Intimacies: A Gender Perspective on Families and Relationships*. Gender Lens Series. Walnut Creek, CA: AltaMira.

Hochschild, Arlie R. 1989. *The Second Shift*. New York, NY: Penguin Books.

Hollister, Matissa N. 2011. "Employment Stability in the U.S. Labor Market: Rhetoric versus Reality." *Annual Review of Sociology* 37(1):305–324.

Jacobs, Jerry A. and Kathleen Gerson. 2016. "Unpacking Americans Views of Mothers and Fathers Using National Vignette Survey Data: SWS Presidential Address." *Gender & Society* 30(3):413–441.

Jones, Jacqueline. 1986. *Labor of Love, Labor of Sorrow: Black Women, Work, and the Family from Slavery to the Present*. New York: Vintage.

Kalleberg, Arne L. 2009. "Precarious Work, Insecure Workers: Employment Relations in Transition." *American Sociological Review* 74(1):1–22.

Landry, Bart. 2000. *Black Working Wives: Pioneers of the American Family Revolution*. Berkeley: University of California Press.

Lane, Carrie. 2009. "Man Enough to Let My Wife Support Me: How Changing Models of Career and Gender Are Reshaping the Experience of Unemployment." *American Ethnologist* 36(4):681–692.

Livingston, Gretchen. "Growing Number of Dads Home with the Kids: Biggest Increase Amongst Those Caring for Family." *Pew Research Center,* June 5, 2014. Retrieved on December 21, 2015 http://www.pewsocialtrends.org/files/2014/06/2014-06-05_Stay-at-Home-Dads.pdf

Milkie, Melissa A., and Pia Peltola. 1999. "Playing All the Roles: Gender and the Work-Family Balancing Act." *Journal of Marriage and the Family* 61(2):476–490.

Mink, Gwendolyn. 1996. *The Wages of Motherhood: Inequality in the Welfare State, 1917–1942.* Ithaca, NY: Cornell University Press.

Munsch, Christin. 2015. "Her Support, His Support: Money, Masculinity, and Marital Infidelity." *American Sociological Review* 80(3):469–495.

Mutari, Ellen, Marilyn Power, and Deborah M. Figart. 2002. "Neither Mothers Nor Breadwinners: African-American Women's Exclusion from US Minimum Wage Policies, 1912–38." *Feminist Economics* 8(2):37–61.

Newman, Katherine. 1993. *Declining Fortunes: The Withering of the American Dream.* New York: Basic Books.

Newman, Katherine S. 1999a. *No Shame in My Game: The Working Poor in the Inner City.* New York: Knopf.

Newman, Katherine 1999b. *Falling from Grace: Downward Mobility in the Age of Affluence.* Berkeley: University of California Press.

Palmer, Phyllis. 1995. "Outside the Law: Agricultural and Domestic Workers Under the Fair Labor Standards Act." *Journal of Policy History* 7(4):416–440.

Pugh, Allison J. 2015. *The Tumbleweed Society: Working and Caring in an Age of Insecurity.* New York: Oxford University Press.

Raley, Sara, Suzanne M. Bianchi, and Wendy Wang. 2012. "When Do Fathers Care? Mothers' Economic Contribution and Fathers' Involvement in Child Care." *American Journal of Sociology* 117(5):1422–1459.

Stainback, Kevin and Donald Tomaskovic-Devey. 2012. *Documenting Desegregation: Racial and Gender Segregation in Private Sector Employment Since the Civil Rights Act.* New York: Russell Sage Foundation.

Stone, Pamela. 2007. *Opting Out? Why Women Really Quit Careers and Go Home.* Berkeley: University of California Press.

Townsend, Nicholas W. 2002. *The Package Deal: Marriage, Work, and Fatherhood in Men's Lives.* Philadelphia: Temple University Press.

Thistle, Susan. 2006. *From Marriage to Market: The Transformation of Women's Lives and Work.* Berkeley: University of California Press.

Wang, Wendy, Kim Parker, and Paul Taylor. "Breadwinning Moms: Mothers Are the Sole or Primary Provider in Four-in-Ten Households with Children; Public Conflicted about the Growing Trend." *Pew Research Center,* May 29, 2013. Retrieved on December 21, 2015 http://www.pewsocialtrends.org/files/2013/05/Breadwinner_moms_final.pdf

Williams, Joan. 2000. *Unbending Gender: Why Family and Work Conflict and What To Do About It.* New York: Oxford University Press.

Zuo, Jiping. 1997. "The Effect of Men's Breadwinner Status on Their Changing Gender Beliefs." *Sex Roles* 37(9–10):799–816.

CHAPTER 8

cVo

Moving On to Stay Put

Employee Relocation in the Face
of Employment Insecurity

ELIZABETH ANN WHITAKER

For over half a century, employee mobility has been part of the professional middle-class experience. After WWII, as US companies grew in size and reach, becoming regional, national, and even global, they began to use employee relocation as a tool for human capital acquisition and development of professional and managerial workers. The practice of corporations placing human resources where they best serve the organization's needs continues today (e.g., see Eby and Russell 2000; Hodson and Sullivan 2002). Businesses today refer to the movement of employees to different communities for work as 'relocation,' with the shorthand reference 'relo' being a well-used term in boardrooms and managerial meetings. This chapter will use the results of qualitative research with relocated families with children to explore several significant ways that the new economy has shifted the employee relocation experience.

Compared with the mid-to-late twentieth century, relocations today include an increasing amount of risk and need for adaptability on the part of employees and their families. In the postindustrial economy, I find that geographic moves are often compelled simply to maintain a family's solvency and standing in middle-class America. I also find that gender plays

a primary role in how relocation is navigated. Gender has long been rec-
ognized as central to how people respond to tensions between work and
family (Gerstel et al. 2002), and employee relocation is certainly a topic at
the intersection of those domains.

I will highlight three aspects of relocation—motivations to moving,
housing, and spouse's work—that speak to the increasing complexity
and potential hazards in the experience. We will see that traditional gender and class ideologies, alone and at their intersection, are often invoked
when family decisions are made under conditions of duress. When people
fall back on ideological notions to help them make decisions in the face
of adversity, they more often find themselves constrained than relieved.
Both women and men can experience the oppressive effects of unequal and
unachievable sets of 'shoulds' and 'ought to's' that are based on traditional
views rather than individual realities. The economy of today can exploit
and derail families on many dimensions, and an analysis of employee relocation exposes the depth and complexity of the effects.

BACKGROUND

In the second half of the twentieth century, a 'relo' was a corporate manager at a major firm. He was the quintessential "Organization Man," who
could expect a job for life as he demonstrated commitment and loyalty to
his employer (Whyte 1956). Relos moved from community to community, jobsite to jobsite, with the confidence that their employers would be
a constant in their changing lives (Kanter 1977). Job-related moves were
opportunities for advancement and upward social mobility, and there was
job security. Moves were accepted with the understanding that there was
reciprocal commitment between worker and employer and that personal
costs borne by an employee and his family as a result of moving would
be rewarded by financial gain (Margolis 1979). In addition to pay raises,
moves were usually accompanied by generous relocation benefits like
bonuses, payment of moving costs, and guarantees by the employer that
the 'relo' would receive fair market value when selling his home. Applying
the term "Organization Man" to typify a relo in the mid-to-late 20th century was no accident. Women were less likely to work, and if they did work,
they were regularly excluded from professional managerial positions and
especially from practices like business travel and relocation (Kanter 1977).
Thus in the past relos were almost exclusively male sole breadwinners who
used employee relocation to climb the economic ladder and solidify their
positions in an organization (Kanter 1977).

The world of work has been changing, and the rate of change has increased with watershed leaps in technological innovation and the strains of global recession in the past decade. We are now well entrenched in a postindustrial, knowledge-based, global economy that has seen a significant decline in long-term employment relationships (see for example Farber 2007, Valcour & Tolbert 2003). Also, women are now active and acknowledged members of the workforce. Working wives now contribute approximately 35 percent of their families' incomes and one in four wives in dual-earner households earns more than her husband (U.S. Department of Labor 2005).

In this postindustrial economy professional workers engage in relocation within a very different context. Working-class and manufacturing jobs are no longer the only jobs subject to layoffs, business cycles, and cost-cutting. Today professional and managerial employees face an uncertain job market characterized by downsizing, corporate reorganization, and an increase in the use of outsourcing and contract labor. Business risk— the uncertainty in profits or danger of loss due to unforeseen events like changes in demand, changes in the price of inputs, natural disasters, etc.— exists in all markets. Corporations' departure from commitment to professional employees is a strategy for transferring business risk to employees by treating them as variable rather than fixed costs of doing business (Cappelli 2008a). Rather than ride out business cycles or accept shocks to the bottom line when risks become reality, employers try to offset financial adversity by reducing labor costs.

Moreover, firms now rarely engage in "Talent Management," the process of developing employees through rotating assignments and mentoring, because the implicit lifelong employment contract for professional workers no longer exists (Cappelli 2008b). Why worry about long-term development of employees if there likely is no long term? Firms want to remain lean—that is, without excess costs in their system, and thus they maintain flexibility in the size of their workforces. They want to be able to bring on and then release workers as needed. With this managerial approach, an employee being moved into a position has no guarantee that the position and the relationship with the company will persist. It is less likely that the position is part of a long-term plan of career development, and more likely that it is instead serving an immediate corporate need. The Great Recession which began in late 2007 exacerbated employment uncertainty and vulnerability and minimized Americans' abilities to choose the circumstances and locations of their employment. To make matters worse, the economic collapse eroded the value of employees' own individual assets (e.g., homes, investments), and it reduced employers' willingness and ability to buffer move costs through generous relocation benefits (see for example Raetz 2012, and Sullivan and McCarney 2011).

Today, as in the past, employee relocations affect entire families, not just wage earners themselves. But the effects of moves on accompanying family members are different now that the relationship between families and major social institutions has changed. The move of one employee is now likely to separate another employee—the spouse—from his or her job. Research shows that approximately 65 percent of domestic corporate transferees are part of dual-career marriages (Marshall and Greenwood 2002).

Past social science research on relocation has been sparse and has emphasized the decision between spouses on whether to undertake a move. However, several exceptional ethnographies offer a glimpse into the past world of employee transfers, and they offer a basis for comparison to today. Kanter (1977) studied a company she called Indsco and was among the first to discuss the role of gender in professional managerial experiences. She found that women were excluded from these positions, but they were expected to support their husbands' routes to achievement by handling the family and home-related operations and by tolerating husbands' moves, travel, long hours, fatigue, and singular focus on work.

Margolis's (1979) qualitative research with corporate managers reinforced the findings that women were assumed to be in the role of accompanying spouse when men climbed the corporate ladder through relocation. Her research revealed that most relocations in the 1970's followed a similar pattern. Relocating "Organization Men" were participants in the "American Dream" of home ownership. Their moves tended to begin with an administratively uncomplicated and sequential process of selling current homes, purchasing larger homes in the destination community, then moving. Margolis found the process generally began in the spring and was finalized in early fall at which time wives took on responsibility for getting the new houses set up. The role of women in the family and the labor force has since expanded, which complicates the challenges and sacrifices women must accept in a corporate relocation. In addition to home- and community-related costs, today's transferred spouses often give up their own employment and interrupt their career trajectories. They are not simply "enjoying the material fruits of their husband's hard work" (Margolis 1979, 154). They may be sacrificing hard-earned gains in work-family balance and the division of labor in their families.

Although times have changed, employee relocation continues to be a common phenomenon. The U.S. Census Bureau estimated that in 2002 about three million people moved to another county, state, or country because employers had transferred or recruited them (Kilborn 2005). The growth rate in transfer activity among current employees is estimated at about 6 percent per year, although there was a slight decline from 2006 through 2009 due to the economic climate (Lamech 2010). Employee transfers make up about 74 percent of relocations, and the additional 26 percent are new hires that occur as a result of deliberate job searches to seek career advancement, to gain better job insecurity, and to replace jobs lost from reorganization and downsizing (ibid.). Importantly, businesses and employees are not the only participants in the relocation process. Annual tracking surveys show that 84 percent of domestic transferees are married and 65 percent have children (Marshall and Greenwood 2002).

Employee relocation emerged as a corporate tool for meeting human resource needs over half a century ago. However, significant changes in the social landscape have taken place since then, and it is important to explore how those changes modify a family's experience of this wholesale change in their daily lives. We need to know how changes in the allocation of risk and responsibility across employers and employees and the increasing need and prevalence of dual-income families affects the already challenging and far-reaching experience of employee relocation.

METHODS

This study is based on qualitative research conducted from February 2008 to August 2009 with both partners in thirty-one families that had relocated for a job at least once in the previous four years. I narrowed the research to those with corporate-paid moves because the research is concerned with the implications of the global nature of the workforce and employers' presupposition of workforce mobility, These are moves where corporations follow hiring practices including: 1) selecting workers, either current employees or new hires, from noncommutable distances from a job site, and 2) funding moves for distant workers.

The class position of workers involved in corporate-paid employee relocation is almost exclusively middle- to upper-middle-class or those struggling to maintain that class standing. In addition, the total of sixty-two people in the sample were all from families with two adult partners and one or more dependent children. Both single-earner and dual-earner families were eligible and included. Looking at this family form allowed the study to find how relocation impacts employees themselves but also how it impacts individuals who are moved but are not themselves directly involved in the work/

worker relationship. Although it may be important to consider other family forms in future research, targeting two-adult relationships with children allowed me to uncover partner interactions and negotiations, impacts on women, and impacts on dual-earner relationships. The approach is further justified because married couples with children do make up the majority of relocations, and available data show that single-parent-headed families comprise only 5.9 percent of these moves (Marshall and Greenwood 2002). Both spouses in each family were interviewed so that the perspective of the employee and the perspective of the accompanying spouse were considered. Although the majority of employee relocations are husband-centered, this sample deliberately included families with wife-centered moves in order to evaluate emerging trends of women's increasing presence in professional careers. The final sample included twenty-one husband-centered moves and ten wife-centered moves.

Twenty-nine of the thirty-one informant couples were white, one couple was African American, and one couple was Hispanic. Therefore, the project does not offer information on potential differences in the relocation experience by race or ethnicity. Similarly, the sample included only heterosexual couples, and so does not provide insights into differences by sexual orientation. Fifteen of the families had moved once for a job since having children, while sixteen families had moved two or more times. The families varied in the age of their oldest child. They also varied in how recently they had moved during the previous four-year period.

Informants were recruited through convenience and snowball sampling using personal connections, real estate brokers, newcomer organizations and stay-at-home parent groups as initial points of contact. The project used two geographic foci for recruiting participants—the state of Michigan and the Chicago Metropolitan Statistical Areas (MSA), which is one of the most active areas for employee relocation (Lamech 2007). The final sample included primarily families from these locations. As a result of snowball sampling, a few families were from elsewhere and some had moved from the recruitment locations, not into them.

Data were gathered through open-ended, semistructured, in-depth-interviews. All of the interviews followed a general interview guide, and lasted between forty-five and ninety minutes, averaging about an hour. Each partner was interviewed separately. Twenty-four couples were interviewed in person, and seven were interviewed by telephone for logistical reasons. The in-person interviews were tape-recorded and then transcribed. The telephone interviews resulted in extensive notes including direct quotes where possible. Transcribed interviews and interview notes were content analyzed to identify common themes.

THE CHANGING MOTIVATIONS BEHIND RELOCATION

The shift from reciprocal commitment between employers and professional employees to market-based employment relationships has created new motivations for taking a job that requires relocation. Historically, professional managerial employees relocated for work to pursue upward mobility and to fulfill their roles in long-term employment arrangements. In the postmodern economy of today, that homogeneity of purpose is gone. This study reveals that the circumstances of corporate relocations today can vary dramatically.

Respondent stories show that macro-structural realties contribute to many, if not all, relocations in some capacity. The state of the economy, the company and the job market come into play, as does the fundamental need to provide for the family. Some families are responding to direct structural influences. These would be workers who move geographically to find replacement employment when a job is lost or there is a known or presumed threat to a current job. In this case, workers are moved by a new employer rather than an existing employer. Other moves are the result of indirect structural influences and are motivated by the overarching sense of insecurity many workers feel today. These would include cases where relocation is accepted because of an employee's desire to make oneself known to be loyal or indispensable should a reorganization or downsizing come along.

Today's workplace is characterized by what Ryan (1999) calls "management by stress". She lists corporate mergers and reorganization with workforce downsizing as major aspects of work reengineering that began in the mid-to-late 1990s. She points out that "while manufacturing jobs have typically been thought of as most vulnerable to layoffs, white collar work is now as insecure." The vulnerability of middle-class, middle-management jobs has persisted from the 1990s into the new millennium as technology has continued to change at an increasing rate. The changes in the organization of work that derive from changes in technology increase the demand for the cognitive and interpersonal skills used by educated professionals and managers, and they reduce the demand for routine analytical and mechanical skills (called "routine tasks") that characterize many middle-educated, white-collar positions and manufacturing production jobs (Goldin and Katz 2007). If a professional managerial job is lost, a worker may find it difficult or impossible to replace it with a similar one. Instead of moving for a voluntary opportunity to achieve advancement and develop one's career, workers take employment where they can and to oblige their employer's preferences.

The informants in this study revealed that workers and their families face uncertainty and vulnerability in employment, and that two ideological norms can play important roles in how they respond. First, these middle-class families adhere to the belief that it is necessary to maintain economic self-sufficiency at the nuclear family level. This is not surprising given that self-reliance has been accorded cultural importance and has been seen as a measure of integrity since the genesis of capitalist society (Ransome 2005). The construct of self-reliance maintains that discrepancy of condition between extended family members and friends is acceptable, and that infringing on kin or friends for financial resources or assistance is only appropriate in dire situations. When exceptional economic resources are needed among the middle class, its members call upon nonfamilial institutions in the form of medical insurance, credit, etc. (Rapp 1999). Husbands and wives in this research, regardless of their own paid-worker status, consistently expressed an urgency to, as a unit, be able to independently meet the needs of themselves and their children. As Donna, age 40, stated simply after relocating twice in eighteen months, "The bottom line is you have to take care of your family."

For many families, traditional gender ideology factored in as well to dictate that the appropriate way to achieve self-sufficiency is by positioning men as primary breadwinners. These findings are consistent with past research on family migration that also found gender roles and gender identity to be a basis of decision making (e.g., Bielby and Bielby 1992; Lichter 1983; Shihadeh 1991). Traditional gender norms assign certain activities and traits to husbands and other traits and activities to wives (Collins et al. 1993). Women are expected to place family ahead of personal goals and have ultimate responsibility for reproductive activities—that is, the work performed within the domestic or private sphere and which helps to sustain a household and reproduce everyday life (e.g., cleaning, cooking, child care and rearing, etc.). Men are expected to act as primary breadwinners and emphasize economic and career success. Kimmel and Ferber (2006) write, "Since the early nineteenth century American manhood has pivoted around the status of breadwinner—the self-made man who supports his family by his own labor" (132). Gender-role theory argues that men's interests in productive labor are favored over women's, given the assumed preeminence of men in that domain.

The stories heard in this research demonstrate that each family is unique yet they are subject to common influences—new forms of economic vulnerability often mediated by old class and gender belief systems. Eight of the thirty-one informant families (25 percent) moved when a primary or sole earner lost a job due to a cutback, reorganization, business failure, or ending contract. Another seven families described circumstances where a primary earner was not out of a job, but a workforce change was impending. In order to preempt the possibility of layoff, the vulnerable worker sought out new employment, either within their own organization or with another employer. Half of the families in the research could point directly to lost or threatened employment as at the root of their decision to relocate.

For example, Ethan, thirty-one, worked for a small software company in Nevada. The company went out of business, and he was practical as he looked for new employment. After multiple interviews in cities across the United States, one company offered him a position in either their California or Michigan office. He accepted the Michigan job strictly based on cost of living factors. He was not moving up the corporate ladder with the job, but instead merely recovering his income. Asked about the context of his recent relocation, he said:

> I worked for [a software company] for about ten years but the company never really went anywhere, it actually went under, backwards instead of forwards. . . . There was nothing really appealing in Michigan, just the economics of California and stuff, so I said what about Michigan?

Mike, 42, was laid off in a reorganization, and he was unemployed for about three months when he got an offer for a job in another state. The offer came when he had some time left on his severance pay, and he was relieved to have that extra cushion to help with move expenses. He had feared his severance would run out before a job came along. The new position paid a similar salary to what Mike had been earning, and he said he was just grateful not to take a pay cut compared with his previous job. Mike, his wife Janet, and their four children ages eight through sixteen made the move from Michigan to another midwestern state so Mike could take the job.

Both Ethan's and Mike's wives gave up good, professional jobs to make the moves. Combining the lateral nature of both men's replacement jobs with the loss of their wives' incomes, both families had lower overall family income after the moves. Still both families maintained economic self-sufficiency as a unit, and both continued on the trajectory of having a male as the primary breadwinner. Janet said, in explanation for going along with the move, "Mike needs to be the breadwinner. It's important to how he sees himself as a husband and a father. I can make anything work but men are different, so what are you gonna do."

Chris was an interviewee who hadn't lost his job, but feared he soon would. He had heard rumors that the facility where he worked in Michigan would be closing, and his wife was a stay-at-home mother to their three children. To be preemptive, he actively pursued several openings at other facilities in the same company. His original suspicions proved correct when the Michigan facility closed three months after he and his family had relocated for a different job within the company. Chris did earn a pay raise in the process, but explained that he had to seek a promotion as justification to his employer for wanting to switch jobs. He expressed with certainty that he would not have taken the new position just for the upward mobility. In fact, he and his family would have preferred he remain in his old job at the lower salary rather than move. Chris appeared to be deliberately vying to climb the corporate ladder, but in fact his actions were the product of structural coercion and fear of losing the status quo.

The male breadwinner ideology was apparent in the relocation decision for Austin, a thirty-one-year-old with an advanced degree who believed his firm was becoming financially unstable. Austin knew that landing a new job in his area of expertise would require moving, and even though he was part of a dual-career marriage, he was not willing to risk unemployment to stay put. After working with a recruiter to find a new position, the family relocated. Austin's wife Kate, thirty, had to give up her own well-paid, professional job so that Austin's role as primary earner would be salvaged. Although Austin secured a pay increase in the process, the family was earning less after the move than when Kate was working. They moved into a substantially smaller home due to both the reduction in overall family income and a large cost-of-living differential compared to where they lived previously. Kate was not willing to engage in a job search upon moving because she felt it was more important to be there for her son after the big change. Kate's masters-level education and her career set her apart from wives in the Kanter and Margolis studies. Still, after the economic climate of business instability forced her family to choose between two careers, Kate, like relocated wives of the past, was relegated to reconcile the shocks of the move on the reproductive sphere.

The stories above recount direct threats to movers' employment and how families used relocation as a response. Further stories will show how a climate of job instability and its attendant stress can factor into a decision on relocation even when there is no particular threat to employment on the horizon. Professional workers today do not have lifelong employment relationships with their employers, and their actions demonstrate an awareness of that reality. For example, Ken and Wren moved from Michigan to the Pacific Northwest. "Ken got a great job offer within his company, a promotion and a big raise, as part of a reorganization, but frankly it was not clear whether there would be any job for him at all if he turned it down," Wren, age 46, said matter-of-factly.

Amber, age 29 and the sole breadwinner in her family, had similar thoughts as Ken and Wren. When offered a move to Michigan, she was not excited at the prospect but ultimately agreed. "This promotion came available and they asked me if I'd be interested and I thought Michigan, cold, snow," she confided. "But anyway, weighing all of the benefits and that they asked me to do it, there's a little more emphasis when they ask you to take a promotion than if you're pursuing one so it's like if I say no, what will happen, will they blackball me? What could be the consequences of saying no?" These families were coerced by a sense of vulnerability to yield to the preferences of their employers.

Mark's story shows both direct and indirect structural influences on his relocation. To avoid a potential layoff, he relocated his family to the Chicago suburbs from another midwestern state only to be downsized from the new position a few months later. At thirty-one years old with a second child on the way, Mark was devastated. He reflected:

> I was there a total of six months when they restructured and terminated me. And that was brutal . . . it was what I was trying to avoid and it was probably one of the worst points in my life that I can remember. Here I was in a new house that cost me twice what it cost me to live [before the move]. We didn't know anybody, I had a new baby, a two-year-old, a stay-at-home wife, and no job. It was horrible. I just remember holing up and crying.

Mark had promised to keep his family within a few hours of where they were living when he had first looked for a new job. After losing that new job, he was much more practical, saying:

> During that time period I was throwing the net out elsewhere and possibly preparing for another move. At that point you have to think about first dealing with the need to earn an income. You need to do whatever you can to take care of your family.

Mark internalized the dictates of traditional gender ideology that his role as husband and father was to provide for his family economically, and he worked strenuously to meet what he saw as his responsibility. He worked long hours and was pursuing an MBA at night. He sought and found a new job to fend off potential loss of his income. Still he found that within a year, despite his hard work and preemptive actions, he could be at risk of unemployment not just once, but twice. Mark's experiences exemplify how dominant cultural notions of masculinity can simultaneously advantage and oppress men. Men's dominance in market-based activities can lead to their work and preferences being prioritized within the family. At the same time, however, societal pressure to provide for a family in a risk-infused, unstable economy can put their sense of relevance and their identities at risk.

In the postindustrial economy, at any given time there is a cadre of managers like Ethan, Mike, and Mark who find themselves unemployed mid-career and in search of new employment. Another cadre of managers like Chris and Austin find themselves vulnerable to up-and-coming reorganizations, mergers, and downsizing, and they fear they will soon join the ranks of the unemployed. A third group has no immediate need for angst, but are well aware that reciprocal commitments are a thing of the past. Recall Ken and Amber. These managers are subject to Ryan's (1999) "management by stress," or the coercive effects of the ever-present threat of workforce reduction. In order to establish themselves as indispensable, as team players, they acquiesce to the demands of the workplace. They work longer hours, respond from home to phone calls and emails, and forgo vacations. And they accept relocation assignments that require leaving their homes and communities with family members in tow.

As the above stories show, the economic motivations behind participating in employee relocation in the new millennium are very different than those found by Margolis (1979) in her study of corporate managers in the early 1970's. Margolis described relocating managers as first and foremost male, but also as first-generation members of the professional middle class taken away by the big corporation from "mining towns, farms and urban ghettos ... and the stultifying narrowness (of) small towns" (144). In 1971, first-generation students represented 38.5 percent of all first-time, full-time college freshman; by 2005, the proportion declined to 15.9 percent. (Saenz 2007). Margolis's informants were presumably willing to sacrifice geographic stability to pursue the "American Dream" after they had "broken away from the proletariat from which they sprang" (145).

My informants, on the other hand, were not pursuing but rather clinging to the "American Dream." For most, the narratives were clear in communicating that, even if they did move up in the process, the motivation behind relocation wasn't about advancement, an innate component of the Dream. It wasn't about attaining middle-class standing on their own terms. Rather relocations were frequently about not losing ground or not losing so much ground that they lost self-sufficiency. And they were about complying with employers' terms instead of their own.

Gender was a noticeable factor in the equation, however. Although the male breadwinner model was not ubiquitously dominant, there were many families for whom male breadwinner dominance in the family was paramount. Many families chose to forfeit their communities and their two-earner terms of living rather than have a male's relative status as family provider be compromised. In several cases, families could have remained in their original communities by restrategizing overall family income with women taking on larger roles and men either leaving the workforce or accepting lower paying, lower-status work. Instead, women deferred their roles as paid laborers and followed their husbands. As families faced decisions about relocation, spouse's interests did not always receive equal weight.

PERSONAL AND FINANCIAL CHALLENGES

Once a family enters into a relocation, it affects nearly every realm of life. Negotiating complete changes in community and home requires a lot of "adaptation work" (Whitaker 2011). Two areas of challenge are especially vulnerable to negative repercussions as a result of the new economic realities in which relocations now take place. Those two include handling the disposal and reacquisition of a residence and the renegotiation of an accompanying spouse's role in terms of paid work and contributions to family income.

Changing residence

During a relocation, families must execute what I have termed the "mechanics of relocation," or the practical and logistical activities of the move, including getting into a new permanent residence. This aspect of relocation has changed with the changing economy, and it can impose serious personal and financial strain. Rather than being a fairly typical experience lasting several months and being fully funded by the corporation as it was for the "Organization Man" of the twentieth century, handling the "mechanics of relocation" has become a diverse experience that varies from being short and smooth over two or three months to being erratic, costly, and worrisome over a period of years. Participation in homeownership, which is usually considered an integral part of the "American Dream," can in today's economy hobble a worker's ability to have the flexibility that the new economy demands.

The duration of the "mechanics of relocation" is a function of many unknowns, especially the state of the housing market and the labor market for a spouse's replacement employment. Today's relocated families may face extended periods of separation between when the relocated employee reports to the new job and when the family is able to join in a permanent residence. Families must be flexible in the face of unknown timelines and the stress of separation. In the past, homeownership and home sale profits were a hallmark of relocation. Those expectations have been replaced by potentially devastating financial losses, concurrent housing payments, and the temptation to forgo homeownership in favor of rental.

In 2010 once an employee accepted a transfer offer, the transferee was allowed about thirty days to report to work at the new work site (Lamech 2010). The time between decision and work start is short and dropping, with the average allowance down ten days from just one year prior (Lamech 2010). Concurrently, the time needed to get a family moved is increasing due to uncertain housing markets and the complexities of managing another adult's career transition. When the time allowed and time needed to report to a new community do not align, spouses and children may have to live separately and/or live in temporary housing situations to fill time gaps.

The state of the real estate market, a component of the overall economy, drives home sale price, average time to sell a home, and availability and cost of homes to purchase. Informants in this study frequently expressed serious challenges related to the real estate market. When those challenges drew out the timeline beyond a few months, it was a stressor for the family.

In addition to the financial strain of dealing with a large financial asset and the separation of family members, the idea of 'home' is value-laden in US culture. Homeownership has long been a staple of the "American Dream." Being in flux regarding one's 'home,' losing one's sense of place yet having that place become an albatross of worry and expense, can create an ambivalence that prevents healthy resettlement. Recall that the class position of workers involved in corporate-paid employee relocation is almost exclusively middle- to upper-middle-class or struggling to maintain that class standing, and that this study focuses on families with children. Professional middle- and upper-middle-class families with children are expected to and usually do participate in homeownership. In this study's sample, all but three couples owned homes prior to their most recent transfer.[1]

The United States has been experiencing a serious housing market turndown since mid-2006. When houses become harder and harder to sell, families' time waiting to complete a move grows longer and longer. The late-2006 'housing bust' followed a period of rapid growth in home prices. Based on a composite index by S&P/Case-Shiller, nationally single-family home prices peaked in the second quarter of 2006 and declined nearly 30 percent by 2010. The Chicago Metro area saw a decline of nearly a third since its peak, and in the Detroit Metro area single family home values dropped by nearly half (Maitland and Blitzer 2012). Price declines cause a reduced demand for transferee homes because they feed into the following phenomena: a reduced appeal of homeownership as a means to wealth, an availability of below-market foreclosure properties as alternatives, and homeowner lock-in to current residences as a result of loss aversion and negative equity positions (Ferreira et al. 2010). The real estate market experienced fifteen-year lows in sales, and average time on the market for single-family homes in early 2010 was double to triple the average time from 2000 to 2006 (Maitland and Blitzer 2012).

The state of the housing market was problematic for the mobile families in my sample, as were other disparities between time allowed and time required to report to work. Many informants found themselves renting or separated from family members for longer periods as homes were not selling, capital for downpayments disappeared, and home ownership became less appealing. The data for this study were gathered during 2008 and 2009, but referenced moves that took place anytime from 2004 (pre-bust) to 2009 (post-bust). Overall, thirteen of the thirty-one families were subject to family separation because the employed spouse moved ahead of the other family members, and twelve of the thirty-one families rented temporarily or permanently post-move. Five families experienced both conditions.

For families who had difficulty selling homes, the work of disposing of the residence expanded to additional tasks, especially identifying alternative options such as renting out the property, leaving the property vacant, modifying sale-price expectations, and considering renting in the destination community. Kate and Austin were separated for five months, during which Kate took on the role of full-time worker and single mom with a house to keep up for marketability. She and their preschool-aged son usually drove five hours each way on the weekends to stay with her husband. She described the circumstances this way:

> So I stayed in Michigan and continued to work. We needed to make money while we were still paying our mortgage in Michigan because the housing market there was not all that fantastic. And then our house actually sold one month after we moved here.

In this sample four families accepted corporate buyouts where their employers, usually facilitated by a relocation service company, purchased their homes at a price just below market value as determined by multiple appraisers. One family rented their home out, and then rented in the destination community. Two left their properties vacant, rented a home in the destination community, and hoped for a sale to materialize. One family left their home vacant and purchased a home in the destination community by borrowing funds from a family member. Yet another left their home vacant and purchased a new home in the destination community after living apart for over a year. Another six months later they allowed the bank to foreclose on the previous home because of their extreme negative equity position even if the house eventually sold.

Homeownership has ceased to be a given for relocators. Two families rented with no plans to buy because they were not convinced that they could build up enough equity to make it economically worthwhile before they might be asked to move again. Brad and Cassie were one such couple. Brad discussed the decision and the difficulty in selling his other home:

> I think both of us, based on the housing market right now, just wanted to rent. And, the fact that, you know, we are only going to be here for a minimum of two years. So it's not a lot of time to build equity in a house or anything. . . . And, um, we put our house down there on the market in February and we just signed on the contract now [in August]. So, it's been, you know, six months of kind of stressing about trying to sell that house and we have to pay rent here and the mortgage down there and everything.

Brad and Cassie went from being homeowners to being renters when economic rationality and uncertainty merged. They rethought the taken-for-grantedness of homeownership and retreated from their commitment to this preeminent milestone of the "American Dream."

Christie and Sam did not lapse in their desire to live in a home they owned even when their financial circumstances didn't support it. At the time of the interview they were struggling financially and emotionally in large part because of a still-ongoing problem with their housing. Initially in the move process the couple spent time apart with Sam moving ahead and staying in the basement bedroom of an extended family member he barely knew. The couple had an offer on their house and were waiting for the sale to finalize. They expected the separation to be brief, but sadly the sale fell through just days before the transaction was finalized.

With a toddler and an infant to care for, Christie was desperate to have the family together. She urged Sam to ask his father for help with a down payment so they could buy a new home while the old one remained for sale. Sam gave in to Christie's request after first refusing. After almost eight months, the couple still had a home for sale several states away, but they had used help from Sam's father to purchase a new home. Sam was dejected about having to borrow from a family member, and seemed resentful of Christie for it. He continually described their housing situation as renting as a reminder that he had not independently provided his family with the home. The psychological impact of the circumstances was great. "There is a part of me that says this doesn't feel like my home yet, something psychological that says it's not yours. Sam says we are renting and in a way we kind of are," Christie said sadly. "But yeah it's been a very stressful year. This has been horrible . . . "

Sam perceived borrowing money from his father as defeat, a loss of self-sufficiency, and a signifier of his inability to provide for his family. Ransome (2005) argues that, according to traditional gender ideology in work-based western societies, successfully performing the provider role is a key marker of what it means to be a male. Sam apparently subscribed to this belief. Christie adhered to it as well, although she and Sam were at odds about acceptable means to the end. She did not see the loan as Sam's failure to provide, but rather as a way of providing. The gendered nature of Christie's actions is even clearer when you realize Christie herself had very high earning potential in a specialized medical field and had previously been the senior earner in the family. As she was imploring Sam to take the loan that caused him so much anxiety, she was refusing to go back to work after the relocation so that she could fulfill her dream of being a stay-at-home mom, itself a product of internalizing traditional gender roles. In accordance with cultural gender scripts, Christie had a strong sense that she 'should' be a stay-at-home mom, and that this role would be inherently fulfilling for her.

Zach and Ashley were another of the many couples in this research who faced protracted difficulty with housing. The couple left a vacant home behind so their family of four could relocate together. Unlike Christie and Sam, they chose to rent until their house sold. They were paying a mortgage in one city and rent in another, but were able to make ends meet by watching their spending. "It was just the stress," Zach lamented, as he explained that the house they were renting was also for sale. "That really worried me. Because it was up for sale and we were on a month-to-month basis. If it got sold we knew we had sixty days probably to get out of the house. It was a constant worry for me." Their house did sell, and they did buy another home in their new community. The interview with this family took place in a charming, even idyllic white picket fence-enclosed home that Zach and Ashley had purchased just days before. It had taken them close to a year to get to there, but they looked on the bright side by emphasizing that the rental period provided time to get to know the community before buying. They remained committed to homeownership as the appropriate end to their journey.

Ironically, by tying relocating families to a geographic location, home-ownership can confound the pursuit of stable employment and upward mobility that facilitate homeownership itself. Also, in the current economy, loss aversion, negative equity, declining loan-to-value ratios that affect credit worthiness, and lengthening of average time-on-market for homes are frequent reasons for relocation offer declines (Ferreira et al. 2010). The majority of homeowning relocators sell or try to sell their properties, while others consciously choose to rent out their homes or become what *Time* Magazine has called "accidental landlords" if their homes fail to sell (Kiviat 2009). Many informants in this sample had relocation benefits from their companies that paid transaction costs on home sales and home purchases, but only a few were offered buy-outs where the employer purchased the home if it did not sell within a designated time frame. Only one was offered loss-on-sale assistance. Over a third of the sample faced challenges from the home sale that imposed significant emotional and financial costs on the family. This is a departure from the experiences with housing for Margolis's subjects who, regardless of other struggles, were almost universally guaranteed bigger homes, home sale profits, and short timelines to resettling together.

SPOUSE'S EMPLOYMENT

With 65 percent of relocating employees married to paid workers (Marshall and Greenwood 2002), relocations today affect accompanying spouses' roles and potentially their sense of identity. With so many moves undertaken as a result of economic uncertainty and vulnerability, the changes that a spouse must negotiate are often not welcome or sought out. In addition, families who are going from two incomes to one may have faced tough decisions about their overall family income composition. Historically, relocating spouses retained their roles and identities as full-time homemakers. The homemaker role came with difficulties of its own when a family moved. Still, there was no role transition, nor did the role create a delay in one's availability to accompany the spouse. Many accompanying spouses still fit it that dynamic, but many do not. Just under 60 percent (eighteen of thirty-one) of relocated spouses in this sample were working for pay pre-move, including eleven of the twenty-one trailing wives and seven of the ten trailing husbands.

This project showed that even if families did not have a traditional male breadwinner-female homemaker configuration prior to a move, traditional gender expectations were often a factor in making decisions about trailing spouses' post-move work. The project had a unique ability to explore the role of gender in relocation because it included both women and men who were moved employees. The evidence suggests that while accompanying men may make sacrifices in their paid-work roles, it is the exception and not the norm. On the other hand, wives who accompany their husbands for a move are very likely to adapt in a way that best serves other family members even if they, themselves, are giving up something they value. As Stone (2007) and Hays (1998) point out, women do not make their labor force decisions in a vacuum. Rather they make decisions during a cultural moment when norms and practices for mothers are very demanding, when the cultural imperative advises mothers, especially middle- and upper-class mothers, to expend a vast amount of time, energy, and money in child-raising.

Ethan and Mike were introduced earlier, and both of their stories exemplify women's sacrifices. Both of their wives had paid work before their moves, and both husbands were contending with layoffs. Ethan's wife Mary was an attorney with a hard-to-find, part-time position in her field. Post-move, she became a full-time, stay-at-home mom and she did not expect to be able to replace her paid position. Although Mary could have supported her family on her own, she was willing to move to have her husband retain that role. She discussed part-time work for mothers in her field:

> As a starting-out attorney, you don't get offers for part-time employment, that's what a lot of women in the field complain about. New attorneys, they want you to work sunup to sundown and women who want kids can't do that; it's a huge problem. It was a good opportunity and I would have stayed. . . . [I didn't become the breadwinner because] he's just so much more driven professionally, even though it seems like I made a huge investment going to law school. To me it's fulfilling to be with my kids, it's something that wouldn't be for him. If he wanted to, he could.

Mike's wife Janet was less indifferent to the sacrifice of her job, but she had seen what Mike's job loss had done to his confidence and sense of identity. She was making a meaningful contribution to the family income and believed Mike could have found a job locally that would have paid enough to combine with her income to make ends meet. To fulfill Janet's wishes Mike would have had to take a pay cut and a job much lower in prestige than the one he lost. Mike ended up finding a job comparable to the one he lost, but the family of six had to move. Janet launched a job search in their new locale and she was the one who ended up with a position that was less prestigious, less satisfying, and much lower-paying. She was not happy about the situation but she was willing to make the adaptation because she saw it as important to her husband's sense of self.

Mike was not indifferent to uprooting his family, but he still clung to his position as primary breadwinner. The couple's early adherence to traditional gender ideology to determine their labor roles had boosted him into the position, and he was committed to staying there. Both Janet and Mike paid a price for this commitment. The cost to Janet was great. It was ubiquitous in her life, costing her a much-loved community and a good job. Mike paid with the intangibles of guilt and fear that are hard to measure against the high costs paid by Janet. Mike felt very guilty for moving the family, especially his two high-school-aged children. He justified his actions with fear, the fear of being unable to send those same two children to college in the near future if the family slipped economically.

Mike also described great fear of being a failure as a father and husband, his definition of which aligned with Townsend's (2002) paradigm of the "Package Deal" that explains good fatherhood as culturally imagined, albeit unrealistically, as a combination of emotional closeness, provision, protection, and endowment of character and opportunity. Middle-class ideology intersected with this gendered construct for Mike as he subscribed to both an unwavering need to fulfill his provider role and the perception that a college education was among the advantages he was obligated to provide. Janet's characterization of the provider role as important to Mike's sense of self was consistent with his own testimony of the situation. The unstable economy conjured the constraints of traditional gender and class ideologies on both of these spouses.

The evidence from this study suggests that relocations for women's jobs are less frequently made under economic duress, which may be why women's trailing spouses were less likely to be placed in difficult positions redetermining their new work roles. Many of the women whose careers led to a relocation were in specialized, high-level, high-skill jobs that are less vulnerable to downsizing. Overall, the moved-employee wives in the study had very high educational attainment. Six of the ten had professional degrees (JD, MD, or PhD) that placed them in the top 3 percent of adults over age 25 in terms of education (U.S. Census Population Survey 2009). As such, their employers were highly invested in getting or maintaining their unique skills within the organization. Specialized skills can give an employee leverage with the employer that other workers do not have. Three of the six highly-educated wives negotiated employment for their husbands as part of the relocation package, making the adaptation process easier for their spouses—one at a university, one at a hospital, and one at a global corporation. Only three of the twenty-one husbands in the husband-centered moves had a J.D., M.D., or PhD, and none of the twenty-one husbands who led a move negotiated new work for their wives. Given the very small sample size and nonrandom nature of the sampling methodology, however, this finding serves only as a directional trend that bears further investigation.

For both trailing men and women, the work-from-home phenomenon that has emerged over the past couple of decades (Richardson 2010) offered a potential counter-balance to the disruptive nature of the relocation. Six of the trailing spouses—three women and three men—were able to minimize their job and role adaptation requirements because their work-from-home job was portable. Tietze and Musson (2010) argue that working from home is not entirely utopian, especially for managerial and office workers. They contend that it introduces conflict and contradiction to the formation of identities related to both home and work. Identity, this argument suggests, is constructed as an ongoing social process, achieved by a subtle interweaving of the many aspects of social and occupational interactions that enable individuals to locate and define themselves in their social environment. Because at-home work, or telework, is less or differently interactive and situated in the contradictory location of home, identity development can become complicated. This research suggests that for relocated spouses the continuity of work and peer contacts from work-at-home arrangements mitigates the disruption to daily lives and sense of identity that result from a move.

Donna used her work-from-home situation as a way to maintain contacts for another time in her life when she is more interested in paid work. At the time of the move she wanted to assist her kids with the transition and not worry about a job. Interestingly, even though Donna did work for pay on a part-time basis, she did not define herself as a worker. She explained it like this, "I was not working. I stopped working after the birth of my first child. . . . I did consulting work and I still do for the company I used to work for. Not a ton, but enough to keep my foot in the door. . . . I was able to keep doing that even after we moved to Chicago because it was a national account. . . . I picked and chose what I wanted to do. My goal was establishing the kids and not myself, well myself too, but not my career."

Evan, who worked as a freelancer in the arts, also continued his paid labor after relocating for his wife's job. "You can do it from anywhere, you just need an email address," he told me. Akira's work role was also undisturbed by the move. In fact, she found that her new home and new community were even more conducive to supporting the business she ran out of her home manufacturing and selling a line of home products. There was more space and the typical wage rates for employees in the area were lower.

Trailing spouse narratives like Donna's, Evan's, and Akira's illustrate that the portability of at-home work can allow accompanying spouses to retain their identities as paid workers. This can reduce the overall strain of the move by eliminating the need for transformation in one important aspect of life.

Among trailing mothers, three of the eleven paid workers were able to continue working for pay because they worked from home; three started a new job; and five transitioned to stay-at-home parent. Among trailing fathers, three of the seven paid workers continued in the same work-from-home job although one of the three scaled back from full-time to part-time hours; two were provided full-time positions with their relocating spouse's employer; one found a new full-time job through his own efforts; and one was offered a job by his wife's employer but elected to stay at home full time with his children to get them resituated. These data are based on the most recent moves for families that have undergone more than one work-related relocation. About equal proportions of trailing men and women underwent a formal role adaptation, but the nature of those changes and the motivations behind them were substantively different. The voluntary nature of most female-led moves in this sample suggests why fewer trailing men reduced their paid-work situations. Moves not prompted by some direct or indirect threat to employment may be more likely to offer a more balanced outcome across spouses. If a move is truly voluntary, devoid of structural coercion, and part of a strategy of upward mobility or career development that originates within the family, the degree to which that strategy serves different family members will likely be greater.

CONCLUSION

The stories told by respondents in this study offer poignant insight into the struggles of professional middle-class workers in the new economy. Since US firms have made shifting business risk from themselves to their employees a standard business practice, it has become harder and harder for professional families to maintain their grip on their middle-class positions. When employment hardship or risk presents itself, families must often respond with high levels of adaptability and even a willingness to leave their communities for what they hope will be lasting opportunity. It is important to note, however, that even when moves are dressed in opportunity's clothing, they may be indirectly coerced by the ever-present sense of employment uncertainty that defines the US workplace today. Workers face the challenges as best they can, enduring loss and navigating housing issues and concerns about second incomes. The families in this sample acknowledged stressors and were persevering, although some expressed hope and others expressed fear and frustration.

Relocation also has the potential to curb advances and commitment to gender equality within the family. Both gender and employee relocation reside squarely at the intersection of work and family, making gender fundamental to how families navigated the experience. In Kanter's and Margolis's studies of the relocation experience, the implications of gender were clear and universal. Men were workers and women were economic dependents and purveyors of reproductive labor who supported their husband's work. Since those studies, women have experienced advancements in the workplace, and western society has adopted increasingly egalitarian views of women. This has changed how women are affected when a family move occurs.

Certainly, this project suggests there have been some improvements in women's position with regard to relocation, even if only by showing that some moves today are for women's jobs. In other ways, however, the project reveals that the economic climate of today can create setbacks for women. Many dual-income families, including those with wives in skilled careers, fell back on traditional gender role beliefs to determine how to proceed when faced with employment challenges. In many cases, men's careers were prioritized and women were compelled to take care of the increased workload caring for and resituating children and home during the major transition. Positioning two careers equally becomes difficult when the economy mandates a national view of the labor market. As a result, men's continued dominance in paid labor can become both more visible and reinforced.

The research argues effectively that reinforcement of traditional gender roles and a gendered division of labor across productive/reproductive lines is oppressive to everyone, to both women and men. Women are clearly injured when ideological imperatives are invoked. Subscribing to the view that women are best suited for caregiving and should be defined by their nurturance subjugates them as secondary family members with little choice and power. When people subscribe to the view that men are best suited for the provider role and we define men by their earnings, this subjects them to a high potential for failure in their own and society's eyes. This is especially true in an economy where good earning positions are scarce and unpredictable. In relocation, where we are studying middle-class professionals, class ideology intersects with gender ideology uniquely so that the need to 'provide' imposes expectations well beyond satisfying basic needs. The economic vulnerability behind so many employee relocations today is reaching into the family to both expose and exacerbate the hazards of traditional class and gender ideology.

Undeniably, relocation has changed from the twentieth century. Overall, families today possess a lower level of power and advantage in the relocation arrangement compared with their employers. Under such conditions, individuals often lose their sense of surety that they are moving forward and that they are living on their own terms.

The decline of individual control exemplified in the phenomenon of employee relocation is situated within the larger context of both political and economic threats and shifts that have pervaded in the twenty-first century. As a result, the last decades have seen an erosion in the dominance of the ideology of the "American Dream" (Stark 2003), and McGuire (2105) has identified the presence in this century of a challenge to the definition of the "American Dream" such that some now dream of security and safety rather than hope and prosperity. It will continue to be important to examine if and how Americans may reshape their aspirations and understandings of success and well-being in the face of change and how progress toward gender equality in the family is affected.

NOTE

1. Two of the couples who were renting before the transfer did so because the relocated spouse was completing a professional degree program. Both anticipated increasing their income dramatically and purchasing a home upon leaving the program. The third had lost their home in a business bankruptcy when the struggling economy caused the wife's business to fail.

REFERENCES

Bielby, William T., and Denise D. Bielby. 1992. "I Will Follow Him: Family Ties, Gender-role Beliefs, and Reluctance to Relocate for a Better Job." *American Journal of Sociology* 97(5):1241–1267.

Cappelli, Peter. 2008a. *Talent on Demand: Managing Talent in an Age of Uncertainty.* Boston: Harvard Business Review Press.

Cappelli, Peter. 2008b. "Talent Management for the Twenty-First Century." *Harvard Business Review* 86(3):74–81.

Collins, Randall, Janet Saltzman Chafetz, Rae Lesser Blumberg, Scott Coltrane, and Jonathan H. Turner. 1993. "Toward an Integrated Theory of Gender Stratification." *Sociological Perspectives* 36(3):185–216.

Eby, Lillian T., and Joyce E. A. Russell. 2000. "Predictors of Employee Willingness to Relocate for the Firm." *Journal of Vocational Behavior* 57(1): 42–61.

Farber, H. S. 2007. "Is the Company Man an Anachronism? Trends in Long Term Employment in the U.S., 1973–2006." Princeton University Working Paper No. 518.

Ferreira, Fernando, Joseph Gyourko, and Joseph Tracy. 2010. "Housing Busts and Household Mobility." *Journal of Urban Economics* 68(1):34–45.

Gerstel, Naomi, Dan Clawson, and Robert Zussman. 2002. "Family Labor and the Construction of Gender." In *Families at Work: Expanding the Boundaries* edited by Naomi Gerstel, Dan Clawson, and Robert Zussman, vii–4. Nashville, TN: Vanderbilt University Press.

Goldin, Claudia Dale, and Lawrence F. Katz. 2007. "Long-Run Changes in the Wage Structure: Narrowing, Widening, Polarizing." *Brookings Papers on Economic Activity* 2:135–165.

Hays, Sharon. 1998. *The Cultural Contradictions of Motherhood*. New Haven, CT: Yale University Press.

Hodson, Randy, and Teresa Sullivan. 2002. *The Social Organization of Work*. Belmont, CA: Wadsworth/Thomas Learning.

Kanter, Rosabeth Moss. 1977. *Men and Women of the Corporation*. New York: Basic Books.

Kilborn, Peter T. 2005. "The Five-Bedroom, Six-Figure Rootless Life." *New York Times*. June 1.

Kilborn, Peter T. 2009. *Next Stop, Reloville: Life Inside America's New Rootless Professional Class*. New York: Times Books.

Kimmel, Michael and Abby L. Ferber. 2006. "'White Men Are This Nation': Right-Wing Militias and the Restoration of Rural American Masculinity." In *Country Boys: Masculinity and Rural Life*, edited by Hugh Campbell, Michael Mayerfeld Bell, and Margaret Finney, 122–137. University Park: Pennsylvania State University Press.

Kiviat, Barbara. 2009. "Accidental Landlords: Renting What Won't Sell." *Time Magazine*. September 19.

Lamech, Miriam. September 2007. "2007 Transfer Volume and Cost Survey." *MOBILITY Magazine*. Washington, DC: Employee Relocation Council.

Lamech, Miriam. September 2010. "2010 U.S. Transfer Volume and Cost Survey." *MOBILITY Magazine*. Washington, DC: Employee Relocation Council.

Lichter, Daniel T. 1983. "Socioeconomic Returns to Migration among Married Women." *Social Forces*. 62(2):487–503.

Maitland, Maureen F., and David M. Blitzer. 2012. *S&P/Case Shiller Home Price Indices: 2011, A Year in Review*. New York: S&P Indices. http://us.spindices.com/documents/research/SP_Case-Shiller_2011_Year_in_Review.pdf.

Margolis, Diane Rothbard. 1979. *The Managers: Corporate Life in America*. New York: William Morrow.

Marshall, Edward L., and Peggy Greenwood. April 2002. "Setting Corporate Policy to Meet the Changing Definition of Family". *MOBILITY Magazine*. Washington, DC: Employee Relocation Council.

McGuire, John. 2015. "Captain America in the 21st Century: The Battle for the Ideology of the American Dream." In *Marvel Comics' Civil War and the Age of Terror: Critical Essays on the Comic Saga*, edited by Kevin Michael Scott, 150–165. Jefferson, NC: McFarland.

Raetz, Leslie. April 2012. "Cutting Costs: A Balancing Act." *MOBILITY Magazine*. Washington, DC: Employee Relocation Council.

Ransome, Paul. *Work, Consumption and Culture: Affluence and Social Change in the Twenty-First Century.* London: SAGE, 2005.

Rapp, Rayna. 1999. "Family and Class in Contemporary America: Notes toward and Understanding of Ideology." In *American Families: A Multicultural Reader*, edited by Stephanie Coontz, 180–196. New York: Routledge.

Ryan, Sarah. 1999. "Management by Stress: The Reorganization of Work Hits Home in the 1990s." In *American Families: A Multicultural Reader,* edited by Stephanie Coontz, 332–341. New York: Routledge. .

Saenz, V. B. 2007. *First in My Family: A Profile of First-Generation College Students at Four-year Institutions since 1971.* Los Angeles: Higher Education Research Institute.

Shihadeh, Edward S. 1991. "The Prevalence of Husband-Centered Migration: Employment Consequences for Married Mothers." *Journal of Marriage and the Family* 53(2):432–444.

Starks, Brian. 2003. "The New Economy and the American Dream: Examining the Effect of Work Conditions on Beliefs about Economic Opportunity." *The Sociological Quarterly* 44(2):205–225.

Stone, Pamela. 2007. "The Rhetoric and Reality of 'Opting Out.'" *Contexts* 6 (4):14–19.

Sullivan, Ellie, and Tim McCarney. April 2011. "The Big Squeeze—After You Think You've Gotten It All: More Policy Savings." *MOBILITY Magazine*. Washington, DC: Employee Relocation Council.

Tietze, Susanne, and Gillian Musson. 2010. "Identity, Identity Work, and the Experience of Working from Home." *Journal of Management Development* 29(2):148–156.

U.S. Census Bureau Population Division. 2009. "December. Table 2: Cumulative Estimates of Resident Population Change for the United States, Regions and Puerto Rico and Region and State Rankings April 1, 2000 to July 1, 2009." NSTEST2009-02.

U.S. Department of Labor, Bureau of Labor Statistics. September 2005. "Highlights of Women's Earnings in 2004." Report 987. Washington, DC. http://www.bls.gov/opub/reports/womensearnings/archive/womensearnings_2004.pdf.

Valcour, P. Monique, and Pamela Tolbert. 2003. "Gender, Family and Career in the Era of Boundarylessness: Determinants and Effects of Intra- And Inter-Organizational Mobility." *The International Journal of Human Resource Management* 14(5):768–787.

Whyte, William Hollingsworth. 1956. *The Organization Man.* New York: Simon and Schuster.

CHAPTER 9

cV&o.

Between Gender Contracts, Economic Crises, and Work-Family Reconciliation

How the Bursting Bubble Reshaped Israeli High-Tech Workers' Experience of Balance

MICHAL FRENKEL

With this bubble bursting, who can afford a child? We are both working so hard and there is so much insecurity around, especially in the high-tech sector. I do not think that bringing a child into this world is a responsible step.

(Amy, 28, married, a British-born Israeli website designer,
Focus Group 10, April 2002)

The twenty-six Israeli high-tech women invited to take part in a focus group on work-family conflicts and strategies were sitting in a large circle, taking turns sharing their stories. It was mid-2002, and the bursting of the high-tech bubble that has shaken the high-technology industry around the globe and brought labor insecurity to an industry that had previously been considered immune to such economic downturns was front and center in their accounts of the work-family challenges they were facing and their depiction of the best way to tackle these challenges. For some participants, the end of the bubble led to a lessening of work-family conflict: a spouse who was laid off and became more available to care for young children or a reduced work load due to fewer projects were some of the reasons mentioned. For others, defending their jobs in a time of major layoffs, or supporting a spouse who had to secure his high-tech job, have made the everyday experience of managing a demanding career while caring for one's family even more challenging than it had been during the halcyon days of the industry, just months before. While the group was somewhat diversified—it included young and older women, married and single, those with children, and those without—the experiences each one of them shared was commonly received with an understanding nod and sympathetic comments. It was in this rather supportive and consensual atmosphere that Amy's comment (cited above) immediately attracted our attention. To the ear of any scholar studying work-family issues in the industrialized world, and to most professional women in advanced economies, Amy's statement would have sounded completely unexceptional. As many of the chapters in this volume have demonstrated, growing economic and labor force insecurity and uncertainty have made men and women in the United States, Japan, and other industrialized societies reconsider or completely forego parenthood. Yet, in the context of Israel, Amy's statement elicited a very different reaction. The room immediately erupted in a collective response, with the same message stated in a different way, namely: "Don't even consider giving up on motherhood for economic reasons."

The group's emotional response may be better understood when we bear in mind that in the previous nine focus groups, the individual interviews we had conducted up to that point, and the open-ended responses to our survey, not a single respondent had made any kind of direct link between the economic crisis and the possibility that she might forego having children in the future. Despite growing economic insecurity, it was clear that, unlike their colleagues in other industrialized societies, Israeli high-tech professionals did not see such security as a precondition for parenthood. Moreover, while studies in the United States, Europe, and Japan (e.g., Lane, 2010, 2016; Pugh, 2015; Alexy, 2016; Gerson 2016) have pointed to a move away from couplehood and parenthood toward self-sufficiency and individualism as a common response to the rise of insecurity and uncertainty in the workforce, my study of workers in the Israeli high-tech industry after the bursting of the bubble indicates a different reaction—namely, a stronger reliance both on the nuclear and extended family to allow one to better navigate economic insecurity, and on parenthood as a core identity and source of meaning in life, and as a strategy for dealing with economic uncertainty.

One explanation for the difference between Israeli professionals and those in the United States and other industrialized societies in their response to economic insecurity may be found in another group member's response to Amy's statement. Rebecca, a twenty-eight-year-old account manager and a mother of two who had migrated to Israel from the United Kingdom eight years earlier, said: "It may have made sense in England to forego motherhood because you are not sure you will have the money to raise them. In Israel it is not like that. You get help from the government, you manage." Relying on her own perception of the conditions in her and Amy's homeland, as compared to those in Israel, Rebecca hints at differences in both the objective provisions offered by the state as part of its welfare policy (known as the defamilialization welfare regime) and in the well-institutionalized, normative division of labor among the state, the market, the extended family, and the nuclear family in caring for children and other family members, also known as "gender contracts." In Rebecca's view, the more generous state provisions in the field of child care in Israel and the social norms in this field allow employees in Israel to stick to the local pronatalist practice, even in times of social insecurity and economic uncertainty.

What Rebecca's comment fails to take into consideration, though, is that the changing constellation and the growing insecurity and instability that characterize both the workplace and the family sphere in the early twenty-first century—as so eloquently depicted by scholars in this volume—have not left Israeli society unaffected. Since the 1980s, Israel has swiftly entered the global economy, replacing its once highly stabilized and highly unionized labor market with a "flexible" one characterized by employers' freedom to lay off their workers as they see fit. The privately owned (often by foreign corporations) high-tech industry was the first to embrace this trend (Senor and Singer, 2011). In line with the spirit of neoliberalism, Israel's once rather generous welfare state has also been subjected to fierce critiques and cutbacks, including severe cuts in unemployment insurance and state-sponsored child support (Maron 2015; Koreh and Shalev 2009), making Rebecca's assertion that "you get help from the government" less persuasive than it had been before. On the family front, divorce rates per 1,000 people have reached 1.8, compared to the OECD average of 2.2 in the early twenty-first century (Kaplan and Herbst 2015), making nuclear family life in Israel almost as unstable as it is in the United States and most of Western Europe. Why, then, was the response of Israeli high-tech workers to growing insecurity brought about by the bubble burst so different from the one documented in other industrialized societies? Drawing on data from focus groups, individual interviews, and surveys of high-tech men and women in Israel during the crash of the early 2000s, this chapter demonstrates how the remnants of the traditional Israeli welfare regime, together with its cultural *heritage*—namely, the institutionalized norms, expectations, and practices that constituted the local *gender contract*, which are slower to change than the objective economic reality—have played a critical role in mediating employees' responses to economic insecurity when it comes to their work-family strategies. After a short theoretical discussion of welfare regimes, gender contracts, and how they may affect employees' responses to economic insecurity, as well as a methodological section presenting the case of Israel, the chapter points to the three main strategies that common work-family Israeli high-tech professionals have developed in the face of the abrupt bursting of the industry bubble: (1) sticking with pronatalism, which was a characteristic mostly of mothers who were balancing work and family before the crisis; (2) returning home, a practice mostly of men who had previously favored work time over family time; and (3) renegotiating their contracts, a strategy employed mostly by women who had favored family considerations over work ones.

WELFARE REGIMES, GENDER CONTRACT, AND ECONOMIC INSECURITY—A THEORETICAL NOTE

States and societies differ in the extent to which they attempt to reduce their members' dependency on the financial and labor markets to secure their own welfare (e.g., Esping-Anderson 1999).

Until the early 1990s, comparative studies of welfare regimes focused on state policies aimed at de-commodification—namely, reducing the extent to which citizens are dependent on the labor market to secure minimal economic security (Esping-Andersen 1990)—but in recent years this line of research has expanded to include policies affecting the dependence of family care providers on their spouses and extended families (defamilialization) (e.g., Esping-Andersen 1999; Daly and Rake 2003; Lewis 1997; Sainsbury 1996; Orloff 1993).

Parallel to the growing interest in defamilialization welfare policies and their impact on gender division of labor and work-family arrangements, a second, closely related body of comparative literature has emerged. It focuses more on "gender contracts"—specifically, the cultural and normative conceptualizations of the desired division of family labor among men, women, the extended family, the community, the market, and the state (e.g., Gottfried 2000, Pfau Effinger 2004b).

Historically, the comparative welfare state literature has identified a strong correlation between decommodification and defamilialization regimes, showing that countries with stronger decommodification policies also tend to adopt a stronger defamilialization approach, reducing the dependency of people with family obligations on both the labor market and their families.

The classification of gendered/family welfare regimes refers to policies and provisions that support women (or care providers in general) during times of precarious employment (such as during pregnancy and after childbirth) and allow them back into the labor market without compromising their children's welfare. The length and extent of coverage of maternity, paternity, family, and sick leaves, together with other policies such as the provision of sponsored and supervised quality early education and afterschool programs, is used to distinguish between liberal, conservative (northern and southern), and social democratic family welfare regimes. A common example of the differences among these regimes is the type of parental leave they offer. In social democratic welfare regimes, the state provides (or forces employers to provide) long and mostly paid leaves for fathers and mothers (encouraging them to share care responsibilities while keeping their jobs). In contrast, conservative regimes have traditionally offered short, fully paid maternity leaves complemented by lengthy but low-paying parental leaves, available mostly to mothers. Finally, the liberal regime is characterized by the minimal availability of state-sponsored and paid leaves, forcing parents of newborn children to go back to work shortly after the child is born and to rely either on the market for the provision of care services (nannies or private day care facilities) or on their families and individual resources. Alternatively, they might have to withdraw from the labor force. Because they differ in the extent of provision offered to various income groups, some regimes may have very contrasting impacts on the work-family strategies of people from different classes. Naturally, the more elaborate a welfare regime is, the less insecure its citizens are likely to feel about the fate of their families in times of personal economic turmoil.

Family welfare regimes and gender contracts are often mutually related. To a certain extent, the state provision of family-related services and allowances is designed to address constituents' needs. Thus when there is a strong norm advocating maternal care for children under three years of age, the state is more likely to offer a stipend that allows mothers to stay at home with their toddlers than it is to sponsor high-quality day care. At the same time, a lack of day care facilities reinforces the norm according to which mothers should stay home with their toddlers because of the lack of other socially acceptable and financially reasonable solutions should they choose to go back to work. The increasing global diffusion of ideas and practices across national boundaries, however, has problematized this tight correlation between family welfare regimes and gender contracts in several ways. On the one hand, owing to pressure from international organizations, many state and regional governments have adopted new laws and regulations aimed at increasing work-family balance and participation in the labor force. In some cases, therefore, states now provide welfare policies that are at odds with existing cultural norms among parents and employers (Frenkel 2013; Walby 2004). At the same time, global market pressures have undermined existing decommodification policies, making all employees, including parents, more vulnerable to economic change and labor insecurities. In these cases, social and cultural frames that had been institutionalized around historical welfare arrangements could be in conflict with the new labor market environment. So far the literature on welfare regimes and gender contracts has largely overlooked the consequences of the changing welfare policies and deteriorating decommodification on individuals' conceptualization of their life plans and the ways in which they rethink their work-family arrangements, given their changing welfare environment.

Naturally, state policies aimed at reducing decommodification and defamilialization are expected to affect employees' experience of labor and economic uncertainty in times of economic crises, and the ways in which employees and job-seekers handle the challenges of economic insecurities when it comes to their work-family considerations and strategies. After all, a lesser dependency on the labor market for providing minimal welfare and family services such as health and education make the challenges associated with losing one's job less threatening.

Labor legislation and the degree of labor flexibility that it lends to employers is part of the welfare regime. While liberal welfare states have tended to allow for greater labor flexibility—for example, allowing employers to lay off their workers as they see fit with very little risk on their part—social democratic and conservative welfare states have more rigid labor legislation that is often reinforced by labor unions. Under these regimes, layoffs are much more complicated and require union cooperation. Under the pressures of neoliberal ideologies and the global market, however, many of the traditionally social democratic and conservative countries have introduced a growing level of labor flexibility. Unionization and unions' ability to protect employers have often been diminished in these societies, increasing the level of labor insecurity in these societies as well. Yet it is important to note that even in countries in which labor protection has decreased, some of the social institutions that have developed around the historical regime endure. In some cases, older employees still maintain their job security, state-sponsored pension plans, and other benefits. Younger employees, who have grown up in a different era, may still develop their life plans and future expectations based on the institutionalized norms that once emerged around the welfare policies but that are no longer available to them.

Analyzing the ways in which Israeli high-tech workers have responded to the accelerating economic insecurity first encountered during the bursting of the high-tech bubble—in a period in which old, relatively generous state provisions were giving way to new, more liberal, and less protective policies—allows us to better understand the extent to which both the existing welfare provisions and the gender contract that was constructed around the old regime have shaped these employees' work-family strategies.

METHODOLOGY

Accounting for the role of gender contracts and welfare regimes in shaping men and women's work-family conceptualizations in times of economic crisis and greater economic insecurity may follow one of two possible research strategies: (1) comparing survey or interview data collected in two different countries characterized by different contracts and regimes but experiencing a similar crisis in the same period, or (2) focusing on the way respondents draw on aspects of their own society's gender contract or welfare regime in their own subjective accounts of the way they have responded to the crisis. While the first strategy tends to assume that the fact that a certain policy is available in a country makes it available and relevant to each and every individual in that country, the second strategy allows us to gain a better understanding of the way men and women experience their own realities and their knowledge of the relevant policies and services provided not only by the state, but by their extended families and communities as well. In this sense, I am more interested in the way people interpret their surroundings and link them to their work-family strategies than in the actual availability of services and provisions. Given the data that were available to me, this chapter follows the second strategy and focuses on the way people take into consideration and interpret their situation when pointing directly to features of the gender regime and welfare state in their environment as factors shaping their reaction to the crisis.

In 2001–2003, in collaboration with the late professor Dafna Izraeli, I conducted a study of the work-family strategies of Israeli high-tech women. The study included personal interviews with sixty men and women working in the field, ten focus group interviews (some of them in mixed and others in gender-segregated groups), and an Internet survey of women only (n=919). The research project was designed during the heyday of this industry in Israel, but by the time we started conducting the focus groups and running the survey, the bubble had burst, and the economic insecurity it triggered was a central topic in many of the focus groups we conducted. While we did not ask any direct questions about the crisis, many participants shared their concerns about and reactions to the new economic situation. For the purposes of this study, I have reanalyzed the qualitative data that emerged from all three sources (interviews, focus groups, and the survey). I have scanned the texts of the transcribed interviews and survey responses, looking for any mention of words and phrases such as "crisis," "bubble burst," "layoffs," and "insecurity." Since no direct question was asked about the crisis in the survey itself, these notions have been found in respondents' replies to these open-ended questions: "What would you find helpful in your attempt to balance work and family?" "What would be a helpful practice at your workplace?" "What would you like to see changed at home to make balancing more feasible?" For the purposes of the present chapter, I draw on the responses that refer specifically to aspects known in the literature to characterize the Israeli middle-class's gender contract and welfare regime at the time. Before we move on to the findings, it is crucial to present these relevant features of the Israeli context.

WELFARE REGIMES, GENDER CONTRACTS, AND THE ISRAELI HIGH-TECH INDUSTRY

With the rejuvenation of the Jewish people after the Holocaust defined as one of the Israeli state's official aims, pronatalist and profamily policies were adopted soon after Israel's independence in 1948 (Berkovitch 1997). Paid maternity leave, the protection of pregnant workers, and a state-sponsored care system (provided by women's organizations) were introduced almost contemporaneously with statehood, making Israel's birth rates the highest in the industrialized world. Simultaneously, the need for professional and educated workers, especially in traditionally feminine occupations, along with a work-centered ideology, led to the normalization of women's and mothers' participation in the labor market, especially among middle-class families. While the actual participation of women in the labor market was rather low and the gender pay gap similar to the one found in the United States at the time, the myth of gender egalitarianism in Israel was dominant in its first decades, and women felt that they had the choice of joining the labor market and drawing on its family welfare provisions or staying at home to care for their families (Herzog 2004; Okun, Oliver et al. 2007). The difficulty for families in maintaining a middle-class standard of living on a single salary (normally quite low at the time) encouraged women in this class to join the labor market as secondary breadwinners. The fact that Israel is a numerically and geographically small society with very close-knit family relations led to the emergence of a gender contract that views men as the primary breadwinners and women as secondary breadwinners and care providers, assisted by the extended family and some state-provided services. Despite the many changes that the Israeli economy and gender division of labor have seen since, this gender contract, which expects middle-class mothers to actively participate in the labor market after a short maternity leave and legitimizes the care of young children in public and private day care centers, continued to characterize Israel in the early 2000s.

With the growing influence of the feminist movement beginning in the 1970s, women were encouraged to assume demanding careers without forgoing motherhood and the responsibility for family care. A combination of the gender egalitarianism myth, the availability of some state-sponsored services, and protection for mothers in the labor market—together with the availability of relatively protected jobs for middle-class women in the public sector—made Israel a leading country in terms of mothers' participation in the labor market, and led women to believe that it is indeed possible to balance the demands of work and family. Since the 1980s, career opportunities for professional women have expanded beyond the public sector, and women have entered less protected careers in which they, much like men, are expected to work longer hours and travel for business. The pressure toward dual-earning families, together with a generational turn and the growing influence of liberal feminism, has led to a growing expectation that fathers will participate in child care, especially among the professional middle class. Together with the features of the Israeli welfare regime, these new cultural expectations determined high-tech parents' conceptualization of work-family integration after the bubble burst.

The political dominance of the labor movement in the state's formative years, the strong social democratic ideology that it introduced, and the unchallenged political power of the local national labor movement (known as the Histadrut), all contributed to the establishment of a socioeconomic regime with minimal labor flexibility, low labor turnover, and exceptionally extensive state intervention in all aspects of residents' everyday life (employment, education, health, pensions, housing, and population dispersion). Health insurance was provided mostly through labor unions and other NGOs, with close to universal coverage. K–12 education for children is free, and private schooling was largely unavailable before the 1990s. Until the mid-1980s, layoffs—at least in the organized primary sector— were almost impossible, and throughout most of this period, the country enjoyed close to full employment and relatively low income inequality. As part of this institutional environment, turning to the state in anticipation of being provided with a minimum level of social security is largely seen as normative.

Global pressures from the International Monetary Fund, the US government, multinational corporations, and global markers, however, have led to the gradual but resolute erosion of the above characteristics of the Israeli welfare regime since the early 1980s, with the high-tech industry leading the charge. Typified by foreign (especially US) multinationals that lack a tradition of unionization, the high-tech industry has offered generous wages and, through stock options, the opportunity to make a lot of money very quickly (Shalev 1999). Given the constant labor shortage in the industry, these conditions have compensated for a lack of job security (Senor, Singer et al. 2009). The industry's young and very high-earning professionals, who often saw themselves as an integral part of a new transnational class, tended to mock the old socioeconomic regime while celebrating their individualistic lifestyles. While they have not foregone building their own families, these young male and female workers have often accepted the long working hours associated with the industry's global corporate culture, pulling the rest of the local professional class along with them in living what they have come to consider the American dream.

Thus the high-tech sector has been the driving force behind Israel's changing labor environment. Drawn to the high-quality and relatively cheap technological manpower in Israel, multinational corporations in the IT field began opening R&D centers in Israel and acquiring local startups. Taking advantage of the new flexibility of the local labor market, these foreign firms have avoided collective bargaining at all costs, while at the same time promising their employees a competitive wage and other benefits that their unionized colleagues could not even have dreamed of. Within a decade, a personal contract in the high-tech industry has, for most Israelis, become the dream job. Working around the clock in a highly competitive environment, constantly traveling overseas for work, driving a new company car, and enjoying high-quality health insurance, food and drink, on-site gym facilities, and luxurious vacations and cultural events at the firm's expense have become part of the standard lifestyle of this new young middle class. Stock options have also become part of the standard fringe benefits that small startups have used to attract talented young workers, and a series of successful "exits" in the late 1990s turned a group of very young (and mostly male) IT professionals into millionaires overnight, further feeding the get-rich-quick dream and tempting other IT professionals to trade in their secure jobs for much more demanding but exciting jobs in local startups (Senor, Singer et al. 2009).

The bursting of the global high-tech bubble in late 2000 shattered this dream. Between March 2000 and the end of 2002, the Israeli high-tech industry lost about 16 percent of its jobs, and the remaining workers suffered an average 10 percent wage cut. But these numbers tell us only part of the story. Stock options, previously seen as the shortest route to becoming rich, became worthless, and as many of my interviewees report, the collapse also smashed their dreams of conquering the tech world and left a void that they found hard to fill without their high-pressure jobs. While the outcome of the collapse may have been similar for young tech professionals in both Israel and the United States, the socioeconomic contexts in which they found themselves were still very different. In Israel, the remnants of the old welfare regime meant that most of them could claim relatively high unemployment payments for one hundred to 135 days (depending on their age and number of dependents), allowing them a degree of flexibility in finding new jobs. Because of the universal health insurance available to them and their families, losing their jobs did not mean the complete loss of their social security; furthermore, because of Israeli labor legislation and the standard wage structure, many of them were entitled to a compensation package that made their redundancy a little less financially devastating. The more relevant aspect for our analysis of the impact of the financial and labor insecurity they encountered on their work-family strategies is the family regime and gender contract in which they were coping with the new circumstances.

RECONCEPTUALIZING WORK-FAMILY RELATIONS IN THE ISRAELI HIGH-TECH INDUSTRY

As mentioned at the beginning of this chapter, the centrality of gender contracts and welfare regimes to the context within which Israeli high-tech workers made sense of the effects of the new economic insecurity on their work-family balancing strategies became visible in the debate that erupted after Amy's suggestion that she might need to forego motherhood, given the new economic insecurity. Organized by means of a mailing list of women in the high-tech list server, which at that time could only handle messages written in English (rather than Hebrew), the group attracted a relatively large number of English-speaking women who had migrated to Israel from such liberal welfare states as the United States, England, Australia, and South Africa.

In the stormy debate that followed, Amy, together with another young immigrant from the United States, voiced her concern that, given the crisis, she and her partner would either be unemployed or would have to work around the clock to be able to support a family. Under such circumstances, she argued, they would not be able to spend enough time with their children or provide the minimal means required to raise them properly. Juxtaposing the Israeli institutional environment with that of their liberal countries of birth, the other English-speaking women evoked different aspects of the Israeli gender contract in an effort to convince Amy to reconsider. For example, pointing to the standards surrounding early childhood education in Israel, Deborah, age 34, a U.S.A.-born marketing manager, said: "Nobody expects you to stay home with a child until he goes to school. There are crèches here and everybody sends their kids there. It is not as if people are going to look at you in a strange way, thinking you are a neglectful mother. If this crisis lasts and you find yourself short of money, they are even subsidized." Others suggested that Amy's Israeli in-laws would probably step in to help with child-care arrangements and their associated expenses.

The reliance on the extended family to provide not only child-care services but also financial assistance was a recurring theme in the group discussions. Nirit, a systems analyst who was married to a middle manager in another high-tech firm, said:

> My mother really encouraged me to have the third child. She knew that I will not be able to care for a third one and work the way my firm requires, so she and my father took early retirement last year. They arrive twice a week to pick up the children from their day care. My in-laws pick up once a week, because they also help my sister-in-law. I can focus on my work because I know that the kids are in good hands, it's within the family.

Later on, Nirit also referred to the financial assistance her parents offered when her spouse lost his job: "My parents had good jobs, my mother as a teacher and my father in a bank. These were the good days, they could retire comfortably and have secured pension plans, so when my husband lost his job, they told us not to worry, and they can help us if we need it. We know that we can count on them."

Israel is by no means one of the most generous family welfare regimes: it does not provide fully sponsored and high-quality early childhood education, as the Scandinavian countries do; nor does it provide long family leaves that allow mothers (and now parents in general) to stay at home with their children until they are three years old on a state stipend close to the minimum wage, as do certain conservative welfare states such as Germany. Moreover, by the early 2000s, middle-class families' access to publicly sponsored day care facilities had declined, and the changes in the length of the workday, especially in the high-tech sector, have made public facilities less accommodating for this industry's workers. However, powerful norms that determine the division of labor between the nuclear and the extended family (especially grandparents) and the state concerning childcare arrangements, along with Israel's strong pronatalist culture, seem to have shaped Israeli high-tech workers' responses to the crisis in a way that excludes foregoing parenthood altogether. The traditional welfare regime, with its high unionization and generous state and employers' provision for unionized middle-class workers, also allowed Nirit's parents to retire early with secured pension payments that allow them to offer financial support to their daughter and her family. The remnants of the old, more secure regime, which no longer applies in the case of Nirit herself, still shapes her life plan and work-family conceptualization through her parents' ability to support her.

This sense of security, which is probably misdirected, may account for the fact that, unlike the Japanese and North American professional women whose stories are documented in this volume, over 85 percent of our survey respondents acknowledged the difficulties in balancing a career in the Israeli high-tech industry with parenting, and expected a wage loss and reduced work schedule for mothers in the sector. However, less than 10 percent presented the challenge as insurmountable.

REDISCOVERING HOME

The unchallenged pronatalist norm in Israel and the importance ascribed to the family in the dominant local public discourse play an important role in shaping the ways in which the most successful high-tech professionals who had been harmed by the crisis made sense of their new circumstances. Yossi, a former international marketing VP of a local startup, who had had to compromise by accepting a lower-paid and far less challenging job as a local marketing manager in a well-established Israeli firm, said:

There was something seductive about that lifestyle. You say to yourself: "I'm a good father, I give them the lifestyle I never had as a kid. I'll spend another year or two or five travelling the world, developing cutting-edge technology, making tons of money, and in five years I'll sell my options and retire before I'm forty, and then we will travel the world together and have whatever we want." But then, it all evaporates in a second and you go back home and realize that you hardly know your own kids. Now I say never again. Yes, I want to have a great job again, but I refuse to spend half of my life flying. (Yossi, former marketing VP of a local startup, Group 2)

As mentioned above, the promise of getting rich quick, together with a sense of great achievement, of being on the cutting edge, flying business class, and living a jet-set life inspired many Israeli high-tech professionals to set aside other aspects of their everyday lives and to invest all of their energy in developing a firm or a product that would one day make them rich and famous like the other entrepreneurs around them. When the bubble burst, the dream burst with it. Thanks to their skills and experience, many of them could find other jobs before unemployment seriously threatened their families' financial stability, but the dream of conquering the world was lost for good. The bursting of this illusion, they argued, led them to reevaluate their lives and realize that family is the only thing that really matters. In a similar vein, Nir, an R&D manager, said:

I was in it since 1987, right out of my military service in a top technological unit. I was at the top of the world. We built this company together and really thought that the big bucks were just around the corner. My wife accepted it. It was not easy for her because she has her own career and I was hardly at home, but there were compensations, you know, a nice home, expensive vacations . . . and then it disappeared. The investors refused to put in even one additional dollar, and we closed within a month. The problem was not financial. I saw my American colleagues who lost their health insurance when they lost their jobs, who had to take their kids out of private schools. This is Israel. Our health insurance is national and nobody sends his kids to private school. I walked away with a nice compensation package and they even let me buy the company car I was using. It was the loss of the dream, and the void it leaves behind. And then you realize that the company is not your family, like we used to think. You have one family, and it is the one you left at home. (Nir, age 42, R&D manager, Group 4)

In Nir's narrative, the Israeli welfare regime plays an important role in preventing the financial disaster that might have befallen him and his family were it not for the remnants of the old Israeli social democratic welfare regime. The challenge he was left with, according to his narrative, was to find a new place for himself in the world. When looking for a new job, he refused anything that required frequent travel, claiming that "I already know that I'm not going to conquer the world, so I realize that I had better get to know my kids before it is too late." In his new job, Nir claims to get home by 5 pm at least once a week and spend time with his two teenage sons.

The other men who referred to the crisis as a turning point in their work-life strategies told very similar stories. Two of them had entered the labor force only a few years before the bubble burst, and while they were prepared to spend every waking moment at the workplace, their dream was shattered before they had even managed to live it. Yet they claimed to have learned the same lesson as their older colleagues, choosing the family track over career as a response. Two of the older ones mentioned looking for high-tech jobs in more traditional companies such as the electric company, where unions are still strong and can offer more job security.

In her *A Company of One*, Carrie Lane (2011) documented the lives and struggles of the bubble burst's victims in Dallas, Texas. While one of her interviewees indeed tells a story of reconstructing his identity around his role as a father and family member when he was unemployed, he treats this identity as a temporary one until he finds another job. Other fathers who discussed their family situations in the context of their unemployment referred mostly to losing their breadwinner status and to their need to protect their job-searching time in order to get back to that position. For some, their unemployment forced their stay-at-home wives to return to the labor market to provide income and health insurance. None of the fathers whose stories were documented has adhered to the "rediscovering home" theme that was so common in the Israeli case. In her own interpretation of the data, Lane refers to the evolution of the "couple self-sufficiency" theme (2011, 119), according to which, instead of sanctifying individual self-reliance, laid-off men take pride in their ability to maintain their independence by temporarily redistributing the work at home. She argues that in the absence of unemployment benefits, pensions, and national health insurance, her interviewees had only themselves and their wives to rely on. As was clear from Yossi and Nir's stories, the fact that unemployment and other welfare provisions were still available to them and that, at the time, more secure jobs were still available in Israel in general in those organizations that were still unionized and adhered to the norms of the historical welfare regime, has allowed for the emergence of a different framework within which they thought about their families in the context of the crisis.

The quite homogenous response of our male participants could be attributed to two different research design biases: (1) the participants of the focus groups joined the groups voluntarily, knowing that the groups would discuss work-family issues. It is quite possible that these men, whose "lessons" were different, were not included in our sample; and (2) one of the disadvantages of focus-group methodology is its sensitivity to a social desirability bias and groupthink (Hollander 2004). In those focus groups in which the theme of disillusion was mentioned, there was an overwhelming consensus that with the bursting of the bubble, the dream was permanently destroyed as well. In fact, the eleven members in this category shared a similar narrative with somewhat similar consequences at the time that the focus groups took place: they all traded in high-powered and extremely demanding careers for smaller or much slower ones that enabled them, for most or at least some of the time, to be more attentive to the needs of their family. At the same time, while three of the eleven have taken jobs that were completely different from their old ones (in teaching and consultancy), the other eight confess that their new jobs are still more demanding than they would have wished. It is possible that the narrative of rediscovering home was a temporary one, allowing these usually high-achieving men to assign new meaning to the inevitable demise of their career dreams. However, the centrality of the family in Israeli culture, together with the growing importance of the father's role in raising his children in general and in the Israeli middle-class gender contract in particular (Gershoni 2004), provided a framework through which these men could make sense of their lives and legitimize their choices.

Orit, a marketing and communications vice president in an Israeli affiliate of a United States-based multinational, was the only woman participating in the focus group to evoke the narrative of rediscovering home. A mother of two, Orit said that she was postponing having a third child for career reasons:

> I slowed down my career to raise the first two, and I was on the fast track again, rising high, making money, traveling all the time, so even though I wanted another one and the biological clock was ticking, I could not make myself slow down. Now, when there isn't much of a chance to fly really high, I think that was really stupid, and I'm going to have a third one and make myself much more present at home.

Orit did not lose her job, but her benefits and chances for promotion decreased considerably. The threat of losing her current job, along with the difficulties of finding an equivalent one, made her reconsider her nontraditional choice to sustain a very demanding career with two young children at home. Since the normative family in Israel expects married couples to have at least three children, and since, at the time, the local discourse did not highlight the high cost of childrearing, Orit and others have seen the crisis as an opportunity to fit in. Of the sixty-one women who referred to the crisis in their responses to our survey, eight also referred to it as an opportunity to have another child. Two of the eight had secured jobs in the government sector and given up hope of moving to better ones in the private sector, and the other six lost their jobs entirely during the crisis. The pronatalist, family-oriented discourse of the Israeli middle class, which before the crisis had forced Orit to constantly defend her ultra-demanding career, now provided a framework in which she could find satisfaction as her career options seemed to deteriorate.

RENEGOTIATING THE GENDER CONTRACT

About half of the relevant sample in our Internet survey and twenty-nine women in our focus groups mentioned the financial crisis as a context in which they found themselves renegotiating their work or family contracts, either at home with their spouses or at work with their employers. The loss of their spouses' jobs, the loss of their own jobs, deteriorating benefits, and difficulties in finding new jobs in an unstable market were all mentioned by these women as reasons to reconsider their earlier work-family arrangements and to try and transform them. The most common theme was the need to renegotiate the division of labor at home in a way that would allow them to better reposition themselves in the labor market after the crisis. Miri, a thirty-five-year-old R&D team head whose spouse was unemployed at the time of the focus group, said:

> The most important thing right now is for my husband to find a job. Because I was the one doing most of the child caring, I did not reach the same level of income and now it is difficult for us to live on my income alone. But our division of labor at home needs to change, too. Now that he is home and spending time with the kids, he is learning how important it is for him and for them, and I am learning how good it is to be able to invest a little more time at work, without the constant need to rush home. I already told him that his next job should allow him to continue being at home part of the week so that when this crisis ends I'll be in a position to negotiate my promotion and get a better salary. Next time a crisis comes around, I want to be indispensable.

Galit, 32, a systems analyst and mother of two, took the need to renegotiate her gender contract at home in a different direction:

> I really don't like my job. I stayed because the kids were young and this company is convenient and close to home, and I always thought that whenever I want,

I can move on to a better job. Now I'm stuck, I'll never be able to get a good job under these conditions, and who knows when I'll be able to move next. I told my husband that it cannot carry on like this. As soon as we can afford it I'm moving to part time and going back to school to finish my MBA so I can move to marketing . . . but he will need to take more of the burden at home to allow me to go back to school and find a job that I'll like afterward.

In both these cases, as well as in fourteen others, the crisis made our group participants realize that the division of household labor—according to which they were the primary caregivers, despite working full time—was holding them back in their careers. While Miri intended to move up to a better-paid and more senior job, Galit, like seven of our other participants, wanted to leave a job that she kept only because of work-family considerations. In both cases, however, the crisis shook their sense that the future was full of opportunities and made them realize that they had to struggle with more determination in order to create a situation at home that would allow them to better position themselves in the work environment when the opportunity arose. The fact that Miri's top-ranking, high-tech professional spouse had lost his job when the bubble burst and was forced to be at home more and depend on her income gave her the opportunity to renegotiate their division of labor. Much like Nir and Yossi, who rediscovered home, Miri's spouse was now claiming to enjoy being with the kids, allowing his spouse to renegotiate her contract in a positive atmosphere.

Another recurrent theme was the urgent need to renegotiate salaries, promotion, and work benefits when the right time came. Irit's words reflect this theme well:

> I was always embarrassed to ask for a raise, or to demand the promotion I deserve. I have two children, so I cannot stay at work until midnight every day, and my husband was making a good salary, so a raise would not be that meaningful. I also always thought that if we ever needed more money, I would have the motivation to fight for it. Now that his income has dropped radically, I cannot ask for a raise, because it is not the right time. But when this stupid recession ends, I'll go after this promotion and the raise I deserve at full speed. Next time a crisis like that hits, I want to be on top of things. (Irit, age 39, team head, Group 7)

When the economy and her husband's income were secured, Irit took for granted the traditional Israeli middle-class gender contract, working full time but choosing to turn down a promotion that would have placed her in a more demanding job and subjected her to the discomfort many women still feel when having to discuss money and raises (Babcock and Laschever

2009). In her own view, the crisis had forced her to reconsider this traditional gender contract and to make sure she did not depend on her spouse's income alone.

Other participants also mentioned an urgent need to renegotiate their work hours and the possibility of working from home when the time to do so was right. Adi, a thirty-three-year-old systems analyst, mentioned that in order to reduce transportation costs, her employers suddenly encouraged her to work from home. She stated:

> I had been begging for a day or two of telecommuting for years, but they weren't very accommodating. Now, when its suits them, they are basically forcing us to do it, but I'm not complaining. I like it a lot. . . . But if they think that when the good times return I'll start working full time from the office again, then they have another think coming. . . .

The changes imposed by the crisis, both at home and in the workplace, seemed to largely determine the lessons that our participants took away from their new experiences. Those who had hoped to improve their situation at work but had put off doing anything about it for work-family reasons were eager to change the division of labor at home so as to allow themselves to make the change at work "when the time comes." Those who experienced their husbands' rediscovery of the home were eager for them to find another job, but did not want this to mean a return to the old division of labor.

Finally, six of our group participants (and one-quarter of our relevant survey responses) reported a decrease in working hours due to the crisis and a reduced demand for their companies' services or products. Enjoying an improved work-family balance because of this slower pace, they stated that they never wanted to return to their previous work schedule. Donna, a product manager in a large Israeli software house, best articulated this feeling:

> In your everyday life, you do not stop to think about how crazy your life is. You are too busy living it, running from one place to the next. And they basically tell you that if you want to work in this industry, you have to be available 24/7. But suddenly everything slows down and you do not have to run all the time. I was lucky, my company did not suffer much, but the urgency of everything has gone, and suddenly you have a life . . . I'm never going back to the rat race.

Both Gerson (2010) and Lane (2011), who study working men and women's responses to growing economic insecurity in the United States, have highlighted the notion of self-reliance and self-sufficiency as a strategy used, especially by women, to face the growing insecurity in the labor market on the one hand, and in the family on the other. Given the growing divorce rates and men's declining interest in starting and supporting a family, a significant number of women in the United States have opted for self-reliance even at the cost of foregoing childbirth and marriage. While the women in our survey and focus groups mentioned the need to secure their future income for their families' sake, at no point have they turned to a full-fledged self-reliance framework, suggesting that they would prefer being independent over having a family. Despite the high divorce rates of the Israeli middle class, and probably due to the safety net the law provides for divorced mothers and the strong family culture—in which the extended family is expected to assist parents in need—self-sufficiency and reliance are not seen as important values shaping people's decisions regarding their work-family strategies.

DISCUSSION AND CONCLUSIONS

Studies of the social consequences of economic crises at both the individual and societal levels rarely look at the effects of such crises on individuals' and families' work-family conceptualizations and life plans. Grounded in a qualitative analysis of focus groups and individual interviews with high-tech workers in Israel, this study has shown that in times of economic crisis and labor insecurity, people draw upon the institutional and cultural resources available to them to make sense of their reality and reorganize their work-family arrangements. At the institutional level, the general welfare regime, which determines the extent of decommodification and people's dependency on the labor market to secure a basic standard of living, as well as the family welfare regime, which focuses more specifically on the extent to which they are dependent on the market and each other to secure an acceptable level of family care, were both found to shape individuals' responses to a crisis. The fact that, in Israel, health insurance and children's education are commonly provided by the state, and that the remnants of the old social democratic welfare regime still provide one hundred to 135 days of income-based unemployment insurance—together with the standard employment contract which, by law, includes a built-in compensation package in case of redundancy—somewhat moderates the immediate financial consequences for the family. Moreover, beyond existing welfare policies, historical ones also determine employees' work-family conceptualizations and strategies. The ability to rely on parents or find jobs in (mostly publicly owned) organizations that still adhere to the old practices allows even those employees that do not have access to these state provisions to count on them. Importantly, this historical welfare regime also played a critical role in shaping the gender contract that survived the partial collapse of the welfare regime itself.

Thus, at the cultural level, the gender contract that expects middle-class men and women to work for pay and develop careers while sharing (however unequally) family responsibilities with the extended family and the state, together with a strong pronatalist tendency that sees childbearing as a national and individual mission divorced from market considerations, seems to shape the ways in which individuals and couples cope with labor insecurity during an economic crisis. In liberal welfare states where the financial burden of raising a child is very high (especially for the middle and upper middle class) and rests almost completely on the parents' shoulders, one immediate response to economic insecurity takes the form of declining fertility rates and the decision to forego childbearing (Hakim 1995; Aassve, Mazzuco, and Mencarini 2005). In social democratic regimes, by contrast, and especially in Israel, state provisions and social norms allow individuals and families greater leeway in making their decisions in both the work and family spheres and to renegotiate their gender and professional identities and their conceptualization of self.

Despite the changes in socioeconomic ideology brought about by globalization, the traditional conceptualization of the state as naturally responsible for securing individuals' well-being also influences individuals' and families' experiences of the crisis. While studies in the United States report a common feeling of personal responsibility for one's layoff, even during an economic crisis, and thus a strong sense of a personal failure (Smith 2002; Lane 2011), our respondents tended to see their situation as an outcome of stronger structural forces beyond their control. While many of them expressed a wish that they would have been better prepared for the crisis by expanding their skill sets and making themselves more indispensable, they often saw it as the responsibility of the state and the employers to bring about economic recovery, which would make their own efforts to overcome the crisis worthwhile. This strong belief in the responsibility of the state for its citizens' general welfare, and for families' welfare in particular was demonstrated during the 2011 social protest movement (the Israeli equivalent of the Occupy Wall Street movement). Whereas in the United States young people's rage was directed at bankers and stockbrokers, the Israeli protest (like the Greek and Spanish ones) was directed at the state, blaming it for abandoning its responsibility for its citizens' welfare. Unlike the Occupy Wall Street protest, the Israeli one garnered comprehensive popular support that crossed generation and class lines. Weeks into the general protest movement campaign, a popular spinoff, called the "strollers' protest," emerged. As part of this campaign, parents (and grandparents) marched all over Israel, calling for more state support for working parents. In fact, this campaign was probably the most successful part of the entire campaign because, unlike other demands that were largely overlooked, the strollers' protest has led to the expansion of state-sponsored child-care services and to an improvement in its quality.

Finally, while this study has looked at a single class and a single industry, it is extremely important to remember that both the welfare state and gender contracts have different consequences for different classes (Mandel and Shalev 2009). Studies that look at the consequences of unemployment for families in different income groups suggest that they have different concerns following income loss and growing insecurity. The fact that most high-tech workers in Israel come from dual-earning families, and that about half of the women in our sample were married to high-income, high-tech men most definitely influenced their responses to the crisis. While in lower-class Israeli families (as in other industrialized countries; see Esping-Andersen 2009) the gender division of labor in child care has not shifted, even in the wake of women's increased involvement in the labor market, for fathers in the local professional class, participation in raising their children has become an aspired-to social norm (Gershoni 2004). This norm makes it easier for men and women to use the context of the economic crisis to rethink their life choices and renegotiate a better work-family contract for themselves.

REFERENCES

Aassve, Arnstein, Stefano Mazzuco, and Letizia Mencarini. 2005. "Childbearing and Well-Being: A Comparative Analysis of European Welfare Regimes." *Journal of European Social Policy* 15(4): 283–299.

Alexy, Allison. 2016. "Laboring Heroes, Security, and the Political Economy of Intimacy in Postwar Japan." In *Beyond the Cubicle: Insecurity Culture and the Flexible Self*, edited by Allison Pugh, 101–128. New York: Oxford University Press.

Babcock, Linda, and Sara Laschever. 2009. *Women Don't Ask: Negotiation and the Gender Divide*. Princeton, NJ: Princeton University Press.

Berkovitch, Nitza. 1997. "Motherhood as a National Mission: The Construction of Womanhood in the Legal Discourse in Israel." *Women's Studies International Forum* 20(5–6):605–619.

Daly, Mary, and Katherine Rake. 2003. *Gender and the Welfare State: Care, Work, and Welfare in Europe and the USA*. Cambridge, UK: Polity.

Esping-Andersen, Gosta. 1990. *The Three Worlds of Welfare Capitalism.* Cambridge, UK: Polity.

Esping-Andersen, Gosta. 1999. *Social Foundations of Postindustrial Economies.* New York: Oxford University Press.

Esping-Andersen, Gosta. 2009. *The Incomplete Revolution: Adapting to Women's New Roles.* Cambridge, UK: Polity.

Frenkel, Michal. 2013. "Toward a Multi-Layered Glocalization Approach: States, Multinational Corporations, and the Transformation of Gender Contracts." In *Themes and Local Variations in Organization and Management: Perspectives on Glocalization,* edited by G. M. Drori, M. Hollerer, and P. Walgenbach, 133–145. New York: Routledge.

Gershoni, Dror. 2004. "New Fatherhood in Israel—a Gender Perspective on Masculinity and Fatherhood in the Institutional and Marital Context." MA diss., Bar-Ilan University. Ramat Gan: Israel.

Gerson, Kathleen. 2010. *The Unfinished Revolution: How a New Generation Is Reshaping Family, Work, and Gender In America.* New York: Oxford University Press.

Gerson, Kathleen. 2016. "Different Ways of Not Having It All: Work, Care, and Shifting Gender Arrangements in the New Economy." In *Beyond the Cubicle: Insecurity Culture and the Flexible Self,* edited by Allison Pugh. New York: Oxford University Press.

Gottfried, Heidi. 2000. "Compromising Positions: Emergent Neo-Fordisms and Embedded Gender Contracts." *The British Journal of Sociology* 51(2):235–259.

Hakim, Catherine. 1995. "Five Feminist Myths about Women's Employment." *The British Journal of Sociology* 46(3):429–455

Herzog, Hanna. 2004. "Women in Israeli Society." In *Jews in Israel: Contemporary Social and Cultural Patterns,* edited by Uzi Rebhun and Chaim Waxman, 195–220. Lebanon, NH: University Press of New England.

Hollander, Jocelyn A. 2004. "The Social Contexts of Focus Groups." *Journal of Contemporary Ethnography* 33(5):602–637.

Kaplan, Amit, and Anat Herbst. 2015. "Stratified Patterns of Divorce: Earnings, Education, and Gender." *Demographic Research* 32(1): 949–982.

Koreh, Michal, and Michael Shalev. 2009. "Dialectics of Institutional Change: The Transformation of Social Insurance Financing in Israel." *Socioeconomic Review* 7(4):553–584.

Lane, Carrie M. 2011. *A Company of One: Insecurity, Independence, and the New World of White-Collar Unemployment.* Ithaca, NY: ILR.

Lane, Carrie. M. 2016. "Unemployed Tech Workers' Ambivalent Embrace of the Flexible Ideal." In *Beyond the Cubicle: Insecurity Culture and the Flexible Self,* edited by Alison Pugh. New York: Oxford University Press.

Lewis, Jane. 1992. "Gender and the Development of Welfare Regimes." *Journal of European Social Policy* 2(3):159–173.

Lewis, Jane. 1997. "Gender and Welfare Regimes: Further Thoughts." *Social Politics* 4(2):160–177.

Mandel, H., and M. Shalev. 2009. "Gender, Class, and Varieties of Capitalism." *Social Politics* 16(2):161–181.

Maron, Asa. 2015. "The Privatization of Social Services in Israel: Processes and Trends." In *Privatization Policy in Israel: State Responsibility and the Boundaries between the Public and the Private,* edited by I. Galnoor, A. Paz-Fuchs, and N. Zion. Jerusalem: Van-Leer Institute (Hebrew). http://www.vanleer.org.il/en/publication/privatization-policy-israel-state-responsibility-and-boundaries-between-public-and.

Okun, Barbara. S., Amalya Oliver, and Oma Khait-Marelly. 2007. "The Public Sector, Family Structure and Labor Market Behavior: Jewish Mothers in Israel." *Work and Occupations* 34(2):174–204.

Orloff, Anna S. (1993). "Gender and the Social Rights of Citizenship: The Comparative Analysis of Gender Relations and Welfare States." *American Sociological Review* 58(3):303–328.

Pfau-Effinger, Brigit. 2004a. *Development of Culture, Welfare States and Women's Employment in Europe.* Aldershot, UK: Ashgate.

Pfau-Effinger, Brigit. 2004b. "Socio-Historical Paths of the Male Breadwinner Model - An Explanation of Cross-National Differences." *British Journal of Sociology* 55(3):377–399.

Sainsbury, Diane. 1996. *Gender, Equality, and Welfare States.* Cambridge, UK: Cambridge University Press.

Senor, Dan. and Saul Singer. 2009. *Start-Up Nation: The Story of Israel's Economic Miracle.* New York: Twelve.

Shalev, Michael. 1999. "Have Globalization and Liberalization 'Normalized' Israel's Political Economy?" *Israel Affairs* 5(2–3):121–155.

Ström, Sara. 2003. "Unemployment and Families: A Review of Research." *Social Service Review* 77(3):399–430.

Walby, Sylvia. 2004. "The European Union and Gender Equality: Emergent Varieties of Gender Regime." *Social Politics: International Studies in Gender, State, and Society* 11(1):4–29.

CHAPTER 10

⌀

Security-Autonomy-Mobility Roadmaps

Passports to Security

JEREMY SCHULZ AND LAURA ROBINSON

WELCOME TO RANCHO BENITO

Taking the highway along the California coast and swinging inland into one of the state's agricultural belts, the hills appear golden in the distance, spotted with gnarled oak trees. Vineyards rise up on either side of the highway, and occasionally cowboys may be seen in the distance herding grazing cattle. Yet as clouds of dust rise from the fields in this agricultural community, the idyllic scene fades dramatically in the town of Rancho Benito, a community wearing the signs of the hard economic times. This once relatively prosperous community is now a place in which many families sit down to dinner in dramatically different circumstances than just a few years ago. After the 2008 recession hit this community, gaping holes appeared in all areas of the economy. Just driving through town, one sees evidence in the strip malls of the failure of one local business after another. Local industry has felt the ravages of the new economic landscape, from a partially empty mall to burgeoning bargain stores. While not all families have endured the same kind or degree of economic insecurity, nonetheless they dwell in a community strongly affected by the Great Recession. While not all have directly felt the effects on their immediate personal circles, all community members live in an environment indelibly stamped by the recession's imprint.

Within this hard-hit community we find Miguel.[1] During his childhood, Miguel's family owned and operated a successful landscaping business catering to the growing tract housing developments in the area. As a youth, he enjoyed playing competitive golf. Miguel's future had appeared clear to him: "I thought that I would get a big time golf scholarship to college." Yet with the damage the Great Recession wrought on his family's finances, his plans changed: "My family hung on for a long time . . . everything went into keeping the business open . . . but we just couldn't make it . . . eventually I had to give up golf." Currently, despite his family's hardships, Miguel still counts himself among the lucky ones. Unlike many of his peers, he is pursuing his goal of becoming an architect by attending a public four-year university: "I found out that colleges outside of California can be a lot cheaper so I'm still going away to school next year." Miguel has adjusted his goals in light of his family's unexpected financial hardship. He has downsized goals in terms of attending a pricey private university and delayed any dreams of becoming a professional athlete. These strategies further Miguel's two-pronged goal. On the one hand, Miguel hopes that a college education will help him recapture his family's middle-class lifestyle. On the other hand, Miguel's decision to forgo an expensive education avoids the financial risk that accompanies reaching for the stars.

Carla is taking another path to minimize risk when planning her future. Unlike Miguel, Carla feels compelled to make financial contributions to her family as soon as possible. Whereas Miguel is reacting to an unexpected reversal of fortune, Carla has never known financial security. Her parents are both fieldworkers who struggle to provide for her and her siblings. By contrast, Miguel's parents attended college and have a circle of educated friends. No one in Carla's family has finished high school; few in her personal community can boast a living wage. While Miguel had to adjust his plans in an attempt to reclaim future security, Carla must venture into uncharted territory to realize a better future. When asked about her plans after high school graduation, Carla explains: "I'm going into the military. I found out that I can get all sorts of skills that will get me a good job when I'm out." In Carla's eyes, gaining vocational skills her parents lack is the recipe for financial security. At the same time, her plan stems from endemic financial insecurity. Carla's planning is both rational and selfless. By joining the military, Carla will immediately bring home a paycheck and will gain what she sees as valuable vocational training: "I will start earning money right away . . . help my family . . . the military gives you job training for free." Carla's sense of duty toward her natal family places an immediate burden on her to contribute financially right out of high school. While this priority lies beyond the experiential horizon of students from the middle classes who have not known unrelenting financial insecurity, it is not uncommon in Rancho Benito.

From this brief sketch it is clear that, while both Miguel and Carla have experienced economic insecurity and deprivation to different degrees, they differ in important and intriguing ways where their responses to this insecurity are concerned. Because of their different family backgrounds and contrasting experiences, both before and after the Great Recession of 2008, Miguel and Carla have developed different perspectives on their futures. But what accounts for this divergence? As we show in this chapter, Miguel and Carla harbor differing visions of their future because of their divergent firsthand and secondhand experiences of economic (in) security, opportunity, and risk. More specifically, they belong to distinctive subgroups of youths in Rancho Benito. The divergent *security-autonomy-mobility* roadmaps articulated by members of these subgroups illuminate the interplay between these experiences and more commonly examined sociological factors.

Miguel belongs to the subgroup of youths adopting what we call a protective reclamation roadmap. Miguel's mobility strategy is best described as a reentry strategy, as it aims to reclaim the lost economic security of the past while protecting his financial future. Unlike Carla, Miguel has some firsthand experience of economic security, even though it lies in the past. Furthermore, the adults in Miguel's circles, particularly his parents, did succeed in scaling the educational ladder and making a stable and comfortable livelihood. By and large, during the years before 2008, their families held secure jobs and took middle-class comforts for granted. From housing to family cars, comforts and basic needs were met on a regular basis. However, for these youths, the stability and prosperity of the prerecession years proved transitory. Even though their families "did things right" in terms of their education and "played by the rules," the Great Recession brought unanticipated reversals of fortune, sweeping away their families' fragile good fortune. During the onset of the recession, protective reclamation youths had a front-row seat to their parents' economic collapse, watching their parents lose their jobs and benefits as well as their houses, cars, and other taken-for-granted possessions. As a result, youths like Miguel desperately wish to recapture the economic security their families enjoyed during the prerecession years. Thus Miguel still desires the long-term economic security which now eludes his stricken parents. At the same time, however, he questions the utility of expensive college degrees as a means of assuring his own future economic viability. Like the other members of this subgroup, Miguel has become more skeptical of the potential of college degrees to act as a buffer against future economic insecurity. For this reason, he also has lost much of his faith in the long-term economic value of pricier college degrees as he believes that no credential will ensure the security he wants. With restrained optimism about the potential of credentialing as a safeguard against financial hardship, protective reclamation youths have downsized their educational aspirations, seeking to minimize the amount of debt incurred in order to finance a college education.

Unlike Miguel, Carla belongs to the subgroup of students who adopt what we call a vocational escalator roadmap. Like Carla, vocational escalator youths have never enjoyed ongoing economic security either before or after the Great Recession. Students like Carla have grown up with an extreme level of precariousness and economic insecurity. Compounding this pervasive firsthand economic insecurity, they also bear witness to the long-standing travails of their parents and other adults in their personal communities that were exacerbated by the Great Recession. Carla has grown up surrounded by parents and other adults who remain stuck at the lowest rungs of both educational and occupational ladders. Lacking any postsecondary training or credentials, the parents of the students adhering to the vocational escalator roadmap have spent their entire lives "living hard" (Howell 1973). They toil in low-level, unstable, and badly paid jobs where they are afforded little autonomy by their bosses and employers. Further compounding this lack of autonomy, their jobs are the first to go when times grow tough and business slows. In the absence of adults who have achieved economic security or have secured educational credentials, vocational escalator students conclude that it is their parents' lack of vocational training and credentials that is ultimately responsible for the precariousness of their lives. This conclusion leads vocational escalator youths to think of vocational credentials as the magic bullet which can assure them the economic security so lacking in the lives of the adults they know. The vocational escalator roadmap is best characterized as an exit strategy that will allow these students to leave behind the precariousness which mars the lives of their parents and other adults in their personal communities.

OVERVIEW OF ROADMAPS

If Carla and Miguel epitomize two subgroups of youths with contrasting roadmaps, they do not exhaust the array of roadmaps evident among Rancho Benito youths. In fact, there are at least two more subgroups which merit their own designation: the academic elevator subgroup and the parental emulator subgroup.

Members of the academic elevator subgroup typically suffer from similar levels of economic insecurity and hardship as their peers in the vocational escalator group. Furthermore, they resemble their vocational escalator peers. Both groups are witnesses to their families' unsuccessful struggles to stay financially afloat even in the best of economic environments. Despite the absence of economically secure adults and substantial levels of continuous privation and hardship, both vocational escalator and academic elevator youths trust in the power of credentialing to ward off financial hardship. However, the resemblance ends there, as the postsecondary plans of the academic elevator youths are vastly more ambitious than the plans outlined by their vocational escalator counterparts. The academic elevator youths stake their hopes on the potential of academic credentials to catapult them into a very different occupational and economic stratum. Unlike the vocational escalator youths who trust in vocational credentialing as the magic bullet, these youths aim to strike out into uncharted territory by pursuing extensive postsecondary educations culminating in BAs or even advanced degrees. Academic elevator youths put their faith in higher education as a pathway to economic security, even if it means taking on educational debt. In contrast to vocational escalator youths, academic elevator youths sign up for a delayed entry into the labor force so that they may complete more ambitious educational goals. The youths who cleave to the academic elevator roadmap sacrifice the possibility of earning money earlier in order to potentially earn more later. The mobility strategy of this subgroup thus trades off early-stage earning opportunities in adolescence for the possibility of a more dramatic break with the circumstances of the youths' families.

The youths who fall into the subgroup outlining a parental emulation roadmap stand apart from the other three subgroups in several respects. First of all, they have come of age in households graced with substantial economic security and minimal hardship both before and after the Great Recession. These youths have observed their parents' steady march to occupational success and economic stability and see no reason to deviate from their parents' paths. After all, the adults have benefited from the dividends of their relatively high-powered academic credentials and socioprofessional networks, dividends which have kept accumulating through easy and difficult times alike. When these parental emulators imagine themselves following in their parents' tracks through the world of higher education, they also envision obtaining similar educational credentials and positions conferring the same durable economic rewards. At the same time, they know from the experiences of their parents and adults in their personal communities that credentials alone cannot guarantee long-term occupational success or economic stability. They recognize that, particularly if they return to Rancho Benito after college, they will need to cultivate the same kinds of social and professional ties that have served their parents so well in building their careers. For parental emulator youths, the crucial challenge is to ensure that nothing stands in the way of securing the appropriate academic credentials and taking possession of the social capital which their parents' personal communities have at their disposal. In their eyes they need to arrive at the doorstep with the necessary credentials and keep the door open with their social networks.

ANALYTIC FRAMEWORK AND RESEARCH QUESTIONS

In this chapter we delve more deeply into each of these four subgroups. We show how these differently positioned youths chart their imagined futures, given their varied positions within a community afflicted by generalized economic insecurity and uncertainty. To illuminate these issues, we compare and contrast the four *security-autonomy-mobility roadmaps* sketched by youths with different experiences of economic insecurity. We map the contours of these *security-autonomy-mobility roadmaps* and trace these roadmaps to the distinctive life circumstances of each of the groups. Exploring how economic security and insecurity resonate through the lives of these youths and how they perceive and respond to the economic circumstances of the adults and peers around them, we investigate the kinds of experiences, preoccupations, and strategies that inform these roadmaps.

One of this chapter's contributions is its focus on a nonurban town located in an agricultural area, a relatively understudied type of community that is culturally and geographically distant from the economically polarized urban centers of the United States. Another contribution is the chapter's emphasis on the role of agency and actors' own strategies for coping with the economic hardships that neoliberalism has posed. Taking a hard look at the consequences of insecurity culture for the imagined futures of planning youths, the chapter probes the links between youths' firsthand and secondhand experiences of economic security and insecurity, both short-term and long-term, and the ways they frame their economic futures. The focus of the analysis is the complex interrelationship between the youths' varied economic circumstances, their class background, and the roadmaps they fashion to give some shape to their futures.

In comparing and contrasting these divergent roadmaps, this chapter pulls together several different strands of scholarly literature: scholarship focusing on youths' imagined futures and aspirational identities (Frye

2012; Schneider and Stevenson 1999; Silva 2012, 2013); scholarly literature on the ways in which families across the class spectrum experience
various forms of economic insecurity (Pugh 2015; Western et al. 2012;
Sherman 2009; Newman 1999 [1988]); and scholarly literature regarding
the emotional and psychic strategies parents and children develop for handling these forms of insecurity (Cooper 2013). Finally, it reveals how the
cultural imperative to see oneself as in control of one's economic circumstances, even in the face of uncertainty and risk, intersects with these varying formative experiences of economic (in)security.

RESPONDENTS: YOUTHS IN RANCHO BENITO

The data are drawn from interviews with high school students attending
two different schools in an agricultural belt of California. Part of a larger
study (Robinson and Schulz 2013), students in our respondent pool are
ethnically and economically diverse. The most economically privileged
youths have professional parents. Many of these parents are college educated and work as teachers, engineers, and administrators in this town's
professional stratum. While slim, the town's professional stratum is joined
by the high flyers in the area's big agriculture industry. Professionals in the
"big ag" sector may sport Wranglers, but they are likely to pair denim with
designer shirts and fancy dress boots (or "shit kickers" to use the patois)
that can cost more than an average family's monthly food budget.

On the other end of the economic spectrum, youths come from families
comprising the working poor. These youths may have parents who cobble
together seasonal work in the fields or have been unemployed since the
meltdown. Many of these youths and their families have been afflicted by
long-term financial hardship as well as long-term material deprivation. For
the youths at the extreme end of this continuum, housing and food can
be scarce resources. Those hardest hit often have no fixed address and rely
on "couch surfing" to keep a roof over their heads. For these youths, life is
marked by constant uncertainty as to where they will reside, what they will
eat, how they will get around town, and even whether the water or power
will be shut off.

In contrast to these youths, other respondents grew up taking for granted
many of the comforts of a middle-class American lifestyle: a family car, a
single-family dwelling, hot food on the table for dinner, etc. This being said,
while many of these families are keeping their heads above water, since the
meltdown they have pinched the pennies to keep a tight rein on their budgets. These families are neither completely secure nor completely insecure.

One or both parents may work in blue- and pink-collar occupations that are heterogeneous along three dimensions: service and manual labor, skilled and unskilled jobs, and licensed and unlicensed professions. For example, one parent may have obtained licensing or specialized training (examples: security guards, welders, real estate agents, and cosmetologists). Another parent may work in unskilled or service occupations such as janitorial and retail (as store clerks). While some parents have fared better than others, most have experienced significant economic stress. Youths have seen their parents slide economically in the face of long-term unemployment, reductions in pay and benefits, vanishing retirements and savings, plummeting home values, "upside-down" mortgages, and a rash of foreclosures.

Finally, to differentiate between these groups' relative financial well-being, it may be helpful to consider what these families regard as a special occasion. Youths from the vocational escalator and academic elevator roadmaps live on the financial edge; for them, a family trip for ice cream is a real treat. As one interviewee recalled, an ice cream sundae splurge for the whole family would be an important occasion and something to remember: "Yeah we were good ... [we would] get all dressed up and do it right." By contrast, for parental emulators, a quick stop at Baskin Robbins is a run-of-the-mill activity. Protective reclamation youths would have once taken such an expenditure for granted. However, in their current circumstances, they no longer take this for granted as a routine and mundane activity undeserving of special attention.

METHODS AND ANALYTIC STRATEGY

In this chapter, our data comes from one-on-one interviews and focus group interviews with several hundred youths attending two high schools in an agricultural of California. Relying on the well-respected tradition of qualitative interviewing (Pugh 2013), we mine respondents' rich narratives replete with details regarding their daily lives, economic circumstances, personal communities, aspirations, and future plans.

In this chapter our goal is to examine the imagined futures of high school students from a working class town in the wake of the 2008 economic crisis. We are particularly interested in how these youths craft their financial and occupational futures in the aftermath of the 2008 economic crisis. For this reason, this chapter focuses on a theoretically revealing subgroup of *planning students* who have given thought to planning their educational and occupational futures.

Planning students attend high school alongside their non-planning counterparts. As this characterization suggests, such planning students stand apart from their non-planning counterparts, who resemble the young women in Julie Bettie's study (2003) or young men in Paul Willis' study (1977). For example, some of the non-planning youths interviewed, common in this economically depressed community, are so engrossed in the everyday struggle to make ends meet that their primary concern is putting food on the table for their families. For such students, meeting immediate needs precludes investing resources in planning their future options. They often find it difficult to imagine let alone discuss a future in which they are acting as "agents" vis-à-vis the individuals and institutions that they will encounter as their adulthood unfolds. Indeed when asked about their futures, some non-planning youths supplied only the vaguest vision such as "I will work more hours" or "I will try to get a better job." Some of these students can also be characterized as oppositional in the same way as the adolescents populating the studies by Bettie and Willis. Such oppositional youths often regard school as an institution designed to thwart them or force them into an ill-fitting mold (Bettie 2003, 102, 137).

Non-planning youths, although worthy of future study, do not take center stage in our analysis. Rather the goal of our chapter is to examine the consequences of formative exposure to economic insecurity for youths' imagined financial and occupational futures, particularly how youths perceive and manage risks and rewards. Therefore we concentrate on the planning youths who have invested in weighing their future options. Our analytic strategy involves the intensive study of planning youths who view the future as something they can anticipate and plan for—at least to some extent—rather than something that simply happens to them. These planning students view educational and occupational institutions as potentially useful steppingstones in their quest for a better future. Planning students believe—rightly or wrongly—that they can engage with institutions to chart their own courses. These students also acquiesce to the neoliberal game of self-directed disciplined striving in the service of improving or enhancing their economic circumstances, implicitly accepting the neoliberal mandate to be economically self-sufficient as adults whatever the obstacles life throws in front of them.

FINDINGS

In this section we present representative cases for each of the four types of roadmaps we identify—namely vocational escalator roadmaps, academic elevator roadmaps, parental emulation roadmaps, and protective reclamation roadmaps. These exemplars have been carefully selected to illuminate ideal typical cases. Through systematic coding, the exemplars have been matched and systematically compared with the larger respondent pool along axes relevant to the study. Previous studies indicate that this matching strategy (Schulz 2012) pays analytic dividends when it comes to illuminating the general patterns characteristic of each type of *security-autonomy-mobility roadmaps* associated with each of the groups of youths. For each of the four groups, representative exemplars are presented. Each group is comprised of two representative youths, one female and one male, who represent the larger patterns in each group of youths who have sketched out roadmaps. The groups are compared and contrasted in order to highlight the ways that past experiences come into play in molding future roadmaps. These exemplars illustrate the complex ties between experiences of economic security and instability and the contours of individuals' *security-autonomy-mobility roadmaps*.

THE VOCATIONAL ESCALATOR ROADMAP

As the case of Carla suggests, youths in the vocational escalator group are no stranger to intensive and prolonged economic insecurity predating the Great Recession. These youths come from "hard living" families compelled to take one day at a time because of the omnipresent unpredictability and insecurities of their precarious livelihoods (Bettie 2003, 13; Howell 1973). Even before the Great Recession, even a modest degree of economic security lay beyond the reach of these youths. Furthermore, very few of the youths who frame this kind of roadmap can look to parents who have any kind of postsecondary training or credentialing. Many of their parents have not attended, let alone graduated from high school. In this group, a high school diploma is a badge of honor. Vocational escalator parents have spent their adult lives working in low-wage jobs offering little in the way of either security or autonomy. The lack of credentials disqualifies them from certified labor such as daycare operator, cosmetologist, auto mechanic, and welder, all jobs that appear to promise a modicum of economic stability. Observing their parents' difficulties in spite of beating the sun to work and valiant efforts to secure some measure of security, the adopters of the vocational escalator roadmap attribute their parents' struggles to their lack of vocational credentials.

The youths who exemplify members of the vocational escalator pathway place their faith in the power of certification and vocational credentialing as an insurance policy in a hostile and uncertain world. By obtaining vocational credentials, they believe that they can escape the economic insecurity and deprivation plaguing the adults in their own families. Youths favoring the vocational escalator roadmap presume that certification and vocational credentialing will insulate them against future economic risk and insecurity and, at the same time, assure them dignity and autonomy in the workplace. Their trust in the power of such credentials often borders on magical thinking. Lacking any firsthand knowledge of the challenges that await even the most vocationally qualified workers, they regard the acquisition of vocational credentials as a potent panacea that can by themselves ensure an upward trajectory and a high degree of economic security. The seed of this idealized vision of certification and vocational credentialing is planted and cultivated by teachers, coaches, and guidance counselors who sing the praises of vocational credentials at school.

Because many of these youths' parents have worked for many years in low-wage jobs where they exercise little power and control over their work conditions, the framers of the vocational exit roadmap show an affinity for occupations where self-employment appears as a tempting and viable option. Young women often idealize the scheduling flexibility of self-employment. Young women are more likely to savor the prospect of working as their "own boss," thereby avoiding the indignities inflicted by supervisors who see employees as nothing more than expenses on their balance sheet. Thus both genders configure their vocational exit roadmaps so that economic security, incremental mobility, and autonomy all figure prominently.

THE VOCATIONAL ESCALATOR ROADMAP: CRYSTAL

The adherents of the vocational escalator roadmap have all witnessed harsh economic realities. They have seen their families, particularly fathers and male relatives, thwarted in their efforts to provide for them and their siblings. Thus vocational escalator women foresee that they will need a steady income in order to provide for their own families and often their natal families as well. Crystal's case illustrates what happens when young women grow up in an economically unstable home environment and seek a vocational escape path.

Women who adopt a vocational escalator roadmap often blame their parents' economic struggles on the heartlessness and bad business sense of employers who are quick to shed workers when the going gets tough, regardless of the commitments made to their employees. Crystal's dad lost his job as an employee of a small local nursery when business dried up. Crystal interprets her father's situation as evidence that it is better to run your own business on your own terms than accept employment at a firm run by someone else who is happy to fire you the moment things turn sour. As she says, "My dad . . . worked hard . . . he was so good with the plants and telling people what to do to make them grow." It wasn't "his fault." Crystal explains that, although money was always tight, her family's situation really deteriorated when the nursery started to founder after the 2008 recession. Borrowing from her father's critiques, Crystal assigns blame to the business owner: "He [the owner] just made all of the employees pay . . . my dad worked there for over ten years . . . and walked away with nothing." During this time of familial hardship, Crystal's mother was unable to right the family ship. For Crystal, her mother's inability to rescue the family from deprivation stems from her lack of marketable skills and vocational credentials: "My mom wanted to run her own day care center but she stopped school early and so she never got the certificate."

Women such as Crystal gravitate toward the possibility of running their own small-scale business, both for the sake of scheduling flexibility and to ensure a greater degree of control over their economic fate. Reviewing her own parents' situation, Crystal has arrived at the conclusion that she needs to earn her certificate in early childhood studies, a credential she will ultimately require to establish her own day care operation. Crystal plans to run her own day care program after earning her certificate at Jefferson, the local community college. Crystal explains: "I just love kids . . . so I wanna work with kids . . . and be a good mom." Unlike youths planning on attending a four-year college and thereby delaying their entry into the labor market, Crystal has decided to enroll in a certification program at the local community college: "It will be better for me to work and go to school at the same time . . . that way I can get my certificate quickly at Jefferson [Community College]."

In assuming the responsibility to provide for her natal family through her own efforts, Crystal is expressing a willingness to step into the breach. Even more important, she is looking into the future to her imagined family. Should her future partner not be able to bring in an income, Crystal can keep the family afloat. As she says: "I want to know that if my guy hits a rough patch . . . you know, so I can still have a job and we'll be ok." Like other such youths who have seen their parents flounder over a long span of time, Crystal presumes that by obtaining skills, she will avoid a similar fate. In her mind, by earning credentials, she will be prepared and able to step in to rescue her family's finances if her husband finds himself unable to work:

I really want a family . . . but like it's scary everyone being out of work . . . made me think of you know what I need to do so like if I have kids . . . get ahead with my education. I would like to have stable money for my family. If I get married and my husband breaks his leg I want to be able to support us financially.

Crystal does not intend to become a stay-at-home mom; her plan is to be a working mother who can provide for her family.

Although Crystal's larger goal appears clear to her, she acknowledges that she cannot look to any adult role models to fill in the blanks. Unable to ask her parents for advice in this realm, Crystal turns to the school's career counselor as an "expert" to help her plan her future strategically: "I didn't know what I could do or how I could do it ... but Ms. Schoefeld was real helpful ... when I told her I was interested in working in having a day care center she told me that I can get my certificate at Jefferson [Community College] after I graduate from high school ... she said I don't even have to leave town and go away to school ... I can do it all right here." Significantly, for Crystal, the guidance counselor serves as an aspirational role model who has already taken the path Crystal sees for herself.

THE VOCATIONAL ESCALATOR ROADMAP: VICTOR

While Victor could count on a roof over his head and food on the table, he never had access to middle-class comforts such as his own bedroom. Even before the Great Recession the adult males in Victor's personal community coped with job losses and inadequate work hours. Long before the Recession's onset in 2008, the "lucky" adults in Victor's personal community had to settle for diminished and more infrequent paychecks. For the "unlucky" adults, long-term unemployment has always been the rule rather than the exception. Victor's father was one of the "lucky" ones: "Until then [2008] my dad had—like you know—steady jobs ... He was working all of the time ... he can fix anything ... so he was the go-to guy at [local hotel] ... for a while he worked at [local plant] fixing whatever they needed." Until the Great Recession, Victor's father provided for his family's basic needs by stringing together jobs from multiple employers. However, with the arrival of the Great Recession, Victor's own living circumstances deteriorated when a steady income eluded his father. Unable to afford the rent, they moved in with their extended family. Victor puts on a bold face: " ... yeah we made it ok ... right now we're with my uncle and aunt."

Victor already holds a part-time job to help out his family. He has already learned firsthand that as an employee he has very little control over his hours and income: "I work at the car wash ... try to get hours ... but never know if my shift is gonna get cut." Victor imagines that as a small-business owner he will be able to gain some measure of control over his finances. By opening his own barbershop, he anticipates a more secure livelihood than his father could deliver: "I think it is better to be my own boss . . . I want to know that I take good care of my family." He reasons that he will never lack for clients as his business fills an ongoing need: "Everybody's got hair, right? Needs to cut it, right? No hair? Still hafta shave . . . so this is a good way to go." At the same time, Victor views entrepreneurship as a means to gaining autonomy so that he can avoid the kind of "shaming" his father experienced at the hands of his employers: "My dad did a real good job for them but it didn't matter . . . they just let him go." Raul, Victor's adult mentor, owns his own shop. Victor feels very fortunate to have discovered such a skilled role model:

> He lets me just watch, so if I'm not working I go there any time that I can. You know just to watch him. It's amazing. Raul is amazing. I can just watch him for hours and hours . . . that's what I want. You know have my own place like that where I can do my art.

Like Crystal, Victor has opted for an educational path centered around vocational classes leading to an occupation-specific state certification, and, ultimately, ownership of his own small business: "I'm going take my classes . . . the problem is getting my kit together . . . it's like $500 bucks to get my kit together . . . once I've got my kit and take the classes, Raul said he would work something out . . . " Victor's relationship with Raul also shows the importance of aspirational role models, particularly the vocationally oriented men who benefit from a local entrepreneur's mentorship.

THE ACADEMIC ELEVATOR ROADMAP

We now turn to the academic elevator roadmap. In many ways, the academic elevator roadmap parallels the vocational escalator roadmap. In both cases, the significant and long-term economic insecurity and hardship marring the lives of the youths have been chronic and unrelenting, even during times of relative economic prosperity. These youths are also accustomed to the chronic unpredictability and insecurities that go hand in hand with hard living. In addition, the parents of both vocational escalator and academic elevator youths lack either degrees or careers which provide either economic autonomy or security.

However, while the same experiences of long-term economic insecurity inform both the vocational and academic elevator roadmaps, the two roadmaps assume divergent forms. The academic elevator roadmap necessitates buying into an objectively riskier proposition, namely that academic credentials alone can propel one into a more secure occupational track. Akin to the upward-looking "prep" students documented in Bettie's study (Bettie 2003), these students attend to their grades and coursework diligently. Thus the students who embrace the academic elevator roadmap are willing to defer economic security for themselves and potentially postpone the immediate financial help they could give to their natal families.

To a much greater degree than their vocational escalator counterparts, the academic elevator youths put their chips down in a high-stakes gamble. They are willing to postpone their entry into the labor market and pay for a four-year college education. In effect they are betting that both the earning opportunities they forfeit in the short-term and the potentially greater debt they incur will ultimately pay off in the end with a white-collar job. For example, whereas vocational escalator youths prepare to plunge into the skilled labor market immediately after earning vocational credentials, academic elevator youths are prepared to defer entry into the labor market in order to seize the golden ring of the BA, even if means that she can't take full-time employment for at least four years. For academic elevator youths, even when it entails the sacrifice of earning opportunities immediately after high school, the opportunities afforded by the BA exert a magnetic pull.

Although they vary by student, there are several, often intertwined, sources of the academic elevator roadmap shared by this relatively small group of students. Often, these students are encouraged by at least one adult mentor, usually teachers and other educators in the school who has taken an interest in them: "Mrs. Smith took me aside after class and told me I could do it . . . " These adult mentors encourage them to exert themselves academically as well as in extracurricular pursuits. Alongside mentoring, the students feel both empowered by and obligated to their parents and siblings to be the first in their family to clear the hurdle of a college education. In addition, friendships with academically oriented peers are yet another complementary factor steering them toward college.

THE ACADEMIC ELEVATOR ROADMAP: MAYA

Maya looks forward to securing a BA en route to a secure and stable white collar career. Maya is well-informed about her occupational options and the necessary educational prerequisites (Schneider and Stevenson 1999) thanks to a special mentoring program for low-income students. Maya expresses certainty about her educational goals: "Right now the big decision. . . [is] where I'm gonna go to school." In her eyes, the important decision facing her as a high school student is how to find a way to pay for her post-secondary degree. Maya announces, "Gotta do it. Better take loans if you have to. Get a job if you have to. But do it. Go straight to a four-year school. If you don't go things can happen." By graduating with her BA, Maya sees a day when she will leave the grinding insecurity and hardship far behind.

Like many students of both genders who place their trust in the power of academic credentials, Maya's personal community has very few adult role models of either gender who have earned the educational credentials to which she aspires. Maya's father is not in the picture at all. Maya's mother, while earning Maya's admiration for her "stick to it" attitude and her unwavering work ethic, has not trodden the road which Maya wants to follow. As Maya sees it, her mother "works so hard—day after day—work, work, work. And nothin's gonna change . . . " Her mother's hard life as a paid caregiver for the elderly makes Maya yearn for a yet unknown degree of economic security. Maya knows that her mother longs for her to join the people who "don't have to struggle just to make ends meet."

In Maya's case adults from the school and her mentoring program played a key role in making the college path seem more attainable. Like Crystal, Maya has turned to educators for the guidance lacking in her personal community. She explains:

> I went to Mrs. Lafitte. She sat me down and explained how she was the first person in her family to go to college too . . . I didn't understand how anything worked . . . She took the time to tell me what I needed to know. She totally helped me . . .

She can also serve as a role model for her younger siblings who aspire to escape their current economic insecurity. By attending college, Maya will pave the way for the younger siblings and ". . . show them they can do it too." Once she has graduated from college and established herself in a career, Maya looks forward to liberating her own mother from economic insecurity: "I can help my mom that way. . . make it better for her so she doesn't have to work so hard." The anticipated rewards of a college diploma weigh so heavily in the balance for Maya that the risks from this path disappear from view.

THE ACADEMIC ELEVATOR ROADMAP: RAFAEL

Like Maya, Rafael has set his sights on securing academic credentials which, in his view, will boost him into a higher and more secure economic orbit than that of his own family and friends. Also similar to Maya, Rafael's eagerness is fueled by a teacher who regularly mentors students. "Mr. Chapelle" leads an annual fundraising effort to take students like Rafael to Washington, D.C. with the goal of broadening their sense of what is possible for them. For many of these students, it is their first trip outside of California or even away from home. Rafael recalls how the trip to the nation's capital was instrumental in shaping his goals: "Mr. Chapelle took us to Washington D.C. talked to us about what we could do . . . made me want to be a teacher."

To accomplish this goal, Rafael believes he must stake everything on going immediately to a four-year college. He believes that this path will open the doors to a secure future. Rafael has seen family members work themselves to the bone, dependent on seasonal work on one of the many "coolers"[2] necessary to the local agricultural industry. He relates: "They always told me I could do anything . . . that they were working hard so that I could do something better." Rafael is highly motivated to go to college and become a high school teacher as a result of his parents' encouragement and having seen their economic struggles.

To keep his eyes on the prize, Rafael refuses to succumb to the temptations of an immediate paycheck attached to a job that may derail his college education, future career, and even his long-term economic security. Rafael frames short-term economic gain from a "dead end" job as an unacceptable risk that might jeopardize his future: "If people aren't careful . . . they just stop going to school. . . . You can't get hooked on a paycheck and wind up not getting your degree." Some academic elevator youths like Rafael have been exempted by their parents from helping support the family through part-time jobs. This dispensation does not come cheaply, but must be achieved with the coin of familial sacrifice on the part of parents struggling to keep the electric and other essential bills paid. With their eyes on the prize of a college education, academic elevator youths forgo immediate income from part-time jobs in order to pursue academics leading to the BA.

Students like Rafael owe a debt of honor toward their family members who are determined to keep them on track for college. To repay this debt, academic elevator youths like Rafael put their shoulders to the wheel to succeed academically. Setting his sights on a full-ride academic scholarship, he has studied hard his entire high school career, taking the hardest classes, going the extra mile to get help, risking the stigma of geekdom, giving up fun activities, etc. Whatever the price of preparing for college, Rafael has willingly paid it both for himself and to honor his family's sacrifice: "Work now. Play later . . . Make my parents proud." Finally, like Maya, Rafael also sees greater earning power as a means to help his natal families: "After I finish college I'm gonna help out my folks . . . that's the way it should be." Rafael invests all of his efforts into earning a college degree, which he sees as the necessary step to securing economic security for himself and his family.

THE PARENTAL EMULATION ROADMAP

Unlike the vocational escalator and academic elevator roadmaps, the parental emulation roadmap stems from different experiential sources and projects a different vision of the future. The parental emulation roadmap revolves around the ideal of replicating the careers and trajectories of parents and other adults. Youths who espouse this understanding of the future treat future economic security and prosperity as guaranteed, as long as they can follow in the footsteps of their parents and other adults in their personal communities.

For those who aspire to emulate their parents, there is nothing unfamiliar about long-term economic security and stability. With substantial and steady incomes derived from their successful law and medical practices or executive positions at local organizations, these parents stand as living proof to their sons and daughters that long-term economic security and prosperity is within their grasp. These optimistic and confident youths have parents who are attorneys, physicians, and local "big ag." These youths have witnessed their own parents and other adults in their personal communities capitalize on their professional networks and organizational positions to enhance their family's standard of living and economic security.

These youths also appreciate the mutually reinforcing advantages conferred by college degrees, postgraduate credentials, and local social capital. They realize that credentials serve only as a gateway to professional success and that a remunerative career stands on other legs besides credentials. Grasping the importance of credentials, they also came to realize the indispensability of their community-specific social capital and local connections. Local connections are often forged through groups and organizations including local private school alumni groups, AAUW, churches, and religious organizations, as well as service groups like Kiwanis and Rotary. Parental emulator youths see their parents knitting local networks together through shared activities such as fundraising barbeques, pancake breakfasts, and a variety of other outreach projects in the community. Parental emulators see their parents making contributions to the local community and also making connections that provide professional benefits.

Parental emulators thus see themselves not only following in their parents' footsteps in terms of education, but also envision capitalizing on similar social and professional networks. Indeed of the many youths who are considering taking up their parents' occupations, many are counting on the very same local socioprofessional networks, which their parents have cultivated in Rancho Benito during their thriving careers.

THE PARENTAL EMULATION ROADMAP: LINDA

Linda exemplifies many of the characteristics that distinguish parental emulators from other types. Because of her parents' professional positions and the substantial incomes that accompany them, Linda has never known either long-term or short-term economic insecurity. Family functions and social events are populated by the local bigwigs: lawyers, doctors, and even judges. Unlike the other youths, Linda has never given a second thought to the family's financial health or standard of living. Even when the economy faltered, her family was relatively insulated and never had to make painful sacrifices.

When asked if she will return to Rancho Benito to start her professional career, she considers "it probably would be easier." Indeed, it would be easier for Linda to join this network than to strike out on her own elsewhere. No matter the professional service needed, Linda's family is bound to know someone who can readily supply an introduction or make a phone call. With a ready supply of references in many life domains, Linda understands that members of the network both benefit from connections and also contribute to them: "It's good to know people. If someone needs something you can put them in touch. Then when you need a favor, they can help you out."

Knowing the benefits conferred by personal connections, Linda is optimistic about her future and the jump-start she will get by letting her career piggyback off of her parents' local connections. Where Linda's aspirations are concerned, it is her mother's career which serves as the guiding light. Linda's mother, a physician with her own local practice, belongs to the town's small but powerful class of professionals. Linda has already mapped out a future path that would look very familiar to her mother's experience: "First college, then med. school, then residency, then maybe my own practice." For Linda, the launching platform for this trajectory has never been in doubt. She "always knew" that she would "go to a four-year right away," as "that's what everyone in my family has done."

THE PARENTAL EMULATION ROADMAP: NICOLAS

Like Linda, Nicolas has little acquaintance with economic instability on account of his parents' lucrative and stable positions within with the town's professional elite. In his case, Nicolas's dad is a pillar of the legal community, representing some of the agriculture firms in the area. Nicolas has grown up in economic circumstances similar to those of Linda, never lacking for either essentials or indulgences. His dad's resilient law practice flourishes in good economic times and weathers the downturns.

Nicolas admires his dad for working hard over the years and sticking to his own ambitious career plan, a plan which got off the ground because of his dad's law degree from a well-known California law school. He also acknowledges his father's talents as a social networker skillful at drumming up business and sustaining his ties to the local community. When Nicolas talks about his father, he characterizes him as a "great guy." Nicolas is aware that his dad ". . . does a bunch of community service and knows a bunch of people." The tight-knit character of the local community is readily apparent to Nicolas, who remarks that "someone always knows someone."

In contemplating his own occupational and economic future, Nicolas embraces the possibility of settling into the same professional and occupational niche as his dad. Planning to first practice as a lawyer, Nicolas aspires to ultimately become a judge. He anticipates putting himself in a position to establish his own law practice in town (or take over his dad's law practice) by spending many years hitting the books at law school. To accomplish his goals, Nicolas knows that he will have to work his way through the ranks and pay his dues: "To make it I will need to work hard. But that is what everyone has to do. So you do it." Like Linda, Nicolas has his eye on an extended educational trajectory comprised of college followed by a postgraduate professional degree. Nicolas explains: "Law school after the BA. Who knows—maybe Harvard Law!"

THE PROTECTIVE RECLAMATION ROADMAP

The youths who belong to the protective reclamation group differ in their relationship with economic insecurity when contrasted with the other groups. Unlike the vocational escalator and academic elevator groups, they have tasted real economic security and a comfortable standard of living for more than short periods. Unlike the parental emulators, however, they have felt the sting of the Great Recession in a direct and personal way. Before the 2008 crisis, their families used to enjoy economic security. Protective reclamation youths can recall what it was like to enjoy a comfortable degree of security and to plan for the future with some degree of confidence. By and large, during the years before 2008, these youths took a middle-class standard of living for granted from housing to family cars to trips to watch baseball at Dodger Stadium. Protective reclamation youths experienced stability unknown to their vocational escalator and academic elevator peers. After the crisis, protective reclamation youths learned to put economic concerns front and center in their future planning.

For protective reclamation youths, the cherished and hard-won economic security provided by their families ground to a halt with the onset of the Great Recession. Without warning, their cocoon of security collapsed, forcing these youths to reevaluate their assumptions about economic security. The sudden reversal of fortune called into question what these youths had believed about their families' economic foundations. It also discredited their families' presumptions about how to create a secure life. In particular, the collapse cast doubt on the power of credentials to guarantee economic security and a middle-class standard of living. Protective reclamation youths recognize that their own parents and other adults had "played by the rules," acquiring college degrees and job experience, but had nevertheless found themselves in dire straits when the going got tough.

For protective reclamation youths, the power of academic credentialing was undermined before their very eyes. For this reason, their attitude toward credentialing stands in opposition to all of the other groups, especially those youths' seeking upward mobility via educational attainment. For these reasons, protective reclamation youths exhibit substantial uncertainty and adopt a risk-averse posture toward the future. These youths express more uncertainty than the others about how they should proceed. They wish to reclaim the lost economic security of the prerecession years, but they have also lost faith in the power of educational credentials to launch them on the path of reclamation. Their risk-averse stance comes across particularly clearly in regards to their stance toward postsecondary schooling. They refuse to countenance the possibility of amassing substantial debt, even if it helps them to obtain marketable degrees in relatively high-paying fields.

THE PROTECTIVE RECLAMATION ROADMAP: DANIELA

Daniela still recalls the halcyon days during her childhood when she dwelt in a roomy and comfortable house in one of the new housing tracts in Rancho Benito. Twice a year her family took her and her siblings to Disneyland, a high point of her life. Daniela recalls feeling very secure before 2008. With the income from her mom's job as an elementary school teacher combined with the income from her dad's successful contracting business, there was always enough money to go around. Unfortunately, the sudden decline in business following the 2008 slowdown dealt a death blow to her father's contracting business, putting him out of work for several years.

In Daniela's view, the only thing holding her family's economic fortune together is her mom's good fortune to have a secure job. She reflects: "We were lucky my mom had her job . . . and that it was a safe job . . . I think it's good to have a job like that." Even with her mom's income, the family's financial situation deteriorated, ultimately causing the family to vacate their home and reluctantly settle into a rental property. Daniela was called upon to make sacrifices in the interest of saving money. Although she is still active in FFA (Future Farmers of America), moving meant that Daniela had to give up raising animals: "I had rabbit hutches in the backyard . . . but I had to find homes for them when we moved."

In her future planning, Daniela is risk-averse and wants to avoid financial uncertainty even as she badly wants to regain lost ground. She is determined to get an "education and someday get a nice house." However, she also fears entering a risky career path. For Daniela, the ideal pathway promises a dependable income. With this goal in mind, Daniela may sacrifice her pre-crisis goal of going into veterinary medicine for a more stable career as a teacher: ". . . it's pretty pricey to become a vet . . . and besides I like kids as much as I like animals. I can still be a teacher and work with 4H or somethin' like that to take care of animals."

Moreover, seeing her parents struggle to pay their financial obligations, Daniela is wary of shackling herself with educational debt and unmanageable student loan repayments. Her wariness leads her to relinquish the dream of immediately attending a four-year college: "Sure it would be nice to go straight to a four-year. But it's too much money . . . I can go to Jefferson [Community College] and transfer." Without even knowing the dollar amounts, Daniela believes that starting out at a four-year college right after high school does not warrant breaking the bank: "It's not worth it to spend all that money just to go to some big school when Jefferson [Community College] has the classes I need . . . besides you end up in the same place."

Like her counterpart Crystal, the student who stakes her hopes on the power of the vocational credential, Daniela aspires to be a provider for her future family and contributor to the family finances. When thinking about her role in a future family, Daniela's believes she can keep the family ship afloat as her mother has done. Daniela strategizes, "It is real important for both people to have a good job so if something happens you can land on your feet. . . take care of your kids." However, Daniela, unlike Crystal, knows what it feels like to experience some measure of economic security and comfort in her daily life. Further, whereas Crystal sees the vocational credential as the ticket to economic security, Daniela does not see educational credentials as magic bullets. While Crystal wants to gain a toehold that will allow her to climb beyond her parents' circumstances, Daniela is willing to downsize her dreams and expectations as a way of reclaiming the economic security she lost in the Great Recession. While Crystal seeks upward mobility and security that her parents have never experienced, Daniela yearns to recreate the economic security her family once enjoyed.

THE PROTECTIVE RECLAMATION ROADMAP: JESSE

Jesse illustrates the protective reclamation roadmap as it manifests itself among the male youths. Both Jesse's father, a successful local chiropractor, and his mother, an accountant, took a hit in the recession. As their client lists dwindled, Jesse's mother took over managing the father's practice as a way to help stretch the overhead budget by reducing payroll. With the crisis, the entire family was forced to revise their expectations about wants versus needs: "My mom says we gotta be thankful for what we've got . . . still got our house, still going to a four-year eventually even if I start out at Jefferson [Community College]."

Jesse's response to the loss of economic security parallels the response of Daniela in many ways. Like Daniela, Jesse remembers better times: "We used to go to Dodger games, go camping . . . it's hard to do that now . . . I want to give my kids those things, and I can't do that if I don't have a good job." Before the crisis, Jesse and his brothers had not yet formulated any concrete occupational aspirations. Witnessing his parents' difficulties weathering the recession, Jesse started to lean toward what he considered a "secure" occupation, namely engineering. Like Daniela, when asked about his future plans, Jesse emphasizes the stability of his future career: "I wasn't really sure what I wanted to do but now I'm thinking engineering . . . I like to build things so I can do that . . . We had a speaker and he told us it is pretty good money and there are a lot of jobs even in hard times." Jesse believes that he can manage risk by choosing a path that affords more security by depending on an employer: "I don't want a rollercoaster. I want a smooth ride . . . I've seen what my parents go through with a small business. No thanks."

Like Daniela, Jesse's desire to recapture the lost economic security of the prerecession years has prompted him to shun risk. In addition to selecting what he believes is a more secure career path, he also is wary of committing to an uncertain educational future: "I don't want to waste my time on a major not related to anything in the real world." In order to reclaim past financial security, Jesse believes he must avoid unnecessary risks that will delay or derail his ability to build a solid financial future: "My dad has told me 'Don't study something useless and don't take loans for a fancy private school unless you want to live on ramen' ... get a degree, get a job, get a life." For this reason, Jesse is reflective about how the price tag of a college education fits into his career plans, "My parents warned me ... still paying off their loans ... I don't want to be in a bunch of debt." Jesse had originally planned to attend his parents' alma mater but has revised these plans in light of the situation. Like so many others guided by this roadmap, Jesse expresses a willingness to trade off personal dreams for greater economic security. He is weighing the idea of taking care of his GE requirements at the local community college unless he is offered generous scholarships and grants: "Sure, I would like to go straight to a four-year. But it's like show me the money. If there is no dinero, then Jefferson [Community College] ... it's my next stop."

DISCUSSION AND CONCLUSIONS

Where it concerns youths' experiences of economic risk, uncertainty, and stability as well as their future plans, Rancho Benito is home to at least four distinct kinds of roadmaps. These four types of roadmap—the vocational escalator roadmap, the academic elevator roadmap, the protective reclamation roadmap, and the parental emulation roadmap—emerge from our systematic comparison of these youths in terms of their past experiences as well as their future orientations and aspirations. As we have seen, each of these types reflects a distinctive outlook on security and mobility on the part of the youths. The various dimensions of these four categories are laid out in Table 10.1.

When we contrast the four groups across the multiple dimensions specified in the table above, we can discern some general patterns. Whereas the economic insecurity and deprivation of the first two groups has stretched on for their entire lives—both before and after the recession years—the economic insecurity of the reclamation-risk aversion group began only after the onset of the 2008 recession. Furthermore, the escalator and elevator groups attribute the economic tribulations of their families to their lack of credentials, and so prize credentials as the magic bullet which can insulate them against the same problems. Lacking adult contacts in these occupations, and hence usable social capital, the youths who frame these roadmaps invest credentials with transformative significance—a vision that is often reinforced by their mentors at school.

Table 10.1 ROADMAPS TABLE

	VOCATIONAL ESCALATOR ROADMAP	ACADEMIC ELEVATOR ROADMAP	RECLAMATION- RISK AVERSION ROADMAP	PARENTAL EMULATION ROADMAP
SECURITY STRATEGY	CHART UPWARD TRAJECTORY	CHART UPWARD TRAJECTORY	REESTABLISH LOST ECONOMIC SECURITY	MAINTAIN ECONOMIC SECURITY

KEY ASPECTS OF ROADMAPS

occupational aspirations	blue-collar and pink-collar jobs, self-employment	white-collar jobs	secure white-collar employment	professional elite white-collar jobs
stance towards education and credentials	vocational credentials are "magic bullet"	academic credentials are "magic bullet"	credentials, risk-averse occupation, low debt all necessary	credentials and social capital both necessary

SOURCES OF ROADMAPS

past and present economic insecurity	chronic long-term economic insecurity that worsened after recession	chronic long-term economic insecurity that worsened after recession	pre-recession economic security and post-recession economic insecurity	continuous economic security pre-recession and post-recession

Parental emulator youths differ the most from the other three groups inasmuch as those youths who adopt the parental emulation roadmap have no firsthand understanding of economic insecurity. Unlike the other three groups, parental emulator youths have experienced long-term economic security. Spectators to their parents' successes, they know how this security can be realized. To the parental emulator youths, the parents' well-trodden path looks like a fail-safe recipe for economic security and a comfortable life.

Finally, members of the protective reclamation group, by contrast, have witnessed the failure of credentials as insurance against economic insecurity. They therefore approach credentials with a skepticism borne of bitter experience. For this group economic security is both extremely desirable and extremely fragile. Things can go right for a long time but then go awry without warning, even when parents have "done everything right." Yearning for the economic dreamland of economically comfortable childhoods preceding the 2008 crisis, these youths evince a skepticism toward a system which has both given and taken away. In this roadmap future autonomy on the job is subordinated to reclaiming the security of the lost economic past. Personal dreams are sacrificed on the altar of financial pragmatism.

CREDENTIALS AND OTHER PASSPORTS
TO ECONOMIC SECURITY

Juxtaposing the four roadmaps allows us to see how different experiences of economic (in)security breed different outlooks on the future among the youths of Rancho Benito. Such a comparison also illuminates the varying roles of what we call *security passports*. In the analysis of the data we can identify three distinct security passports: credentials (both vocational and academic); occupational autonomy (running one's own business or working as a freelancer); and social capital.

The credential passport is the most central passport across all four groups. Both vocational escalator youth and academic elevator youths pin their hopes on the credential passport. Their faith is bolstered by the educators' claims on behalf of credentials. Albeit to varying degrees, each of the four groups sees credentialing as necessary. The occupational autonomy passport resonates with two of the four groups. For vocational escalator youths, credentials in the form of vocational certifications operate synergistically alongside occupational autonomy. Aspirations for occupational autonomy as exemplified by an entrepreneurial orientation appeal to members of the vocational escalator group. In their eyes, once they are properly trained and equipped with a certificate or license, the door will be open to running a successful business and creating a relatively secure and prosperous future. For the women in this group, such a role also promises more freedom and flexibility than working for a boss. For the men in this group escaping the clutches of a boss and running one's own shop carries the intoxicating whiff of masculine self-reliance. On the other end of the spectrum, parental emulators also see the value of the occupational autonomy passport, particularly those who aspire to their own medical or law practice. By contrast, neither the academic elevator nor the protective reclamation youths prioritize the occupational autonomy passport. Credentials are the indispensable passport for the vocational elevator youths. To them, credentials are the only passport that can facilitate entry into an occupation largely unfamiliar to their personal communities. Vocational elevator youths rely neither on occupational autonomy nor social capital passports—for them, vocational credentials carry almost the entire weight of their future plans. Conversely, protective reclamation youths regard both the credential and occupational autonomy passports with skepticism. While they believe they must earn a college degree, they are nonetheless wary of succumbing to the same reversal of fortune as college-educated parents. These youths thus do not pin their hopes on credentials in the same way as do vocational elevator youths. At the same time, they are also wary of the occupational autonomy passport, particularly when they have seen parental businesses that faltered during the meltdown. Because many of these youths doubt the capacity of small businesses to survive in a bad economy, they have lost faith in the potential of occupational autonomy to deliver a secure and stable life.

In terms of social capital, this passport plays a marginal role in all of the roadmaps with the exception of the parental emulator roadmap. Significantly, while social capital may play a role for reclamation youths, they are well aware that social capital did not suffice to salvage their parents' financial well-being. By and large, they cannot bank on their own social networks or their families' social networks to enhance their future job prospects or prospects of economic security.

In tandem with credentialing and occupational autonomy passports, the social capital passport plays a central role in the roadmaps of the parental emulator youths. These fortunate youths give each passport a specific role. While the credential gets them past the first hurdle, occupational autonomy – particularly when combined with social capital—gets them to the finish line. These youths know well that credentials may be enough to crack open the door to stability, prosperity, and security, but they are not enough to keep the door open over the long haul. So these youths bank on both occupational autonomy and social capital in local networks to help them carve out a successful and secure future in the decades ahead.

Finally, among the findings that emerge from our research on Rancho Benito youths are some insights into the relationship between these roadmaps and gender. Overall, the two genders converge closely in terms of their experiences of economic (in)security as well as their imagined futures. If we contrast the roadmaps of the male youths to those of the female youths across the four types of roadmaps, gender divergence stands in the shadow of gender convergence. This convergence is especially striking in the case of the youths who embrace the protective reclamation roadmap. All the youths in this group have grown up in dual-earner middle-class households in which women have shared responsibility for the family's economic well-being alongside men. These youths, whether female or male, thus view two incomes as a necessary hedge against economic risk and insecurity.

Several of these groups do manifest some unexpected gender divergences. Probably the most striking divergence characterizes the members of the academic elevator group. While the women and men in this group alike express great enthusiasm for the prospect of a secure and stable white-collar job, the women are more concerned about the costs of missing the academic elevator. Many of the academic elevator women entertain grave concerns about their futures should they miss their ride. This concern is fueled by their skepticism about the male breadwinner model, as well as their goal of strengthening their bargaining position within their own future household. Finally, many of these young women had heard encouraging words from female role models and mentors at school who were themselves anxious to help the students travel down this road. Thus, even more than the men, the women maintain a laser-like focus on the potential of higher education to unlock the kinds of jobs and careers capable of making them financially independent.

This chapter opens a new and revealing window onto the past experiences and future visions of the youths from agricultural California. In chronicling their attempts to exert agency vis-à-vis an uncertain future, the chapter sheds light on this often forgotten population: working-class communities far from urban America. As the youths' vivid narratives illuminate, their divergent experiences have led them to very different understandings of potential futures. Each of the four groups sees both the future's opportunities and constraints in a different light, depending on their past experiences of economic security and insecurity. Despite the differences among the groups, however, they have all, to one degree or another, witnessed the unseen but powerful forces unleashed by the 2008 meltdown that have reshaped the economic landscape beneath their feet. Perhaps most importantly, all four groups are grappling with the collision between the neoliberal ideal of economic self-reliance and the neoliberal realities of risk, insecurity, and uncertainty.

NOTES

1. All names are pseudonyms. Grammar has been corrected only when necessary for clarity.
2. The "cooler" refrigerates freshly picked fruits and vegetables so that they can be transported.

REFERENCES

Armstrong, Elizabeth, and Laura Hamilton. 2013. *Paying for the Party: How College Maintains Inequality.* Cambridge, MA: Harvard University Press.

Bettie, Julie. 2003. *Women without Class: Girls, Race, and Identity.* Berkeley: University of California Press.

Cooper, Marianne. 2013. *Cut Adrift: Families in Insecure Times.* Berkeley: University of California Press.

Frye, Margaret. 2012. "Bright Futures in Malawi's New Dawn: Educational Aspirations as Assertions of Identity." *American Journal of Sociology* 117(6):1565–1624.

Howell, Joseph T. 1973. *Hard Living on Clay Street: Portraits of Blue-Collar Families.* Garden City, NY: Anchor.

Newman, Katherine. 1999. *Falling from Grace: Downward Mobility in the Age of Affluence.* Berkeley: University of California Press.

Pugh, Allison. 2004. "Windfall Child Rearing: Low-Income Care and Consumption." *Journal of Consumer Culture* 4(2):229–249.

Pugh, Allison. 2013. "What Good Are Interviews for Thinking about Culture? Demystifying Interpretive Analysis." *American Journal of Cultural Sociology* 1:42–68.

Pugh, Allison. 2015. *The Tumbleweed Society: Working and Caring in an Age of Insecurity.* Oxford: Oxford University Press.

Robinson, Laura, and Jeremy Schulz. 2013. "Net Time Negotiations within the Family." In *Special Issue: ASA Communication and Information Technologies Section 2013. Information, Communication, and Society* 16(4):542–560.

Schneider, Barbara L., and David Stevenson. 1999. *The Ambitious Generation: America's Teenagers, Motivated but Directionless.* New Haven, CT: Yale University Press.

Schulz, Jeremy. 2012. "Talk of Work: Transatlantic Divergences in Justifications for Hard Work among French, Norwegian, and American Professionals." *Theory and Society* 41(6):603–634.

Sherman, Jennifer. 2009. *Those Who Work and Those Who Don't.* Minneapolis: University of Minnesota Press.

Silva, Jennifer. 2013. *Coming up Short: Working-Class Adulthood in an Age of Uncertainty.* New York: Oxford University Press.

Silva, Jennifer. 2012. "Constructing Adulthood in an Age of Uncertainty." *American Sociological Review* 77(4):505–522.

Western, Bruce, Deirdre Bloome, Benjamin Sosnaud, and Laura Tach. 2012. "Economic Insecurity and Social Stratification." *Annual Review of Sociology* 38:341–359.

Willis, Paul. 1977. *Learning to Labor: How Working Class Kids Get Working Class Jobs.* New York: Columbia University Press.

CHAPTER 11

✺

Intimate Inequalities

Love and Work in the Twenty-First Century

SARAH M. CORSE AND JENNIFER M. SILVA

The central features of the American economy changed significantly near the end of the twentieth century, and those changes are intensifying in the twenty-first century. Globalization and the attendant financialization of the global economy have fundamentally rearranged industries, organizations, and jobs. Most workers now have less stability than in the past and are more likely to face job changes and disruptions such as downsizing and industry-level reorganizations. Many changes in the labor market have had especially profound effects on working-class Americans. Routine, less-skilled work, especially in manufacturing, has been outsourced to developing countries, and the American economy increasingly rewards skilled labor and advanced degrees (Kalleberg 2009). Simultaneous changes in the political and cultural realm have emphasized individual self-reliance and the privatization of risk through mechanisms such as the rise in self-employment, the decline of defined benefit programs, and disappearance of organizational commitments to employees (Hacker 2006). The result of these changes is that work has become insecure for many if not most workers.

Insecurity, however, varies across type of work. Education is the main credential sorting workers into jobs and occupations: it serves as the gateway to class mobility and determines suitability to and success in the knowledge economy.[1] The work insecurity faced by a high school dropout looking for a minimum wage job is different than that faced by a lawyer doing a contract job for a legal temp agency. Inequality thus operates through education in contemporary America. Massey (2008) shows the increased centrality of education to inequality, demonstrating that education explained 62 percent of income differences in 2005 compared to only 18 percent in 1950. The resources that individual workers can muster to address insecurity also vary by class (Cooper 2014).

Middle-class workers with college educations and above have material, cultural, and intellectual resources that both make them more competitive in a global economy and help make them resilient in the face of insecure work and its effects. Although college-educated workers face un- and underemployment, they do so at significantly lower rates than less-educated workers and with more resources to respond to the effects of work insecurity.[2] Their discretionary income; their savings and investments that protect against economic shocks; their linguistic and expressive capacities; and their knowledge about and comfort with institutions and experts all hedge against the risks generated by insecure work.

Less-educated workers face significantly more problems. Work insecurity for less-educated workers means the loss of full-time work and especially family wage work; the sharp decline of labor unions and a concomitant disappearance of employer subsidized health insurance and other benefits; and even the ability to count on jobs of any kind. Less-educated workers not only face more insecurity, as low-skill jobs are outsourced, but they face insecurity of a more fundamental nature, affecting basic needs such as food and housing (Edin and Shaefer 2015). Given the necessity and centrality of work to people's lives—and the close cultural coupling between what people *do* and who they *are*—we would expect that massive transformations in work would affect people's behavior, identities, and expectations in other realms of their lives (see also Pugh 2015).

In particular, we examine how this insecurity at work translates to the world of intimate relationships. New forms of work emphasize flexibility, adaptability, and short-term "projects," and deemphasize loyalty, stability or routine, and institutional continuity (Sewell 2009). As people adapt themselves to these new demands at the workplace, do their expectations, metrics, and relationship skills change in the domestic realm as well? Do they bring their work experiences of short-term flexibility and flux home? We demonstrate that people's experiences at work do in fact affect their desires and capabilities in other parts of their lives. Insecure work changes our nonwork lives.

We cannot understand the effects of work insecurity on intimacy without thinking about the mediating effects of class position. Both the types of insecurity and the resources with which to respond to insecurity vary by class (Cooper 2014). Drawing upon in-depth interviews and surveys with working- and middle-class men and women, we investigate the mechanisms by which the characteristics and processes of insecure work seep into intimate relationships. We demonstrate how material resources and work patterns interact with emerging cultural definitions of a "good relationship." We find that class-based resources like linguistic skills, emotional vocabularies, knowledge about social institutions, and access to social and symbolic capital produce very different outcomes in people's personal lives. We also explore the strategies and emotions with which people respond to insecurity at work and at home. Middle-class workers, we argue, are more able to recover from the destabilizing effects of insecure work than the working-class, many of whom have few resources to help mediate the effects of the new global economy.

THE MEANING OF INTIMACY

The primary form of intimate relationships in America in the last several hundred years is marriage. However, marriage as a social institution has undergone drastic transformations in the latter half of the twentieth century. As Furstenberg asserts: "It is no exaggeration to say that the American, and more broadly the Western, family changed more dramatically in the latter half of the twentieth century than in any comparable span of time in our history" (2011, 192). No-fault divorce, cohabitation, nonmarital childrearing, multipartnered fertility, and voluntary fatherhood represent just some of the massive changes that have recently befallen American families (Carlson and England 2011). And family patterns have not only changed, but have also become more unequal by education and other measures of social class, creating a two-tiered family system (Furstenberg 2011). Today highly-educated people are more likely to marry, less likely to divorce, more likely to have children within marriage, less likely to have children with more than one father, and more likely to wait to have a family until they are financially stable than their less educated counterparts. Thus marriage and its benefits are implicated in inequality, as stable marriage becomes a distinctive social institution marking middle-class status.

In order to understand these changes, scholars have examined the shifting legal mandates and cultural logics that underlie the institution of marriage (Gillis 1996; Coontz 2006). In the United States, the rise in the 1920s of the idea of "companionate marriage" (Simmons 2009) replaced older forms of commitment, envisioned as vehicles for economic and childrearing purposes whose primary goal was the stability and reproduction of property rights and family networks. The emotional dynamics of earlier forms of marriage involved clearly delineated gender duties and mutual obligations to kin networks, and were rooted in male authority, backed by both religious and legal mandates (Coontz 2006). "Companionate" forms of marriage envisioned the couple as a "single entity defined by common interests" (Furstenberg 2011, 209), a lifelong entity, and an indissoluble union. Lifelong commitment was shored up by external legal, religious, and moral norms that restricted birth control and abortion, dealt with premarital pregnancy with shotgun marriage, and limited access to divorce.

However, cultural understandings of a "good marriage" have shifted to reenvision marriage as an institution dedicated to the couple as equal individuals committed to emotional and personal growth and expressiveness. Newer forms of "therapeutic" marriage became detached from concerns of family and property to focus on the happiness, equality, mutuality, and self-actualization of individuals with marriage itself subordinated to individual needs and freedoms (Simmons 2009; Bellah et al. 1985; Illouz 1997; Cherlin 2009). Despite the dominance of new forms, most contemporary marriages show at least some signs of older forms, in part because of the legal implications of marriage for shared property and child rearing and in part because of the persistence of gendered forms of labor and identity.

Although the shift in the definition of marriage meant increased independence for women and liberated many people from sterile, abusive, or unfulfilling situations, it also means that the pressure on marriage is much higher. While staying married used to be an assumption supported by social norms and institutions, it is now an individual responsibility. Marriage that needs to grant happiness, equality, mutuality, and self-actualization takes enormous individual resources, such as a linguistic skills, the habit of self-reflexivity, time for in-depth conversation, and perhaps psychological counseling or other expert help as well.[3] Furthermore, such marriages are constantly required to "measure up" to the needs of each participant and when they fail to do so, the prevailing cultural logic dictates divorce (Bellah et al. 1985; Illouz 1997; Cherlin 2009). Marriage in its contemporary manifestation, then, becomes both more equitable (in terms of gender) and more fragile (Giddens 1992; Illouz 1997).

Americans across the class spectrum highly value romantic commitment: according to the Pew Research Center, only 4 percent of never-married adults ages 25 to 34 say they don't want to get married (Wang and Parker 2014). Why, then, are working-class men and women less likely to get married, stay married, and have children within marriage? We argue that rising cultural expectations of a good relationship have made marriages more difficult to sustain for everyone. For people struggling with insecure work, limited time, and constrained material and emotional resources, the individual work required to meet cultural demands of marriage is especially difficult to undertake (Silva 2013). Thus, in exploring the effects of work insecurity on intimacy, we consider both how insecurity varies by class and how resources for sustaining intimacy vary by class.

DATA AND METHODS

This chapter draws on data from two projects. The first project involved both (1) face-to-face interviews with one hundred working class young adults, aged 24–34, in Massachusetts and Virginia (Silva 2013) and, (2) a supplemental expansion of these interviews intended to create a comparative middle-class sample administered via a web-based open-ended survey. The web-based survey was open to young adults across the country seeded by a snowballing effort via Facebook and garnered 158 responses from 24–34 year olds, 129 of whom were middle class and twenty-nine of whom were working class. The second data set involved 120 face-to-face interviews with young adults, aged 18–22, and at least one of their parents. These interviews were collected in sites across the country including, for example, California, Texas, Ohio, Minnesota, and Oregon. In order to recruit respondents, we visited working-class and middle-class neighborhoods and workplaces, including service industries, police and fire stations, factories, restaurants, community centers and nonprofits, and recreation venues like gyms, videogame halls, and bars. We also went to community, regional, state, and private colleges. Interviews generally lasted 1.5 to two hours and focused on education, work, and relationship histories as well as experiences and definitions of "good" relationships, aspirations, and conflicts. Overall, we draw on data from 378 respondents, roughly split between men and women, hailing from thirty-five of the fifty states, and including white, African-American, Latino, and Asian respondents.

Although defining class is difficult in the United States as most scholars consider class to be a combination of education, occupation, income, and wealth, we operationalized class dichotomously as the father's educational attainment either below college graduation or college graduation and above, due to the overriding importance of education in today's economy (for an extended discussion of class operationalization see Lareau and Conley 2010). Our middle-class respondents are thus defined as those holding college degrees, but the sample also includes many upper-middle-class respondents. Conversely, our respondents whose fathers have less than a college degree are defined as working class although the sample also includes lower middle-class, upwardly mobile working-class, and truly disadvantaged respondents (Silva and Putnam 2015).[4]

INSECURE WORK AND INTIMACY IN THE WORKING CLASS: DISILLUSIONMENT AND DEFEAT

Family scholars identify a specific set of economic, social, and cultural forces that shored up the strong norm and practice of marriage in post-war America (Coontz 2006). In this era of full employment, high wages, and broadly shared prosperity, a significant number of fully employed, generally male, blue-collar workers were able to earn enough money to get married, buy a house, and raise a family in relative comfort (Danziger and Ratner 2010). These stable wages, enabled in part by unions, supported the widespread rise of the "traditional" family—the breadwinner/homemaker model in which men took on the responsibility of earning the family's livelihood and women devoted themselves to domestic and family concerns.

However, the economic foundations upon which these "traditional" marriages rested have crumbled. The disappearance of stable, unionized, full-time jobs with benefits for people who lack a college degree and the concomitant "privatization of risk" are hallmarks of the contemporary economy (Kalleberg 2009). In part because of the decline in labor unions, real wages for the non-college educated have fallen dramatically in the last 40 years. Johnson (2002) reported that real wages for working-class jobs declined by 12 percent for those with a high-school diploma and 26 percent for those with less than a high school degree between 1973 and the end of the twentieth century. The loss of good jobs for those without a college degree was also driven by the decline in the US manufacturing sector as those jobs were shipped overseas.

Increasingly the jobs available to those without a college degree are service-sector jobs, many of which are short-term and/or part-time and lack benefits (Kalleberg 2009). Lacking benefits, especially health insurance, is a major cause of poverty. Estimates are that 60 percent or more of personal bankruptcy filings are a result of medical bills due to a lack of or insufficient health insurance (Himmelstein et al. 2009). Even for jobs that do offer health insurance, the cost of that insurance has increased by 50 percent or 60 percent since the early 1970s (Warren 2006). Pensions are another important benefit that is increasingly privatized so that, rather than receiving a defined benefit, workers are required to save and invest for themselves, bearing market risk and information costs individually (Hacker 2006).

The end result of these changes is that working-class jobs are harder to find, pay less, pay less consistently, and provide fewer benefits and less protection against any unexpected costs—in short, they are insecure (see Warren 2006 on the decreased disposable income of working families compared to their forbears). Over the same period, working-class young men and women have become less trusting of others and more socially isolated (Snellman et al. 2015). As we will demonstrate, rising economic and social insecurity in the public sphere have had profound consequences for the achievement of intimacy in the private sphere.

Our interviews with working-class men and women today suggest the unworkability of the traditional breadwinner/homemaker model of intimate relationships in the face of severe changes in the labor market for those without college degrees. Some men and women strive to make the breadwinner/homemaker model of gendered intimacy function despite the lack of jobs offering "family" wages to breadwinning men. A number of men and women we spoke with conveyed a deep sense of betrayal by the failure of this model. Others envision relationships whose goal is emotional expressiveness and mutual self-actualization, with an assumption of joint financial responsibility. Frequently, however, these relationships seem equally unattainable as many respondents lacked the material and cultural resources needed to construct such time- and resource-intensive partnerships.

Overall, we heard that for working class people with insecure work and few resources, little stability, and no ability to plan for a foreseeable future, concerns for one's own survival threaten the ability to imagine being able to provide materially and emotionally for others. Trust is in short supply when instability and insecurity are the norm and intimate betrayal a very real risk. In such conditions, the material obligations required by older forms of marriage may be untenable while the emotional and psychological commitment required by contemporary ideals of marriage become, not a hedge against external risks, but instead one demand too many given the already limited resources available to the postindustrial working class.

Our conversations with those without a college degree show that material constraints create or exacerbate other types of constraints, leading our interviewees both to express feelings of distrust or even fear about intimate relationships, and to have difficulty imagining being able to provide for others. Many men doubt their competence as providers and therefore their attractiveness as potential partners and express a fear of enduring commitment. Women express more varied tensions, ranging from those who continue to desire a more traditional security rooted in the male provider model but are stymied by "unreliable men," to those who desire independence in work and value communication, emotional expressive-ness, and mutual growth in their romantic lives. Regardless of which pat-tern they follow, women struggle to achieve either model.

Cindy, for example, is a white woman in her mid-forties living in the same small Ohio town in which she was raised. Growing up, her dad had stable factory work and she remembers a secure childhood in which her mother packed her dad's lunch "every day," Sundays and birthdays were marked by special events in the family home, and summers held family car trips. Cindy contrasts her secure childhood with her own daughter's child-hood. She explains, "I did my part as a woman," supporting her husband through her domestic labor and emotional care, but her husband didn't do "his job as a man" by getting—and keeping—a job. Cindy's model of her own father's stable manufacturing work is much less viable in early twenty-first century Ohio. Although her town had a sizeable manufacturing base in the 1960s and 1970s when her father was working, the percent of the area labor force employed in manufacturing fell from a high of 40 percent to under 20 percent between 1970 and 2010. In 2010, the unemployment rate was over 10 percent, roughly one-third higher than the national aver-age. After her husband deserted her, Cindy moved in with her parents, but when they died shortly thereafter, she was left a single mother with a five-year-old, no home, and a minimum-wage job in a convenience store. Desperate for security and afraid of losing her daughter, Cindy married a man who became physically abusive to her and her daughter. With two failed marriages behind her, Cindy has no plans to marry her current live-in: "Twice is enough, I'm not ready for marriage." Nonetheless, she hasn't given up on the idea of long-term commitment and a rewarding intimate relationship. Although she hopes for it, Cindy is not optimistic. Speaking of her disappointments with her husbands and boyfriends, Cindy says "[M]en . . . it's like raising kids all over again." Cindy's narrative shows the difficulty of depending on a traditional breadwinner/homemaker model of gendered labor in twenty-first-century working-class life. Although this schema worked for Cindy's parents, it is a much less viable model today.

Megan, Cindy's now twenty-year-old daughter, lives with her mother and her mother's boyfriend. Having never finished high school, Megan can't even find a job in the service economy, but dreams of becoming a model. Although she wants children, she wants to wait until her life is "stable physically, mentally, and financially" before having them. Unfortunately, her first serious boyfriend "split her head open." Because she'd seen her mother's abusive second marriage, however, Megan knew this meant she should end the relationship and she did. Her current boyfriend is in jail and, anyway, not particularly committed to her. Megan says she "can't trust anyone" because people "use you," although she considers herself "super close" to her mother. She still hopes, however, to find a husband and have a family. It is difficult to imagine how Megan will find a husband who earns enough to support a family or that she will succeed in the world of modeling.

The story of Cindy, her parents, and her daughter is a story of declining stability down three generations, as well as a story of increasing disconnection from meaningful social institutions (Putnam et al. 2012). Cindy's parents were stable and strongly nested within institutions such as lifelong marriage, the Church, his labor union, and their local neighborhood. Cindy herself is more loosely attached; she has married twice and has had years of (low-paying) jobs as well as having lifelong friends in the community (although she complains that the dire economy has changed her friendships for the worse). Megan, however, has little if any social, economic, or cultural capital—an unstable childhood with multiple disengaged "dads"; a several-year stint living elsewhere that uprooted her from childhood friends and the neighborhood; multiple unsuccessful attempts to finish her high-school education; and no experience with, or even opportunity for, employment. The stable structures undergirding her grandparents' lives are gone, leaving chaos and insecurity in the possibilities for both Megan's work and intimate lives.

Kelly, like Cindy, has had no experience with enduring intimate relationships. Unlike Cindy, however, she provides us with a narrative that categorizes intimate relationships primarily as a threat to a hard-won independence and self-sufficiency. Kelly is a white woman in her late twenties whose chaotic childhood led to a ten-year battle with drug addiction, which reduced her to living in her car several times. Having overcome her addiction problems, she is currently sober, working as a line chef, and living independently—although on the edge of insolvency—in the greater Washington, DC area. Kelly says "I like the idea of being with someone, but I have a hard time imagining trusting anybody with all of my personal stuff, which is a really big part of being in a relationship." Kelly dislikes the self-editing she does to maintain relationships, as her vision of an intimate relationship is based not on a traditional gendered division of labor, but on an ideal of trust, communication, and mutual self-realization. That vision seems unattainable however, as her fear of losing the independent self she painstakingly constructed from the chaos of her childhood and the rubble of her addiction constrains her willingness to enter into the give-and-take of intimate relationships: "I'd rather be alone and fierce than in a relationship and be milquetoast." Unlike Cindy, Kelly isn't looking for a man to provide for her; she can support herself financially, if precariously. But like Cindy, Kelly has no model of a successful and attainable relationship. For her, the choice of intimacy carries with it a threat of self-destruction; without emotional skills to construct boundaries and manage trust or the resources to work with experts such as therapists, she can't risk her tenuous stability.

Juan, a Central American immigrant to Southern California, also struggles with the tension between the two models of marriage. In his fifties, Juan is a widower raising four boys eighteen and under on a housepainter's wages. He has not had a serious relationship since his wife died of cancer eight years ago because "being a good dad" means paying rent, buying food, and putting his children's welfare first which, given his limited resources, precludes remarriage. Juan says "la comunicación" is key to intimate relationships, which confounds his eighteen-year-old son who is helping translate the interview because the son, Carlos, has just described his father as stoic, silent, and emotionally closed. Juan thus embodies the very tension he discusses. On the one hand, Juan lives by traditional understandings of the male as provider of material resources, concentrating his efforts on his children's material welfare—and his inability to achieve security means that he is not "marriage material" by his own calculations. However, he also acknowledges the importance of a more contemporary understanding of intimacy as rooted in expressive emotional sharing, even as his terseness and emotional distance are evident in both the interview and his son's descriptions of their home life. Juan demonstrates the gap between an awareness of socially valorized practices and the ability to perform and sustain them. As we will demonstrate, middle-class men and women embrace strategies such as pursuing higher education and hiring professional experts such as therapists to achieve these desired communication skills and the romantic stability they promise—yet the daily insecurity of Juan's life prohibits such costly investments.

Brandon is an African American man in his mid-thirties who, like Cindy, subscribes to a gendered model of intimate relationships. Describing himself as an "old school Southerner [who] wants to take a woman out dancing and to dinner," Brandon confesses he has not had a relationship in several years. "No woman wants to sit on the couch all the time and watch TV and eat at Burger King," says Brandon, but his employment situation makes him unable to offer anything more. Brandon has an MA but also $80,000 of educational debt. Unable to find a job utilizing his expensive and hard-won educational credentials, he works as a night manager in retail. His salary barely covers his living expenses and debt service. Brandon is fatalistic about his situation; although he thinks he's "missing out on life," he reasons that "I can only take care of myself right now."

Brandon takes full responsibility for his situation, not blaming women or characterizing them as materialistic but acknowledging the difficulty of marriage and especially kids without stable and sufficient employment: "Money isn't love, but you need to be stable to be in a relationship. And once you start with kids you can't go back." Much more than most of the people we spoke with, Brandon explicitly ties the failure of his intimate life to the failure of his work life.

While Brandon approaches his inability to sustain a romantic commitment with resignation, other working-class men express anger at a cultural system that evaluates men based on their ability to achieve security and success in the realm of work. The vast majority of never-married American women (78 percent) today believe that "a steady job" is an essential quality in a mate, compared to only 46 percent of never-married men (Wang and Parker 2014). Thus, even as the rise of the global information economy has been brutal to working-class men, expectations of men as providers persist. Nathan, a twenty-five-year old African American, works the night shift as a medical biller. Although he jokes that "[age] twenty-five might be the year for monogamy," he fumes when pushed to discuss the possibility of marriage: "women say 'I need a ring' but you don't need that really. . . . It's a hustle." Although Nathan may seem angry at individual women, we would argue that Nathan feels trapped by the gendered obligation to provide expensive material goods in order to prove his worthiness as a man. Faced with the impossibility of succeeding at the breadwinner role given his precarious financial independence, Nathan feels betrayed by a cultural logic that discounts other qualities that he may have to contribute to a partnership, such as loyalty or support.

Many working-class respondents believe that commitment is too risky. An eighteen-year-old Latina living with her family in Southern California, Serena doesn't want to get married until she is thirty because she wants to concentrate on college. However, she's currently working retail and trying to save the $45/credit-hour she needs to pay for community college courses. Serena's father lost his work as a housepainter when the housing market crashed, impoverishing the family; she and her parents now live with extended family. The cost of her hoped-for college career is her responsibility, as is the planning of it—neither of Serena's parents even graduated from high school so they have little advice or help to offer her in her pursuit of an education. Serena's parents have been married for twenty-plus years, but she herself doesn't even date and has taken a class on abstinence at her church because she fears ending up single and pregnant like so many of her friends. Intimate commitment for Serena, then, is not a hedge against the external risks of the economy, but one more potential risk. Serena sees the traditional breadwinner-homemaker model as irrelevant for her current vision of success, but she faces an uphill battle marshaling the resources she needs to achieve an independent life through education and work.

Finally, Douglas, an unemployed twenty-five-year-old, epitomizes much of what we heard from our working-class respondents. After talking about his own failed and short-term relationships, he says wistfully, "People used to get married at twenty-one. You don't see that anymore. Trust is gone. The way people used to love is gone." This sense of loss, or even despair, over the possibilities for ongoing intimate commitment infused our conversations with working-class people. Their disillusionment with any possibility of long-term success in the labor market was matched by a pervasive sense of disillusionment about the possibility of meaningful, enduring relationships.

Although we are certainly not arguing there is a perfect correspondence between stable work and long-term relationships, most of the more optimistic working-class respondents we spoke with were among the small minority with stable, decent-paying work with benefits. For a minority of our respondents—primarily those with blue-collar civil service jobs and those in the military—reliable, secure work with benefits created stability, allowing for planning and facilitating trust. These men, and they were predominantly men[5], experienced themselves as able to offer something meaningful to a potential partner. For example, Dave, a white twenty-three-year-old non-college graduate, says "I'm currently living with the woman I intend to marry. I just need to save up for the ring. I love being in the [Armed Forces]." He not only expects to "spend twenty years in the military," but also hopes to "complete an officer commissioning program." Dave earns a low salary as an enlisted soldier, but he also receives room, board, and a clothing allowance as well as health insurance and paid vacation. If he does stay in the military for twenty years, his salary and benefits will increase substantially and he will earn a guaranteed pension with healthcare. If he becomes an officer, he will do even better. The stability of his work allows him to imagine himself moving into a foreseeable future that has shape and promise, unlike the majority of our working-class respondents who have little or no sense of what the future might hold. His work stability and the promise of not only continued employment but career development, facilitate Dave's ability to plan and commit to a long-term relationship. The military, police, and firefighters are some of the few remaining bastions of secure blue-collar work that provide benefits and a family wage. Competition for these jobs is, however, fierce and getting fiercer.[6]

INSECURE WORK AND INTIMACY IN THE MIDDLE
CLASS: RESOURCES AND RESILIENCE

Issues of work and intimacy under contemporary economic conditions play out differently among our middle-class respondents. Middle- and upper-middle-class jobs have also been affected by changes in the postindustrial economy, especially in some sectors. Lifelong employment with a single firm is increasingly rare and corporate mergers and downsizing increasingly common, leading to prolonged un- and underemployment for many potential or erstwhile middle managers. The effects of the recession on those in the residential and commercial development professions have been especially severe (Pugh 2015). An increasing number of professionals are contractors rather than employees (e.g., outside legal counsel, freelance writers, and consultants of various kinds) with the reduced certainty and benefits that designation entails. The effects of this increased insecurity on intimacy are mediated, however, by a wide range of resources mobilized by the middle class to create resiliency in the face of threats from work insecurity.

Earl and his wife live in the Pacific Northwest with their two children. Earl has worked in the natural resources industry and been successful with both his own company and his real estate investments. Earl and his wife Jan married when he graduated from college. She left before getting her degree to return with him to his hometown where he was starting a business with some family members. They waited to have children until they were "stable"—they owned their own house and had started a college fund for their as-yet-unborn children. Earl told his wife he would "work as many jobs as it took" to ensure that she could stay home with the kids. Although his wife has never worked outside the home, Earl works long days, starting at 5:00 am during the week, and thus leaves the work of raising their two children to Jan. However, Earl and Jan prioritize both their marriage and their family, eating dinner as a family most nights, scheduling couple's "date nights," spending family weekends at their vacation cabin disconnected from electronics, and travelling together at least once a year.

Earl and Jan's story is a story of considerable resources marshaled in support of marriage and family. In addition to the flexibility to schedule nightly dinners, weekends, and vacation time, there are numerous other resources to support the family. When their daughter began to run with "the wrong crowd," Earl and Jan built a barn, bought their daughter a horse, and switched her to a private school with an equestrian focus to get her back on track. As they've aged, Earl and Jan have recommitted themselves to remaining vital in and focused on their marriage. When he turned fifty, they sat down and, after acknowledging that their focus has been on the children for the last twenty years, asked each other how do we "make it for another fifty years together and have a life?" Jan has since returned to finish her college degree while Earl has joined a gym, both taking these steps in order to stay attractive to each other. Sustaining this type of commitment draws on psychological and emotional resources, such as therapeutic languages of self-actualization, as well as the obvious material ones. But for Earl and Jan, "spending" those resources on their marriage enables intimacy and bonding, prioritizing their commitment and stability and securing that stability for their children.

For Earl and Jan, the traditional model of breadwinner/homemaker has worked well, perhaps especially because they have the resources that allow them to fortify that model with a more contemporary focus on companionate marriage and Jan's development outside of her roles as wife and mother. Unlike Cindy, Jan's reliance on her husband's earnings has produced a comfortable life and two children strongly launched on successful trajectories. Unlike Cindy's husband, Earl's ability to embrace the traditional model was facilitated by familial, educational, and social capitals that helped start and maintain his successful (hometown) business. His own sense of competence and success as a businessman, as a provider for his wife and children, and as a good husband and father, have in turn helped protect the stability of his marriage and family.

Neil, a married African American in his early thirties, also faces work insecurity as he is self-employed, running his own educational consulting business. He and his wife Celeste, a full-time professional, have been married for almost four years. As a couple, Neil and Celeste share many activities: they run together, play tennis, volunteer for Habitat for Humanity, and put on college fairs at the local high school. At the same time, they are passionate about self-growth—Neil just finished reading an Oprah Book Club favorite called *A New Earth: Awakening to your Life's Purpose*—and they support each other's quests to be firmly autonomous individuals by spending hours discussing their personal goals. Neil and Celeste don't have children and, in fact, have turned a room they thought would be the baby's room into "the relaxation room, we go in there and journal and read." Despite the potential insecurity of self-employment, Neil and Celeste experience their lives very differently than our working-class respondents. They draw on their money, their educations, and their familiarity with therapeutic culture to "mak[e] sure our lives are full of purpose, not accepting just anything but really making sure it's in line with the goals and visions we both have." They privilege their sense of selves, committing their resources to a self-reflexive relationship: "You know for a time my wife didn't work for three months, she was trying to find what she wanted. I said, take your time, don't just take anything, decide what you want. Don't settle . . . it will spill over." Neil and Celeste's lives are marked by the cultural and material resources common to our upper-middle-class respondents. They spend time and money hedging against the risks of settling, disappointment, and ultimately marital dissolution by self-consciously discussing, planning, and working on their relationship. These "investments" help insure them against the risks and disappointments of intimate life, as their health and pension benefits help insure them against old age and illness.

Despite their resources, middle-class people are obviously not immune to work insecurity and intimate disruptions. Their ability to manage the disruption and the long-term effects of the disruption are, however, fundamentally different than the working class. Marnie is a white woman in her fifties who lives in the urban Northeast. She is just about to get married for the third time. She has two children in their late teens from her second marriage; they live with her and her fiancé in a beautiful home in a wealthy suburb. After her second marriage to an entrepreneur failed, Marnie struggled to combine her well-paying but time-intensive job with her increased responsibilities at home. She started her own consulting business to facilitate her flexibility while raising her two girls. Although she faced increased risk doing this, it was nonetheless an option open to her through mortgaging her house, unlike her more poorly educated counterparts who struggle to combine work and parenting without such resources. Note that for Marnie, the flexibility of consulting was, although risky, also a major benefit, as it allowed her time with her daughters while stacking work into times they were busy elsewhere.

Marnie's commitment to being married, despite her first two failed marriages, is profound. She talks in great detail about her work in therapy to overcome her difficult childhood with an alcoholic mother and unreliable father. She has continued working with a therapist to integrate her new fiancé with her daughters. Similarly, when one of her daughters was struggling academically and emotionally after the divorce, Marnie assembled multiple experts to assess and treat the daughter. Thus, although Marnie faces difficulties from marital dissolution, the challenges of balancing demanding work and parenting, and the financial pressures of starting a new business, she has significant resources that both shield and help herself and her children psychologically and financially. Her knowledge of and skills at interacting with institutions—such as school systems, potential corporate clients, testing and psychological experts, and financial institutions—are nonmaterial resources that allow Marnie to leverage her assets in the face of risk to benefit her life and that of her children.

GENDER'S ROLE IN INTIMATE INSECURITY

One striking differences between our working-class and middle-class interviews was the explicitness with which a number of women in the middle class constructed their intimate lives as a "haven" or hedge against the risks of work disappointments. For example, a twenty-seven-year-old white middle-class college graduate says she is hopeful about the future because she is "confident that [I've] found a compatible life partner, so we'll make anything work." She points out how much "easier to feel hopeful when you can depend on someone." Although she is grateful to have found someone she can "depend on," it doesn't seem surprising to her that she would. This is in stark contrast to working-class respondents such as Cindy. Cindy has never found someone she could depend on financially or emotionally.

Similarly, in stark contrast to Megan, Cindy's daughter, who is unsuccessfully looking for both a committed relationship and work, a thirty-year-old white upper-middle-class respondent who recently completed an advanced degree says:

> I know that I am talented and that I will have another job eventually, but it's hard to remember that when I keep interviewing for jobs and then they go to someone with ten more years of experience than I have. I know that in a different economy, I would have a new job by now . . . this period in my life is teaching me new things about myself. . . . I'm glad that I'm in a stable and committed relationship, heading toward marriage, because I know that I would definitely be stressed about that if it wasn't happening.

This upper-middle-class woman not only has more reason to be hopeful about her future employment than Megan, but she can rely on her upcoming marriage as well. Her own resources, material and symbolic, are complemented by the availability of her partner's—and she and her resources will in turn be available if he's in need. Stable relationships, especially those with the legal protections of marriage, buttress middle-class lives, shielding individuals from at least some of the exigencies of postindustrial life.

Echoing this sentiment, another young middle-class woman says, "my feelings of hope about the future have definitely changed since graduating college and graduate school; I now put more emphasis on health, family, and friends than I do career advancement. My work is very important to me, and I want to have a 'successful' career. But I now base my identity and sense of happiness and hope much less around my job and more around other areas of life: health, community, and relationships." For these women, all of whom have invested in their educations and are committed to working, the realm of intimate relationships nonetheless serves to cushion their disappointments or failures in the world of work by offering alternative financial support and meaningful symbolic achievements.

Neither the working-class nor middle-class men we spoke with valued their intimate relationships as a specific hedge against the downside in the realm of work. However, recent survey data from the Pew Research Center finds that the number of stay-at-home fathers has risen significantly, rising to two million in 2012 from 1.1 million in 1989 (Livingston 2014). About a quarter of these fathers report that their primary reason for staying at home is because they are "unable to find work." It is possible that increasing insecurity at work—especially in the wake of the Great Recession—may disrupt traditional gender expectations of men, creating space for alternative models of achievement.

NEW MODELS, PERSISTENT INEQUALITIES

Our in-depth qualitative interviews demonstrate the complexities of the interaction between class and intimate relationships. Because the changing conditions of labor in the new economy vary by class (as old ways of working varied by class although in different ways) the consequences for romantic and family life also differ by social class. New images of marriage, especially successful marriage, rely on narratives of self-awareness and self-actualization, whose achievement requires both material and cultural resources that may be in short supply among working-class populations. Older images of marriage as a route to respectability and children, rooted in a gendered division of labor and a pragmatic sensibility, hold little appeal for most of our respondents, yet the idealized companionate marriage sustained by therapeutic discourse may be an elusive enterprise even for those with the time, money, and skills to work on it.

The demands of postindustrial labor are also extensive for the highly educated, but for many there are, in addition, significant material and cultural rewards. Although many couples are dual-career professionals, significant space still exists for stay-at-home mothers supported by well-paid professional fathers, at least while children are young. For those who do continue working, women especially discuss the seemingly irreconcilable nature of work-family conflicts, but for those with money, subcontracting the labor of childrearing and especially housework is a readily available option. Middle- and upper-middle-class respondents express high expectations for their marriage and a family life centering on self-fulfillment, deeply engaged parenting by both parents, and an articulated psychoemotional awareness. However, they also express feelings of safety, comfort, and benefit derived from their home lives. Women especially experience intimate life as a potential counterweight to the disappointments and difficulties of the paid labor force.

Both middle-class men and women, however, express anxiety about the uncertainties and demands of the twenty-first-century economy, and see those as potential threats to the security provided by their intimate lives. They insure themselves against the possibilities of marital complacency, conflict, and dissolution through private material and emotional investment. Building a relaxation room, scheduling a weekly therapy appointment, taking college classes, and spending time on "date nights," are all investments in marriage and intimacy that help protect against the risks and uncertainties inherent to the contemporary demands on individuals and relationships. These forms of "private insurance" though are too "costly" for most working-class couples, even though they are at greater risk of divorce to begin with and have fewer safety nets to catch them if they do fall. Ultimately, the material and symbolic benefits of marriage—pooled income and assets, less financial risk in making large purchases, shared childrearing labor, trust, and love itself—accrue to those already at the top of the class distribution.

NOTES

1. Education is usually seen as the key marker of social class in America because of its profound effects on income, employment, family stability, and lifestyle (see Massey 2008).
2. As the Bureau of Labor Statistics (2013) reports, the unemployment rate in 2012 was 12.4 percent for people with less than a high school degree, 8.6 percent for people with just a high school degree, 4.5 percent for people with a bachelor's degree, and only 2.1percent for people with a professional degree (see United States Department of Labor, "Employment Projections 2015." Bureau of Labor Statistics. Washington, DC, http://www.bls.gov/emp/ep_chart_001.htm).
3. The best estimates we've found are that in 2005, roughly 12 percent of people in the United States experienced talk therapy of some form in the previous year and that there is more likelihood of doing so if you are younger, not a minority, and not poor (Wang et al. 2005). Therapeutic language may also be acquired through self-help groups, AA type support groups, reading, and other forms of popular culture such as certain types of TV shows (e.g., *Oprah*).
4. To provide some context on income inequality, in 2011, the top 40 percent of family households in the United States earned above $75,000 annually. The top 20 percent of family households earned over $115, 866 annually. The top 5 percent of family households earned over $205,200 annually. These figures are just about *earned* income, they don't include money from investments; money that adds enormously to rich people's overall income but barely affects the income of people at

lower levels. All data from United States Census Bureau. Washington, DC, http://www.census.gov/hhes/www/income/data/historical/families/, accessed January 8, 2013.

5. For example, women comprise only 15 percent of the US Armed Forces (Patten and Parker 2011).

6. For example, in 1999, approximately 98 percent of enlisted recruits had a high school degree, compared to roughly 81 percent of the general population aged 18–24 (Watkins and Sherk 2008; National Center for Education Statistics 2011).

REFERENCES

Bellah, Robert N., Richard Madsen, William M. Sullivan, Ann Swidler, and Steven M. Tipton. 1985. *Habits of the Heart: Individualism and Commitment in American Life*. Berkeley: University of California Press.

Carlson, Marcia, and Paula England. 2011. *Social Class and Changing Families in an Unequal America*. Stanford: Stanford University Press.

Cherlin, Andrew. 2009. *The Marriage Go-Round: The State of Marriage and the Family in America Today*. New York: Vintage.

Coontz, Stephanie. 2006. *Marriage, a History: How Love Conquered Marriage*. New York: Penguin.

Cooper, Marianne. 2014. *Cut Adrift: Families in Insecure Times*. Berkeley: University of California Press.

Danziger, Sheldon and David Ratner. 2010. "Labor Market Outcomes and the Transition to Adulthood." In *Transition to Adulthood. Special Issue of the Future of Children* 20(1), edited by Gordon Berlin, Frank Furstenberg Jr., and Mary C. Waters, 133–158.

Edin, Kathryn, and Maria Kefalas. 2005. *Promises I Can Keep: Why Poor Women Put Motherhood Before Marriage*. Berkeley: University of California Press.

Edin, Kathryn, and H. Luke Shaefer. 2015. *$2.00 a Day: Living on Almost Nothing in America*. Boston: Houghton Mifflin Harcourt.

Furstenberg, Frank. 2011. "The Recent Transformation of the American Family: Witnessing and Exploring Social Change." In *Social Class and Changing Families in an Unequal America*, edited by Marcia J. Carlson and Paula England, 192–220. Stanford: Stanford University Press.

Giddens, Anthony. 1992. *The Transformation of Intimacy: Sexuality, Love and Eroticism in Modern Societies*. Stanford, CA: Stanford University Press.

Gillis, John R. 1996. *A World of Their Own Making: Myth, Ritual, and the Quest for Family Values*. Cambridge, MA: Harvard University Press.

Hacker, Jacob. 2006. "The Privatization of Risk and the Growing Economic Insecurity of Americans." SSRC. June 7. Accessed on January 6, 2013 http://privatizationofrisk.ssrc.org/Hacker/.

Himmelstein, David, Deborah Thorne, Elizabeth Warren, and Steffie Woolhandler. 2009. "Medical Bankruptcy in the United States, 2007: Results of a National Study." *American Journal of Medicine* 122(8): 741–746. Doi:10.1016/j.amjmed.2009.04.012.

Illouz, Eva. 1997. *Consuming the Romantic Utopia: Love and the Cultural Contradictions of Capitalism*. Berkeley: University of California Press.

Johnson, Jennifer. 2002. *Getting By on the Minimum: The Lives of Working-Class Women.* New York: Routledge.

Kalleberg, Arne L. 2009. "Precarious Work, Insecure Workers." *American Sociological Review* 74(1):1–22.

Lareau, Annette, and Dalton Conley. 2010. *Social Class: How Does It Work?* New York: Russell Sage Foundation.

Livingston, Gretchen. 2014. "Growing Number of Dads Home with the Kids." Washington, DC: Pew Research Center's Social and Demographic Trends. June 5. http://www.pewsocialtrends.org/2014/06/05/growing-number-of-dads-home-with-the-kids/.

Martin, Steven P. 2004. "Growing Evidence for a Divorce Divide? Education and Marital Dissolution Rates in the United States since the 1970s." Working Papers Series on Social Dimensions of Inequality. New York: Russell Sage Foundation.

Massey, Douglas. 2008. *Categorically Unequal: The American Stratification System.* New York: Russell Sage Foundation.

National Center for Educational Statistics. 2011. 2012-026. "America's Youth: Transitions to Adulthood." Institute of Education Sciences. Washington, DC: US Department of Education. December 2011. http://nces.ed.gov/pubs2012/2012026.pdf

Patten, Eileen and Kim Parker. 2011. "Women in the U.S. Military: Growing Share, Distinctive Profile." *Pew Research Center,* accessed May 5, 2016. http://www.pewsocialtrends.org/files/2011/12/women-in-the-military.pdf.

Pugh, Allison J. 2015. *The Tumbleweed Society: Working and Caring in an Age of Insecurity.* New York: Oxford University Press.

Putnam, Robert, Carl Frederick, and Kaisa Snellman. 2012. "Growing Class Gaps in Social Connectedness Among American Youth, 1970–2009." Harvard University, Kennedy School of Government. July 12. Accessed January 8, 2013. http://www.hks.harvard.edu/saguaro/pdfs/SaguaroReport_DivergingSocialConnectedness.pdf

Sewell, William Jr. 2009. "From State-Centrism to Neoliberalism: Macro-Historical Contexts of Population Health Since World War II." In *Successful Societies: Institutions, Cultural Repertories, and Health,* edited by Peter Hall and Michèle Lamont, 254–287. Cambridge, UK: Cambridge University Press.

Silva, Jennifer M. 2013. *Coming Up Short: Working-Class Adulthood in an Age of Uncertainty.* New York: Oxford University Press.

Silva, Jennifer M., and Robert D. Putnam. 2015. "Methodological Appendix: The Stories of Our Kids." In *Our Kids: The American Dream in Crisis,* by Jennifer M. Silva and Robert D. Putnam, 263–279. New York: Simon and Schuster.

Simmons, Christina. 2009. *Making Marriage Modern: Women's Sexuality from the Progressive Era to World War II.* New York: Oxford University Press.

United States Census Bureau. Washington, DC. http://www.census.gov/hhes/www/income/data/historical/families/, accessed January 8, 2013.

United States Department of Labor. "Employment Projections 2015." Bureau of Labor Statistics. Washington, DC. http://www.bls.gov/emp/ep_chart_001.htm.

Wang, Philip S., Michael Lane, Mark Olfson, Harold A. Pincus, Kenneth B. Wells, and R. C. Kessler. 2005. "Twelve-Month Use of Mental Health Services in the United States: Results From the National Comorbidity Survey Replication." *Archives of General Psychiatry* 62(6):629–640.

Wang, Wendy, and Kim Parker. 2014. "Record Share of Americans Have Never Married." Washington, DC: Pew Research Center's Social & Demographic Trends. September 24.

Warren, Elizabeth. 2006. "Rewriting the Rules: Families, Money, and Risk." June 7. Retrieved on January 6, 2013. Available at: http://privatizationofrisk.ssrc. org/Warren/.

Watkins, Shanea, and James Sherk. 2008. "Who Serves in the US Military? The Demographics of Enlisted Troops and Officers." Center for Data Analysis Report #08-05 on National Security and Defense. August 21. Retrieved on May 29, 2013. Available at: http://www.heritage.org/research/reports/2008/08/who-serves-in-the-us-military-the-demographics-of-enlisted-troops-and-officers.

AFTERWORD

CHRISTINE L. WILLIAMS

Recent changes in the economy and family structure have upended many lives. Downsizing, unemployment, divorce—these have become unremarkable and even anticipated events in the average life course. In this era of social turbulence, adaptability and flexibility are replacing loyalty and stability in our jobs, our relationships, and our cultural values. In this volume, Allison Pugh has gathered together a group of outstanding scholars to take us "beyond the cubicle" to understand how people are coping with these vexing social conditions.

For an earlier generation of sociologists, this scholarly effort to link the organization of society and the economy to the individual's inner feelings, needs, and desires was called the "social structure and personality" perspective. Talcott Parsons (1970) was best known for this approach; it was revived by Nancy Chodorow in her study of the reproduction of mothering (1978). But since then, serious attention to the internal dimension of social life has fallen out of favor among social scientists. As a discipline, sociologists tend to emphasize structural causes for social behavior, giving short shrift to the origins of those structures in human creativity and emotion. Consequently, we know very little about how people think and feel about the many social upheavals impacting their lives.

As the authors of this volume demonstrate, people do not passively absorb all that life throws at them. Individuals who suffer the traumas of job loss, divorce, and heartbreak struggle to make sense of them and to navigate a way through them. Understanding the meaning of these events takes us into the internal realm of unconscious conflict, longing, and inhibition, and forces us to reckon with individual differences.

In this volume, the authors explore how macro-level social and economic forces impact the lives and loves of real people on the ground. Through intimate portraits and finely calibrated surveys, they reveal extensive personal and collective efforts to cope with financial crisis. They demonstrate how the breakdown of the traditional employment contract—which guaranteed job security in return for loyal service—has wreaked havoc on people's emotional lives. And they show the limits of conventional narratives used to make sense of lost jobs and relationships.

As Pugh writes in her introduction, the changing emotional geography of the new economy is "drenched in gender meanings," evident in several of the chapters in this volume. For example, Carrie Lane introduces us to men who are struggling in deeply personal yet highly gendered ways to cope with losing their jobs in the high tech industry. They feel guilt, shame, and sadness. Yet, at the same time, they identify with their employers and accept the seeming inevitability of their plight. Without their employers to blame, they blame themselves and their "irrational" expectations of job security. They are supposed to be *men*, after all, not "annoying children" with weak, dependent, and immature needs.

Lane's interviews reveal an internal side of the economic crisis. Society teaches that "real men" must be autonomous, in control, and independent— the proverbial "self-made man." Always more fantasy than reality, today these qualities are terribly out-of-sync with an uncertain and fickle job market. Yet the male breadwinner ideal continues to hold sway, causing untold psychological hardship for the many who try—and inevitably fail— to live up to its demands. The enduring appeal of this icon is evident among both the winners and the losers in the new economy, among men as well as women. It crops up among Gerson's singles in Silicon Valley, who take pride in their self-reliance by abjuring adult relationships altogether. We see this ideal reflected again in Whitaker's peripatetic middle-class families, who cling desperately to the view that husbands control their fates, even as they are flung around the country in search of elusive job prospects. The powerful appeal of the independence narrative is even evident among Utrata's single mothers in Russia, who, in an almost complete gender-reversal, characterize themselves as strong and self-reliant in contrast to weak, dependent, and unreliable men. For these single mothers, their only claim to dignity is through repudiating social and emotional support.

All of these stories reveal the untenable and sometimes painful consequences of the masculine ideal. By denying the need for care, companionship, and durable bonds, this model of selfhood may be adapted to the vagaries of the new economy, but it denies our basic humanity. As Pugh writes, "children still have to be raised, the elderly still have to be tended."

In none of the world's wealthy countries are more than two-thirds of adults in the labor force—let alone all of them—yet this has become the new dystopian ideal. A society that celebrates independence and scorns dependence on others leaves people bereft and unmoored, especially in times of crisis. When layoffs occur and economic disaster looms, where do people turn? Facing few job prospects, the people in this volume move, get divorced, self-medicate, or go back to school. Ironically, a popular choice of several of the individuals we meet in this book is business school, where the myth of the self-made man is enshrined in the curriculum. Nowhere, it seems, is the human need for connection with others acknowledged, let alone encouraged and nurtured.

Nowhere, that is, except for in the bonds of motherhood. As adult relationships become more fragile, mother-child relationships remain the only reliable safety net. The task of fulfilling our emotional need for connection with others increasingly falls to mother and mother alone. Sociologist Sharon Hays (1996) has documented the overwhelming pressures faced by women in the middle class to practice an especially selfless form of intensive mothering, while psychoanalyst Barbara Almond (2010) has explored the cultural taboo that prohibits mothers from expressing any ambivalence whatsoever about their children. The cultural ideal of the all-sacrificing mother is the necessary counterpart to the myth of the self-made man. These two gendered archetypes are flipsides of the same coin: The radical individualism of the ideal worker depends on the invisible reproductive labor of a home-based caregiver. In the Fordist past, women expected to be compensated for their caregiving through their marriages to breadwinning men. Today, without the support of secure jobs or stable marriages, caring for others has become a reckless and irresponsible choice.

Yet this volume is full of stories of mothers making sacrifices for their children. They are forced to give up their careers, their communities, their adult relationships, even their feminist values to support their children in an unyielding and precarious job market. In one particularly poignant example, Corse and Silva recount the experience of Megan. Unemployed and reeling from a series of failed relationships with men, Megan trusts no one, except for her mother Cindy who has taken her in, just as Cindy's mother did for her a generation earlier. But who, I wonder, is taking care of the mothers? In a culture that does not value or reward caregiving, they are often bereft, raising children alone on meager incomes. It is no wonder that many women forgo motherhood altogether.

The decision to have children should be a deeply personal one, but it is never made in a cultural vacuum. Pronatalism, it seems, can soften the blow of economic crisis, as Frenkel's study of Israeli women suggests. In their society, where the myth of self-reliance is not a driving force, public support is strong for social welfare policies that encourage caring and connection to others.

In the past, strong unions in Israel further buttressed workers' demands for family accommodations from employers. But as in other traditional social democratic and conservative countries, union strength has diminished in Israel under the pressures of neoliberal ideologies and the global market—although Israeli workers maintain their high expectations for hard-won benefits like pensions and job security.

In contrast, most workers in the United States are neither in unions nor do they expect to be protected from the ravages of the precarious job market. This is not necessarily a sign of worker apathy, but rather the result of a concerted effort by government officials and corporations to destroy unions, chip away at labor rights, and curtail workers' expectations. Employers have done an excellent job convincing workers to demand very little of their jobs. Management consultants, career counselors, and "happiness" experts recast downsizing and job insecurity as opportunities for personal growth and fulfillment. At the University of Texas at Austin, where I work, the business school offered a webinar during a recent economic downturn on the topic of "Turning job loss into long-term happiness, better health, and a more fulfilling career." As documented by Cabanas and Illouz in this volume, this "happiness" discourse demands from workers absolute self-control, self-regulation, and self-efficiency in return for a chance at economic stability. From this Orwellian perspective, it is impossible for displaced workers to express anger or even frustration at their employers without sounding like "annoying children."

Workers have a difficult time imagining and articulating an alternative discourse. They may long for decent jobs, or at the very least, husbands with decent jobs who can support them, but they have no idea where to find them. Scholars, too, sometimes lapse into nostalgic longing for the golden era of the Keynesian bargain, when unions were stronger and wage inequality was much less than it is today. But this is a gendered nostalgia, based on the traditional division of labor between breadwinning husbands and homemaking wives. It is also a racialized nostalgia: as Branch points out, black men were excluded from the traditional labor contract that guaranteed job security and the family wage to white men. As a result, most black women never got the chance to be stay-at-home moms. Black femininity, she writes, "was defined by the expectation (and often necessity) to work on behalf of the family."

The civil rights movement pressured employers to stop their preferential hiring of white men. But as it turned out, the resulting increased diversity in the workforce coincided with the rise of employment insecurity. The Keynesian bargain was called off almost as soon as white women and minority men and women began leaving their jobs in the periphery and obtaining access to white men's jobs in the once secure core. Similarly, in Japan, it seems that the traditional labor bargain is being scaled back just as women's demands for equality at work are finally being heeded. Interestingly, however, young people in Japan reject the traditional pathway to success. As Alexy reports, the much heralded "salaryman"—the loyal male worker who was once the proud source of Japan's economic miracle—is now being stereotyped as a pathetic belligerent drunk. The new cultural ideal of a "freeter" that is taking his place offers the potential for meaningful work and greater gender equality, but not stability and security.

What would inspire workers to take to the street to demand economic security? Today, many individuals are fearful of losing their jobs or becoming unemployable, which makes them unwilling to demand much from their employers. In my own research, I see this fear everywhere, among low-wage retail workers as well as among highly paid professionals (Williams 2006; Williams, Muller, and Kilanski 2012). "Everyone knows" that the question is when—and not if—the layoffs will occur, but nobody knows what to do about it, aside from working harder, "leaning in," and engaging in an endless and often fruitless cycle of self-improvement.

Political solutions seem especially elusive, granted the prevailing culture of cynicism toward government in the United States. However, governments elsewhere have responded to the financial crisis by implementing new programs, including "flexicurity" in Denmark and the "beyond employment" approach advocated by the European Commission (Vosko 2010). These programs are based on the assumption that workers should not bear the economic and emotional burdens of precarious employment. If employers are to be allowed to expand and contract their workforces in response to global competition, then workers must be insured a stable livelihood during periods of unemployment. Furthermore, individuals should be able to move in and out of the labor force depending not only on employer needs, but also depending on their personal needs for care and training, without being made vulnerable to financial and psychological ruin.

For workers in the United States to demand such changes, James Jasper (2014), an expert on social movements, argues that a shift from fear to indignation may be needed. Workers must overcome their fear about losing their jobs and feel entitled to better treatment. Two mechanisms are required to bring about this shift: first, workers must identify a villain to blame for their plight rather than blaming themselves or God (or, in this case, "global capitalism," which can seem as inscrutable and omnipotent as

God); second, workers must develop a sense of pride and worth in themselves as workers. Neither will be easy to engineer given the widespread employer ideology that blames displaced workers for their plight and treats every person and every job as expendable.

Since the damages wrought by our insecurity culture fall disproportionately on women, feminism has an important role to play. Helping women survive insecurity culture requires good jobs and living wages, which are the traditional demands of the feminist movement. But women also need increased time, recognition, and compensation for the indispensable care they provide—a need that cuts across divisions of class, race, and even gender. If, as Jasper claims, developing a sense of entitlement is key to social change, it is critical to cultivate a sense of pride and worth among everyone involved in caring for others.

Historically, scholars have supported emerging social movements by helping to articulate their purpose and values. This volume represents a pioneering effort to do just that. By connecting personal troubles to social conditions, identifying the winners and losers in the new economy, and criticizing the existing gendered and racialized discourses about work, Allison Pugh and the authors in this book are crafting a new framework that can restore hope and dignity to workers. Ideally, *Beyond the Cubicle* will stimulate more researchers to join this worthy effort.

REFERENCES

Almond, Barbara. 2010. *The Monster Within: The Hidden Side of Motherhood.* Berkeley: University of California Press.

Chodorow, Nancy. 1978. *The Reproduction of Mothering: Psychoanalysis and the Sociology of Gender.* Berkeley: University of California Press.

Hays, Sharon. 1996. *The Cultural Contradictions of Motherhood.* New Haven, CT: Yale University Press.

Jasper, James. 2014. *Protest: A Cultural Introduction to Social Movements.* Malden, MA: Polity.

Parsons, Talcott. 1970. *Social Structure and Personality.* New York: Free Press.

Vosko, Leah F. 2010. *Managing the Margins: Gender, Citizenship, and the International Regulation of Precarious Employment.* Oxford: Oxford University Press.

Williams, Christine L. 2006. *Inside Toyland: Working, Shopping, and Social Inequality.* Berkeley: University of California Press.

Williams, Christine L., Chandra Muller, and Kristine Kilanski. 2012. "Gendered Organizations in the New Economy." *Gender & Society* 26(4):549–573.

INDEX

and high-tech workers, 243
as ideal, 184–87, 188–89, 196–98
in Israel, 237
and middle-class families,
   295–96, 299
and relocation, 211–12, 214–15,
   218–19, 221–22, 225
and self-reliance, 210
and working-class families, 288–89,
   289–90, 292–93
See also gender contracts;
   neo-traditional work-care
   arrangements
management by stress, 209, 214
managerial status
   and age cohort, 60
   and emotional exhaustion, 66–67
   and emotional impacts of job
      insecurity, 66, 70
   and timing of knowledge about
      mergers, 66–67t
   and well-being outcomes, 62
Margolis, Diane Rothbard, 206, 214
Marienthal (Jahoda et al), 1–2
marriage
   and autonomy, 171
   changes in, 156, 158, 285–87, 299
   companionate marriage, 285–86,
      296–97, 299
   and complementary
      incompetence, 112–13
   and educational levels, 156
   emotional/psychological resources
      required for, 286, 289, 295–97,
      299–300
   in post-bubble Japan, 120–22
   and salarymen, 12, 111–14, 120
   and women's careers, 101–2, 111
   See also intimacy
Maryanski, A. R., 112
Marzano, Michela, 40–41
masculinity
   and breadwinning status, 180,
      184–87, 190–91, 196–98, 213–14
   cracks in armor of, 187–88
   in Japan, 124n12
   in Russia, 133, 134, 140, 141–42
   and salarymen, 106, 118–20
   and tyranny of gender norms, 192–93
   See also femininity; gender

Maslach Burnout Inventory (MBI), 57
Maslow, Abraham, 33
Maslow's Pyramid of Needs, inversion of,
   26, 32, 33, 35–36, 43
Massey, Douglas, 284
maternity leave. *See* parental leave policies
McGuire, John, 226
mergers, knowledge about, 11–12
   and generational cohorts, 62–65
   timing of, 60–62, 66–67t
   unexpected announcement of, 55–56
military
   as stable employment, 254, 294
mindfulness, 40
minimum wage legislation, 181
mobility
   and relocation, 209, 211–13,
      214, 225–26
   See also security-autonomy-mobility
      roadmaps
Moen, Phyllis, 11–12
   chapter by, 51–70
mother-child relationships, 307
motherhood. *See* family life; single
   mothers, Russian
movement, constant
   as attribute of self-reliant women, 137
   See also relocation
Munsch, Christin, 193
Musson, Gillian, 223

neoliberalism
   and autonomy, 37–41
   characteristics of, 25
   and flexibility, 41–43, 91,
      138–39, 145–47
   and insecurity culture, 6–7, 12,
      133–35, 143–44
   and positive psychology, 29–30,
      43, 138–39
   in Russia, 129–31
   and self-reliance, 130–31, 148–49
   work ethic of, 31–33
neo-traditional work-care arrangements,
   87, 157–58, 159–62, 170–71, 182
New York Times, 2, 75
Newman, Katherine, 80, 197

objective job uncertainty, 52
Occupy Movement, 91, 95, 249